DUMBARTON OAKS STUDIES

XXVI

TIME IMMEMORIAL: ARCHAIC HISTORY AND ITS SOURCES
IN CHRISTIAN CHRONOGRAPHY
FROM JULIUS AFRICANUS TO GEORGE SYNCELLUS

TIME IMMEMORIAL
ARCHAIC HISTORY AND ITS SOURCES
IN CHRISTIAN CHRONOGRAPHY
FROM JULIUS AFRICANUS TO GEORGE SYNCELLUS

William Adler

Dumbarton Oaks Research Library and Collection
Washington, D.C.

Library of Congress Cataloging-in-Publication Data

Adler, William, 1951–
    Time immemorial : archaic history and its sources in Christian
chronography from Julius Africanus to George Syncellus / William
Adler.
        p.   cm. — (Dumbarton Oaks studies ; 26)
    Bibliography: p. 239
    Includes index.
    ISBN 0-88402-176-9
        1. Chronology, Ecclesiastical.   2. Time—Religious aspects—
Christianity.   3. History (Theology)—History of doctrines—Early
church, ca. 30–600.   4. History, Ancient—Chronology.   I. Title.
II. Series.
CE25.A35 1989
907'.2—dc19   88-13942

Contents

Acknowledgments

It is my pleasant duty to acknowledge the several people and institutions who assisted me during the preparation of this book.

Professor Robert Kraft of the University of Pennsylvania directed the doctoral dissertation that forms the basis of most of the material in the present volume. Professor Michael Stone suggested the topic and invited me to speak to his graduate seminar at the Hebrew University of Jerusalem on various aspects of Christian chronography. Professors Otto Neugebauer and O. A. W. Dilke were kind enough to answer my inquiries on technical aspects of ancient chronography and geography. Professors Louis Feldman, Anthony Grafton, Sebastian Brock, and my colleagues Bruce Mullin and James VanderKam read the manuscript at various stages in its development and offered many helpful improvements in style and content. Professor David Auerbach and Nancy Overbeek assisted at the final stages of the preparation of the manuscript.

I wish to thank North Carolina State University for its financial and material support. Professor Robert Bryan, head of the Department of Philosophy and Religion, granted me a reduced teaching load in the fall semester of 1986 in order to finish the writing and research of this book. The Interlibrary Loan Department at D. H. Hill Library was always prompt in tracking down obscure books and articles. I also owe acknowledgments to the College of Humanities and Social Sciences Research Committee for approving a subvention for the publication of the book.

It is my pleasure finally to express my gratitude to the staff of Dumbarton Oaks, especially Professor Robert Thomson, Director, and Frances Kianka, Manuscript Editor. I am also grateful to the anonymous readers of the manuscript and to Christopher Dadian who did an extraordinary job in copyediting it.

I dedicate the book to the memory of my father.

Raleigh, North Carolina

Introduction

Measured by the rigorous standards of accuracy that Thucydides applied to the written monuments of former generations, the Christian universal chronicle would fall far short of the mark. After experimenting with primordial history, Greek chronographers had concluded, not without reason, that their own sources for this period were either incredible or inadequate. But their Christian counterparts were as likely as not either to dismiss these concerns as simple narrow-mindedness or to exploit this caution for their own purposes; if the Greeks could not know the past with certainty, it was, they said, only because the Greeks themselves were once notoriously negligent archivists, forcing their posterity to make do with erratic and contradictory records.[1] Christian chronographers, on the other hand, far more optimistic even about the remotest segment of world history, rarely succumbed to such doubt. Even Eusebius, with whom we associate the most candor in acknowledging the ambiguities of primordial chronology, never goes so far as to consign it to the realm of the "mythical" or "unknowable." Nor is he prepared to attach much of the blame to Moses. Granted, he acknowledges in the introduction to the *Canons*, there are obstacles to devising an absolute chronology of events from Adam; but this is principally because the records of the Greeks and barbarians for this period were so spotty.[2]

---

[1] Among the many works written on the Greek treatment of primordial history, see the excellent discussion by Arnaldo Momigliano, "Time in Ancient Historiography," *History and Theory,* Beiheft 6 (Middletown, 1966), 14–22; idem, "Historiography on Written Tradition and Historiography on Oral Tradition," *Studies in Historiography* (London, 1966), 211–20.

[2] See Jerome's Latin translation of Eusebius' introduction in *Die Chronik des Hieronymus* 11–12F, ed. R. Helm, 2nd ed., GCS 47, *Eusebius Werke* 7.1–2 (Berlin, 1956) (hereafter *Canons*). There he states as one of his reasons for beginning his *Canons* from Abraham the fact that for the preceding period "nec Graeca nec barbara et, ut loquar in commune, gentilis invenitur historia." In the first part of his Chronicle, Eusebius does, however, acknowledge the existence of variations in different versions of Genesis. For Eusebius' treatment of the chrono-

From its very inception, Christian chronographers canvassed a much larger field of human history than their Greek counterparts. Whatever scepticism they might have inherited from the Greeks about the accessibility of the remote past was quickly overruled by the grandiose expectations that they brought to the discipline. One of the reasons why Greek historians felt uncomfortable about venturing into the primordial past was simply because, in the words of Momigliano, it left so many "empty periods."[3] Such gaps would have been far less daunting to the Christian chronographers. They were, after all, guided, at least initially, by a different τέλος, and one for which the simple ordering of events would have proved sufficient.[4] For example, behind the plan of Julius Africanus (ca. 160–ca. 240) to write a chronicle that encompassed the whole sweep of past history lay a single theological motive: to comprehend the course of human history in a single millennialist scheme.[5] In this scheme, historical meaning lay not in the intrinsic content of the events described or even their relationship to one another, but rather in their order, succession, and chronological scope. Eusebius later would find millennialist chronography distasteful, reminding his readers of Jesus' interdiction against such speculation in Acts 1:7.[6] But Africanus did not stand alone. "We whom the sacred Scriptures instruct to the knowledge of truth," wrote the Latin apologist Lactantius in the fourth century, "know the beginning and the end of the world."[7]

Other factors also pressured the chronographers to push back the frontiers of the knowable past. In the propaganda war against Greek culture, apologists never ceased reminding their Greek detractors that, compared to "barbarian" peoples, they were as children; what better way to exemplify this than by contrasting their short and erratic historical records with what everyone, even the Greeks, liked to believe were the carefully pre-

---

logical problems for pre-Abrahamic history, see below, Chap. 2, pp. 46–50, 69–71. The text of Eusebius' first book survives in an Armenian recension; see *Die Chronik aus dem Armenischen übersetzt,* trans. J. Karst, GCS 20, *Eusebius Werke* 5 (Leipzig, 1911). All references to Eusebius' first book are from Karst's translation (hereafter *Chronica*).

[3] Momigliano, "Time in Ancient Historiography," 16.

[4] For a useful differentiation between "chronology" and "history," see James William Johnson, "Chronological Writing: Its Concepts and Development," *History and Theory* 2 (1962–63), 125–26.

[5] For discussion, see below, Chap. 1, p. 19.

[6] *Chronica* 1.30–2.6.

[7] Lactantius *Divine Institutes* 7.14. As Momigliano points out, Eusebius' strictures against it did not succeed in stamping out chiliastic chronography; millennialism is also present in the work of Bishop Hilarian and Sulpicius Severus, both writing in the late 4th century; see Arnaldo Momigliano, "Pagan and Christian Historiography in the Fourth Century A.D.," *The Conflict between Paganism and Christianity in the Fourth Century* (Oxford, 1963), 85.

served eyewitness documents of the barbarians? Even so narrow an undertaking as the uniform dating of holy days might produce the same effect.
Alexandrian chronographers, from as early as Clement, had experimented
with the idea of the era from the creation of the cosmos. But when in the
fifth century they had finally achieved this objective, part of its motivation
was, in the words of Otto Neugebauer, a matter of "church politics,"
namely, to reckon the date of Easter independently of the celebration of
the Jewish Passover. If it was the first day of creation that marked the first
date of the first 532-year Easter cycle, the principle that lay behind this
design was to confirm the doctrine that Christ's resurrection and the first
day of creation occurred on precisely the same day.[8]

One important by-product of the Christian chroniclers' desire for inclu-
siveness was their preservation of a large and heterogeneous corpus of
extra-biblical sources, especially for primordial history. It did not take long
for chronographers to recognize that the first ten chapters of Genesis, albeit the ultimate authority, could only provide a scaffolding for the creation of a chronology of antediluvian history. Whatever reservations a
chronicler might have had about competing chronologies of primordial
history, the fact remained that, if he wanted his work to be considered a
"universal" chronicle, he was constrained to consider other sources for this
period, for example, the antiquities of the Babylonians, Egyptians, and
Phoenicians. Moreover, Genesis itself was silent on a number of questions
that had always intrigued chronographers: How long did Adam stay in
Paradise? Which chronology of Genesis was more accurate—the Septuagint, the Samaritan Pentateuch, or the Hebrew Bible? Did Methuselah
survive the flood? How did the ancients calculate the duration of the year?
Questions such as these might provide the justification to examine other
works that spoke more directly about them. From their Hellenistic predecessors, for example, Christian chronography had inherited a fondness for
speculating about εὑρήματα, that is, the origins of the arts and sciences,
especially as this matter pertained to the foundation of the precise reckoning of time. But although Genesis had something to contribute on this
subject, the Christian chroniclers were to find in the Hellenistic ethnic
histories a much richer lode of information; describing the origins of civilization was, after all, one of the main reasons why many of these histories
were composed in the first place.[9]

The requirements of the genre allowed the Christian chronographer a

---

[8] Otto Neugebauer, *Ethiopic Astronomy and Computus, Sitzungsberichte der Österreichische Akademie der Wissenschaften,* phil.-hist. Klasse 347 (Vienna, 1979), 8.

[9] For discussion, see below, Chap. 4, pp. 107–13.

latitude in examining non-biblical sources and wisdom that might have been unheard of in other Christian literature. Yet at the same time this was always held in check by certain built-in restraints. When the Christian chronographer consulted extra-biblical sources to supplement Genesis—be it a Jewish apocalypse such as the *Book of Enoch,* or the antiquities of Berossus and Manetho—he operated within a very limited paradigm. What defined the use of these sources was usually the same, that is, either to find in these works independent corroboration for Genesis, or to enlarge on matters that Genesis left ambiguous or unsettled altogether. What did one do, then, with a source that clarified and confirmed Genesis in some cases, but positively undermined it in others?

Chronographers applied a variety of methods to mediate between the two extremes, methods almost invariably tendentious. As we shall see, chroniclers of Alexandria resorted to "allegorical" explanation to account for what might appear to us to be the irreconcilable discrepancy between the 432,000 years of Berossus' pre-flood chronology and the mere 2,242 years of the Septuagint. Offensive portions of a text were excised, on the pretext that such material was not fit for unsophisticated readers, or had, in the words of Syncellus, been adulterated by "Jews and heretics."[10] At the more extreme level, sources might undergo emendation, interpolation, or in some cases wholesale reworkings. What is in any case clear is that not until Joseph Scaliger (sixteenth century) did anyone seriously challenge the very presuppositions that this approach assumed.[11]

Standing at the end of a long discussion of this question in Antiquity, stretching almost six hundred years before him, is the Ἐκλογὴ χρονογραφίας of George the Syncellus.[12] Composed in Constantinople at the beginning of the ninth century, under the patriarch of Constantinople Tarasius (784–806),[13] it was originally meant to extend from the creation of the world to the time of Tarasius; but its author died before

[10] Sync. 27.11.

[11] For discussion of Scaliger's departure from this tradition, see Anthony Grafton, "Joseph Scaliger and Historical Chronology: The Rise and Fall of a Discipline," *History and Theory* 14 (1975), 164–73.

[12] Herein referred to only as Syncellus. The whole title of the work according to the Paris manuscript is "Ἐκλογὴ χρονογραφίας συνταγεῖσα ὑπὸ Γεωργίου Συγκέλλου γεγονότος Ταρασίου πατριάρχου Κωνσταντινοπόλεως ἀπὸ Ἀδὰμ μεχρὶ Διοκλητιάνου." All citations from Syncellus' chronicle are from the recent edition of Alden A. Mosshammer (Leipzig, 1984); this edition replaces the older one by W. Dindorf, *Georgius Syncellus et Nicephorus Cp.,* 2 vols., CSHB (Bonn, 1829).

[13] The office of σύγκελλος was that of an advisor to the patriarch. For biographical information on Syncellus, see Leo Allacci, *De Georgiis et eorum scriptis diatriba* (23), in J. A. Fabri-

completing the work, and the chronicle stopped with the beginning of the reign of the Roman emperor Diocletian (285 C.E.).[14]

Joseph Scaliger's first edition of portions of Syncellus' chronicle in the seventeenth century brought to light a vast collection of source material, otherwise all but unknown in the West. Although Scaliger himself had nothing but contempt for Syncellus, he immediately recognized that the chronicle was a *thesaurus* of ancient sources, some of which had up to that time been known only in passing references.[15] Quotations, for example, from the lost chronography of Julius Africanus were preserved by Syncellus.[16] Equally important were Syncellus' extracts from Eusebius. Before the discovery of Syncellus in the West, for example, European chronographers had known from Jerome's translation of his *Canons* that Eusebius had also composed a *prior libellus*. Jerome had unfortunately elected not to translate this book into Latin, however, and scholars in the West could only speculate as to its contents. Thrilled to discover that Syncellus' chronography contained numerous references to the otherwise lost first book of Eusebius' chronicle, Scaliger went so far as to suggest, prematurely as it turned out, that Syncellus' work was largely a transcript of Eusebius, from which one could reconstruct in large part the contents of the lost first book.[17]

Contained in Syncellus' chronicle were also long extracts from various ethnic histories composed in Greek in the early Hellenistic period. Interest in the antiquities of Berossus and Manetho had at the time been stimulated by the appearance of the highly suspect works published by the Italian monk Annius of Viterbo, texts soon exposed as fraudulent. Annius aside, Syncellus' chronicle represented in the seventeenth century the single most important witness to the abridgments of Berossus' *Babyloniaca*

---

cius, *Bibliotheca Graeca* 10 (Hamburg, 1809), 630–41; Heinrich Gelzer, *Sextus Julius Africanus und die byzantinische Chronographie*, 2 vols. (Leipzig, 1885–88; rpr. New York, 1967), 2. 176–89 (hereafter *SJA*); R. Laqueur, "Synkellos" (1), *RE* 4.2 (zweite Reihe), 1388–91.

[14] The work was subsequently continued by Theophanes up to the year 813 (the reign of Michael I); edition of Theophanes by C. de Boor, 2 vols. (Leipzig, 1883–85). For discussion of the relationship of Theophanes to Syncellus, see Harry Turtledove, *The Chronicle of Theophanes* (Philadelphia, 1982), xi–xii.

[15] Scaliger published material from Syncellus in his *Thesaurus Temporum*, 2 vols. (Leiden, 1606; rpr. Osnabrück, 1968). Most of Scaliger's observations on Syncellus are to be found in his notes to the scattered Greek witnesses to Eusebius (2. 241–63).

[16] Excerpts from Africanus' chronicle preserved in Syncellus and other sources are collected by M. J. Routh, *Reliquiae Sacrae*, 2 (Oxford, 1846), 238–309.

[17] For Scaliger's use of Syncellus to reconstruct Eusebius, see most recently Alden A. Mosshammer, *The Chronicle of Eusebius and Greek Chronographic Tradition* (Lewisburg, 1979), 40–41; Jacob Bernays' biography, *Joseph Justus Scaliger* (Berlin, 1855; rpr. Osnabrück, 1965), 94–95, gives a good summary of Scaliger's attempts to use Syncellus in recovering Eusebius' chronicle.

by Alexander Polyhistor, Abydenus, and (ps-)Apollodorus. For Egyptian chronology, Syncellus preserved as well the epitomes of Manetho in the varying recensions of Eusebius and Africanus; the mysterious *Book of Sothis*, pseudepigraphically attributed to Manetho; and the so-called *Ancient Chronicle*, said by Syncellus to have antedated Manetho and to have been "the source of his error."[18] It was in fact Syncellus' excerpts from these sources that contributed to the ultimate discrediting of the Annian forgeries.[19]

No less sensational were Syncellus' extracts from Jewish pseudepigrapha. Undoubtedly stirring the greatest excitement were the citations from *1 Enoch*, both because of the putative antiquity of the work and because of the apparent influence that this book had once exerted in the early Church. Scaliger's initial reaction to these excerpts was a mixture of contempt and native curiosity. While repelled by its content ("piget, taedet, pudetque"), he recognized that the apparent antiquity of the work, and its use by Tertullian and Jude, gave it a certain status.[20] Only a few years before the publication of Syncellus, a Capuchin traveler and explorer, Gilles de Loches, had contributed further to interest in this apocalypse by bringing back from Ethiopia a book that he claimed was an Ethiopic text of Enoch.[21] The claim was subsequently and conclusively refuted by the German orientalist Ludolf, but not without first whetting the European appetite for writings attributed to this patriarch.[22] Syncellus' excerpts, following on the heels of this premature report of an Ethiopic text of Enoch, provided for the first time a portion of a work known only in a few scattered reports in the church fathers.[23]

Scholarship on Syncellus has been mainly guided by his perceived value

[18] Sync. 56.19. For discussion of these works, see below, Chap. 2, pp. 55–65.

[19] On the Annian forgeries, their influence on Renaissance chronography, and Scaliger's attempt to recover the true fragments of Manetho and Berossus, see Grafton, "Joseph Scaliger and Historical Chronology," 164–73, and the works cited there.

[20] *Thesaurus Temporum*, 2. 245.

[21] The account of de Loches' discovery of (ps-)Enoch was reported by Pierre Gassendi, *Viri illustris Nicolai Claudii Fabricii de Peiresc, senatoris Aquisextensis, Vita*, 3rd ed., (Quedlinburg, 1706–8), 2.4, 284 (for the year 1633). In the beginning of the 16th century, Guilliame Postel also claimed to have seen a copy of Ethiopic Enoch; for discussion, see Nathaniel Schmidt, "Traces of Early Acquaintance in Europe with the Book of Enoch," *JAOS* 42 (1922), 50–51.

[22] See his *Historia Aethiopica* (Frankfurt, 1681), 347. After examining its contents, Ludolf recognized that the author of the work, entitled *Book of the Mysteries of the Heavens and the Earth*, did not claim to be Enoch at all, but a certain Bakhayla Mīkā'ēl. The work does contain, however, material that is found in *1 Enoch*. For an account of the circumstances attending the discovery of the book, see Budge's introduction to his English translation (London, 1935), xiii–xix.

[23] Syncellus' text of *1 Enoch* was known first in the original Greek form as it had been

as a witness for reconstructing from these excerpts earlier works, either
Eusebius, Africanus, the Alexandrian chronographers Panodorus and Annianus, or the various Greek and Hellenistic sources surviving fragmentarily through him.[24] When, therefore, other documents were discovered that
were thought to represent better witnesses to many of these sources, interest in his chronicle inevitably declined. The discovery of the Armenian
version of Eusebius, for example, revealed that his chronicle contained an
earlier version of many of the same excerpts from Manetho and Berossus
as Syncellus, often attesting a more original text. And Syncellus' excerpts
from the Jewish pseudepigrapha now constitute only a small fraction of
the available witnesses to them. In the case of *1 Enoch,* for example, we
now have, in addition to Syncellus' excerpts, another large Greek fragment
from that work, a small citation in Syriac, several Ethiopic manuscripts,
and the recently discovered Aramaic fragments from Qumran.

If his chronicle is now treated as a mostly depleted mine of ancient
source material, Syncellus himself must bear partial responsibility. Like
many other Byzantine chronographers, he is often more adept at compiling sources and excerpts than he is at analyzing or accounting for them.
Standing at the end of a long tradition of textual transmission, Syncellus
is removed from the original text of many of his sources by two, three, or
even more intermediaries. Whatever motive may have inspired one of Syncellus' predecessors to consult a source has sometimes been lost in the
process of transmission. In many cases we must assume that the sheer
weight of tradition, a fondness for cataloguing sources, or a simple desire
to parade erudition were the only motives that Syncellus had for citing his
sources.[25]

---

published in *Thesaurus Temporum,* and then in a Latin translation by the German polymath
Athanasius Kircher, published in several different works; see, for example, his *De Arca Noe*
(Amsterdam, 1675), 5–8. Early analysis of Syncellus' text of *1 Enoch* is a chapter in the history
of this work that has yet to be written. Among the many scholars after Scaliger to examine
these excerpts, the more important are: Johann Heidegger, *De historia sacra patriarcharum
exercitationes selectae* (Amsterdam, 1688–89), 10.7–10.11 (272–78); August Pfeiffer, *Henoch, descriptus exercitatione philologica ad Gen. 5.22.23.24* (Wittenberg, 1670), 4.5–8; Thomas Bang,
Caelum Orientis et prisci mundi triade exercitationum literariarum representatum (Hauniae,
1657), 25–29; Johann Ernst Grabe, *Spicilegium ss. patrum,* 2 vols. (Oxford, 1698–99), 1. 347–
54.
    [24]Thus, in his important study of Byzantine chronography, Gelzer used Syncellus and the
other Byzantine chroniclers principally to recover Africanus and the Alexandrian chronographers; for discussion of Gelzer's views on Syncellus' dependence on Panodorus and Annianus, see below, Chaps. 5 and 6, pp. 134–35, 160–63.
    [25]Thus, in the antediluvian portion of his chronicle, Syncellus will often quote from
sources whose credibility he completely rejects. Among the reasons he names for citing them
are "for the sake of curiosity" (cf. 5.26), or lest someone might deem his work "incomplete
(ἀτελές)" (16.33).

But it would be unfair to say that Syncellus operates only as an anti-quarian. One may argue about the substance of his treatment of Eusebius, Africanus, and his Alexandrian predecessors; Scaliger considered most of it petty, and Gelzer tended to the view that where it was not trivial, it was derived from other sources.[26] But the fact remains that, unlike many other Byzantine chronicles, Syncellus does not defer to the authority of his predecessors. He knows of the claims of his predecessors on critical mat-ters such as the date of the creation of the universe, the flood, and the incarnation, and he does not shrink from criticizing them for their failings. Critical detachment from his sources is especially true of Syncellus' treat-ment of antediluvian history. No one will praise Syncellus here for clarity in presentation of his sources; but neither is the work only a catalogue of "herrenlosen Kleinigkeiten."[27] When, for example, Syncellus furnishes an excerpt from the *Babyloniaca*, he does so only in the context of a larger discussion of the treatment of this work by his predecessors, whom he compares and evaluates. It would not be an exaggeration to say that if one wanted to write a descriptive history of the use and interpretation of the sources for primordial history by Christian chronographers from the third to the ninth century, Syncellus would be the single most important wit-ness.

SCOPE AND METHOD OF THE PRESENT STUDY

The approach to the subject taken in the present study requires a brief explanation. As the research on this subject progressed, it became increas-ingly evident that, inasmuch as Syncellus is in constant dialogue with his predecessors, his authorities had to be treated before proceeding to Syn-cellus himself. Many of the sources that Syncellus consulted had under-gone a long prior transmission and interpretation, and the only way to develop a controlled picture of Syncellus' own treatment of the question is to discuss his predecessors first. As a result, the actual analysis of Syn-cellus is deferred until the final chapters. Anyone perusing the table of contents will also recognize that many Christian chronographers have been excluded—Theophilus and Hippolytus, for example. This is so only because this study is defined by the chronographers whom Syncellus ex-pressly identifies as his predecessors in the primordial portion of his chron-icle—Julius Africanus, Eusebius, Panodorus, and Annianus.

[26] For discussion of modern assessments of Syncellus, see below, Chap. 5, pp. 132–36.
[27] Eduard Schwartz used this expression to refer to the various unattributed fragments found in Byzantine chronicles. See his article s.v. *Chronicon Paschale, RE* 3.2, 2475.

I have been using the words "primordial" and "archaic" to delimit the chronological period treated in this study. These terms, not at all self-defining, demand some clarification. Broadly speaking, I mean a remote segment of world history, knowledge of which was believed to be restricted by the available sources. But this would have meant different things for different chronographers. For Greek chronographers, it might have extended to everything before the Trojan War, the flood at the time of Ogygus, or the reign of the Assyrian king Ninus. In Eusebius' *Chronicle*, it might have meant anything before Adam's expulsion from Paradise; or in the *Canons*, it might have comprehended the period before Abraham. Africanus and the Byzantine chronographers would, of course, have reasoned differently.

One has, therefore, to be satisfied with a fluid understanding of the term. For the present investigation, I have attempted to avoid arbitrarily delimiting the field of study with boundaries such as "pre-flood" or "pre-Abraham," electing instead to proceed inductively from the chronographers themselves. In Christian chronography, Eusebius was to set the standard for later work by clearly defining what he considered to be the problems of pre-Abrahamic history; they involved the proper use of non-biblical sources (primarily Babylonian and Egyptian), the reconciliation of conflicting recensions of the Bible (Septuagint, Hebrew, and Samaritan Pentateuch), and the proper way to handle Genesis' account of creation and Adam's life in Paradise. Eusebius' reservations about this period represented not only a departure, probably deliberate, from Africanus; they seem also to have stimulated subsequent chronographers in Alexandria in the fifth century to undertake both a revision and a critique of Eusebius. Although it is clear from Syncellus' discussion of them that their critique of Eusebius extended to a great variety of subjects, from Syncellus we know most about their criticism of his handling of sources for the antediluvian period. In the process of mounting this critique, these Alexandrians introduced a whole new set of sources (principally Jewish pseudepigrapha) and problems. What Syncellus preserves in the ninth century are both his impression of the history and development of the question and his own views about it.

CITATIONS FROM EARLIER SOURCES IN SYNCELLUS' ANTEDILUVIAN CHRONOLOGY

The following is a complete inventory of Syncellus' attributed citations from earlier sources in the antediluvian portion of his chronicle (1.1–43.3).

References to sources that are not explicitly attributed are not included. Citations are listed here in order of their first appearance in Syncellus. Each entry contains the following information: (a) name of author cited; (b) location of citation(s) (page and line number in Mosshammer's edition); (c) Syncellus' identification of the author cited; (d) title of citation, if this exists; (e) summary of contents of this citation; (f) probable origin of citation.

1. Gregory of Nazianzus: (a) 2.18–2.21 (ὁ μέγας ἐν θεολογίᾳ Γρηγόριος), on the measurement of time; source specified only as "somewhere (που)" = *Second Oration on Theology* 8; (b) 32.23–28 (κατὰ τὸν θεῖον Γρηγόριον), on idolatry, polytheism, and the worship of natural objects; from Gregory's *Second Oration on Theology* 14.

2. Julius Africanus: (a) 3.1–2 (ὁ Ἀφρικανός), on the "noetic first day"; source not specified; (b) 10.10–11 (κατὰ τὸν φυσικὸν λόγον Ἀφρικανοῦ), on the significance of the name "Enosh"; (c) 17.28–18.10 (Ἀφρικανοῦ), "On the mythical chronology of the Egyptians and Chaldeans (περὶ τῆς τῶν Αἰγυπτίων καὶ Χαλδαίων μυθώδους χρονολογίας)"; probably from Africanus' chronicle; (d) 19.23–20.4 (Ἀφρικανοῦ), "On the Watchers," probably from his Chronicle; (e) 20.8–13 (ὁ Ἀφρικανός), on Africanus' dating of the flood in the year 2262, probably refers to his Chronicle; (f) 21.26–22.11 (Ἀφρικανοῦ [in the margin of ms. A]), on the question of the age of mankind after the fall of the Watchers, probably from his Chronicle.

3. *Jubilees:* (a) 3.14–18 (ἐν λεπτῇ φέρεται Γενέσει, ἣν καὶ Μωϋσέως εἶναί φασί τινες ἀποκάλυψιν), on the twenty-two works of creation, equal to the number of Hebrew letters, the books of the Hebrew Bible, and the number of patriarchs from Adam to Jacob; also the creation of the "heavenly powers" on the first day of creation = *Jub.* 2:2, 23; (b) 4.21–22 (ἐκ τῆς λεπτῆς Γενέσεως), on Adam's and Eve's naming of the animals and their life in Paradise; cf. *Jub.* 3:1–35; (c) 7.28–8.10 (Ἐκ τῶν λεπτῶν Γενέσεως), on Adam's seven years in Paradise (cf. *Jub.* 3:17, 32) and the snake's talking to Eve with a human voice (lacuna in Eth. Jubilees here; cf. Charles' note to *Jubilees* at 3:23, *APOT* 2. 17, note 23); (d) 27.34–28.4 (ἐν τῇ Μωυσέως λεγομένῃ ἀποκαλύψει), on the persecution of Noah's offspring by the demons, the offspring of the Watchers; cf. *Jub.* 10:1–12.

4. John Chrysostom: 3.19–22 (ὁ ἅγιος Ἰωάννης καὶ μέγας ἐν διδασκάλοις Χρυσόστομος), on the one day spent by Adam in Paradise;

attributed by Syncellus to his "interpretation of the Gospel according to Matthew (ἐν τῇ ἑρμηνείᾳ τοῦ κατὰ Ματθαῖον εὐαγγελίου)" = *Homilies on Matthew* 59.1 (on Mt. 18:7).

5. *Life of Adam:* 4.21–22 (τοῦ λεγομένου Βίου Ἀδάμ; see also 4.23; 5.26), on the duration of time spent by Adam and Eve in Paradise (4.29– 5.25). The work is not attested outside of Syncellus; for discussion, see Hermann Rönsch, *Das Buch der Jubiläen* (Leipzig, 1874) 279–81.

6. Josephus: (a) 4.20 (Ἰουδαϊκὰς ἀρχαιολογίας), probable reference to Josephus' *Antiquities;* (b) 8.1–2 (ὁ Ἰώσηππος), on the punishment of the serpent; cf. Josephus, *Ant.* 1.1.4.

7. Leviticus: 5.17–25 (ὁ θεὸς διὰ Μωϋσέως ἐν τῷ Λευιτικῷ), on the laws of purification after childbirth = Lev. 12:2–5; 15.19; the origin of the laws is traced to Adam and Eve's entry into Paradise (cf. *Jub.* 3:8–14).

8. *Apocalypse (Testament) of Adam:* 10.14–24 (ὁ Ἀδὰμ ἔγνω δι᾽ ἀποκαλύψεως), on Adam's revelations about the Watchers, the flood, repentance, the divine incarnation, and the prayers for each hour of the day. More complete text in George Cedrenus 1. 17.18–18.7 (ed. I. Bekker, 2 vols., CSHB [Bonn, 1838–39]). The fragment is similar in content to a Syriac pseudepigraphon called the *Testament of Adam*. For text and English translation of Syriac and Greek recensions, see Stephen Edward Robinson, *The Testament of Adam*, SBLDS 52 (Chico, 1982). A Greek text of the *horarium*, attributed to Apollonius of Tyana, is also preserved in a document dealing with magic (see F. Nau, *Apotelesmata Apollonii Tyanensis*, Patr. syr. 2 [1907], ed. R. Graffin, 1362–1392).

9. *First Enoch* (also known as *Ethiopic Enoch* or *Books of Enoch*): (a) 11.19– 13.19 (Ἐκ τοῦ πρώτου βιβλίου Ἐνὼχ περὶ τῶν ἐγρηγόρων), on the fall of the Watchers and their corruption of and revelations to the daughters of men = *1 En.* 6:1–9:5 (*APOT* 2 [Oxford, 1913]). A condensed form of this excerpt appears in Cedrenus 1. 19.12–20.2; (b) 24.10–27.7 (Ἐκ τοῦ λόγου Ἐνὼχ: Τὰ λοιπὰ περὶ ἐγρηγόρων); 27.8 (ἐκ τοῦ πρώτου βιβλίου Ἐνὼχ περὶ τῶν ἐγρηγόρων), divided into three parts—24.12–26.8, on the punishment of the Watchers = *1 En.* 9:1–10:15; 26:9–25, on the savagery of the Giants = *1 En.* 15:8–16:2; 26:26–27:7, on the burning of Mount Hermon, not attested in preserved witnesses to *1 Enoch*. R. H. Charles traced this last excerpt to the so-called "Apocalypse of Noah," a work which he believed was interwoven with *1 Enoch;* see his note to *1 En.*

16:2 (*APOT* 2. 198). More recently J. T. Milik traced it to the *Book of the Giants,* a part of the Enoch corpus that survives only fragmentarily; see his *The Books of Enoch* (Oxford, 1976) 72, 317–20; (c) 34.16–19 (ἐν τῇ Βίβλῳ αὐτοῦ Ἐνώχ), apparently a summary of *Book of Heavenly Luminaries* = *1 En.* 72–82; cf. also George Cedrenus 1. 21.11–13 (ed. Bekker); (d) for another possible reference, see 33.1–3, on revelations of Chorabiel (Χωραβ-ιήλ = Eth. "Kokabi'el") to mankind about the orbit of the sun (cf. *1 En.* 6:7).

10. Genesis: (a) 3.24–25 (ὁ θεόπτης Μωϋσῆς), on Genesis' chronology of Adam's life in Paradise; (b) 8.25–9.2 (Τῆς θείας γραφῆς περὶ τοῦ γένους Κάιν) = Gen. 4:17–18; (c) 13.20–26 (ὁ . . . θεόπτης Μωυσῆς ἐν τῇ Γενέσει), on the fall of the sons of God = Gen. 6:2 ff.; (d) 16.7–13 (ὁ θεόπτης Μωϋσῆς ἐν τοῖς μετὰ τὸν κατακλυσμόν), on the founding of Babylon by Nimrod = Gen. 10:8; (e) 21.23–25 (ἡ γραφή) = Gen. 6:3.

11. Second Epistle of Peter: 13.27–31 (ὁ . . . κορυφαῖος καὶ ἀπόστολος Πέτρος ἐν ἐπιστολῇ δευτέρᾳ), on God's punishment of the fallen angels and the flood at the time of Noah = 2 Peter 2:4–5.

12. Zosimus (fourth-century alchemist of Panopolis): 14.2–14 (Ζωσίμου τοῦ Πανοπολίτου φιλοσόφου), from his "writings to Theosebeia in the ninth book of Imouth (ἐκ τῶν γεγραμμένων αὐτῷ πρὸς θεοσέβειαν)," on the teachings of the fallen angels. The quotation is attributed by Syncellus to the ninth book of the work called *Book of Imouth.* The excerpt is not preserved elsewhere in Greek, but does survive in a Syriac manuscript; French translation in *Histoire des sciences. La chimie au moyen âge,* 3 vols. ed. M. P. E. Berthelot, R. Duval (Paris, 1893; rpr. Osnabrück, 1967) 2. 238.

13. Ephrem Syrus: 15.11–31 (ὁ θεῖος Ἐφραΐμ, ἡ ὠκεανόβρυτος γλῶσσα), on the location of Paradise, attributed by Syncellus to his "dogmatic discourses on Paradise (ἐν τοῖς εἰς τὸν παράδεισον δογματικοῖς αὐτοῦ λόγοις)." Highly paraphrastic Greek translation from Ephrem's *Hymns on Paradise* 1.10–11, ed. E. Beck, CSCO 174, Scriptores Syri 78 (Louvain, 1957).

14. Eusebius: (a) 20.14 (Ὁ . . . Εὐσέβιος), on the age of Methuselah and the date of the flood (A.M. 2242); cf. Eusebius' *Chronica,* 38.23–26 (ed. Karst); (b) 41.23–28 (ὁ Εὐσέβιος ὁ Παμφίλου), on the succession of primordial Egyptian kings. Attributed by Syncellus to Eusebius' Chronicle; cf. *Chronica* 62.11–65.2 (ed. Karst).

15. Berossus: (cf. 14.22: Βήρωσσος ὁ τῆς Χαλδαϊκῆς ἀρχαιολογίας συγγραφεύς; 32.4: Βηρώσσου τοῦ τὰ Χαλδαϊκὰ ψευδηρογοῦντος). Although Syncellus refers to Berossus at various places (14.22; 16.4; 17.3–4; 17.13; 32.4–5), he, like Eusebius before him, only knows Berossus from excerpts of the *Babyloniaca* in later sources—Alexander Polyhistor, (ps-)Apollodorus, and Abydenus.

16. Alexander Polyhistor: 28.17–32.3 (᾽Εκ τοῦ ᾽Αλεξάνδρου τοῦ Πολυΐστορος), "On the ten Chaldean kings who ruled before the flood, and the flood itself, and Noah and the ark, in which he also inserts some fabulous stories, as they are recounted by Berossus (περὶ τῶν πρὸ τοῦ κατακλυσμοῦ βασιλευσάντων ι΄ βασιλέων τῶν Χαλδαίων καὶ αὐτοῦ τοῦ κατακλυσμοῦ, καὶ περὶ τοῦ Νῶε καὶ τῆς κιβωτοῦ, ἐν οἷς καί τινα διὰ μέσου τερατώδη φάσκει, ὡς τῷ Βηρώσσῳ γεγραμμένα)." The same excerpt is found in the Armenian translation of Eusebius' *Chronica* 6.14–11.34.

17. Abydenus: 39.1–27 (᾽Εκ τῶν ᾽Αβυδενοῦ), "On the kingdom of the Chaldeans (Περὶ τῆς τῶν Χαλδαίων Βασιλείας)" = Eusebius, *Chronica* 15.27–16.29.

18. (Ps-)Apollodorus: 40.5–25, on Berossus' succession of Chaldean kings before the flood (cf. Eusebius' *Chronica* 4.18 ff.).

19. Manetho: (a) 18.21–19.17 (Μανεθῶ ὁ Σεβεννύτης ἀρχιερεύς), "Concerning the ancient history of the Egyptians (Περί τῆς τῶν Αἰγυπτίων ἀρχαιολογίας)," a table of primordial Egyptian kings from Hephaestus to Zeus. This list is not attested outside of Syncellus, possibly belonging to (ps-)Manetho's *Book of Sothis;* (b) 41.11–19: "Letter of Manetho of Sebennytus to Ptolemy Philadelphus (᾽Επιστολὴ Μανεθῶ τοῦ Σεβεννύτου πρὸς Πτολεμαῖον τὸν Φιλάδελφον)." According to Syncellus (41.7–9), this letter, addressed to Ptolemy II Philadelphus, introduced the *Book of Sothis* (ἐν τῇ βίβλῳ τῆς Σώθεως).

20. Panodorus: Although Panodorus is named in several other places (35.7; 35.31), there is only one passage that is unambiguously attributed to him (ὁ Πανόδωρος . . . λέγων; 41.30–42.20); the passage is an extract from Panodorus' interpretation of (ps-)Manetho's (i.e., the *Book of Sothis*) primordial history. In other places in which Syncellus might be quoting Panodorus, Syncellus uses only φησί or similarly ambiguous language (cf. 32.32–34.2, which appears to be excerpted from the work of one of Syncellus' Alexandrian predecessors).

21. Annianus: 36.21–37.11 (φησὶν ὁ Ἀννιανός), concerning the 532-year Paschal cycle, and Annianus' criticisms of Eusebius for his omission of 290 years.

22. Epistles of Paul: 27.12–18 (ὁ μακάριος Παῦλος), three quotations from Paul to legitimize use of the apocrypha on the grounds that Paul also cites from apocryphal works: (a) 1 Cor. 2:9 (attributed by Syncellus to the "Apocrypha of Elijah (Ἠλία ἀποκρύφων)"; (b) Gal. 5:6, attributed by Syncellus to the "Apocalypse of Moses (ἐκ τῆς Μωυσέως ἀποκαλύψεως)"; (c) Eph. 5:14, attributed by Syncellus to "the so-called Apocrypha of Jeremiah (ἐκ τῶν Ἰερεμίου λεγομένων ἀποκρύφων)."

CHAPTER ONE

Primordial History in Christian Chronography up to Eusebius

ʿΟ ἄδηλος χρόνος: ARCHAIC CHRONOLOGY AND ITS CONVENTIONS IN GREEK HISTORIOGRAPHY

"Nearly all writers of history," observes Orosius in the first chapter of his *Seven Books of History against the Pagans,* commence their narrative with Ninus, the supposed first "world" monarch and king of the Assyrians.[1] If anything notable had occurred before Ninus, Orosius complains, it passed unnoticed, relegated instead to pre-history and outside the realm of legitimate inquiry.[2]

The convention of beginning historical narrative in the "middle period" might have appeared myopic to Orosius, but it had not been arrived at lightly.[3] To be sure, Greek antiquarians were not averse to appealing to their mythic past for moral lessons or faint glimpses of the way things once were.[4] But because of the paucity and unreliability of their records even for relatively recent events, Greek chronographers were known to tend toward conservatism in defining the frontier between history and prehistory.[5] When, for example, in the third century B.C.E., the chronographer Eratosthenes (275–194 B.C.E.) undertook to develop a continuous chronology of Greek history, he determined that all that had occurred before the Trojan War (1184 B.C.E.) was "mythical"; and for the purposes of establishing an absolute chronology of events, the first Olympiad (776 B.C.E.)

---

[1] Orosius 1.1, ed. C. Zangemeister, CSEL 5, (Vienna, 1882).
[2] Ibid., 1.2–3. Orosius (1.5) dates Ninus 3,184 years after Adam. For the dating of Ninus' accession in Greek historiography, see below, note 15.
[3] Orosius complains that the approach revealed historical tunnel-vision (*opinione caeca*).
[4] See A. E. Wardman, "Myth in Greek Historiography," *Historia* 9 (1960), 403–13.
[5] For the difficulties facing Greek chronographers, see Felix Jacoby, *Atthis* (Oxford, 1949), 169–225.

was assumed to be the earliest secure date.[6] Eratosthenes' practice did find later advocates.[7] Like him, the Roman chronicler Varro would also acknowledge the insufficiencies of Greek history for the period before the first Olympiad. In his tripartite segmentation of Greek history, Varro treated as "historical (ἱστορικός)" only those events that had occurred after the first Olympiad.[8] All else, including even the Trojan War, was consigned either to the "mythical (μυθικός)" or, for even more remote periods, the "indeterminate (ἄδηλος)."[9] But the inadequacies of this "Greek-colored view of ancient history" would have been immediately evident, especially to those chroniclers who were aware that oriental civilizations claimed to have in their possession dated and continuous records stretching back well before that time.[10]

Why Assyria was assumed to be the oldest datable civilization, and not one of the other civilizations of the ancient Near East, is a matter of conjecture. In his *Persica,* the Greek historian Ctesias had first espoused this view, and although Ctesias' unreliability was widely recognized, his views on the ancient Near East had established, in the words of Drews, "a vulgate tradition of Assyrian history."[11] Largely under the influence of Ctesias, the chronological priority of Assyrian civilization was assumed in the several world histories and chronicles of the second and first centuries

[6] On the work of Eratosthenes, see Ed. Schwartz, "Die Königslisten des Eratosthenes und Kastor mit Excursen über die Interpolationen bei Africanus und Eusebios," *Abhandlungen der königlichen Gesellschaft der Wissenschaften zu Göttingen,* phil.-hist. Klasse 40.2 (1894–5), 1–96, esp. 22–54. Timaeus of Tauromenium, whose chronological system was also based on the Olympiad, fixed the date of the Trojan War somewhat earlier than Eratosthenes; see Truesdell S. Brown, *Timaeus of Tauromenium,* University of California Publications in History 55 (Berkeley, 1958), 125 (note 6); for discussion of the various Greek eras, see E. J. Bickerman, *Chronology of the Ancient World* (Ithaca, 1968), 70–78, esp. 75–76.

[7] Most notably in the chronicle of Apollodorus (2nd century B.C.E.); see Felix Jacoby, *Apollodors Chronik,* Philologische Untersuchungen 16 (Berlin, 1902), 10–12.

[8] Quoted by Censorinus, in *De die natali* 21.1–2, ed. F. Hultsch (Leipzig, 1867).

[9] According to Varro, the "indeterminate" period extended from the beginning of mankind to the first flood, at the time of the "autochthon" Ogygus, according to tradition the earliest name in Attic history. The "mythic" period encompassed the period from this flood to the first Olympiad.

[10] See Ben Zion Wacholder, "Biblical Chronology in the Hellenistic World Chronicles," *HTR* 61 (1968), 451.

[11] Robert Drews, "Assyria in Classical Universal Histories," *Historia* 14 (1965), 130. For doubts about Ctesias' credibility, see, for example, Plutarch: Ctesias filled his books "with a great farrago of nonsense" (*Artax.* 1.4). For modern assessments of Ctesias' sources and reliability, see Jacoby, "Ktesias" (1), *RE* 11.2, cols. 2041–55, esp. 2047; A. R. Burn, *Persia and the Greeks* (New York, 1962), 11–13; Paul Schnabel, *Berossos und die babylonisch-hellenistische Literatur* (Leipzig, 1923), 184. For more favorable estimates of Ctesias, see, for example, T. S. Brown, *The Greek Historians* (Lexington, 1973), 77–86.; Robert Drews, "Assyria," 138–42. Drews maintains that Ctesias had access to authentic Babylonian archives.

B.C.E.[12] Although Ninus may have had predecessors in Asia, he was the first monarch about whom anything certain could be said, and the first king to emerge as a true world ruler. "The first man," writes Diodorus, "to be handed down by tradition to history and memory for us as one who had achieved great deeds is Ninus king of the Assyrians."[13]

By the fifth century the convention of writing universal histories from Ninus' accession to power was securely entrenched, held, or so Orosius claims, by "virtually all historians, both Greek and Latin."[14] Two developments helped to promote its use. When in the first century B.C.E., the Greek chronicler Castor of Rhodes had determined to give Greek civilization an antiquity extending beyond the Trojan War, it was Ctesias' *Persica* that he had used as his source for the ancient Near East, and Ninus was the first monarch with whom he had synchronized the reign of Aegialeus, supposedly the first to rule in Greece.[15] The synchronisms that Castor had formulated were to furnish the basis for later chronography, both Christian and pagan, with the result that it would have proved difficult to replace Ctesias without having first reestablished chronological relationships between Greek kings and their oriental counterparts. The theory of

[12] For discussion of Ctesias' influence, see Drews, "Assyria," 134–38. Of the Assyrian part of Diodorus' history, Drews (134) says that it was "little more than a digest of the first three books of Ctesias' *Persica*."

[13] Diodorus 2.1.4 (trans. C. H. Oldfather, 12 vols., LCL, [Cambridge, 1968]). See also Castor of Rhodes, who, while acknowledging that Belus, Ninus' father, was also king of Assyria, asserts that the "years of his reign have not been handed down clearly" (in *FrGH* 2B, 250 F1). The particular significance of Ninus' reign lay in the belief that he was the first monarch to establish an empire in Asia. In his epitome of the universal history of Pompeius Trogus (ed. Otto Seel [Leipzig, 1935]), Justin allows that the Scythian and Egyptian kingdoms preceded the Assyrian. But he does not consider them true world empires because they did not expand their sphere of control (cf. 1.6–7; 2.1 ff.). Ninus was the "first to substitute the ancient and ancestral custom of the nations with the novelty of a lust for empire" (1.4; cf. 2.1 ff.; also cited in Augustine *City of God* 4.6). For discussion, see most recently J. M. Alonso-Núñez, "An Augustan World History: The *Historiae Philippicae* of Pompeius Trogus," *Greece and Rome* 34 (1987), 66–67.

[14] Orosius 1.1. In addition to Castor, the world historian Cephalion also commenced his chronology from Ninus and Semiramis (cf. Photius, *Bibliotheca*, Cod. 68.34a [PG 103.166A]). Varro himself must have also accepted it. According to Augustine, Varro, in his *De gente populi Romani*, had traced the beginnings of Greek history to the first king of Sicyon, who was believed to be Ninus' contemporary (in Augustine *City of God* 18.2E). For discussion, see Drews, "Assyria," 134–36. One should not assume, however, that this practice had hardened into dogma. Other starting points continued in use; see Jean Sirinelli, *Les vues historiques d'Eusèbe de Césarée*, Université de Dakar, Faculté des Lettres et Sciences Humaines, Publications de la Section de Langues et Littératures 10 (Paris, 1961), 48–49.

[15] Castor dated the accession of both kings to the year 2123 B.C.E. On Castor's work as a chronicler, see especially Schwartz, "Die Königslisten," 1–22; Kubitschek, "Kastor" (8), *RE* 10.2, 2347–57; see also Wacholder, "Biblical Chronology," 464–65; Drews, "Assyria," 133; fragments from Castor's chronicle are collected in *FrGH* 2B, 250 FF 1–20.

the four monarchies was bound to have even more far-reaching conse-
quences. Dating back at least to the second century B.C.E., this theory
sought to schematize all of universal history according to a succession of
world monarchies. Although the empires that were believed to make up
this succession were not always uniform, Assyria was normally treated as
the first, of which Ninus was considered the first true king.[16]

CHRISTIAN CHRONOGRAPHY: ITS ADAPTATION AND CRITIQUE OF THE CLASSICAL TRADITION

Christian universal chroniclers did not hesitate to take over many conventions of Greek chronography. The Olympiad, first developed by Timaeus and Eratosthenes, was extensively used by Africanus and Eusebius,
who quickly perceived its value in standardizing and systematizing Greek
history.[17] Castor's chronology also exerted an influence; Eusebius, for example, used his synchronisms between Greek and Assyrian kings as the
secular basis for his own chronological canons. Even Orosius, who had
complained about the parochialism of beginning a historical narrative
with Ninus, would himself, like other Christian historians, use the theory
of the four monarchies (starting with Ninus and Assyria) as the organizing
principle for most of his work. Indeed, he is one of its best representatives.[18]

If, however, by Orosius' time, pagan historians had "disregarded or not
known" what had preceded the reign of Ninus, the same cannot be said
of their Christian counterparts, the universal chroniclers. In general, it
may be said that Christian historians were far more reluctant to exclude as
"unknown" a whole segment of world history. Such reluctance is not difficult to understand. Those historians, writes Orosius, who ignored the
first period of history, "would have us believe that the world and the creation were without beginning."[19] Although this was only an inference on

---

[16] The earliest attested use of this theory in the West is Aemilius Sura (early 2nd century
B.C.E.). For discussion, see Joseph Ward Swain, "The Theory of the Four Monarchies: Op-
position History under the Roman Empire," *CP* 35 (1940), 1–21; Arnaldo Momigliano, "The
Origins of Universal History," *Settimo Contributo alla Storia degli Studi Classici e del Mondo
Antico*, Storia e Letteratura, Raccolta di Studi e Testi 161 (Rome, 1984), 87–92.

[17] On the use of the Olympiad in the chronicles of Africanus and Eusebius, see Alden
Mosshammer, *The Chronicle of Eusebius*, 136–46, 154–58.

[18] See Swain, "Four Monarchies," 20–21. Christian historians became progressively more
influenced by this theory. Africanus does not appear to have used it, and it is unclear whether
Eusebius, Jerome, or an intermediary was responsible for imposing the theory on the Latin
text of the *Canons*.

[19] Orosius 1.2.

Orosius' part, it is clear that for the pagan historian uncertainty about the precise age of the universe was one of the reasons why chroniclers chose to avoid it. "Whether," wrote Varro, "the first period had a beginning or existed always cannot be known." For that reason, he says, it should be considered ἄδηλος—indeterminate.[20]

Christian chronography proceeded from different premises. In the shape that Julius Africanus had given it, chronography was largely an extension of Jewish/Christian millennialism, according to which all of human history was to be subsumed under a 6,000-year chiliastic scheme.[21] Such a scheme would have precluded the segmentation of history into the categories that Varro had prescribed. Even after the millennialist applications of chronography had fallen into disfavor in some quarters, chronographers found other grounds for extending chronology beyond the conventional limits. Orosius himself would give one reason for parting with the established norms. By commencing history with Ninus, and failing to treat the 3,184 years before his reign, his pagan contemporaries began their narratives from the "middle period," thereby emptying history of its meaning.[22] For if they had started their histories from the first period, they would have recognized that the "wars and calamities" which made up the content of their works had existed from the very creation of man, and were the way in which the "world had been disciplined by alternating periods of good and bad."[23]

A second factor was purely polemical. From the very outset, Christian chronographers had recognized the value of their discipline in the ideological war against Greek culture. There could be no better way to demonstrate the lateness of Greek civilization than by pushing the chronological limits well beyond what the Greeks considered historical. Tatian, Clement, Eusebius, and Africanus are only the better known early Christian writers to employ fairly elaborate chronological arguments to establish that the Greeks arrived on the scene only belatedly.[24] Africanus is typical of the

---

[20] In Censorinus, *De die natali* 21.2 (Hultsch): "Primum tempus, sive habuit initium seu semper fuit, certe quot annorum sit non potest comprehendi."

[21] Africanus' *Chronographiae*, which narrated in five books world history from the birth of Adam to his own time, survives only fragmentarily in later sources. On Africanus' millennialism, see in particular, Heinrich Gelzer, *SJA*, 1. 24–26; Mosshammer, *The Chronicle of Eusebius*, 146–47. For a recent discussion of the presuppositions of Christian chronography, see Brian Croke, "The Origins of the Christian World Chronicle," in *History and Historians in Late Antiquity*, ed. Brian Croke and Alanna M. Emmett (Sydney, 1983), 116–31.

[22] Orosius, 1.11.

[23] Ibid., 1.10–11. For discussion, see Hans-Werner Goetz, *Die Geschichtstheologie des Orosius* (Darmstadt, 1980), 16–20.

[24] Clement *Stromateis* 1.21–1.29; Tatian *Discourse to the Greeks* 36–41.

approach. He calculates 1,020 years as the interval between the first Olympiad, "from which period the Greeks thought they could fix dates accurately," and Ogygus, supposedly the first man in Attica, and a contemporary of Moses.[25] Moreover, as was widely acknowledged, the intervening period between Ogygus and the first Olympiad was one, not of history, but of legends: Prometheus, Io, Europa, and the affairs of Troy, among others. "Whatever special event is mentioned in the mythology of the Greeks because of its antiquity," Africanus concludes, "is to be found to be later than Moses."[26]

There is very little original in these arguments; as Africanus acknowledges, he had largely developed the chronology from Greek and Hellenistic Jewish authorities.[27] Indeed, the purpose in such arguments was not to innovate, but rather to convict the Greeks of newness by appealing to chronological data whose accuracy they themselves had vouchsafed. But while Christian chronographers could claim support for their case in the traditional universal histories of the Hellenistic period, they found in works largely ignored by their Greek counterparts an even richer deposit of documentary material. These latter sources were the native oriental histories of the Egyptians and Babylonians.

BABYLONIAN AND EGYPTIAN ANTIQUITIES

The Oriental Chronicle and Christian Apologetic

"I have examined," Eusebius states in the prologue to the *Chronica*, "various documents of the histories of the Ancients: what the Chaldeans and the Assyrians report, what the Egyptians also write about specific subjects, and what the Greeks narrate as well, insofar as this can be known with certainty."[28] This last qualification—"insofar as this can be known with certainty"—is an important one; it embodies a sentiment that was widespread in both Jewish and Christian history and apologetic, namely, that in matters of primordial history the records of the Greeks were not reliable. Unlettered until Cadmus and ever prey to natural calamity, the

---

[25] In Eusebius *Praeparatio Evangelica* (hereafter *PE*), 10.10.7 (488d). Ed. Karl Mras, GCS 43.1; *Eusebius Werke* 8.1 (Berlin, 1954–56).

[26] In Eusebius *PE* 10.10.19 (490cd). Trans. E. H. Gifford (Oxford, 1903).

[27] Among his sources, Africanus names Philochorus, Theopompus, Polemo, and Josephus. On the contribution of Hellenistic Judaism to apologetic chronography, see Wacholder, "Biblical Chronology," 458–77.

[28] *Chronica* 1.2–5 (trans. Karst). Unless otherwise specified, all citations are from Book 1 of Eusebius' chronicle.

Greek past, Eusebius claims, was mostly blurred.[29] Africanus had expressed the same view earlier. "Until the Olympiads," he wrote, "there is nothing precise in the stories of the Greeks. Before this time everything is confused and there is mutual agreement on nothing."[30]

The poor quality of Greek records for primordial history was in itself hardly controversial; Greek chroniclers themselves lamented over the paucity and unreliability of the documents upon which they had to depend. But when Christian and Jewish historians and apologists made the same observation, they often meant to make an additional polemical point as well: the unreliability or non-existence of Greek records for primordial history proved that the Greeks were not fit to write about the remote past.

In what Momigliano has termed "one of the most important discussions on historiography left to us by Antiquity," Josephus makes the connection graphically.[31] "My first thought," he writes in the prologue to *Against Apion*, "is one of intense astonishment at the current opinion that in the study of primordial history, the Greeks alone deserve serious attention."[32] A balanced view of things would demand a much lower regard for their work. In the writing of history, the Greeks had no cause for boasting. In an earlier age, the Greeks took no measures to preserve a record of their deeds of posterity. The writing of history, not to say writing at all, was among the last things which the Greeks learned how to do. As a result, when the Greek historians first set about writing down the past, they found themselves without documentation, thereby forced either to fabricate or copy from one another. "Anyone can easily discover from the [Greek] historians themselves that their writings have no basis of sure knowledge, but merely present the facts as conjectured by individual authors."[33]

In the ancient world, superior antiquity was often taken to imply cultural priority as well. It is clear that Josephus' indictment of the Greek historians in *Against Apion* formed part of a larger attempt to invalidate Greek culture by proving that it was strictly derivative of other more ancient cultures. There was no better way to illustrate this point than to contrast the historical records of the Greeks with the older and supposedly better kept records of the oriental peoples.

---

[29] Ibid., 2.20–23.
[30] Quoted by Eusebius in *PE* 10.10.1–2 (487d) (trans. Gifford).
[31] Arnaldo Momigliano, "Time in Ancient Historiography," 19; see also Tessa Rajak, "Josephus and the 'Archaeology' of the Jews," *JJS* 33 (1982), 468–69.
[32] Josephus *Against Apion* 1.6. Trans. H. St. J. Thackeray, LCL, vol. 1 (London, 1976).
[33] Ibid., 1.15.

Here, too, Josephus had a long literary tradition to draw upon. In Plato's *Timaeus,* an Egyptian priest had rebuked Solon for his arrogance about the achievements of Greek civilization:

> O Solon, Solon, you Greeks are always children. There is no such thing as an old Greek. . . . You are young in soul, every one of you. For therein you possess not a single belief that is ancient and derived from old tradition, nor yet one science that is hoary with age. . . . And if any event has occurred that is noble or great or in any way conspicuous, whether it be in your country or in ours or in some other place of which we know by report, all such events are recorded from of old and preserved here in our temples; whereas your people and the others are but newly equipped, every time, with letters and all such arts as civilized states require; and when after the usual interval of years, like a plague, the flood from heaven comes sweeping down afresh upon your people, it leaves none of you but the unlettered and uncultured, so that you become young as ever, with no knowledge of all that happened in old times in this land or in your own.[34]

In Hellenistic apologetic the Egyptian's rebuke became a kind of *topos.* Eusebius, who was fond of belittling Greek civilization, cites the passage approvingly in the prologue to the *Chronica.*[35] Speaking on behalf not just of the Jews, but of all non-Greek eastern peoples, Josephus would make even more extensive use of the motif in *Against Apion.* In the Greek world, he writes, "everything will be found to be modern and dating, so to speak, from yesterday or the day before."[36] Josephus knows the same reason for this as the Egyptian priest in the *Timaeus:* periodic catastrophes and Greek laxity in preserving a record of their deeds and discoveries for their posterity. Against this, he will contrast the various older civilizations of the Orient (i.e., "the Egyptians, Chaldeans, and the Phoenicians—for the moment I omit to add our nation to the list"[37]). A temperate climate and care in maintaining records for posterity ensured that these peoples preceded the Greeks in all aspects of culture: "the foundation of their cities (κτίσεις πολέων)," the "invention of the arts (τὰς ἐπινοίας

---

[34] *Timaeus* 22C–23B. Trans. R. G. Bury, LCL (Cambridge, 1975).
[35] *Chronica* 2.25–28; see also Clement *Stromateis* 1.29.
[36] *Against Apion* 1.7.
[37] Ibid., 1.8; cf. 1.215.

τῶν τεχνῶν)," the "compilation of a code of laws (τὰς τῶν νόμων ἀναγραφάς)," and most of all "care in historical composition."[38]

Josephus had a vested interest in championing the chronicles of the orientals. The grammarian Apion, Josephus' opponent and the occasion for the work, had earlier pointed to the fact that few Greek historians mentioned the Jews in their treatment of primordial history; this was proof, he said, that the Jews were a people lacking both a history and an original culture. The oriental chronicles were far more favorable witnesses, and Josephus could find in them attestation not only for the antiquity of the Jews, but validation for the Bible as well. Christian chroniclers had similar concerns. Tatian, for example, a Syrian apologist whose interest in archaic chronology was governed almost entirely by his animus against the Greeks, would also speak in praise of the accuracy of the oriental chronicles. The reason differed little from Josephus', namely, to prove that Moses was "older than the ancient [Greek] heroes, wars, and demons. And we ought rather to believe him, who stands before them in point of age, than the Greeks, who without being aware of it, drew his doctrines [as] from a fountain."[39]

As Josephus admits, he did not have access to the original "sacred texts" of the Egyptians and the Babylonians. Nor were these sources available to the chroniclers. What they knew of oriental history was almost entirely from secondary sources, among others the *Babyloniaca* of Berossus and the *Aegyptiaca* of Manetho. These two works, which Josephus describes somewhat loosely as "translations" or "paraphrases" from the original documents,[40] constituted the main source of information for Babylonian and Egyptian antiquities for both Josephus and the Christian chroniclers from Africanus even up to the Renaissance.[41]

---

[38] Ibid., 1.7–8; for an example of this same theme in early Christian literature, see Clement *Stromateis* 1.16, which gives a long catalogue of the various arts and sciences first developed by non-Greek peoples.

[39] Tatian *The Discourse to the Greeks* 40. Trans. J. E. Ryland, *ANF* 2. 81.

[40] *Against Apion* 1.73.

[41] The fragments from Berossus' *Babyloniaca* have been collected in *FrGH* 3C 680 FF 1–22; an earlier collection of these excerpts is in *FHG* 2. 495–510. An English translation of the *Babyloniaca* based mainly on the Greek text in Syncellus was done by Stanley Mayer Burstein (*The Babyloniaca of Berossus*, Sources from the Ancient Near East 1.5 [Malibu; 1978], 13–35). The major work on the *Babyloniaca* is still P. Schnabel's *Berossos und die babylonisch-hellenistische Literatur;* see also Ed. Schwartz, "Berossos" (4) *RE* 3.1, 309–16; W. v. Soden, "Berossos," *RGG* (3), 1. 1069; W. Spoerri, "Bero(s)sos," *Der kleine Pauly*, 1 (1964), 1548; Franz Susemihl, *Geschichte der griechischen Litteratur in der Alexandrinerzeit*, 2 vols. (Leipzig, 1891–2) 1. 605–7; Friedrich Cornelius, "Berossus und die altorientalische Chronologie," *Klio* 35 (1942), 1–16; François Lenormant, *Essai de commentaire des fragments cosmogoniques de Bérose*

Berossus, Manetho, and the "Twin Tradition"

The tradition about the composition of these two works is curiously symmetrical and not entirely beyond suspicion.[42] The *Babyloniaca* and the *Aegyptiaca* are both said to have consisted of three books, spanning the entire course of Egyptian and Babylonian history from its beginning.[43] Both works were officially commissioned, the *Babyloniaca* by Antiochus I Soter, and the *Aegyptiaca* by Ptolemy II Philadelphus, a Ptolemaic king known for his interest in exotic works. Manetho, says Syncellus, was "almost contemporary with Berossus, or a little later (κατὰ τοὺς αὐτοὺς σχεδόν που χρόνους ἢ μικρὸν ὕστερον)."[44] Both Berossus and Manetho were priests, educated in Greek culture,[45] who claimed to have composed

---

(Paris, 1871). See, more recently, Robert Drews, "The Babylonian Chronicles and Berossus," *Iraq* 37 (1975), 39–55; and G. Komoróczy, "Berosos and the Mesopotamian Literature," *AAAScHung* 21 (1973), 125–52.

For fragments of the *Aegyptiaca*, see *FrGH* 3C 609 FF 1–28. Waddell has collected and translated the surviving portions of the work, along with other fragments from other sources attributed to Manetho (LCL [Cambridge, 1940–64]). The major works on Manetho include the following: Jacob Krall, *Die Composition und die Schicksale des Manethonischen Geschichtswerkes, SitzungsberAkWien*, phil.-hist. Classe 95 (1879[1880]), 123–226; Hans Wolfgang Helck, *Untersuchungen zu Manetho und den ägyptischen Königslisten*, Untersuchungen zur Geschichte und Altertumskunde Aegyptens 18 (Berlin, 1956); R. Laqueur, "Manethon (1)," *RE* 14.1, 1059–1102; Susemihl, *Geschichte der griechischen Litteratur*, 1. 608–16. Among the older works, several are still valuable; see, for example, George Friedrich Unger, *Chronologie des Manetho* (Berlin, 1867); H. Vollot, *Du système chronologique de Manethon* (Beaune, 1867); A. Böckh, *Manetho und die Hundssternperiode* (Berlin, 1845); Robert Fruin, *Manethonis Sebennytae Reliquiae*, Dissertatio philologica inauguralis (Leiden, 1847); Franz Joseph Lauth, *Manetho und der Turiner Königspapyrus* (Munich, 1865); H. von Pessl, *Das chronologische System Manethos* (Leipzig, 1878); Richard Lepsius, "Über die Manethonische Bestimmung des Umfangs der aegyptischen Geschichte," *AbhAkBerlin*, phil.-hist. Klasse (1857), pp. 183–208.

[42] For modern suspicions about this "twin tradition," see in particular Ernest Havet, *Mémoire sur les écrits qui portent les noms de Bérose et de Manéthon* (Paris, 1873); also Alfred and Maurice Croiset, *Histoire de la littérature grecque*, 5 vols (Paris, 1887–99) 5. 99; also Waddell, *Manetho*, viii (note 1).

[43] According to Eusebius (*Chronica* 63.17–21), Manetho "composed his account in three books. These deal with the gods, demi-gods, and spirits of the dead, and the mortal kings who ruled Egypt down to Darius, king of the Persians" (trans. Waddell, fr. 1). Although the epitomes of Manetho in both Africanus and Eusebius contain 31 dynasties, the 31st dynasty is generally considered to be a later addition. Cf. Waddell, *Manetho*, fr. 75(a), (note 184). As for the *Babyloniaca*, Schnabel (*Berossos*, 16–29) conjectures that Berossus treated Chaldean wisdom in the first book; the second and third books, the historical segment of the work, took the form of a continuous record of kings from the period of the ten antediluvian Chaldean kings to the accession of Alexander. For a conflicting reconstruction of the arrangement of the subject material in this work, see Schwartz, "Berossos," 310.

[44] Sync. 17.4.

[45] According to Josephus (*Ag. Apion* 1.73), Manetho was "both a native of Egypt and proficient in Greek learning (τῆς Ἑλληνικῆς μετεσχηκὼς παιδείας)." Berossus, he says, was "familiar in learned circles (γνώριμος . . . τοῖς περὶ παιδείαν ἀναστρεφομένοις) through his publication for Greek readers of works on Chaldean astronomy and philosophy" (*Ag. Apion* 1.129).

their works on the basis of temple records to which they, as priests, had privileged access.

The authors of these works did not shrink from tailoring their histories to a Greek audience. In the *Babyloniaca*, Babylonian deities were identified with their Greek counterparts; it is Bel/Zeus, for example, who warns Xisuthrus, the Babylonian flood hero, about the imminent deluge. Similarly, in his symbolic interpretation of the Babylonian cosmogony, Berossus attempts to accommodate the rationalizing inclinations of the learned Greek reader; after recounting the myth of Bel's creation of heaven and earth from "Thalath," the primordial woman, Berossus urges his reader to in terpret the story "allegorically."[46] Nor does Berossus report this myth as part of the historical narrative; it is rather revealed to the primitive Babylonians by Oannes, a primordial sea monster who appears to mankind at the beginning of Babylonian civilization. As Gelzer has observed, Berossus employed this literary device to avoid historicizing the Babylonian myth of creation, and thus inviting the ridicule of the Greek reader.[47]

As much as they were historians, Manetho and Berossus were apologists, bent on extolling both the antiquity and continuity of the cultures on whose behalf they wrote. In addition to his cosmogonic revelations, Oannes is credited by Berossus with the introduction of all those τεχναί that, as Josephus would insist in *Against Apion*, the Greeks had only gotten much later: "the knowledge of letters (γραμμάτων), and sciences and crafts of all types (τεχνῶν παντοδαπῶν) . . . how to found cities (πόλεων συνοικισμούς), establish temples (ἱερῶν ἱδρύσεις), introduce laws and measure land (γεωμετρίαν). It also revealed to them seeds and the gathering of fruits and in general it gave man everything which is connected with the civilized life."[48] In tracing the origins of civilization to antediluvian Babylonia, Berossus was not only satisfying a characteristically Hellenistic fascination with εὑρήματα;[49] he was also implying that the Greeks, as well as all other peoples, had derived their culture from Oannes'

[46] *Chronica* 8.17. Karst gives the following translation of the Armenian text: "Sinnbildlicherweise aber, sagt er, und in übertragener Bedeutung sei solches mythologisiert worden über die Naturen" (ad loc.); Syncellus' text of the *Babyloniaca* here has: ἀλληγορικῶς δὲ φησι τοῦτο πεφυσιολογῆσθαι (30.9–10). Later, the neo-Platonist Damascius (6th cent. C.E.), in his work *Difficulties and Solutions of First Principles*, ventures a Platonizing interpretation of the same creation myth; he casts "Tauthe" (= Ti'āmat) and "Apason" (= Apsū) as "first principles"; their offspring "Moymis" (= Mummu) as the "mental world (νοητὸς κόσμος)"; and Bel/Marduk as the demiurge. For English translation and discussion, see Alexander Heidel, *The Babylonian Genesis*, 2nd ed. (Chicago, 1951), 75–76.

[47] Cf. Gelzer, *SJA*, 2. 26. For further discussion, see below, Chap. 4, pp. 110–11.

[48] Sync. 29.11–16 (trans. Burstein, *Babyloniaca*, B.1.5, 13–14).

[49] On the theme of the culture-hero in Hellenistic world-history, see A. Momigliano, "The Origins of Universal History," 83–85.

primordial revelations: "from the time of Oannes," he writes, "nothing further has been discovered (οὐδὲν ἄλλο περισσὸν εὑρεθῆναι)."[50]

Manetho, writes Josephus, promised to "translate (μεθερμηνεύειν) the history of Egypt from the sacred books (ἐκ τῶν ἱερῶν γραμμάτων)."[51] Oriental histories of the Hellenistic period often characterized themselves in this way. The *Babyloniaca*, Josephus writes, was a faithful rendition of its sources, as was the Jewish *Antiquities:* "I have translated" the *Antiquities*, Josephus writes, "from the sacred books."[52] Such claims will strike the modern reader as extravagant, since all three writers did not hesitate either to embellish upon their native records or excise material that would invite derision from Greek readers.[53] But the motive behind the hyperbole is plain. If Greek historians had no sound documentary base upon which to work, compelled thereby to present the facts "as conjectured by individual authors," oriental historians had merely to reproduce in Greek carefully preserved records to which they, as priests, had privileged access.[54]

Native loyalty meant too that both Berossus and Manetho were, like

[50] Sync. 29.16.

[51] *Against Apion* 1.228. Josephus says earlier (1.73) about the *Aegyptiaca* that Manetho "wrote it in the Greek tongue . . . having translated (μεταφράσας—paraphrased?) it from the sacred books."

[52] *Against Apion* 1.54; see also *Antiquities* 1.17, where Josephus promises neither to "add to nor subtract from" what is found in Scripture. Of the *Babyloniaca*, Josephus says that its author "followed the most ancient records" (*Against Apion* 1.130). In introducing the *Babyloniaca*, Alexander Polyhistor, who had transcribed large portions of that work, reports that Berossus translated "many books which had been preserved with great care (μετὰ πολλῆς ἐπιμελείας) at Babylon" (in Sync. 28.22–23). For other oriental writers in Greek who putatively took pains to establish their fidelity to their sources, see Porphyry's description of the composition of the *Phoenician History* of Philo of Byblos; the work, he says, was a translation into Greek of the history of Sanchuniathon, supposedly a contemporary of Semiramis, who "made a complete collection of ancient history from the records in the various cities and from the registers in the temples" (in Eusebius *PE* 1.9.21 (31b) [trans. Gifford]). See also Josephus' description of Menander of Ephesus (*Ant.* 8.144; 9.283; *Ag. Apion* 1.116); for discussion, see Rajak, "Archaeology," 473. Sometimes, the claims about care and accuracy in preservation and translation reached absurd proportions, as, for example, in the case of (ps)-Manetho's *Book of Sothis;* for the supposed conditions under which the *Book of Sothis* of (ps-)Manetho was written, see below, Chap. 2, pp. 57–59.

[53] For discussion of this question as it relates to Josephus' *Antiquities*, see Louis H. Feldman, "Hellenizations in Josephus' Portrayal of Man's Decline," in *Religions in Antiquity*, Studies in the History of Religions 14, ed. Jacob Neusner (Leiden, 1968), 336–53; see also Rajak, "Archaeology," who rightly recognizes this motif as having its origins "among the later Greek exponents of Oriental cultures" (472). The only work for which the description "translation" is apt is the Septuagint. But even here the Jewish apologist (ps-)Aristeas overstates the case; on several occasions, his language is ambiguous enough to leave the impression that what the seventy-two Jewish sages did was simply to prepare a critical edition of the Pentateuch, not a translation at all; for discussion, see G. Zuntz, "Aristeas Studies II: Aristeas on the Translation of the Torah," *Studies in the Septuagint: Origins, Recensions, and Interpretations*, ed. Sidney Jellicoe (New York, 1974), 213–24.

[54] *Against Apion* 1.15. Josephus, writes Momigliano, was "quite right in saying that the Jews had better organized public records than the Greeks. . . . What he did not know was that

Josephus, sensitive to what Greek historians had written about their respective civilizations. For Josephus the particular offense of the historians against the Jews was virtual neglect. Berossus and Manetho had their own complaints. When the *Babyloniaca* and *Aegyptiaca* appeared in Greek in the beginning of the third century, Greek historians were not well informed about Egypt and the Near East. It followed from this neglect or misinformation that both historians conceived their task at least in part as that of disabusing Greek historians of what they considered were misconceptions about the age and accomplishments of the civilizations that they represented.

Since Herodotus, Greek historians had not overlooked Egypt. But Manetho was far from satisfied with what had been written on the region, particularly by Herodotus. Manetho, Josephus tells us, had "convicted Herodotus of having erred through ignorance on many points of Egyptian history."[55] We are told elsewhere that he had even composed a separate work meant as a critique of Herodotus.[56] Berossus' own grievance concerned that very historical datum that was to dominate the historians of Orosius' day, namely, the Ctesias-inspired confusion of Babylonia and Assyria, and the resulting assumption that Ninus was the first notable monarch in Asia. Against this, Berossus recorded a succession of Chaldean kings antedating Ninus by thousands of years. Along with this came as well some unkind words for the Greek historians who clung to these views. In the third book of the *Babyloniaca*, Josephus writes: "he [Berossus] censures the Greek historians for their deluded belief that Babylon was founded by the Assyrian queen Semiramis and their erroneous statement that its marvellous buildings were her creation."[57]

---

public records kept by priests need to be looked into very carefully" ("Time in Ancient Historiography," 19).

[55] *Against Apion* 1.73.

[56] Two preserved fragments from that work in Waddell, *Manetho*, fr. 88.

[57] *Against Apion* 1.142 (trans. Thackeray). In evaluating Berossus' criticism of Ctesias, Schnabel has remarked, "One of the greatest services of Berossus remains that he set the genuine native tradition over against the false reports of Ctesias and his successors and made these traditions available to the Greeks" (*Berossos*, 184). It cannot be assumed, however, that the "native traditions" which Berossus offered as an alternative to Ctesias were in every instance more accurate. Berossus was hardly a critical reader of his sources, and recorded numerous factual errors; to what extent the *Babyloniaca* was an improvement over the *Persica* is still a matter of dispute. For recent discussion of this question, see T. S. Brown, *The Greek Historians*, 83–84. Burstein (*Babyloniaca*, 8) notes that the *Babyloniaca* contained a "number of surprising errors of simple fact of which certainly the most flagrant is the statement that Nabopolassar ruled Egypt." Berossus, Burstein suggests, "offered only the most superficial explanations of the events he recorded and made no attempt to compensate for the biases of his sources." For a comparison of Berossus and Ctesias, see A. v. Gutschmid, "Zu den Fragmenten des Berosos und Ktesias," *Kleine Schriften*, 2. 97–114; Drews, "Assyria," 138–42.

The Pagan Reception of Berossus and Manetho

There is probably no better illustration of the tenacity with which historical conventions persisted in Antiquity than the almost wholesale neglect of the *Babyloniaca* and *Aegyptiaca*. If, as has been suggested, Berossus
and Manetho had hoped to supplant previous histories as the definitive
works on Egypt and the Near East, they were notable failures. Neither
work seems to have aroused more than a passing interest among Greek
writers on the Orient. Although Susemihl's observation that the *Aegyp-*
tiaca "received not the slightest attention in the literary world of the
Greeks and Romans"[58] is probably an exaggeration, it is clear that few
classical Greek and Latin authors took note of the *Aegyptiaca*. The *Baby-*
loniaca hardly fared any better. The work did receive sporadic and scattered attention from Greek authors, notably Alexander Polyhistor in the
first century B.C.E. and later Abydenus (first century C.E.) and Juba of
Mauretania.[59] For the most part, however, the *Babyloniaca,* and along with
it Berossus' strictures against Ctesias and his *epigoni,* were ignored by later
historians. Castor, the first Greek chronographer to incorporate the early
chronology of the Near East, continued to use Ctesias, as was also true of
the several universal histories that appeared in the first century B.C.E.—
those of Diodorus Siculus, Pompeius Trogus, and Nicolaus of Damascus.[60] Even those historians who knew the *Babyloniaca* seem to have been
curiously immune to his criticisms of Ctesias. Polyhistor, the principal
source of the *Babyloniaca* for the Christian chroniclers, felt no remorse in
consulting Ctesias for his treatment of archaic Assyrian history, thus per-
petuating the confusion of Assyria with Babylonia which Berossus had
tried to correct.[61] Berossus would have been most disturbed by Abydenus'
easy conflation of the *Babyloniaca* with Ctesias. Struck by Berossus' lack of
interest in the rule of Ninus and Semiramis, Abydenus simply supplemented this deficiency with material from Castor and Ctesias; the end
result was that Abydenus, like Castor, began his "historical" narrative with
Ninus.[62]

[58] F. Susemihl, *Geschichte der griechischen Litteratur,* I. 611.
[59] Excerpts from Abydenus' treatment of Babylonian history in *Chronica* 15.27–20.32. Tatian (*Discourse to the Greeks* 36; cf. Eusebius *PE* 10.11.18 [493b]) notes that "Juba in his treatise
Concerning the Assyrians says that he has learned the history from Berossus."
[60] See Drews, "Assyria," 134.
[61] Cf. Schnabel, *Berossos,* 150–54; Burstein, *Babyloniaca,* 8.
[62] In Eusebius *Chronica* 25.31–26.11; cf. Drews, "Assyria," 131 (note 13); in Eusebius's highly
condensed text of Polyhistor/Berossus' Babylonian history before the accession of the Medes,
there is a passing reference to the rule of Semiramis over Assyria.

There are many reasons why the *Babyloniaca* and the *Aegyptiaca* failed to gain the attention that their authors had hoped they would. It would appear to be a combination of Greek attitudes toward the Orient and the composition of the works themselves. It has been suggested that Manetho's annalistic approach to his subject failed to satisfy the literary inclinations of the Hellenistic period for fanciful stories about non-Greek peoples.[63] The *Babyloniaca* suffered from its own internal problems: the many incomprehensible and foreign Babylonian names,[64] and the extravagantly long chronology of Babylonian history,[65] which would have proved difficult for a Greek historian to incorporate into a Greek universal history. As a recent writer on the *Babyloniaca* has maintained, the critical weakness of the *Babyloniaca,* and hence the reason for its neglect, lay in the fact that the Greek text of the work was little more than a "veneer covering the essentially unexplained Babylonian content."[66]

The neglect of these works by Greek and Latin historians certainly had little to do with lack of interest or even a disposition to slight the accomplishments, antiquity, and wisdom of Eastern peoples. Hellenistic writers and historians on Egypt and the Near East were guilty of none of these things. But—and this has been amply demonstrated—their interest in non-Greek peoples tended largely toward exotic and edifying tales, preferably recounted by Greek, not native, historians. For Egypt and the Near East, there already existed several histories that came closer to satisfying these tastes than the *Aegyptiaca* and the *Babyloniaca*—not just Ctesias and Herodotus, but the *Aegyptiaca* of Hecateus of Abdera as well (ca. 300 B.C.E.). This latter work, which Jacoby has aptly described as more a "philosophical romance" than a history, enjoyed a popularity among Hellenistic readers far surpassing Manetho's work of the same name.[67]

Berossus and Manetho were not unknown names in Antiquity. To the contrary, both writers enjoyed a considerable cachet in learned circles. It was, however, not as historians that they were celebrated, but rather for their contributions to culture and wisdom. Josephus was already aware of this when he first mentioned Berossus in *Against Apion*. Although Jo-

[63] Cf. Waddell, *Manetho,* xxv; Susemihl, *Geschichte der griechischen Litteratur,* I. 611.

[64] Schwartz, "Berossos," 314.

[65] Cf. Schnabel, *Berossos,* 29–32.

[66] Burstein, *Babyloniaca,* 9. Burstein cites as an example of this the myth of Oannes and his revelations to mankind, which, he says, the Greeks would have considered unbelievable. Not all Greeks appear to have found this story incredible, however; cf. Julian, *Against the Galileans* (176AB), who affirms his belief in the existence of Oannes when he extols the wisdom of the Chaldeans. For further discussion, see below Chap. 4, pp. 110–11.

[67] Cf. F. Jacoby, "Hekataios" (4), *RE* 7.2, 2758; Waddell, xxiv–xxv.

sephus would introduce him as a historical witness, he acknowledged that Berossus was familiar to his Greek readers not as a historian, but for his publication of numerous writings on Greek astronomy and astrology.[68] By the third and fourth centuries C.E., both Berossus and his younger contemporary Manetho were credited with numerous discoveries and works, largely undeserved, in the fields for which the Chaldeans and Egyptians were most celebrated, the astral sciences. To this extent, what pagan writers remember of these two authors is not unlike what they remember of other revered figures from the Orient—Zoroaster, Solomon, and Moses, for example. Like them, Berossus and Manetho had become a type of the oriental sage.[69]

The Greek reaction to the *Babyloniaca* and the *Aegyptiaca* contrasts sharply with the reception of these works in Hellenistic Judaism and Christianity. For Josephus and the chroniclers, Berossus and Manetho were preeminently historians, not sages. Far surpassing anything that the Greeks had to contribute to the study of ancient Egypt and the Near East, both histories were, next to Genesis itself, looked to as documentary evidence for a period that Greek chronographers considered largely unknowable.

THE CHRISTIANIZATION OF THE ORIENTAL CHRONICLE

Christian historians were often impressed, sometimes even dismayed, by similarities, both real and imagined, between Genesis and the ethnic histories of the Babylonians and Egyptians. Syncellus, himself no admirer of these sources, felt it necessary to account for these parallels. In his judgment, plagiarism was the only explanation. Though the histories of the Chaldeans and the Egyptians, he writes, may "appear to agree with divine Scripture in part," this is so only because those "who have composed these

---

[68]*Against Apion* 1.129; Schnabel (*Berossos*, 20) believed, however, that Josephus was referring here to the *Babyloniaca*.

[69]The astronomical material associated with Berossus has been collected by Schnabel, *Berossos*, 256–60 (pt. 6); also in *FrGH* 3C 680 FF 15–22. According to a tradition preserved by Vitruvius in his work *De architectura*, Berossus, the "expositor of the Chaldean Discipline" (9.2.1), began to teach the Greeks about Chaldean science (i.e., astronomy and astrology) when he moved from Babylonia to the island of Cos (9.6.2). For the tradition about Berossus' invention of the sundial, see Vitruvius *De architectura* 9.8.1. The accuracy of the tradition is doubtful.

Manetho "attained the acme of wisdom," writes Aelian (*De natura animalium* 10.16), apparently on the basis of hearsay. Like Berossus, Manetho was associated with various works on Egyptian religion and science; for excerpts from these works, see Waddell, *Manetho*, frs. 76–87. For discussion, see below, Chap. 2, p. 62 (note 76).

histories have taken every worthwhile idea (πᾶν νόημα χρηστόν)" from Scripture.[70] One of the examples that Syncellus adduces in support of this charge has to do with the Babylonian cosmogony, as it was revealed by Oannes. In Syncellus' excerpts from the *Babyloniaca*, the monster Oannes is reported to have revealed to "mankind that there was a time in which all was darkness and water."[71] For Syncellus, alert to the parallel between this and Gen. 1:2, there was no other conclusion than that the Chaldeans had stolen the doctrine from Moses, only superficially changing (μετέπλασε) the wording in order to seduce the less sophisticated.[72]

There is some irony in the charge, because this very passage was probably not original to the *Babyloniaca*. As has been suggested elsewhere, the word "darkness (σκότος)" was interpolated by a Jewish scribe, eager to enlarge upon similarities between the *Babyloniaca* and Genesis.[73] That Syncellus should later take this passage as evidence of fraud on the part of Berossus illustrates the extent to which his impressions of his sources had been colored by many centuries of prior transmission by Jewish and Christian scribes.

The *Babyloniaca* and the *Aegyptiaca* survive almost entirely in fragments, excerpts, and references in Josephus and the chroniclers. In many cases, their knowledge of these sources has been filtered through several stages of redaction. Both Eusebius and Africanus, for example, know of the *Aegyptiaca* only through chronological epitomes of that work appearing several centuries after its publication.[74] And although direct excerpts from the *Babyloniaca* do survive, none of the chroniclers knew the work firsthand, depending instead on Polyhistor's abridgment of it.[75] By the time that Syncellus, in the ninth century, was polemicizing against the *Babyloniaca*, the excerpts that he knew had already passed through several hands, including Polyhistor, Eusebius, and the Alexandrian chroniclers.[76] For these reasons, it must be recognized that what survives from these two ethnic histories is almost entirely governed by the editorial discretion

[70] Sync. 23.35–24.2. See also 32.8, where Syncellus asserts that the Chaldean teratology "took its point of departure entirely" from Scripture.

[71] Ibid., 32.15.

[72] Ibid., 32.17.

[73] Schnabel (*Berossos*, 156) argued for interpolation on the grounds that Oannes' allegorical explanation of the cosmogony posits creation only out of moisture; see also Burstein, *Babyloniaca*, 14 (note 11).

[74] For discussion of these epitomes, see below, pp. 33–34.

[75] Eusebius makes this explicit; the excerpts from the *Babyloniaca* begin as follows: "From Alexander Polyhistor concerning the writings of the Chaldeans" (*Chronica* 4.9). For discussion, see Schnabel, *Berossos*, 154–68.

[76] Cf. Schnabel, *Berossos*, 162–68.

of Jewish and Christian witnesses, none of whom hesitated to embellish these sources for overtly tendentious purposes.

It is not difficult to discover the motives that impelled Josephus and his Christian successors to use and edit the sources as they did. Validation of the biblical narrative was one reason. In discussing the plausibility of the Genesis narrative about the longevity of the antediluvian patriarchs, Josephus appeals not only to the view, widespread among ancient writers, that primitive mankind led a more virtuous and salubrious life than subsequent generations; he adds as well the fact that his words are confirmed by other "historians of Antiquity," including "Manetho, the annalist of the Egyptians," and "Berossus, the compiler of the Chaldean traditions."[77] Just as important were the polemical/apologetic applications of these sources. It was Josephus who first recalled Berossus' and Manetho's strictures against the Greek historians. These sources, he observes, discredit Greek historians on the basis of ancient and supposedly eyewitness sources, and prove that the Jews, at the very least, surpassed the Greeks in antiquity. Thus, after his excerpt from the *Aegyptiaca*, putatively about the expulsion of the Jews from Egypt, Josephus concludes: "Manetho has thus furnished us with evidence from Egyptian literature . . . and that we left it at a date so remote that it preceded the Trojan War by nearly a thousand years."[78] Tatian later offered the same reason in his *Address to the Greeks*. "Berossus is a very trustworthy (ἱκανώτατος) man," he writes. What particularly commends the *Babyloniaca* to him is Berossus' reference to Nabuchadnezzar's war against the Jews, and thus his indirect corroboration of Moses' antiquity.[79]

Virtually all of the editing by Jewish and Christian writers who used the *Babyloniaca* and the *Aegyptiaca* was intended to enhance the corroborative value of these sources. If only a fraction of their original works survive, it is because narrowly apologetic and chronographic interests had determined what was and what was not worth transmitting. Thus, in *Against Apion,* Josephus' extracts from Berossus and Manetho treat only a few select periods in Babylonian and Egyptian history: namely, that material which could be used either as independent confirmation for the antiquity of the Jews or of the biblical narrative.

Since, by its very nature, Christian chronography examined a broader range of world history than Josephus, both Africanus and Eusebius set

[77] Josephus *Antiquities* 1.107 (trans. Thackeray); see also Eusebius *PE* 9.13.5 (415d).
[78] *Against Apion* 1.103–104 (trans. Thackeray).
[79] Tatian *Discourse to the Greeks* 36; cf. Eusebius *PE* 10.11.9 (493b); Clement *Stromateis* 1.21.

their sights on the entire chronological span of Berossus' and Manetho's histories. But the synopses of the *Babyloniaca* and the *Aegyptiaca* that their chronicles preserve are highly condensed and edited versions of these sources, excluding much historical material deemed either irrelevant or inappropriate in a biblically based chronology. The result of this editing is reflected clearly in the shape of the material from Berossus and Manetho preserved by the chroniclers.

Only one segment of the *Babyloniaca* consisted of material that was strictly historical narrative; much of it was given over to a discussion of Chaldean wisdom. The *Babyloniaca,* says Polyhistor, "contained the histories of heaven (and of earth) and seas and the first birth and the kings and their deeds."[80] After describing the revelations of Oannes, Berossus promises to "discuss these matters in the book of kings."[81] Yet, in the form of the *Babyloniaca* that we know from Eusebius, very little of this Chaldean wisdom survives. Presumably a Jewish or Christian editor found it irrelevant or altogether unacceptable. In his own extracts from the *Babyloniaca,* Eusebius himself does not conceal the fact that he had abridged the text of the work as he knew it from Polyhistor. In enumerating the postdiluvian Babylonian kings from Xisuthrus up to the "accession of the Medes," for example, Eusebius reports that Polyhistor mentions each one of them by name "on the authority of the book of Berossus."[82] Eusebius' excerpts, however, furnish the names of very few of them. As a rule, most of the historical notices that Eusebius retained from Polyhistor concerned only the deeds of the better known Babylonian and Assyrian kings and those recognizable from allusions and parallel reports in the Bible.

Selectivity is even more visible in the chroniclers' use of the *Aegyptiaca.* The highly abbreviated epitomes of that work in Eusebius and Africanus, containing no citations directly attributable to Manetho, are of a strikingly different character from the long narrative quotations from the *Aegyptiaca* preserved by Josephus.[83] Indeed, if one were to base his conception of the original form of the *Aegyptiaca* strictly on the state of its preservation in Eusebius and Africanus, he might erroneously assume that Manetho was not a historian at all, but only a compiler of lists of kings. Divided into

[80] *Chronica* 6.20–23 (= Sync. 28.24–26).

[81] Ibid., 7.25–26 (= Sync. 29.19–20).

[82] Ibid., 12.20–24 (trans. Burstein, *Babyloniaca,* C.4.2, 21); see also 15.15–17.

[83] Africanus' epitome of Manetho's *Aegyptiaca* is preserved only in Syncellus' chronicle. Eusebius' epitome survives both in Syncellus, who compares and contrasts it with Africanus' epitome, and in the Armenian translation as well. Both epitomes are included in Waddell's edition and translation.

three "tomes (τόμοι)," the epitomized *Aegyptiaca* was essentially a chronological synopsis of the whole *Aegyptiaca*, cast in the form of running lists
of Egyptian kings, the length of their rule, and the dynasty to which they
belonged. Taking the form of lists of kings, these epitomes were composed
well after the publication of the *Aegyptiaca*, distilling from that work a
chronological conspectus of all of Egyptian history.[84]

By furnishing a handy conspectus of the relevant chronological material
in the *Aegyptiaca*, which could be compared and synchronized with the
chronologies of other peoples, the epitomes were mainly intended to assist
the work of chronography. With the exception of the earliest dynasties,
Africanus' and Eusebius' epitomes give only the sparsest information, and
this is, as already noted, mainly chronological; for some dynasties not even
the reigns of individual kings are dated, only the length of the whole dynasty. This paucity of historical material applies even to those Egyptian
dynasties about which much was known in Antiquity, and about which
Manetho himself apparently wrote a great deal. The fully developed narrative in Josephus' authentic excerpts from Manetho's account of the reign
of the "shepherd-kings" contrasts sharply with what Africanus and Eusebius say about their rule. The latter two give only the names and the total
years of their rule.[85] What historical notices do appear in the epitomes are,
predictably, largely synchronistic in nature.[86] At the eighteenth dynasty,
for example, a dynasty which Unger has termed "the most well-known of
all the dynasties,"[87] the epitomes describe events only of significance for
Jewish and Greek history—the exodus of Moses from Egypt, the flood at
the time of Deucalion, and the conquest of Argos by Danaus.[88]

Simple condensation was not the only method that Jewish and Christian
historians applied to these sources. Interpolations, forgeries, artificial syn-

---

[84] Unger (*Manetho*, 6–9), however, believed that Manetho himself had composed the epitome as a kind of chronological appendix to the historical work. For discussion, see also J.
Krall, *Die Composition*, 208–21; R. Laqueur, "Manethon," *RE*, 14.1, 1080–89; synopsis of
Laqueur by Waddell, *Manetho*, xix–xx. Krall considered these epitomes the work of Egyptian
chronographers (210–13); Gelzer regarded them as Jewish or Christian compositions (*SJA*, 1.
205–6; 2. 53–54).

[85] Cf. *Against Apion* 1.93–105 with Africanus' and Eusebius' version of the 15th to 17th
dynasties (ed. Waddell, frs. 44–48).

[86] It is mainly for the earliest dynasties of human kings that the epitomes provide historical
information of antiquarian interest only. After this, the narrative becomes decidedly less detailed—a feature which can be attributed either to the fact that a redactor of the epitome lost
interest in the nonchronological parts of the *Aegyptiaca* (so Unger, *Manetho*, 13), or to the
greater intrinsic interest of early Egyptian history.

[87] Unger, *Manetho*, 6–8.

[88] Cf. frs. 52 and 53 (ed. Waddell).

chronisms and fanciful interpretations were all literary techniques that Jewish and Christian writers appear to have employed to enhance the corroborative value of Berossus and Manetho. In certain cases, this took the form of developing parallels, often imagined, between these sources and the Bible. Doubtless the reason Eusebius elected to retain so much of Berossus' treatment of antediluvian history was that here he had discerned some of the more suggestive parallels with Genesis. In Berossus' narrative of the ten antediluvian Chaldean kings, Eusebius recognized a parallel with the ten pre-flood generations of Genesis. And Berossus' story of Xisuthrus, the hero who had survived the flood in an ark, bore a close resemblance to the Genesis account of the same event; "Xisuthrus," Eusebius wrote, "is the same one who is called Noah by the Hebrews."[89] Josephus earlier had endorsed the same identifications, adding as well some of his own. In his account of the period immediately after the flood, Berossus had referred to a "righteous man experienced in celestial affairs." This anonymous figure, concluded Josephus, must have been none other than Abraham.[90]

One of the most forced of Josephus' interpretations appears in the discussion of his first excerpt from the *Aegyptiaca*. In that excerpt, Manetho had recounted the conquest of Egypt by the Hyksos, the tribe of shepherds who had overrun and ravaged Egypt during the reign of Tutimaeus. For Josephus, the Hyksos could have been no other people than the Jews, because Manetho had reported that after their expulsion the Hyksos "built a city in the country now called Judaea . . . and gave it the name of Jerusalem."[91] In this way, Manetho was cast for Josephus as a favorable witness to the antiquity of the Jews: "Manetho has thus furnished us with evidence from Egyptian literature for two most important points: first, that we came into Egypt from elsewhere, and secondly, that we left it at a date so remote in the past that it preceded the Trojan War by nearly a thousand years."[92]

Zeal to enhance the corroborative value of these sources occasionally

---

[89] *Chronica* 10.13. Josephus goes so far as to say that Berossus has "like Moses described the flood . . . and told of the Ark, in which Noah, the founder of our race, was saved when it landed on the heights of the mountain of Armenia" (*Ag. Apion* 1.129–30). For Eusebius' likening of the ten antediluvian Chaldean kings with the ten pre-flood biblical generations, see *Chronica* 9.31–34. Other parallels between Berossus and Genesis have been investigated by Marshall D. Johnson, *The Purpose of the Biblical Genealogies*, SNTS Monograph Series 8 (Cambridge, 1969), 28–31.

[90] Cf. *Antiquities* 1.158. See also *Against Apion* 1.128–133.

[91] *Against Apion*, 1.90.

[92] Ibid., 1.103–4.

could lead to tendentious interpolation of them. Corruption of the text of the *Babyloniaca* is found almost immediately after its appearance.[93] In the form of the *Babyloniaca* that he had received from Polyhistor, Eusebius discerned what he considered striking substantiation of Genesis 11:1–9. "Polyhistor," Eusebius observes, "agrees with Moses' writings regarding the building of the tower [of Babel]."[94] The passage to which Eusebius refers is a quotation in the midst of Polyhistor's transcript of Berossus' account of the rebuilding of Babylon after the flood: "When all men spoke the same language, they built the enormous tower, so that they could ascend to heaven. But the all-powerful God sent a wind and destroyed the tower and divided man's language; because of this, the city was called Babylon. But after the flood, there existed Titan and Prometheus, and Titan also made war with Kronos."[95]

It is extremely unlikely that this euhemeristic account of Babylon's re-establishment after the flood existed in the original text of the *Babyloniaca*. It should first be noted that, with the exception of Polyhistor and Abydenus, this legend, and the several variations of it, survive only in Jewish, Samaritan and Christian sources.[96] Commentators on this passage have suggested that the story, which, in its various manifestations, involves a blending of Genesis 11 with Hesiod and other oriental mythologies, owes its origin to a syncretistic form of Judaism or Samaritanism of the hellenistic period.[97] Polyhistor himself, in another work, entitled Περὶ Ἰουδαίων, cites a very similar version of this story from an anonymous Samaritan author whom he incorrectly identifies as Eupolemus, a Jewish historian of the second century B.C.E.[98] Moreover, although Polyhistor

---

[93] For discussion of these corruptions, see Schnabel, *Berossos*, 155–62.

[94] *Chronica* 12.6–7.

[95] Ibid., 12.10–15.

[96] For Abydenus' version of the same story see *Chronica* 17.11–24 (= Sync. 46.10–16). For Christian and Jewish versions of the legend, see (ps-)Eupolemus, in Eusebius PE 9.16.2–17.9 (418c–419d); *Sibylline Oracles* 3.97–161, ed. J. Geffcken, GCS 8 (Leipzig, 1902); Moses of Chorene, *History of the Armenians* 6, trans. Robert W. Thomson, Harvard Armenian Texts and Studies 4 (Cambridge, Mass., 1978). In Moses' account, the author, allegedly on the authority of Berossus, adds the Persian god Zurvan into the mix; for discussion, see Robert W. Thomson's note to his English translation (p. 78, note 4). A variant of this story that does not include the Tower of Babel motif is found in various Hellenistic world chronicles and histories (see Drews, "Assyria," 133, note 20 for references). For further discussion, see below, Chap. 4, pp. 112–13.

[97] Cf. Martin Hengel, *Judaism and Hellenism*, 2 vols. in 1 (Philadelphia, 1974), 1. 88–90.

[98] On (ps-)Eupolemus, see in particular Wacholder, "Pseudo-Eupolemus' Two Greek Fragments on the Life of Abraham," HUCA 34 (1963) 83–113; Nikolaus Walter, "Zu Pseudo-Eupolemus," *Klio* 43/45 (1965) 282–90; Jakob Freudenthal (*Alexander Polyhistor und die von ihm erhaltenen Reste jüdischer und samaritanischer Geschichtswerke: Hellenistische Studien Heft 1* [Breslau, 1874–75] 85–86) was the first to argue that (ps-)Eupolemus was a Samaritan.

includes this legend of the tower of Babel among his excerpts from Berossus, he does not attribute it to Berossus. Instead he identifies the "Sibyl" as its source. A comparison of Polyhistor's quotation with the extant fragments from the Sibylline oracles reveals that Polyhistor was quoting from material now found in the third book of the Sibyllines, that is, the so-called "Jewish Sibyl."[99]

Schnabel has proposed that Polyhistor's personal interest in locating associations between the archaic history of the Babylonians and that of other oriental peoples (in this case, the Jews) prompted him to insert the tower of Babel story at what he deemed was an appropriate place in Berossus' narrative.[100] Another explanation is that the text of the *Babyloniaca* had already undergone interpolation. Evidence for this is found elsewhere in Polyhistor's extracts from Berossus. In Polyhistor's account of Berossus' narrative of the ten kings who reigned before the universal flood, he includes a quotation from "Apollodorus" on the same subject.[101] If the Apollodorus being referred to is the Greek chronicler, the reference cannot have existed in the original text of the *Babyloniaca*. Apollodorus lived over a century after the appearance of the *Babyloniaca;* moreover, it is unlikely that Apollodorus' chronicle included material from Babylonian preflood history, since Apollodorus' chronicle did not attempt to establish a chronology for events before the Trojan War. Although the identity of (ps-)Apollodorus is unknown, his apparent identification of the Babylonian flood story with the one "about which Moses also makes mention" has suggested to some scholars that he was a Jew.[102]

Most of these interpolations into the *Babyloniaca* occurred sometime shortly after the publication of the work and before Polyhistor set about transcribing the work for Greek readers. Polyhistor's own relatively neutral and antiquarian posture toward the work guaranteed the survival of much original material from the *Babyloniaca*. And although the Christian chroniclers sifted out much material which they considered extraneous,

---

[99] *Sibylline Oracles* 3.97–161. For discussion of the relationship of the Jewish Sibyl to Berossus and Chaldaism, see W. Bousset, "Die Beziehungen der ältesten jüdischen Sibylle zur chaldäischen Sibylle," *ZNW* 3 (1902), 23–49.

[100] See Schnabel, *Berossos,* 69–76.

[101] *Chronica* 4.18 ff.

[102] Ibid., 4.27–28; this same Apollodorus is also mentioned in the account of the succession of antediluvian Chaldean kings. Schwartz conjectures that (ps-)Apollodorus was a Jewish historian writing about the year 100 B.C.E. who hoped to improve upon Berossus' and Manetho's credibility by attaching their chronologies of Babylonia and Egypt to the widely respected chronicle of Apollodorus; see Schwartz, "Apollodorus" (61), *RE* 1.2, 2860–62; for the Jewish background and date of (ps-)Apollodorus, see also Wacholder, "Biblical Chronology," 464–65.

they transmitted large portions of the work relatively unaltered from the form in which they received it from him. What does survive in the chronographers from the *Babyloniaca*, therefore, preserves a good picture of the contents and shape of the original work. The same cannot be said of the *Aegyptiaca*, however. If by the first century C.E. the *Aegyptiaca* was, in the words of Laqueur, the "object of numerous literary analyses" in the context of Jewish/Egyptian polemic, what the *Aegyptiaca* suffered afterwards is such thoroughgoing corruption that the original chronology standing behind the various Christian recensions of it has often been all but erased.[103]

The reasons for this have to do with the circumstances of the work's transmission. Aside from a highly suspect letter of Manetho to Ptolemy II Philadelphus,[104] the only direct quotations from Manetho's history are in Josephus' *Against Apion;* these constitute only a small fraction of the whole work, and contribute little information about the overall plan of the work or the background of the author. Moreover, Manetho lacked a sympathetic excerptor comparable to Polyhistor. As Laqueur has shown, the *Aegyptiaca* appears to have had little use other than as an instrument for polemic, apologetic, or chronography. Nor did the form in which the chronographers knew the *Aegyptiaca* enhance its chances for accurate transmission; by their very nature, the chronological epitomes of the work which Africanus and Eusebius consulted were highly vulnerable to textual corruption.[105]

Syncellus himself found the extent to which Eusebius' epitome of the *Aegyptiaca* diverged from Africanus' grounds for undertaking a detailed comparison of these two "most famous recensions (δύο τῶν ἐπισημοτάτων ἐκδόσεις)" of Egyptian history, so that "with proper application one may apprehend the opinion which approaches nearer to Scriptural truth."[106] Predisposed to fault Eusebius anyway, Syncellus would find in his deviations from Africanus one more reason to prefer Africanus. "It must be noted," he writes elsewhere, "how much less accurate (ὁπόσον

---

[103] In addition to Eusebius' and Africanus' epitomes, Syncellus knows a third, widely divergent, recension of Manetho's chronology, thought to derive from the pseudepigraphic *Book of Sothis* (see below, Chap. 2, pp. 57–60). The so-called *Excerpta Latina Barbari* (given this name by Scaliger because of its many corruptions) also preserves a form of Manetho's chronology (fr. 4, ed. Waddell). For discussion of the sources of the *Excerpta*, see Gelzer, in *Zeitschrift für wissenschaftliche Theologie* 26 (1910), 500 ff.; idem, *SJA*, 2. 316–26.

[104] See below, Chap. 2, pp. 57–58.

[105] "The astonishing variations between their figures [Africanus and Eusebius] are an eloquent testimony to what may happen to numbers in a few centuries through textual corruption" (T. Eric Peet, *Egypt and the Old Testament* [Liverpool, 1923], 25–26).

[106] Sync. 59.12–15.

... λείπεται ἀκριβείας) Eusebius is than Africanus in the number of kings he gives, in the omission of names and in dates, although he practically repeats the account of Africanus in the same words (αὐταῖς λέξεσι)."[107]

One of these reworkings, which struck Syncellus as especially glaring, occurred in Eusebius' account of the seventeenth Egyptian dynasty, the so-called "shepherd kings." "It was in this time (the rule of the shepherd kings)," Eusebius wrote, "that Joseph was appointed regent over Egypt." In comparing Eusebius' epitome of Manetho with the parallel version of Africanus, Syncellus recognized that Africanus' epitome of Manetho assigned these kings to the fifteenth dynasty. "Notice," he says, "how Eusebius for his own purposes (πρὸς τὸν οἰκεῖον σκοπόν) asserts that the kings who were reported by Africanus to be in the fifteenth dynasty belonged to the seventeenth dynasty. For it is agreed by all (ἐπὶ ... πᾶσι συμπεφώνηται) that Joseph exercised his rule over Egypt at the time of Apophis. But Eusebius, since he was unable to place Joseph's rule during the reign of someone else, transposed Apophis from the fifteenth to the seventeenth dynasty, shortening (κολοβώσας) the years of his rule from 61 to 30 years. And he substituted only 103 years for the 151 years of the whole dynasty, and instead of six kings gave only four."[108]

Normally a critic of Eusebius, Syncellus was inclined to assume that Eusebius was in almost all cases inferior to his predecessor, from whom he had copied. Syncellus notwithstanding, it is unlikely that Eusebius himself was responsible for reworking a form of Manetho which he had received from Africanus. Although Africanus is in all a more faithful witness to Manetho, in some cases Eusebius preserves a chronology closer to the original. Even where tendentious editing is unmistakable in Eusebius, these corruptions appear in independent witnesses to Manetho.[109] Eusebius was, moreover, generally fastidious in citing intermediaries, not

---

[107] Ibid., 65.18–20 (fr. 21(a), trans. Waddell).

[108] Ibid., 69.1–7. Syncellus inferred a synchronizing motive from a comment which he found in Eusebius' account of the 17th dynasty: "It was in this time (the rule of the shepherd-kings) that Joseph was appointed regent over Egypt." In order to preserve the chronological integrity of this synchronism, Eusebius (or his source) had to move the time of the rule of the shepherd-kings from the 15th to the 17th dynasty (for discussion, see Laqueur, "Manethon," 1087–88). Syncellus later suggests that Eusebius removed names and subtracted years from the 15th Egyptian dynasty in order to tamper with Africanus' dating of the reigns of the early Greek kings Inachus and Cecrops. By making Inachus a predecessor of Moses and Cecrops contemporary with him, Eusebius, Syncellus says, not only corrupted his Egyptian sources, but also departed from the accurate tradition established by many earlier Jewish and Christian authorities (cf. Sync. 70.23–71.27).

[109] The transposition of dynasties 15 and 17, for example, occurs also in a scholium to Plato's *Timaeus* (ed. Herman, 21E; fr. 49, ed. Waddell); cf. Unger, *Manetho*, 19.

shrinking to acknowledge, for example, his indebtedness to Polyhistor for his excerpts from the *Babyloniaca*. Although it is uncertain whether Eusebius' source for the chronology of the *Aegyptiaca* was based directly on Africanus, Eusebius himself considered this source an authentic work of Manetho, and this is the way he characterized it.[110]

For the most part, Josephus and the Christian chronographers considered Manetho and Berossus corroborative sources, and their use and editing of these sources were meant to reflect and enhance this. For the purposes of establishing the antiquity of the Jews, the accuracy of the Bible, the folly of the Greek historians, and the newness of their civilization, both Jewish and Christian historians had, as we have seen, attached great value to these works. Minor deviations or material deemed irrelevant to the aims of apologetic or chronography could either be suppressed or reworked. Far more difficult to absorb, however, were those parts of the oriental histories that flatly contradicted these aims.

Already in *Against Apion,* Josephus had to confront in Manetho a witness that could prove on at least one occasion to be positively hostile. Josephus might have been gratified to find that Manetho had fixed the chronological origins of the Jews well before the Trojan War. But, in what was to become a well-known explanation of the origin of the Jews, Manetho had traced their descent to a "crowd of Egyptian lepers and others, who for various maladies, were condemned, as he asserts, to banishment from the country."[111] Aided by the inhabitants of Jerusalem (that is, the Hyksos, who had earlier been expelled from Egypt), they conquered Egypt, finally to be routed by Amenophis and his son Rampses.[112] At the end of this excerpt comes the widely circulated slander that their leader Osarsiph, "when he went over to this people, changed his name and was called Moses."[113]

[110] It is likely, however, that Eusebius' epitome was derived indirectly from Africanus'. At the fourth dynasty, for example, Africanus says about the reign of King Suphus, the third ruler of this dynasty, that he composed the *Sacred Book,* "which I acquired on my visit because of its great renown." The statement about the purchase of the book was probably inserted by Africanus himself, who had in fact traveled to Egypt to visit the bishop of Alexandria. In Eusebius' notice about the same king, he says that the "Egyptians hold the *Sacred Book* in high esteem"; here, the epitomator has assimilated Africanus' own observation about the *Sacred Book* into material purportedly from Manetho himself (fr. 14, ed. Waddell). For discussion, see Laqueur, "Manethon," 1085–86; Krall (*Die Composition,* 210) believes that Africanus himself had already found the remark about the purchase of the book in the epitome that he consulted.

[111] *Against Apion* 1.229 (trans. Thackeray).

[112] Ibid., 1.243–251.

[113] Ibid., 1.250.

Whether this slander against the Jews belonged to the original text of the *Aegyptiaca* or, as Laqueur has suggested, a later form of the text heavily interpolated by an editor hostile to the Jews was not the pertinent question for Josephus.[114] He was confronted with the problem of accounting for anti-Jewish invective from a work which he had earlier praised as an accurate "translation from the sacred texts of the Egyptians." The only explanation that he could offer was that, in this particular instance, Manetho had strayed from the original archives. As long as Manetho followed "the ancient records (ταῖς ἀρχαίαις ἀναγραφαῖς)," Josephus says, "he did not go far wrong."[115] The slander against Moses and the Jews, however, was not based on authentic records, but rather "unauthorized" and fictitious rumors. When Manetho "had recourse to unauthenticated legends (ἀδεσπότους μύθους), he either concocted from them a most improbable story, or else trusted the statements of prejudiced opponents."[116]

The Christian chronographers also found a great deal in the histories of Berossus and Manetho that ran counter to their own purposes. To be sure, their accounts of the remote past helped to falsify the Greek contention that this period was largely indeterminate and undocumented. But the supposedly eyewitness records upon which these sources were based could, if taken seriously, falsify Genesis as well. What proved to be the single most taxing question was reconciling the widely divergent archaic chronologies of Berossus and Manetho with Genesis.

The difficulties confronting the Christian chronographer were in some ways already anticipated by analogous ones faced much earlier in Greek chronography. As Jacoby has observed, a Greek universal chronicler, having as his raw material only local town records, lacked "a uniform, or authoritative, thread, on which to string the single facts." In order to fashion a single chronology of the Greek people, it was first necessary to "create a chronological scaffolding" for the individual towns, and then to choose "among the local lists . . . (and) reconcile with them as well as he

---

[114] For the argument that this invective against Manetho belonged to the original text of the *Aegyptiaca*, see Raymond Weill, *La fin du moyen empire égyptien* (Paris, 1918), 70–76, 101; Victor Tcherikover, *Hellenistic Civilization and the Jews* (Philadelphia, 1959), 362–64; Menahem Stern, *Greek and Latin Authors on Jews and Judaism* 1 (Jerusalem, 1974), s.v. "Manetho." Richard Laqueur ("Manethon," 1064–80) contends that Josephus initially consulted a text of the *Aegyptiaca* that was neutral toward the Jews. Later, however, he became aware of another edition of that work which contained many interpolations and expansions, alternately favorable and hostile to the Jews; for a synopsis of Laqueur's reconstruction, see Waddell, *Manetho*, xvii–xix. See also Eduard Meyer, *Aegyptische Chronologie* (Berlin, 1904), 71–79; John Gager, *Moses in Greco-Roman Paganism*, SBLMS 16 (Nashville, 1972), 116–18.

[115] *Against Apion* 1.287.

[116] Ibid., 1.287.

could the dates of the other lists, i.e. to create synchronisms."[117] *Mutatis mutandis,* the Christian chronographer confronted the same challenge for archaic history; only here his sources were not local town records, but the competing and divergent chronologies of the Egyptians and Chaldeans.

To be sure, his non-biblical sources for archaic history were mostly free of chronological lacunae and were in all cases written. In this respect, he was relieved of the task earlier faced by the Greek chronographer, who had to give chronological form to what were, in many cases, only oral reports and undated legends. Nor did the Christian chronicler have to decide, as the Greek chronographers had to, often arbitrarily, which chronology was to serve as the basis for comparison; Genesis was in all cases determinative. But, even so, the chronology of Genesis was itself a matter of uncertainty, and once this question was resolved, there was the broader question of showing how its relatively meagre chronology could be reconciled with the far more grandiose chronologies of other competing sources. If it required several centuries for Greek chronographers to establish a uniform chronology *ab origine populi,* it should be no surprise that Christian chronographers were for an even longer time unsure how, out of the confusion, to establish a chronology *ab origine mundi.*

[117]Jacoby, *FrGH* 3B 27, F 92, 381. "The difficulty put before the Greek chronographer," Jacoby observes, "may be compared to that which the World Chronicles had to overcome, the various peoples being for these records what the various Greek towns were for the Greek chronographers."

CHAPTER TWO

Africanus, Eusebius, and the Problem of Primordial History

CHRISTIAN CHRONOGRAPHY AND THE ERA
AB ORIGINE MUNDI

An era, writes the Muslim chronographer al-Bīrūnī, "means a definite space of time, reckoned from the beginning of some past year." They may vary, he notes, but what is broadly constitutive of all eras is that they mark some memorable occurrence—a natural catastrophe, a recurring celestial event, the appearance of a prophet or the reign of a famous king: "By such events the fixed moments of time are recognized. Now such an era cannot be dispensed with in all secular and religious affairs. Each of the nations scattered over the different parts of the world has a special era. . . . And thence they [the nations] derive the date which they want in social inter-course, in chronology, and in every institute which is exclusively peculiar to them."[1]

Among the several eras that he names, the one al-Bīrūnī hails as the "most famous" is the era from creation.[2] Yet he knows as well that reck-oning of dates from the creation is precarious. In the first place, none of the groups who use such an era—the Jews, the Christians, and the Magi-ans—agree as to the proper way to date from the creation. Besides, over the course of so many years things must have gotten muddled. "Every-thing, the knowledge of which is connected with the beginning of crea-tion and with the history of bygone generations, is mixed up with falsifi-cations and myths, because it belongs to a far remote age; because a long interval separates us therefrom, and because the student is incapable of

---

[1] Al-Bīrūnī, *The Chronology of Ancient Nations* 16.13–20, trans. Edward Sachau (London, 1879).
[2] Ibid., 16.21–22.

keeping it in memory and of fixing it (so as to preserve it from confusion)."[3]

Few Byzantine chronographers would have been daunted by these problems; for them the era of creation was a fixed and immutable point. The first-formed day, writes Syncellus, will serve as an "unshakable foundation (θεμέλιον ἀρραγῆ)" for his narrative.[4] There was, however, far less certainty among Syncellus' predecessors, both Jewish and Christian.

One problem—and one that interested the philosophers as well—involved determining if time (that is, measured time) and creation were coeval. "No one who thinks clearly" on this matter, writes Syncellus, will dispute the view that the first day of creation marks the beginning of "chronological movement."[5] But the Jewish and Christian Platonists of Alexandria believed otherwise. Although only rarely did commentators on Genesis deny the basic contention that time did not exist before the creation of the world,[6] there was less unanimity as to whether or not the first day of creation inaugurated "temporal movement." Already, in his *On the Creation of the Universe*, Philo had denied categorically that when Genesis said, "In the beginning God created the heaven and the earth," the expression was meant in a "chronological sense (κατὰ χρόνον)."[7] In the first place, it would be wrong to suppose that God required six days to complete the process.[8] Moreover,

> it is quite foolish to think that the world was created in six days or in a space of time at all. Why? Because every period of time is a series of days and nights, and these can only be made such by the movement

[3] Ibid., 16.26–17.2.
[4] Sync. 2.23.
[5] Ibid., 2.8.
[6] For discussion of this question in Antiquity, see Richard Sorabji, *Time, Creation and the Continuum* (Ithaca, 1983), 98–130, 193–209, 232–52. The subject aroused lively controversy. In the *Timaeus* (37D), Plato described time as a "moving image of eternity," progressing "according to number. Wherefore, . . . with a view to the generation of Time, the sun and the moon and five other stars, which bear the appellation of 'planets,' came into existence for the determining and preserving of the numbers of Time" (*Timaeus* 38C, trans. Bury). But not all writers after Plato were prepared to acknowledge that time only had its beginning with the creation of the universe. According to Cicero (*De natura deorum* 1.9), an Epicurean by the name of Velleius had ridiculed the whole notion. Perhaps the measurement of time did not exist, but "it is," he writes, "inconceivable that there was ever a time when time did not exist" (trans. H. Rackham, LCL [Cambridge, 1979]). Some of the Rabbis also seem to have accepted the idea that time existed before the creation; see L. Ginzberg, *The Legends of the Jews*, 7 vols. (Philadelphia, 1909–38), 5. 6–7 (note 14).
[7] Philo *On the Creation of the Universe* 7.26 (trans. F. H. Colson and G. H. Whitaker, LCL [London, 1971]).
[8] Ibid., 3.13.

of the sun as it goes over and under the earth; but the sun is a part of heaven, so that time is confessedly more recent than the world. It would therefore be correct to say that the world was not made in time, but that time was formed by means of the world, for it was heaven's movement that was the index of the nature of time.[9]

Instead, Philo maintains, not a little cryptically, that the Mosaic hexaemeron refers only to the order (τάξις) by which God simultaneously (ἅμα) created the world.[10] It followed from his Platonizing interpretation of Genesis 1 that in this order of creation what God had done on day one was to create incorporeal "models (ἰδέαι)" and "patterns (τύποι)" for the creation of the intelligible world. The uniqueness of this "noetic first day" was further suggested to Philo by the expression which Moses used to refer to it: not the first day, but day one, "an expression due to the uniqueness of the intelligible world and to its having a natural kinship to the number 'One.'"[11]

This explanation of Genesis 1:1 was a convenient one, because by it Philo succeeded in circumventing the obvious problem that the heavenly luminaries, which according to the *Timaeus* had come into existence for the "determining and preserving of the numbers of Time," had, on the first day, not yet been created.[12] It was presumably under the influence of Philo that the Christian Platonists of Alexandria formed the same conclusion. In his *Homilies on Genesis*, Origen, for example, had, like Philo, concluded that Genesis 1:1 does not refer to a "temporal beginning," since "time begins to exist only with the following days."[13] Philo's views seem to have exerted influence on Origen's associate, Julius Africanus, as well; he too used the same nomenclature to describe the first day of creation: "noetic."[14] Indeed, Africanus must have found the whole problem of the chronology of creation sufficiently obscure to deter him from reckoning events from the first day. For although he had included in his chronicle an account of the Mosaic cosmogony,[15] his era was not, as is sometimes

---

[9] Philo *Allegorical Interpretation of Genesis* 1.2 (trans. Colson and Whitaker, LCL [London, 1971]); see also *On the Creation of the Universe* 7.26.

[10] *On the Creation of the Universe* 7.27–28. For discussion of Philo's simultaneous, but ordered, creation, see Sorabji, *Time, Creation and the Continuum*, 208–9.

[11] Philo *On the Creation of the Universe* 9.35.

[12] Cf. *Timaeus* 38C.

[13] Origen *Homilies on Genesis* 1.1.

[14] In Sync. 3.1–2.

[15] Of Africanus' chronicle, Photius says: ἄρχεται δὲ ἀπὸ τῆς Μωσαϊκῆς κοσμογενείας (*Bibliotheca* Cod. 34.7a [PG 103. 66C]).

thought, *ab origine mundi,* but rather *ab anno Adam.* In choosing as his point of departure not the beginning of the universe, but rather the beginning of human history, Africanus revealed his own reservations about this most primordial period in history.[16]

EUSEBIUS' CHRONICLE AND THE ANTEDILUVIAN NARRATIVE OF GENESIS

From the fragments of his chronicle that survive in Syncellus, it is clear that Africanus was well aware that primordial chronology after Adam raised doubts. But none of them was beyond resolving.[17] But Eusebius, Africanus' successor and a chronicler of more modest pretensions, approached archaic history with far greater caution. What preceded Adam's expulsion from Paradise—not just the events of Adam's life there, but the "creation of the heavens and the earth and the universe" as well—must be consigned, he writes, to the "indeterminate."[18] This is so owing to uncertainty about the period of time that had elapsed from Adam's creation to his expulsion from Paradise. "No one is able," he writes, "to determine the period of time spent in the so-called Garden of God."[19] Eusebius' own conclusion was that Paradise did not refer to an earthly habitation, nor did Moses describe the life of an earthly man in Paradise; rather he referred to the collective condition of all of humanity living in a more blessed state than that of mankind after the Fall.[20] The allegorical interpretation of

[16] "This distinction between Adam-years and world-years may appear pedantic to many," writes Gelzer (*SJA,* 1. 35), "but there is more here than meets the eye. Africanus' sense of history is seen in the fact that he does not date from the creation of the universe, but from Adam; thus history is the history of mankind. The story of the creation is not, to be sure, ahistorical, but prehistorical." On Africanus' sense of history as evidenced in his choice of the era *ab Adam,* see also Jean Sirinelli, *Les vues historiques,* 42.

[17] One such problem in Genesis' pre-flood chronology that concerned Africanus was Gen. 6:3, dealing with the limiting of man's age to 120 years. "Let it not be deemed a subject of dispute (ζήτημα)," he writes, "because men lived afterward a longer period than that." The answer to this ἀπορία lies in the fact that God issued the injunction 100 years before the flood only to the sinners of that time, who were then 20 years of age (in Sync. 21.26–22.2). Africanus' solution recalls the treatment of Gen. 6:3 by the Targums; cf. *Targum Onkelos* ad loc.: "I will give them an extension of time, 120 years, to see if they will repent." See also Jerome *Hebraicae Quaestiones* (on Gen. 6:3; in CC Series Latina 72.1.1 [Turnholt, 1959]). "Many go astray," he writes, in inferring from this punishment that "human life was abbreviated to 120 years"; the 120 years refer instead to the period of time given to that generation for the purpose of repentance. For a comprehensive discussion of the ancient solutions, see Louis Ginzberg, *Legends of the Jews,* 7 vols. (Philadelphia, 1909–38), 5. 174–75 (note 19).

[18] *Chronica* 36.16–17. Eusebius allows that there were some chronographers who believed it possible to date from creation, but he does not identify them by name.

[19] Ibid., 36.16–17.

[20] Ibid., 36.17–24.

Genesis 2, recalling Origen's own interpretation of the story, here has a practical consequence for chronology. When, says Eusebius, Moses speaks of the 930 years of Adam's life, he means only the earthly Adam after the expulsion. What precedes it is "ur-history."[21]

Even for the period after Adam's expulsion from the Paradise there were numerous uncertainties. The critical problem here had to do with the reliability and contradictions of the sources for pre-flood history. Most Greek Christian chronographers tended to prefer the authority of the Septuagint over other sources for the period.[22] But the Septuagint chronology for pre-flood history presented internal inconsistencies. One such inconsistency, which Jerome called a "very celebrated problem," had to do with Methuselah's age when he fathered Lamech and the duration of time that Genesis had assigned to the period from Adam to the flood.[23] Following the Septuagint, Eusebius and most of the Greek chronographers after him reckoned the period as 2,242 years. But by this reckoning, Methuselah would have survived the flood by 14 years. As Syncellus observes later in an excellent summary of the whole question, Africanus and some of the copies of the Septuagint added 20 years to this period apparently in order to avoid the difficulty.[24] Some of the copies [of the Septuagint], Syncellus writes:

> report the birth of Lamech in the 187th year of this same Methuselah. And Africanus, following them, calculates the flood at the time of Noah in A.M. 2262. This does not seem to us to be sound. For it seems to me that Africanus reckoned the year of the flood in the 2,262nd year of the world because of the fact that the 969 years of Methuselah's life, beginning from the year A.M. 1287, extend to the year 2256 and beyond the 2,242 year limit.

[21] Ibid., 37.7–9. On Eusebius' belief that the Garden of Eden referred to a place outside of temporal and physical existence, see also PE 7.18.7–10 (332cd). For the influence of Origen on Eusebius' treatment of this matter, see Glenn F. Chesnut, The First Christian Histories, 2nd ed. (Macon, 1986), 68. Traces of Eusebius' approach to pre-Adamic history survive in the Byzantine chronographers; see, for example, Michael Glycas, who says that "Adam after his expulsion from Paradise (for at this time [τηνικαῦτα] chronography has its beginning) lived 930 years" (227.5–6; ed. I. Bekker, CSHB [Bonn, 1836]). A Greek extract of Eusebius' views on the question survives in the Ἐκλογὴ Ἱστοριῶν 166.17–167.5 (ed. John Anthony Cramer, Anecdota Graeca 2 [Oxford, 1839]).

[22] For Eusebius' high regard for the Septuagint, see Chronica 37.32–36.

[23] See Jerome Hebraicae Quaestiones (on Gen 5:25).

[24] Already in the 3rd century B.C.E., Demetrius, a Hellenistic Jewish chronographer, had, on the basis of the Septuagint, assigned 2,264 years to antediluvian history (in Eusebius PE 9.21.18 [425c]). Like Africanus, his motive might have been to avoid having Methuselah survive the flood.

But Eusebius says about Methuselah that the period of his life happened to exceed this flood. And we know that some of the manuscripts have it that he lived another 782 years (after the birth of Lamech). In this way, he did not see the flood. And this is what Eusebius also says. But if someone grants this as true, Methuselah will be found to have completed in all 949 years. And his grandfather Jared, who lived to be 962 years, will have greater longevity than him. But everyone agrees that Methuselah was the longest-lived of all men, and that he died in the flood. Therefore, one might suppose that Methuselah was born in the 153rd year of Enoch, that is in the 1,273rd year of the world. Adding to these the 969 years of Methuselah's life makes 2,242 years, in which year the flood occurred, during which Methuselah died.[25]

What proved to be a more fundamental question for Christian chronographers was the existence of so many other conflicting sources and chronologies for primordial history. Eusebius was studious in cataloguing most of them—not just the various versions of Genesis (the Samaritan Pentateuch and the traditional Hebrew text), but the chronologies of the Babylonians and the Egyptians as well.

The difference between the pre-flood chronology of the Hebrew and Greek Bible—656 years in all—arose mainly from a discrepancy in dating the birth of the patriarchs. For six of these patriarchs, the Hebrew text and the Samaritan Pentateuch were almost consistently 100 years lower than the Septuagint. The discrepancy was so glaring that it attracted the attention of numerous Christian interpreters, who characteristically blamed it on the Jews. Among the motives cited by chronographers for Jewish tampering with the chronology of Genesis was their desire to prove that the Messiah had not yet arrived. "The Hebrews," writes Jacob of Edessa, "wanting to pervert the computation of years, in order to show that Christ had not yet arrived, subtract 100 years from Adam before he fathered Seth."[26] Augustine has one of the most subtle discussions of the whole matter. The idea, he says, that the Jews "made certain alterations in

---

[25] Syncellus 20.7–25; cf. Eusebius *Chronica* 38.22–26. Augustine (*City of God* 15.11) knows of some chronographers who maintained that for the period that Methuselah lived after the flood he was "alive but not on earth . . . in the company of his father, who had been translated."

[26] In G. S. Assemani, *Bibliotheca Orientalis*, 3 vols. in 4 (Rome, 1719–28), 1. 65. In this same notice, Jacob claims also that in his time there were certain Hebrew manuscripts that confirmed the Septuagint chronology.

their version to diminish the authority of ours (the Septuagint)" is implausible: "No matter how great their depravity and spite," he writes, no intelligent person could think that the Jews "could have effected all this in so many and so widely scattered codices." The minor numerical divergences (for example, the difference in the age of Lamech at his death) Augustine attributes to a "mere scribal error," committed by the first copyist of the Septuagint, "from which the mistake spread more widely." After all, he says, numbers are particularly susceptible to corruption. But the consistency in the difference between the Septuagint and the Hebrew Bible as to the birthdates of the antediluvian patriarchs led Augustine to suspect a deliberate design. In his own time Augustine knew of chronographers who, following a well-known tradition, believed that the earliest years were only 1/10th of the modern solar year, so that Adam lived only to be 93 solar years, not 930 years. The scribe, Augustine writes, who added 100 years to the date of the birth of the patriarchs also assumed that these archaic years were only 1/10th of a modern year. But he recognized as well that this would mean that when Adam fathered Seth at age 130, he was only 13 years of age. "It was doubtless for these reasons that he added a hundred years in the cases where he did not find the age suitable for engendering children, and after their birth subtracted a like number to make the total tally."[27]

Eusebius too seized on the standard explanation that the Jews had tampered with the text of Genesis, contributing his own peculiar opinion that the Jews deliberately lowered the years when the patriarchs fathered their first child in order to legitimize early marriage and childbirth![28] Far more difficult to explain, however, were the chronological discrepancies between Genesis and the primordial narratives of the Egyptians and the Bab-

[27] *City of God* 15.13 (trans. Philip Levine, LCL [Cambridge, 1966]). For the idea that the archaic year was only some fraction of the modern solar year, see below, Chap. 3, pp. 75–78. For modern discussion of the question, see Ralph W. Klein, "Archaic Chronologies and the Textual History of the Old Testament," *HTR* 67 (1974) 255–63; Wacholder, "Biblical Chronology" 452–58. Wacholder suggests that there was a Jewish school of chronography in Alexandria, of which Demetrius was a representative; the disparity arose from a desire on the part of the translators to lengthen the duration of biblical history in order to rival the antiquity of the other civilizations (457–58); but the addition of a mere 800 years to pre-flood chronology hardly seems like a credible effort to compete with the Babylonians and Egyptians, whose archaic histories extended many thousands of years.

[28] *Chronica* 40.13–20; cf. Sync. 95.16–25. The hundred year difference in the Hebrew text, Eusebius says, could have been the "product of Jews who in support of early marriage ventured to shorten and hasten the period of time before procreation. For if the men of most ancient times had lived long lives of many years, thereby arriving at marriage and procreation sooner, as the reading in their text shows, who would not take after them and imitate the custom of early marriage?" (translation according to Greek text in Syncellus).

ylonians. From his epitome of the *Aegyptiaca*, Eusebius knew that Manetho had assigned to the reigns of the gods and demigods of Egyptian archaic chronology some 25,000 years; and to the ten pre-flood Chaldean kings alone Berossus ascribed 432,000 years.[29] Both numbers were seemingly totally asynchronous with the 2,242 years that the Christian chronographers had reckoned from the birth of Adam to the flood.

Synchronizing Babylonian and Egyptian chronology with what Africanus had termed the "more modest" mind of the Hebrews was a challenge that was to engage the energies of Christian chronographers for centuries thereafter. Although the vigor and acrimony with which they pursued this question may at first seem curious, it becomes less so once it is recognized that what was at stake was not simply reconciling different chronologies, but rather different views about the age and origin of the universe.[30]

BABYLONIAN AND EGYPTIAN ANTIQUITIES AND "COSMIC" HISTORY

For a Greek ethnographer, probably the single most striking aspect of the chronicles of the Egyptians and Babylonians was the enormous time span that they encompassed. In particular, the chronological scope of these chronicles, extending back to the remotest period of human history, helped to establish the chronological, and hence cultural, priority of the Orientals.

While it is doubtful that Greek writers were prepared to accept the claim that the chronological priority of the Orientals proved their overall cultural superiority, there was one side of the argument that did command widespread assent. This was the belief that the Chaldean and Egyptian priests had accurate astronomical observations well before the Greeks. For if the reigns of the first Babylonian and Egyptian kings were reckoned in years, months, and days, these priests had in their custody a continuous

---

[29] The number 432,000 is a fairly fixed tradition in the pre-flood chronology of the *Babyloniaca*. Ancient authors give conflicting accounts of the entire period of time encompassed by his work. Syncellus' Greek text gives the impossible figure of 150,000 years (Sync. 28.24); the extracts in the Armenian text of Eusebius give 2,150,000 years (*Chronica* 6.19–20); Africanus, probably referring to Berossus, 480,000 (in Sync. 18.4); Pliny 490,000 years (*NH* 7.56.193). The traditions about Manetho's chronology of Egyptian mythic history are more diverse; Eusebius assigns to Manetho's archaic chronology 24,900 years (*Chronica* 64.4–7); for other witnesses to Manetho's chronology, see frs. 2–5 (ed. Waddell).

[30] The following discussion follows what I have said in a previous article on the same subject: "Berossus, Manetho and *1 Enoch* in the World Chronicle of Panodorus," *HTR* 76 (1983), 419–42.

record of celestial movement stretching several thousand years. It was this that evidently led the Egyptian priests in Herodotus to list the discovery of the solar year as one of the many things imparted to the Greeks by the Egyptians.[31] Herodotus could acknowledge the merit of this boast, not only because the Egyptian calendar seemed "more clever" than the Greek, but because these priests could produce astronomical records extending 11,340 years and including observations of four heavenly shifts.[32] Much the same thing was said about the Chaldeans. Porphyry recalls that Callisthenes, the student of Aristotle, had sent to his teacher Babylonian astronomical observations extending over 31,000 years.[33] According to Cicero, the Babylonians maintained that the availability of astronomical records encompassing 470,000 years meant that the Chaldean method of divination was based on 470,000 years of experience.[34]

One consequence of the enormous duration of the oriental chronicles was that these sources were regularly used to promote particular views about the origin and creation of the world. Thus, Simplicius, the sixth-century Aristotelian, in his commentary on Aristotle's De caelo, asserts that the records of the Chaldeans and Egyptians attest to the constancy and hence the eternity of the universe. "I have heard," he writes, that: "the Egyptians have recorded astronomical observations not less than 630,000 years, and the Babylonians 1,440,000 years. For such a span of time, from which histories have been handed down, the record is no different than now concerning the heavens, or the number of stars, or their size or color, or their movement in revolutions."[35]

For the Platonists, interest in these sources appears to have been determined mainly by their perceived value in the calculation of astronomical or "Great Year" cycles—fixed periods of time required for the celestial bodies to return to the same position that they had at the beginning of the cycle.[36] It was ostensibly because of its cyclic nature that the Great Year came to be linked by the Pythagoreans and neo-Platonists with the belief

[31] Herodotus 2.4.

[32] Ibid., 2.142.

[33] Quoted by Simplicius in his commentary on Aristotle's De caelo 2.12 (226b); in Commentaria in Aristotelem Graeca 7. 506.10–16 (ed. I. L. Heiberg [Berlin, 1893]).

[34] Cicero De div. 1.19. The number 470,000 may be based on the Babyloniaca.

[35] Simplicius Commentary on Aristotle's De caelo 1.3 (54b) (ed. Heiberg, 7. 117.24–30).

[36] For modern studies of the origins and varieties of the doctrine of the Great Year, see especially B. L. van der Waerden, "Das grosse Jahr und die ewige Wiederkehr," Hermes 80 (1952), 129–56; R. Van den Broek, The Myth of the Phoenix, Études préliminaires aux religions orientales dans l'Empire Romain 24 (Leiden, 1972), 67–112; Bernhard Sticker, "Weltzeitalter und astronomische Perioden," Saeculum 4 (1953), 241–49; Franz Boll, et al., Sternglaube und Sterndeutung, 4th ed. (Leipzig, Berlin, 1931), 200–5.

in cosmic periodicity and the eternal regeneration of the cosmos.[37] Although the duration of the cycles was calculated differently,[38] the governing principles were that these revolutions would be completed at fixed intervals, and that the course of these cycles would be marked by regularly recurring natural catastrophes, floods or fires.

In his *Timaeus,* Plato, one of the first Greek authors to describe world cycles in this way, characterizes the "perfect year" as that duration of time required for all of the celestial bodies to return to the same position that they had at the beginning of the cycle.[39] When, in that same dialogue, the Egyptian priest rebukes Solon for his arrogant and groundless belief that Greek civilization was superior to the wisdom of the Orientals, he too reverts to the idea of cosmic shifts in order to demonstrate the superiority and continuity of Egyptian culture. "There have been," he says, "and there will be many and diverse destructions (φθοραί) of mankind, of which the greatest are by fire and water. . . . After the usual interval of years, like a plague, the flood from heaven comes sweeping down afresh upon your people, (and) it leaves none of you but the unlettered and uncultured, . . . with no knowledge of all that happened in this land or in your own."[40] By contrast, cultural continuity is assured for the Egyptians. This is so not only because of their diligence in preserving the memory of any event "that is noble or great or in any way conspicuous;"[41] just as important is the fact that a temperate climate protects Egypt from the extremes caused by heavenly shifts.

By this argument the priest intended to show that because of Egypt's immunity from periodic destructions, "what is here (in Egypt) preserved is the most ancient." A theme adapted by many non-Greek peoples,[42] the

---

[37] See van der Waerden, "Das grosse Jahr," 129–32.

[38] Censorinus (3rd cent. C.E.), by far the most learned witness on the subject, catalogues Great Year cycles ranging from nineteen (the Metonic cycle) to several thousand years (cf. *De die natali* 18). Cicero, aware of many different versions of the Great Year cycle, refuses to offer an opinion about the duration of this cycle; the whole issue, he writes, was "a matter of great controversy (*quaestio magna*)" (*De natura deorum* 2.20).

[39] *Timaeus* 39D: "The complete number of time fulfils the perfect year (τὸν τέλειον ἐνιαυτόν) when all the eight circuits, with their relative speeds, finish together, and come to a head when measured by the same and similarly moving."

[40] Ibid., 22C–23B (trans. Bury LCL).

[41] Ibid., 23A.

[42] Including Hellenistic Judaism. Josephus employs it in the prologue to *Against Apion* (see above, Chap. 1, pp. 22–23). In the *Antiquities* (1.68–71), Josephus assimilates the flood at the time of Noah to the doctrine of Great Year cycles; in order to preserve antediluvian science from floods and fires, Seth and his descendants erected monuments for subsequent generations, one of brick (in case of fire) and the other of stone (in case of flood). Philo also appears to adopt the idea of alternating catastrophes; in his *Life of Moses* (2.263), he states that

supposed continuity of the oriental chronicles, which figured so importantly in their claim to cultural priority, could be exploited as well to demonstrate the superiority of the Orientals in matters of astronomical observation and prognostication. For if accurate, the long duration of these archives would then be invaluable in the prediction of future and regularly recurring cycles.

A good illustration of this is Seneca's well-known discussion of the periodic catastrophes brought about by these cycles. Expanding on the analogy of the Great Year to a solar year, some had supposed that the periodic floods and fires would occur during its seasons, the flood in the winter and the fire in the summer.[43] Amid great speculation regarding these "seasonal" disruptions, Seneca credits Berossus, the "priest of Bel," with having being been able to predict exactly the times of the floods and fires of the Great Year:

> Berossus, the interpreter of Bel, says that these catastrophes occur with the movements of the planets. Indeed, he is so certain that he assigns a date for the conflagration and the deluge. For earthly things will burn, he contends, when all the planets which now maintain different orbits come together in the sign of Cancer, and are so arranged in the same path that a straight line can pass through the spheres of all of them. The deluge will occur when the same group of planets meets in the sign of Capricorn. The solstice is caused by Cancer, winter by Capricorn; they are signs of great power since they are the turning points in the very change of the year.[44]

In this passage, Berossus' analogy of the cosmic year to the solar year contains an element of astral determinism only hinted at in earlier speculations on this subject. Berossus reasons that since the summer solstice occurs when the sun is at its maximum northern latitude in the celestial sphere (the sign of Cancer), the ἀποκατάστασις would occur when all the celestial bodies conjoined in this sign of the Zodiac. Conversely, since

---

mankind forgot the Sabbath because of such catastrophes, which obliterated the memory of earlier generations; for the influence of this conception on Jewish apocalyptic, see most recently Martin Hengel, *Judaism and Hellenism*, 2 vols. (Philadelphia, 1974), 1. 191–93; also Louis Feldman, "Hellenizations," 351–52. Traces of the doctrine of the Great Year may also be discernible in the priestly narrative of Genesis; see Johnson, *Biblical Genealogies*, 31–36.

[43] Censorinus (*De die natali* 18.11) credits Aristotle with being the first to have theorized that in the summer of the Great Year cycle the world would be consumed by a fiery conflagration (*incendium mundi*); in the winter, by a flood (*diluvium*).

[44] Seneca *Quaestiones naturales* 3.29.1 (trans. Thomas Corcoran, LCL [Cambridge, 1971–72]).

the winter solstice of the solar year occurs when the sun is at its maximum southern position in the celestial sphere, so would the winter of the Great Year begin when the planets, the sun, and the moon come into conjunction in the sign of Capricorn.

Seneca does not attribute this prediction to a particular work of Berossus, nor do any such prognostications survive in the preserved fragments of the *Babyloniaca*. But Berossus' own treatment of pre-flood Babylonian history would have provided some justification for this inference. In his summary of Polyhistor's excerpts from Berossus, Eusebius states that he "describes individually . . . the ten kings from Alorus the first king up to Xisuthrus, during whose time, he (Berossus) says, the great and first flood took place," implying by this statement that Berossus looked forward to a second universal cataclysm.[45] Moreover, as van der Waerden has shown, the 432,000 years that Berossus assigns to this period represent either a Great Year or some fraction of it.[46] Since Berossus' chronicle recorded the exact time of one of these cosmic catastrophes, it followed that Berossus would be equipped to know the time of subsequent and regularly recurring cataclysms of the Great Year cycle.[47]

Even if, as Lambert has suggested, Seneca had gotten this information from a "garbled summary of the *Babyloniaca*,"[48] the contents of this report reveal a characteristic inclination of pagan writers to mine the oriental chronicle for its speculative content. We should not conclude, however, that this was merely a case of willful misreading. For while it is unclear whether Manetho, Berossus' counterpart and younger contemporary, periodized his history according to Great Year cycles, Egyptian priests and chroniclers after him, eager to prove the primacy of their race in astron-

---

[45] *Chronica* 4.27. On the basis of this passage, Schnabel reversed his earlier position (in *OLZ* 9 [1910], 401–2) that the *Babyloniaca* made no reference to an *inundatio futura*; for Schnabel, this passage presupposes a future ἐκπύρωσις (Berossos, 95); see also Herman L. Jansen, *Die Henochgestalt* (Oslo, 1939), 75.

[46] B. L. van der Waerden, "Das grosse Jahr," 142. For discussion of Berossus' speculations about cosmic cycles, see also J. Bidez, "Bérose et la Grande Année," *Mélanges Paul Fredericq* (Brussels, 1904), 9–19; K. F. Smith, "Ages of the World," *ERE* 1 (1926), 199; P. Schnabel, "Apokalyptische Berechnung der Endzeiten bei Berossos," *OLZ* 9 (1910), 401–2.

[47] See Pliny *NH* 7.123, who asserts that the Athenians erected a statue to Berossus "ob divinas praedicationes." Note also that Josephus makes a similar observation when he states that the antediluvian generations had to live at least the duration of a Great Year in order to be able to predict the future with certainty (*Ant.* 1.104–6).

[48] Cf. W. G. Lambert, "Berossus and Babylonian Eschatology," *Iraq* 38 (1976), 171–73; Jacoby also assigned this passage, as well as many other astronomical and astrological traditions attributed to Berossus, to (ps-)Berossus (see *FrGH*, 3C 680, FF 15–22). For arguments in favor of the essential accuracy of Seneca's representation of Berossus, see P. Schnabel, *Berossos*, 17–19; 94–96; Robert Drews, "Babylonian Chronicles," 51–55; Burstein, *The Babyloniaca*, 15, 31–32.

omy, worked actively to encourage the speculative use of their native chronicles as well.

THE GRECO-EGYPTIAN CHRONICLE IN LATE ANTIQUITY

There is a passage from Africanus' chronicle preserved by Syncellus in which Africanus speaks reproachfully of the chronicles of the Egyptians. Egyptian "priests and astrologers," he complains, have "put forth an account (of their past) . . . in far-fetched cycles and myriads of years (περιττὰς περιόδους καὶ μυριάδας ἐτῶν)."[49] No amount of chronological manipulation, however, could conceal what was, in Africanus' eyes, the true motive behind the supposed longevity of these chronicles; it was, Africanus comments, simple ethnic boasting (ἐπὶ τὸ κομπωδέστερον).[50]

We have no indication from this excerpt what the astronomical cycles were according to which the Egyptian astrologers had periodized their past. But the speculative character of the Egyptian chronicle emerges very visibly in two Egyptian chronicles of Hermetic provenance. Preserved again by Syncellus, they probably were made known to him from Panodorus, an early fifth-century Christian universal chronicler of Alexandria. Indeed, the proper interpretation of one of these Egyptian chronicles— the *Book of Sothis*—was destined to become a point of contention between Syncellus and his Alexandrian source.[51]

There is, Syncellus writes, an anonymous chronicle called the *Ancient Chronicle* (τὸ παλαιὸν χρονικόν), which circulates "among the Egyptians (φέρεται . . . παρ' Αἰγυπτίοις)."[52] The chronicle, he says, encompassed the "immense (ἄπειρον)" period of 36,525 years, the largest portion of which belonged to the reigns of the mythic period.[53] The number 36,525 has, Syncellus adds, an astronomical significance:

> If this total is broken up or divided 25 times into 1,461 years, it reveals the periodic return of the Zodiac which is commonly referred to in the Greek and Egyptian books, that is, its revolution from one point to that same point again, namely the first minute of the first degree of the equinoctial sign of the Zodiac, the ram as it is called by them, according to the account given in the *Genika* of Hermes and the

[49] In Syncellus 17.30–32.
[50] Sync. 17.30.
[51] See below, Chap. 3, pp. 78–80.
[52] Sync. 56.23. Syncellus knows the same work by other names: "a certain old chronography (παλαιόν τι χρονογραφεῖον)" (56.18) and the "so-called [more] Ancient History of the Egyptians (ἡ παλαιοτέρα νομιζομένη Αἰγυπτίων συγγραφή)" (57.26).
[53] Ibid., 56.19–22.

Books of the Cyrranides. Hence, it was, I suppose, that Ptolemaeus announced that the ready tables should be calculated in periods of 25 years.[54]

Syncellus believed that the work predated Manetho; in fact, he says, the *Ancient Chronicle* was the source of Manetho's "error" (ἐξ οὗ καὶ Μανεθῶ πεπλανῆσθαι νομίζω).[55] However, the references to the *Genika* of Hermes Trismegistus and the significance of the number 36,525 in the Hermetic literature suggest that the work was composed in the Hermetic environment, probably, as has been suggested elsewhere, in the third or fourth century C.E.[56] The notable thing, however, is the chronicle's periodization of history. The 1,461 years referred to are the well-known Sothic cycle, the period of time required to reconcile the Egyptian solar and civil calendar.[57] Although the significance of this period in the ancient Egyptian calendar has been overrated, the Sothic cycle, or a multiple of it, was often thought to represent a Great Year cycle.[58] "Among the Egyptians and Greeks," Syncellus states, the period of time encompassed by the *Ancient Chronicle* was a whole cosmic revolution from "one sign of Aries and back again."[59]

[54] Ibid., 57.12–57.19 (trans. Waddell, *Manetho*, app. iii, 231).

[55] Ibid., 56.19.

[56] The authenticity of the *Ancient Chronicle* was first questioned by A. Des Vignoles, *Chronologie de l'histoire sainte*, 2 vols. (Berlin, 1738) 2. 659, 663. For the date and the composition of the *Ancient Chronicle*, see Gelzer, *SJA*, 2. 215–17; Unger, *Chronologie des Manetho*, 20–28; Böckh, *Manetho und die Hundsternperiode*, 40–57. I see no reason to accept Gelzer's claim (*SJA*, 2.215) that the *Ancient Chronicle* was a Christian or Jewish composition.

[57] In addition to a lunar and solar calendar, the ancient Egyptians possessed a "civil calendar," consisting of 365 days (three seasons of four months each), with an additional five epagomenal days. This discrepancy meant that every four years, the civil calendar would begin one day before the solar calendar. At the end of 1,461 civil years, or 1,460 solar years, the civil year would have moved "backwards" through every day of the solar year. This cycle was known as the Sothic cycle, because the beginning of this cycle was calculated on the basis of the heliacal rising of the star Sothis, the Egyptian name for Sirius. On the Sothic cycle and its relationship to the Egyptian calendar, see Richard A. Parker, *The Calendars of Ancient Egypt*, Studies in Ancient Oriental Civilization 26 (Chicago, 1950), 51–56.

[58] See Otto Neugebauer, "Die Bedeuteungslosigkeit der 'Sothisperiode' für die älteste ägyptische Chronologie," *AO* 17 (1938), 169–95; idem, "The Origin of the Egyptian Calendar," *JNES* 1 (1942) 396–403. Van den Broek (*The Myth of the Phoenix*, 26–32) gives a summary of 19th-century opinions about the role of the Sothic cycle in the ancient Egyptian calendar. For the connection of the Sothic cycle with the Great Year, see Tacitus (*Annals* 6.28), who associates the cycle with the life of the Phoenix, known for its regenerative powers; Firmicus Maternus (*Praef. Astron.*), who links the cycle to the period of time during which the sun, moon and the five planets return to their original position. Michael Psellus knows a Great Year of 1,753,200, evidently 1,200 Sothic cycles; cf. M. Tannery, "Psellus sur la Grande Année," *REG* 5 (1892), 206–11; J. Bidez, "Bérose et la Grande Année," 13.

[59] Although Syncellus does not explain the significance of the number 25 in this computation of the cosmic revolution, it probably refers to the period of the Egyptian lunar cycle (see Parker, *Calendars*, 13–17). The number 36,525 appears to have great significance in Her-

Characteristics similar to the *Ancient Chronicle* are found in the *Book of Sothis*, a chronicle of Egyptian history that appears to have constituted Panodorus' principal source for Egyptian history, at least for the primordial period. Although the *Book of Sothis* purports to be composed by Manetho himself, it is now generally regarded as a classic piece of ancient pseudepigraphy, composed sometime before the fifth century.[60]

In introducing the *Book of Sothis*, Syncellus states that the work was a translation of antediluvian inscriptions left by "Hermes Trismegistus" in the "Seriadic land" and cached away in the temple shrines of Egypt:

> It remains now to give a few extracts concerning the dynasties of Egypt from the works of Manetho of Sebennytus. In the time of Ptolemy Philadelphus, he was styled high-priest of the pagan temples of Egypt, and wrote from stelae in the Seriadic land (ἐν τῇ Σηριαδικῇ γῇ), stelae inscribed, he says, in a priestly dialect and hierographic characters (ἱερᾷ . . . διαλέκτῳ καὶ ἱερογραφικοῖς γράμμασι) by Thoth the first Hermes and translated (ἑρμηνευθεισῶν) after the flood from the priestly tongue into the Greek language in hieroglyphic characters (ἐκ τῆς ἱερᾶς διαλέκτου εἰς τὴν Ἑλληνίδα φωνὴν γράμμασιν ἱερογλυφικοῖς). When the work had been arranged in books by Agathodaimon, son of the second Hermes, and father of Tat, in the *adyta* of the temples of Egypt, Manetho dedicated it to this same king Ptolemy II Philadelphus with the following words.[61]

What follows is a letter from Manetho addressed to Ptolemy Philadelphus, outlining the proposed contents of the *Book of Sothis:*

> To the great king Ptolemy Philadelphus Augustus (βασιλεῖ μεγάλῳ Πτολεμαίῳ Φιλαδέλφῳ σεβαστῷ). Greeting to my lord Ptolemy from Manetho, high priest and scribe of the sacred shrines of Egypt, born at Sebennytus and dwelling at Heliopolis. It is my duty, almighty king, to reflect upon all such matters as you may desire me to investigate. So, as you are making researches concerning the future of

---

metic speculation. Iamblichus states, on the authority of "Manetho," that the Hermetic corpus consisted of 36,525 books; cf. *De mysteriis* 8.1 (ed. Edouard des Places [Paris, 1966]). The Sabians are said by Shahrastani to have described a world-cycle of 36,425 years, probably a corruption of 36,525; cf. D. Chwolson, *Die Ssabier und Ssabismus*, 2 vols. (St. Petersburg, 1856) 1. 768 (note 4). Whether Syncellus or his source was responsible for equating this astronomical period with the "precession of the equinoxes" is unclear; see Böckh, *Manetho und die Hundsternperiode*, 54–55.

[60] For further discussion, see below, Chap. 6, pp. 172–73.

[61] Sync. 40.31–41.9 (trans. adapted from Waddell, App. 1).

the universe (περὶ τῶν μελλόντων τῷ κόσμῳ), in obedience to your command I shall place before you the Sacred Books which I have studied, written by your forefather Hermes Trismegistus (τοῦ προπάτορος τρισμεγίστου Ἑρμοῦ).

Farewell, I pray, my lord king.[62]

When seeking to determine the existence of fraud, little confidence is inspired in a manuscript reported to have been hidden for thousands of years in a library or a temple shrine, only recently finding the light of day. The circumstantial details attending the discovery of *Book of Sothis,* and the elaborate and farfetched literary pedigree with which the author endows the *Book of Sothis,* both of which were meant to enhance the work's credibility, place it squarely in the category of literary imposture.[63] The pseudonymous character of the work is barely concealed by the several historical anachronisms in the introductory letter to the work. There, (ps-) Manetho extends his greetings to "Ptolemy Philadelphus Augustus," to whom the work is putatively dedicated; "Augustus (σέβαστος)," however, was never applied to a Ptolemaic king, coming into currency only in the Roman Empire. In his account of the origin of the book, the author again betrays himself as a forger: "I shall place before you the Sacred Books which I have studied, written by your forefather Hermes Trismegistus." Here, too, the historical anachronism exposes the late date of the work; the term "trismegistus" does not appear as an epithet for Hermes until the first century B.C.E.[64]

The motives lying behind the composition of this letter are largely transparent. What the author wants to establish above all are the primordial

---

[62] Ibid., 41.12–19 (trans. Waddell, App. 1).

[63] See W. Speyer, *Die literarische Fälschung im heidnischen und christlichen Altertum,* Handbuch der Altertumswissenschaft 1.2 (Munich, 1971), 81, 255; R. Laqueur, "Manethon," 1100–1. The inconsistencies of this account of the work's origins have already been amply treated by Walter Scott (*Hermetica* 3 [Oxford, 1926], 491–92. Among the peculiarities of its description is the incredible statement that the stelae were "translated after the flood into Greek with hieroglyphic characters," which Scott believes was omitted by a copyist and then reinserted in the wrong place later (491, note 2). Scott also suggests that the long discussion of the work's origin (starting with ἐκ τῶν and continuing to ἐν τοῖς ἀδύτοις τῶν ἱερῶν Αἰγύπτου) introduces a breach in continuity, and should be excised (491–92, note 6); cf. R. Reitzenstein, *Poimandres* (Leipzig, 1904), 139. For an opposing view, see Garth Fowden, *The Egyptian Hermes* (Cambridge, 1986), 31 (note 108).

[64] On the basis of certain similarities with a report in Varro (in *City of God* 18.3), Festugière suggested that the letter may have drawn on a tradition originating sometime before Varro. See his *La Révélation d'Hermès Trismégiste,* 4 vols. (Paris, 1949–54), I. 74–75. Böckh (*Hundsternperiode,* 15) argued that the letter could not have been written before the 3rd century C.E. For early testimonies to the name "Hermes Trismegistus," see also Fowden, *The Egyptian Hermes,* 216–17.

and esoteric origins of the work, the divine sponsorship of its translation into Greek, and the inaccessibility of the original revelation upon which it is based. The description of the origins of the *Book of Sothis* recalls other accounts of the origin of Hermetic books. Iamblichus states, for example, that Bitys, the "prophet of Ammon," explained the teachings of Hermes which he "found in the *adyta* of Sais in Egypt," written in hieroglyphics.[65] The original revelations of Hermes Trismegistus are no longer accessible, having been composed in an obscure language and set up in the land of Seir, a place usually thought to lie in a very remote region of the world.[66]

As noted earlier, oriental historians liked to contrast the putative accuracy and antiquity of their records with the late and contradictory records of the Greeks. To do so, they regularly minimized their own role as original authors, presenting themselves instead as simple translators of ancient archives carefully preserved either in temples or public monuments. In the case of the *Book of Sothis*, the supposed care with which the original revelation was preserved and rendered into Greek approaches the absurd. The motif of stelae left for postdiluvian generations was a device commonly employed by oriental historians to explain the survival of pre-flood wisdom after the flood. In the closest extant parallel to this stelae legend, recounted in Josephus' *Antiquities* and numerous Christian chronographers, Seth and his descendants were also said to have erected brick and stone monuments before the flood and deposited them in the "land of Seir."[67] Their intention was to ensure the protection of primordial learning from destruction by flood or fire. The labored account of the circumstances attending the translation of *Sothis* after the flood suggests as well that the author wanted to impress his readers with the accuracy of the final published work. First translated into Greek "with hieroglyphic characters" and deposited in temple shrines by Agathodaimon, it was later presented in Greek letters to Ptolemy. In his zeal to stress the antiquity of the archives upon which the *Book of Sothis* was based, the author of the work has thus robbed Manetho of any originality: all that Manetho does is transliterate the text of *Sothis* into Greek letters.

A comparison of Josephus' genuine excerpts from the *Aegyptiaca* with the contents of the Hermetic *Book of Sothis* reveals the extent to which the

[65] Iamblichus *De mysteriis* 8.5 (ed. des Places).

[66] In Christian sources, Seir was sometimes described as a mountain lying in the far eastern corner of the presently inhabited world. For discussion of the location of Seir, see G. J. Reinink, "Das Land 'Seiris' (Šir) und das Volk der Serer in jüdischen und christlichen Traditionen," *JSJ* 6 (1975), 72–85.

[67] *Ant.* 1.68–70.

speculative and pseudo-scientific concerns of late Antiquity have reshaped the character of the Hellenized Egyptian chronicle. Unlike the continuous historical narrative that makes up the content of Josephus' excerpts from Manetho, both the *Book of Sothis* and the *Ancient Chronicle* are merely running lists of kings; rather than to describe the Egyptian past, their purpose seems mainly to celebrate its longevity. Indeed, the *Book of Sothis* has even more grandiose pretensions. The reference to "Sothis" in the title suggests that the work, like the *Ancient Chronicle,* was periodized into Sothic "Great Year" cycles. And in his letter of introduction, "Manetho" dedicates the chronicle to Ptolemy Philadelphus, supposedly in response to the latter's inquiries "about the future of the universe (περὶ τῶν μελλόντων τῷ κόσμῳ)."

RELIGIOUS SYNCRETISM IN THE *BOOK OF SOTHIS*

One can only guess as to the intentions of the author in concocting such a work and foisting it upon Hermes and Manetho. Rivalry with Chaldaism, especially as it was embodied in the *Babyloniaca,* may be one reason. A particularly illustrative example of the same rivalry is found already in the first century C.E., in the course of a polemic against Chaldaism written by the Egyptian Stoic Chaeremon and preserved by Michael Psellus.[68]

Psellus includes this extract in order to settle the dispute between the Egyptians and Chaldeans concerning the antiquity of their respective civilizations. The Chaldeans, Psellus writes, "date their own wisdom back about 400,000 years into history, while the Egyptians surpass even this number in their traditions. And the Chaldeans present themselves as the teachers of the Egyptians, whereas the Egyptians boast that it was the Chaldeans who wished to become disciples of them. . . . Now, when I read the wise Chaeremon, . . . I found that the wisdom of the Chaldeans is older than the one zealously practiced among the Egyptians, but that neither people was the teacher of the other, but that both have their own champions."[69]

Chaeremon, Psellus goes on to say, explains the reason why the Chaldeans spread the lie that they instructed the Egyptians in astronomy. Al-

---

[68] The excerpt was first published by E. N. Sathas, "Fragments inédits des historiens grecs n. 1: Chaeremonis *Aegyptiaca,*" *BCH* 1 (1887) 121–33, 194–208; also in *FrGH,* 3C, 618 F 7 and 665 F 193; recent edition and English translation of this excerpt by Pieter Willem van der Horst, *Chaeremon: Egyptian Priest and Stoic Philosopher,* Études préliminaires aux religions orientales dans l'Empire Romain 101 (Leiden, 1984), fr. 2.

[69] Fr. 2 (trans. van der Horst).

though the Egyptians had possessed an indigenous knowledge of this science from ancient times, the Nile had once flooded, destroying all the astronomical data that the Egyptians had collected in books. Forced to turn to the Chaldeans for knowledge of conjunctions and eclipses, they received maliciously distorted information from their Chaldean rivals, who had "altered the times in their calculations and given out the movements of the planets and fixed stars contrary to their natural order (παρὰ τὴν φύσιν)." The Egyptians, now "in great uncertainty concerning the principles," became disciples of the Chaldeans. When the Egyptians recovered the truth about the universe, they later took precautions against future catastrophes by engraving the "true knowledge of reality on baked bricks (τὴν ἀληθίνην γνῶσιν τῶν ὄντων ἐν ὄπταις πλίνθοις)." In this same excerpt, Chaeremon singles out the *Babyloniaca* for special derision, most notably Berossus' legend of Oannes, the Chaldean culture-bringer. He was a charlatan, claims Chaeremon, who, "dressed in the garb of a fish," deluded the earliest Egyptians with false teachings and threatened to cause an eclipse of the sun if the Egyptians refused to make him king.[70]

Chaeremon's references to the flood and stelae appear anomalous in a work purportedly of Egyptian origin, since there is no evidence that a universal flood figured in the native mythology of the Egyptians, and since Egyptian apologetic often trenched on the alleged immunity of Egypt from periodic floods and fires brought about by cosmic cycles.[71] Presumably, Chaeremon adopted both these motifs and the story of Oannes from Chaldean mythology (via Berossus' *Babyloniaca*) both to explain the origin and evolution of Egyptian wisdom and to denigrate the Chaldeans.[72] In

---

[70] Probably, the false teachings include astronomy and astrology. For Oannes' revelations about the celestial sciences, see also Hyginus *Genealogiae* 247.16: "Oannes qui in Chaldaea de mari exisse dicitur astrologiam interpretatus est." Oannes is presented in this excerpt from Chaeremon as nothing more than a charlatan, whose real name was Ioannes. He is given a most peculiar pedigree: a descendant from Hermes and Apollo and the 14th ruler after Ninus, who according to Chaeremon was the author of Chaldean wisdom. The fact that he is cast as the ruler of the Egyptians may arise from a confusion on Psellus' part. In the original text of the *Aegyptiaca*, Chaeremon could have been describing the circumstances of the rule of "Ioannes" in Babylonia. In another excerpt, whose authenticity is doubtful, Oannes is also reviled as a man who became king of the Egyptians through deception and was worshipped as a god (fr. 16D, ed. van der Horst); on the authenticity of this passage, see van der Horst, 64 (note 1, on fr. 16D).

[71] Cf. Herodotus 2.142; Diodorus 1.10.4–7; Proclus *Commentary on Timaeus* 22 A5–B3 (ed. Diels); Varro (in Augustine *City of God* 18.10); cf. Böckh, *Hundsternperiode*, 81. On the significance of the flooding of the Nile in Egyptian mythology, see Dierk Wortmann, "Kosmogonie und Nilflut," *Bonner Jahrbücher des Rheinischen Landesmuseums* 166 (1966), 62–112.

[72] Another story about the preservation of Egyptian culture through the flood is found in Ammianus Marcellinus (22.15.30), who says that the Egyptians buried the "most ancient rites"

noting many of the same foreign motifs in the *Book of Sothis,* several commentators have also suggested that "Asian or Chaldean" elements have penetrated the work.[73] Clearly, there is much here that resembles the composition of the *Babyloniaca.* In the *Book of Sothis,* (ps-)Manetho attributes the original revelation to Hermes/Thoth, the Egyptian counterpart to Oannes.[74] According to the *Babyloniaca,* antediluvian writings were preserved through the flood by being buried underground; *Sothis'* Hermes engraves his revelations on stelae. Credit for the final compilation of the work would then naturally go to Manetho. As one roughly contemporary with Berossus, he was the natural candidate to whom to attribute the work.[75] Manetho was, moreover, credited in late Antiquity with the writing not just of histories, but of Hermetic and astronomical works as well; the *Book of Sothis* thus joins the ranks of a large collection of literary frauds of late Antiquity ascribed to the Egyptian priest.[76]

The parallels between the *Book of Sothis* and the *Babyloniaca* extend as

---

in the earth, "since they had fore-knowledge that the deluge was coming and feared that the memory of the ceremonies might be destroyed" (fr. 28D, trans. van der Horst). This tradition, which may also go back to Chaeremon (for discussion, see van der Horst's note on fr. 28D, p. 73 note 1) shows very close affinities with Berossus' story of Xisuthrus; before the flood, Xisuthrus received a command from Cronus to "bury the beginnings and the middles and the ends of all writings in Sippar" (trans. Burstein, fr. C.2.1). After the flood, these buried writings were dug up in Sippar and distributed to mankind.

[73] See, for example, M. Plessner, "Hermes Trismegistus and Arab Science," *Studia Islamica* 2 (1954), 55–57. But Plessner exaggerates the importance of the *Book of Sothis* in saying that it is the "missing link" (56) between the Arabic stories of Hermes and the Babylonian flood myth. See also M. Fr. Lenormant, *Essai de commentaire des fragments cosmogoniques de Bérose,* 269.

[74] When, for example, the emperor Julian assails the Jews and Christians for not having produced any contributors to culture, he contrasts them with the Chaldeans and Egyptians, who have, he says, Oannes and Hermes respectively (*Against the Galileans* [176AB]).

[75] Syncellus himself seems to be aware of rivalry between Manetho and Berossus, for he says that each accuses the other of lying about the antiquity of his race in order to glorify his own fatherland (Sync. 38.20–21).

[76] Several other pseudepigraphic works, some of Hermetic provenience, circulated in the name of Manetho. Eusebius says that Manetho wrote a work called the *Sacred Book* (Ἱερὰ Βίβλος), which expounded the "whole history of Egypt and especially the details of Egyptian religion" (in Eusebius PE 2 Proem. 44c). Two works on astronomy and natural science circulated in antiquity under the name of Manetho—the so-called *Epitome of Physical Doctrines,* and the *Apotelesmatica,* an astrological poem composed in hexameters. The first work is generally regarded as authentic, its purpose being to present Egyptian views on the physical properties of the universe (see the fragments from the work in Waddell, *Manetho,* frs. 82,83). Waddell (xxvii) speculates that the purpose of the work was to familiarize Greeks with the fundamentals of Egyptian science. The *Apotelesmatica,* first attested by Hephaesteon of Thebes in the fourth century, is clearly pseudepigraphic. As Köchley and Kroll have shown, it is a composite work, the earliest portion of which was composed about the 2nd century C.E. See H. A. Köchley, *Manethonis Apotelesmaticorum qui feruntur libri vi* (Leipzig, 1858); W. Kroll, "Manethon" (2), *RE* 14.1, 1102–6.

well to the kings to whom these works were supposedly dedicated: the *Babyloniaca* to Antiochus Soter, *Sothis* to his contemporary Ptolemy Philadelphus. It should first be recalled that the oft-repeated claim that Manetho dedicated the *Aegyptiaca* to Ptolemy Philadelphus owes its origins not to the *Aegyptiaca* at all but to the pseudepigraphic *Book of Sothis*. In fact, the only other ancient author even to mention the date of Manetho is Plutarch, who says in his *On Isis and Osiris* that Manetho lived during the reign of Ptolemy I.[77]

There is little reason to trust what the *Book of Sothis* reports here. Ptolemy II Philadelphus was a king credited with having officially sponsored the translation into Greek of numerous foreign books.[78] Stories of his contributions to learning were not always well founded, however. One good example of this is, of course, the supposed conditions surrounding the translation of the Torah from Hebrew. In order to validate the authority of this translation, the Jews of Alexandria circulated a legend, according to which Ptolemy II Philadelphus had officially commissioned the undertaking. Whether the translation was undertaken with official sponsorship, however, is a matter of legitimate doubt.[79] Syncellus himself reports what must be rejected as the wholly incredible claim that Philadelphus, "a man wise in all things (ἀνὴρ τὰ πάντα σοφός) and extremely industrious, collected all Greek, Chaldean, Egyptian, and Roman (sic) books; having translated (μεταφράσας) the foreign ones into Greek," he placed 100,000 books in the Alexandrian library.[80]

These legends about Ptolemy's learning and philanthropy share the same motives. Egyptian chauvinism accounts for the glorification of Ptolemy Philadelphus as benevolent monarch and polymath. In point of fact, Ptolemy Philadelphus seems to have evinced very little interest in native Egyptian writings. Unlike his predecessor, "in this reign," writes Tarn, "all interest in native Egypt was dropped, and a little later Alexandria appears

[77] Cf. Plutarch *On Isis and Osiris* 28.362 (fr. 80, ed. Waddell). In Plutarch's account, Manetho is reported to have helped decipher a dream vision experienced by Ptolemy Soter.

[78] See W. W. Tarn, "Ptolemy II," *Journal of Egyptian Archaeology* 14 (1928), 252–54.

[79] For a summary of modern scholarly views on the reliability of the tradition about royal sponsorship, see Sidney Jellicoe, *The Septuagint and Modern Study* (Oxford, 1968), 52–58, and works cited there. Although there was some ancient uncertainty about the Ptolemaic king who sponsored the translation (cf. Clement *Stromateis* 1.149), it was generally believed to be Philadelphus. For discussion of the ancient witnesses, see Elias Bickerman "The Septuagint as a Translation," *Studies in Jewish and Christian History* 1 (Leiden, 1976), 167–70, and works cited there.

[80] Sync. 327.17–21. No credence can be placed in the claim that Ptolemy had Latin works translated, since, as Bickerman has observed (apropos of this passage), "for us, at least, Latin literature began with a play of Livius Andronicus produced in 240 B.C.E."; see his "The Septuagint as a Translation," 174 (note 17).

as merely an object of hatred to many Egyptians."[81] Moreover, there was no better way to validate a translation's authenticity than to trace its origins to official and/or divine sponsorship. This was what spurred apologists for the Septuagint to manufacture the fabulous legend about Philadelphus' interest in the Septuagint.[82] (Ps-)Manetho had the same thing in mind when he composed the dedicatory letter to the *Book of Sothis*. We have little grounds for concluding, however, that this Hellenized Egyptian of late Antiquity was accurately representing the conditions under which the historical Manetho wrote his own work.[83]

The *Book of Sothis* has left a curious legacy. Syncellus, who had no reason to doubt that the work was genuine, was himself struck by the symmetry between Manetho and Berossus. For him, there was no other explanation than that Manetho had copied from Berossus. "What Manetho of Sebennytus," Syncellus says, "wrote to Ptolemy Philadelphus about the Egyptian dynasties is full of lies and composed in imitation of Berossus about the same time or a little later (κατὰ μίμησιν Βηρώσσου πεπλασμένα κατὰ τοὺς αὐτοὺς σχεδόν που χρόνους ἢ μικρὸν ὕστερον)."[84] In modern studies of Hellenistic literature, Berossus and Manetho are commonly treated as contemporaries and literary "twins," the latter doing for Egyptian what the former did for Babylonian culture and history. While no one would seriously suggest today, as Croiset once did, that the symmetry in the tradition about the *Babyloniaca* and the *Aegyptiaca* proves that they were the fabrications of one oriental apologist,[85] it is salutary not to forget that Syncellus is the single most important witness to this tradition. And when he reports that Manetho was Berossus' literary twin, he says it in reference not to the *Aegyptiaca*, but to the *Book of Sothis*. To the extent that he is representing the *Book of Sothis*, a forgery of late Antiquity possibly influenced by and in competition with the *Babyloniaca*, Syncellus is accu-

[81] "Ptolemy II," 254.

[82] A curious tale told by Zosimus the alchemist (4th century) shows that even the story of the translation of the Septuagint could get wound up with Egyptian Hermetism. Zosimus knows a legend according to which the high-priest Asenas had sent Hermes to Ptolemy in order to translate the Bible into Greek; cf. Fowden, *The Egyptian Hermes,* 31 (note 108).

[83] Doubts about the supposed contemporaneity of Berossus and Manetho were already expressed by C. Mueller (*FHG* 2. 511). Another pseudepigraphic work of later Antiquity foisted upon Manetho and supposedly dedicated to Ptolemy Philadelphus is the *Apotelesmatica;* for the pseudepigraphic character of this work, see above, note 76.

[84] Sync. 17.2–4.

[85] A. Croiset, *Histoire de la littérature grecque,* 5. 99. See also E. Havet, *Mémoire sur les écrits,* passim.

rate; whether it is an accurate biographical report about the historical Manetho is, however, another matter.

THE ORIENTAL CHRONICLE AND PAGAN/CHRISTIAN POLEMIC

Modern writers on Manetho like to draw a sharp distinction between Manetho the historian and Manetho the sage. But (ps-)Manetho's *Book of Sothis* resists such neat categorizations. Although scholars in the nineteenth century tended to treat the chronicle as a historical work belonging in the same class as the *Aegyptiaca,* it is now more commonly included in the *Corpus Hermeticum.*[86] Greek writers of late Antiquity were no less uncertain about the proper way to classify chronicles like the *Book of Sothis* and the *Ancient Chronicle:* should they be treated as ethnic histories or as esoteric works offering revealed wisdom about the future course of the universe?

The inclination seems to have been to the latter view. In his commentary on Plato's *Timaeus,* the fifth-century neo-Platonist Proclus writes of having learned from his colleague Iamblichus that the "Assyrians" had in their possession chronicles that extended over whole Great Year cycles. The report moved Proclus to conclude that the oriental chronicle belongs in an entirely different class of literature from what he calls, perhaps contemptuously, the "much celebrated archeology (πολυθρύλητος ἀρχαιολογία) of the Greeks."[87] Whereas Greek historians were satisfied to record the history of a particular region or city, the Egyptians and Assyrians had recorded monuments that encompassed whole cosmic cycles.[88]

---

[86] See Walter Scott, *Hermetica,* 3. 492–93; A.-J. Festugière, *La Révélation d'Hermès Trismégiste,* 1. 74–75; Reitzenstein, *Poimandres,* 139; Fowden, *The Egyptian Hermes,* 29–31. The categorization of the *Book of Sothis* as "Hermetic" arises, of course, from the character of the dedicatory letter, which reads like a standard description of the origins of the Hermetic writings. August Boeckh, struck by the contrast between the grandiose pretensions of the introductory letter and the simple list of kings that follows, has suggested, unconvincingly, that the *Book of Sothis* contained a lost fourth section of purely speculative material; see *Hundsternperiode,* 13. Scholars of Hermetism who have analyzed the letter of (ps-)Manetho are often unaware that the letter introduces only an Egyptian chronicle, with little apparent connection to Hermetism.

[87] Proclus, *Procli Diadochi in Platonis Timaeum Commentaria,* ed. E. Diehl, 3 vols. (Leipzig, 1903), 1. 100.29–101.4 (on *Timaeus* 22AB).

[88] Proclus *Commentary Tim.* 1.101.1–6 (on *Tim.* 22AB). Proclus, commenting later on *Timaeus* 40AB (ed. Diehl, 3. 125.27–126.1), has the following to say about the records of the Chaldeans: "But the men I particularly speak of are the Chaldeans, who had observations of whole cosmic cycles and irrefutable predictions both of private and public occurrences. Why, therefore, should we adduce as testimony the records of a few observations, and views that are youthful and not accompanied with such great accuracy, when they [the Chaldeans] bear witness to the teachings of the ancients concerning the motion of the fixed stars?"

By their neglect of Berossus and Manetho, the Greek historians gave silent assent to the same view. Pagan writers, as we have seen, were oddly at variance with their Christian counterparts in viewing these men not as historians, but rather as sages. Even their historical works are seen largely as repositories of oriental wisdom.[89] Although this perception arises at least in part from a characteristically Hellenistic penchant to romanticize the East, the pseudonymous author of the Hermetic *Book of Sothis* has done nothing to correct this view. Offering to Ptolemy Philadelphus Hermetic prognostications about the future of the universe, "Manetho" here plays the role of Hermetist far better than he does the Egyptian annalist; one should not be surprised, therefore, to see that in late Antiquity Manetho is normally understood in just this way.[90]

Christian chronographers could hardly be comfortable with this transformation, for it undermined the very reason why they appealed to Berossus and Manetho in the first place—namely, the antiquity of the archives upon which they were based. True, the tremendous longevity of their chronicles promoted the case for the superiority of oriental culture and historiography. But what Africanus had termed the "cycles and myriads" of these chronicles posed a direct challenge to Genesis' account of creation. Indeed, we know that already by the second century C.E., the putative antiquity of the oriental chronicles was used by Greek polemicists in the pagan/Christian controversy about the age of the universe. In order to demonstrate the errancy of Moses' account of creation, the anti-Christian polemicist Celsus adduced the case of the Egyptians. The Egyptians, he states, are best suited to speculate about the creation of the universe and its cycles because they have a continuous record of their civilization, undisrupted by periodic floods and fires.[91] By contrast, Moses, who lived after the flood and had no record of antediluvian history, failed to recognize that the cataclysm at the time of Noah was only one of the more

---

[89] So see Pliny *NH* 7.56.193. The several hundred thousand years of Berossus' history interest him not because of the historical information contained therein, but because they contained uninterrupted astronomical observations from primordial times. Pliny, who probably did not know the *Babyloniaca* firsthand, seems to have benefited very little from its historical content.

[90] See above, Chap. 1, pp. 29–30. The same observation would apply equally well to Berossus. The *Babyloniaca*, writes Drews, "has been customarily considered a work of history, and I do not doubt that it was presented as such. . . . The only thing in it which was of value to Josephus and Eusebius was what Berossus had to say about the history and chronology of Babylon. . . . But in Hellenistic and Roman times, when his work was still known, the subjects with which Berossus was identified were 'astronomy and the philosophical doctrines of the Chaldaeans'" ("The Babylonian Chronicles and Berossus," 53).

[91] Celsus, in Origen's *Against Celsus* 1.19–20; 4.9–13; 4.21.

recent of a long series of cyclically recurring calamities.[92] As a consequence, his account of creation was little more than a distortion of doctrines he had borrowed from the Egyptians.[93]

The immunity of the Egyptians from natural calamity is an old motif, appearing, as we have seen, already in Plato's *Timaeus*. Clearly, the circulation of such works as the *Ancient Chronicle* and the *Book of Sothis*—the latter the work of an antediluvian sage extending several thousands of years—made an effective case for Celsus' contention that the Egyptians had the most accurate knowledge about the age of the universe. What is most significant is the similarity of Celsus' argument to one that Josephus had mounted earlier against the Greeks in *Against Apion:* that the Greeks, unlike the Orientals, had no historical records extending before the most recent flood or fire.[94] The use of the same argument on both sides of the controversy illustrates that the presumed antiquity of the Chaldean and Egyptian chronicles was a double-edged sword. Although these chronicles helped to demonstrate the "newness" of the Greeks and the unreliability of their histories for primordial history, at the same time they called into question the accuracy of the biblical account of the age of the world.

In response, Christian chroniclers began to demur. No longer was the putative longevity of the oriental chronicles automatic confirmation of their reliability; to the contrary, it could signify their unreliability. The Chaldeans, writes Lactantius, were at "liberty to speak falsely about primordial history, because they knew that the Greeks were ignorant about this period." When, he observes, Plato and the other philosophers said that "many thousands of ages had passed since this beautiful arrangement of the world was completed . . . in this they perhaps followed the Chaldeans, who as Cicero has related in his first book respecting divination foolishly say that they possess comprised in their memorials 470,000 years."[95]

No better reversal of attitudes can be found than in Augustine's views on the matter. Confronted with the long duration of Egyptian history, Augustine found himself an advocate of the superior credibility of Greek history on precisely those grounds for which Josephus had impugned it,

[92] Celsus (in *Against Celsus* 4.21) also conjectures that the story of Sodom and Gomorrah was an allegory of the universal conflagration; he likens this story to the legend of Phaethon, which in the *Timaeus* (22C) is also presented as an allegory of the world fire.

[93] *Against Celsus* 1.19–20; 4.11; 4.21. Origen's response to this is that Moses was older than those who formulated the doctrines about universal cycles (4.11–12).

[94] See above, Chap. 1, pp. 21–23.

[95] Lactantius *Div. inst.* 7.14.

namely its modest duration. In the course of his critique of arguments in favor of world cycles and the eternity of the universe, Augustine reports about a portion of an Egyptian chronicle which Alexander had reportedly sent to his mother Olympias. Where this could be compared with Greek accounts (based on Ctesias) of the same events, Augustine noticed that the Greek narrative was invariably shorter in duration. "We have," he writes, "a reason to give credit to Greek history, in that it does not exceed the true tale of years that appears in our truly sacred histories."[96]

It need hardly be stressed that the problem of Chaldean and Egyptian chronology was especially acute for the Christian universal chronicler who conceived his task as the writing of a continuous record of the world from its creation. Naturally, it was in the treatment of archaic history that the problem was sensed most sharply, since it was to the mythic or antediluvian portion of their chronicles that Berossus and Manetho had assigned the longest duration of time. Here, too, Christian chroniclers had to work mostly on their own. Since Manetho and Berossus were largely ignored by Hellenistic historians, there existed for the Christian chroniclers no one like Castor of Rhodes to provide for them ready-made chronological comparisons. As a consequence, the problem was destined to generate enormous controversy, starting already with Africanus, and persisting for many centuries thereafter.

"The Jews," writes Africanus, ". . . having been taught a modest mind (ἀτυφότερον . . . διδαχθέντες), and one such as becomes men (ἀνθρωπίνως) together with the truth by the spirit of Moses, have handed down to us, by their extant Hebrew histories, the number of 5,500 years as the period up to the advent of the Word of salvation." "Why then," he asks, "is it necessary to speak of the 480,000 years" of the Chaldeans, from whom the Jews "derive their origin as descendants of Abraham?" It is "an absurdity (λῆρον)," belonging in the same category of folly as the idle boasting of the Egyptians about their own antiquity.[97] Against the background of Africanus' own perception of the purpose of chronography, this uncompromising rejection of Babylonian and Egyptian antiquities is understandable. For Africanus, Christian millennialism depended on accurate chronology. It was best, therefore, to avoid chronologies that jarred so violently with the more modest chronology of the Bible.

---

[96] Augustine *City of God* 12.11 (trans. Levine).
[97] In Sync. 18.3–9 (adapted from trans. in *ANF*, 6. 131).

Compared to Africanus' apodictic denunciation of Egyptian and Babylonian antiquities, Eusebius' treatment of this question appears as the model of sobriety. Yes, Eusebius acknowledges, the Egyptians do recite a "long series of foolish myths."[98] And Berossus' 432,000 years of pre-flood history, like the legend of Oannes, can hardly be taken literally.[99] But perhaps a clever chronographer might find a way to prove chronological harmony. As for himself, Eusebius would make no pretensions to having succeeded in accomplishing this, contenting himself only with a few modest proposals.[100]

But this is all they were. Indeed, in the purely chronological segment of his chronicle, the Χρονικοὶ κανόνες, Eusebius was prepared to adduce such problems as a warrant for bracketing pre-Abrahamic chronology altogether. Although occasionally willing to accommodate a reader's interest in knowing the dates ab Adam, Eusebius was far more comfortable with the era that was to become the backbone of these tables—the era of Abraham.[101] This decision to date events ab Abraham marked as well an implicit acquiescence to the conventions of Greek chronology. Abandoning the less traditional Babyloniaca, Eusebius in his Canons reverts to the chronology of the Near East as it had been established by Castor and Ctesias. The fila regnorum of these tables commence with Ninus, the king of Assyria and the "first to rule over Asia," and it was with his reign that Eusebius synchronized the birth of Abraham.[102]

Eusebius' concession to Greek chronography should not be understood to mean that he was prepared thereby to accept all its implications. Greek chronographers who sought to demarcate chronological periods sometimes appealed to categories like "mythic" and "poetic" to refer to segments of history beyond the scope of their inquiry. To this extent, it would probably be an exaggeration to say that Eusebius, in reverting to the era of Abraham in the Canons had, like his Greek counterparts, relegated this earlier period to the "ahistoric." For even while acknowledging the difficulties attaching to primordial history, Eusebius never doubted its histor-

---

[98] Chronica 2.32–34.

[99] Ibid., 9.8 ff.

[100] For discussion of Eusebius' attempted solutions, see below, Chap. 3, pp. 77–78.

[101] In Jerome's Latin translation of Eusebius' introduction to the Canons, he says that he supplies the dates from Adam only to satisfy the curiosity of a reader (ed. Helm, 14.20–15.7). For discussion, see Gelzer, SJA, 2. 91. For discussion of Eusebius' use of the era ab Abraham, see Sirinelli, Les vues historiques, 46–52.

[102] Eusebius says of him that "Ninus the son of Bel was the first to rule over Asia, with the exception of India" (Canons 20a, ed. Helm). For discussion of the chronological significance of the reign of Ninus in Eusebius' chronicle, see Sirinelli, Les vues historiques, 47–49.

icity. His treatment of primordial history does not embody the misgivings of a historian who considers the period outside the scope of history. To the contrary, he takes pains to vindicate the accuracy of the Septuagint chronology against the other versions, and to prove the historical veracity of the many events recorded in the first ten chapters of Genesis; fossils surviving to this day from the flood, he even says in one place, are tangible proof of the "credibility of this ancient history."[103]

The uncertainties attaching to pre-Abrahamic history arose instead from what Eusebius deemed the intrinsic limitations imposed upon him by the discipline of chronography and by the nature of the sources used. This measured treatment of his sources in the first book of his Chronicle, wrote Quasten, reveals the judgment of an "author skilled in textual criticism."[104] His approach reflects the temperament of a thinker who, when confronted with disagreement or uncertainty, felt more comfortable in setting out various options than in devising his own.[105] But other less disinterested motives may have been at work as well. By including in his treatment of archaic history so many other, only partially synchronized, chronologies, Eusebius succeeded in heightening uncertainty about the prospects for establishing an absolute chronology of events for it. One suspects that, by maximizing the variables involved in developing an absolute chronology from Adam or from creation, Eusebius expected to dampen the use of chronology in speculation about the age and future duration of the world. In the chronicle of his predecessor, Julius Africanus, chronography functioned largely as a subset of Christian apocalypticism; in Eusebius' time as well, there were adherents to the view that biblical chronology made it possible to acquire an exact knowledge of the beginning and end of the world.[106] It was this application of chronography that Eusebius, himself no friend of Christian chiliasm, expressly cau-

---

[103] Cf. *Chronica* 41.19–29; Sync. 96.4–12. For discussion, see Sirinelli, *Les vues historiques,* 47.

[104] J. Quasten, *Patrology,* 3 vols. (Westminster, 1984), 3. 312.

[105] Eusebius' decision to begin with Abraham, and not some more remote event or person, shows, wrote Gelzer, that in the *Canons* Eusebius the historian had prevailed over Eusebius the apologist. It would have been dissembling if Eusebius had on the one hand polemicized against the errors and flaws of non-biblical sources, and then overlooked the similar problems in Hebrew archaic history. Gelzer suggests as well that Eusebius' sensitivities to chronological problems had been sharpened by his learned opponent Porphyry, a scholar who was skilled in identifying inconsistencies in biblical chronology (*SJA,* 2. 91). Eusebius shows the same reticence for archaic Greek history. Rather than offering a precise date for Homer, for example, he simply lays out a cross section of views (*Canons* 66a, ed. Helm); for discussion, see Mosshammer, *Eusebius,* 85.

[106] See, for example, Lactantius *Divine Institutes* 7.14.

tioned against in the preface to his own work. Jesus' warning to the disciples in *Acts* 1:7—"It is not for you to know times or seasons which the father has fixed by his authority"—applies, he says, not only to the reckoning of the end-time, but to all times.[107] Chronography, cautions Eusebius, cannot claim to be an exact science.

[107] *Chronica* 1.30–2.6. For discussion of the anti-apocalyptic tone of Eusebius' chronicle, see Ed. Schwartz, "Eusebios" (24), *RE* 6.1, 1379; also R. Helm, *Eusebius' Chronik und ihre Tabellenform*, *AbhAkBerlin*, phil.-hist. Klasse 4 (1923), 30 ff.; Jean Sirinelli, *Les vues historiques*, 38–41; Dorothee König-Ockenfels, "Christliche Deutung der Weltgeschichte bei Euseb von Cäsarea," *Saeculum* 27 (1976), 352–54. For a good general discussion of Eusebius' perspective on Christian eschatology, see G. Chesnut, *The First Christian Histories*, 164–74.

CHAPTER THREE

Panodorus as a Critic of Eusebius

EUSEBIUS' CHRONICLE AND ITS LEGACY

Of the fate of Eusebius' *Chronicle* in the West, we are reasonably well informed. In the year 381, Jerome undertook to translate the *Canons* into Latin, updating the work with more recent events from Roman history, and possibly conforming the work even more narrowly to Greco-Roman practice by organizing the *fila regnorum* around the scheme of the four monarchies.[1] For reasons that are not altogether clear, however, Jerome elected not to include Eusebius' more theoretical first book, leaving his successors in the West to speculate on the contents of Eusebius' *prior libellus*. Deprived of a valuable corpus of source material for archaic history, Latin historiography suffered as a consequence. When, for example, Orosius, in the fifth century, set about discrediting the view that "kingdoms and wars began with Ninus, as if forsooth the human race had existed up to that time in the manner of beasts," he might have found useful documentary support in the excerpts from the *Babyloniaca* in the first book of the *Chronicle;* as we have seen, Berossus composed this latter work for much the same reason.[2]

Unlike Jerome, Christian chronographers in the East did not confine themselves to translating and augmenting the *Canons.* Syriac chronogra-

---

[1] In Jerome's translation, the sequence of kings was arranged in the second column, so as to conform to the pattern of the four monarchies. Since this scheme was absent in the Armenian recension, Swain ("Four Monarchies," 19) suggested that the "introduction of the theory of four monarchies and a fifth into Christian historiography was due primarily to Jerome." Karst believed, however, that although this form might have been lacking in the original text of the *Canons* (on the basis of which the Armenian translation was made), Eusebius had imposed this structure on the second edition of the work; see the introduction to his translation of the Armenian text, xix-xxiii. See also A. Mosshammer, *The Chronicle of Eusebius,* 58–59, 69.

[2] For the continuation of Eusebius' chronicle in the West, see Brian Croke and Alanna M. Emmett, "Historiography in Late Antiquity: An Overview," in *History and Historians in Late Antiquity,* 3–4.

phy reveals pervasive influence from the first part of Eusebius' chronicle, which, from as early as the late sixth century, was epitomized and translated into Syriac.[3] It was a Syriac translation that served, at least in part, as the basis for the subsequent translation of the *Chronicle* into Armenian, today the single most important witness to the first book of that work.[4] The Byzantine chronographers, who knew the work either firsthand or through an Alexandrian redaction, also preserve portions of the *Chronicle*.[5] Although Scaliger's initial impression that Eusebius' chronicle could be reconstructed from Syncellus and other Byzantine witnesses was premature, Syncellus' work remains of enduring value both as a witness to Eusebius and to the reception of his work by Christian chronographers after him.

The reaction to the *Chronicle* was hardly favorable. Some of Eusebius' successors, Syncellus writes, were far from satisfied with his inconclusive handling of archaic chronology, sharply rebuking him for his failure to understand fully his profane sources for pre-flood history. "Out of respect" for these men, he will not disclose their names, but he soon relents on this promise, identifying these historians as two early fifth-century Alexandrian monks, Panodorus and Annianus. Syncellus says of these men that they were contemporaries (ὁμοχρόνοι), writing separate chronicles at the time of Theophilus, "the twenty-second archbishop of Alexandria" (388–416 C.E.).[6]

Panodorus and Annianus are names that, as G. F. Unger observed over a century ago, are "often connected to one another in an ambiguous way."[7] Until new witnesses are found, this will probably always remain true. Syncellus, our principal source for the lost chronicles of these monks, furnishes an account of their contents that is not entirely consistent. On the

---

[3] A Latin translation of the Syriac epitome of the Chronicle is included in Alfred Schoene's *Eusebi Chronicorum Libri Duo*, 2 vols. (Berlin, 1866–75), 1. 50–57, App. 3 (First Book); 2. 201–19 (Canons). Another Syriac epitome of Eusebius is found in a chronicle pseudonymously attributed to Dionysius of Tell-Mahre; text edited by I.-B. Chabot, *Chronicon Pseudo-Dionysianum vulgo dictum*, CSCO 91, 104 (Scriptores Syri 43, 53); Latin trans. CSCO 121 (Scriptores Syri 66). On Eusebius' chronicle in Syriac, see esp. Paul Keseling, "Die Chronik des Eusebius in der syrischen Überlieferung," *Oriens Christianus*, Series 3, 1 (1927), 23–48, 223–41; 2 (1927), 33–56. Also Karst, lii-liii; A. von Gutschmid, "Untersuchungen über die syrische Epitome der Eusebischen Canones," *Kleine Schriften*, 1. 417–47; 483–529; Mosshammer, *The Chronicle of Eusebius*, 50–51.

[4] On the composition of the Armenian translation, see Karst's introduction, xxxiv-liv; Mosshammer, *The Chronicle of Eusebius*, 40–51; 73–75.

[5] Schoene has collected many of the sources in his edition of Eusebius.

[6] Sync. 34.24–25; 35.6–8. Of Panodorus, Syncellus says later (396.12–13) that he flourished during the time of the emperor Arcadius (383–408 C.E.).

[7] Unger, *Chronologie des Manetho*, 38.

one hand, he makes it clear that the two works were far from identical; yet at the same time, the similarities that Syncellus discerned between them are so striking as virtually to preclude the possibility that the two works, composed at the same time and place, were written independently of one another.

If one had to decide strictly on the basis of Syncellus which of the two writers was more original, the evidence would weigh heavily in favor of Panodorus.[8] Syncellus rarely mentions Annianus except in conjunction with Panodorus, his elder contemporary. And when he sets out excerpts from their work, it is Panodorus whom he ordinarily cites.[9] It can be inferred from Syncellus' own witness that Panodorus possessed an originality and independence far surpassing his colleague, so much so that Syncellus, although admiring Panodorus' skill in theoretical matters, would later, and on more than one occasion, call Panodorus' orthodoxy into question.[10]

Of all the similarities that Syncellus had discerned in these two chronicles, the most notable of them extended to their jointly held conviction that Eusebius' chronicle was badly flawed. Repeatedly, Syncellus uses the word καταμέμφειν to characterize their repudiation of him.[11] Syncellus, himself no admirer of Eusebius, had no reason to question the validity of most of their criticisms;[12] but on at least one question he rushes to Euse-

---

[8] See Gelzer, *SJA*, 2. 189–93.

[9] See, for example, Sync. 41.29–42.19; 88.24–89.6. In one case, however, Syncellus (36.20–37.11) quotes from Annianus concerning Eusebius' miscalculation by 290 years of the period from Adam to Constantine.

[10] Although Syncellus has admiration for both chroniclers, he clearly prefers Annianus' work to that of Panodorus. He speaks, for example, of Annianus "the most blessed monk (εὐλαβεστάτῳ μοναχῷ) and his contemporary Panodorus" (34.24–35). Of the two chroniclers, Annianus was "more succinct, accurate, and aligned with patristic and apostolic teaching (ἐπιτομωτέραν καὶ ἀκριβεστέραν τῇ ἀποστολικῇ τε καὶ πατρικῇ παραδόσει ἀκόλουθον)" (35.20–22). By contrast, Syncellus' assessment of Panodorus is more restrained. On the one hand, he praises Panodorus as a man "not unskilled in the precise reckoning of time (οὐκ ἄπειρος χρονικῆς ἀκριβείας)" (396.12–13), whose work contained "much useful material (πολλὰ χρήσιμα)" (35.31–32). On the other hand, he criticizes Panodorus for being "repetitive in many places" (35.35); above all, Syncellus repudiates Panodorus for his error in calculating the birth and death of Jesus, an error that Syncellus ascribes to Panodorus' zeal for the speculations of "pagan sages," and which Annianus managed to avoid. For further discussion, see below, Chap. 6, pp. 161–63.

[11] Ibid., 17.19–21; 36.5–6; 37.12.

[12] Among the other criticisms of Eusebius were Eusebius' failure to include the second Cainan in his biblical genealogy, and his neglect of the interregnal period of foreign kings in the time of the judges (36.30–37.15). Syncellus makes the similarity between the two writers clear when, after giving a reprise of Annianus' critique of Eusebius (36.16–37.11), he says: "This is exactly (ἐπὶ λέξεως) what Annianus states when he rightly (δικαίως) criticizes Eusebius, 'son' of Pamphilus, for his omission of 290 years; regarding these things, Panodorus is in agreement in his indictment of him" (37.12–14).

bius' defense. To censure Eusebius for failing to recognize the chronological harmony of Berossus and Manetho with Genesis was, he argues, "futile (μάτην)," an "empty criticism."[13] Panodorus was singularly culpable. He "is wrong," Syncellus contends, "in finding fault (μέμφεται) with Eusebius here on the grounds that Eusebius failed to explain the meaning of the historians. . . . In this he criticizes Eusebius, not understanding that these arguments of his, which are incapable of proof or reasoning, have been proved against himself and against truth."[14]

GRECO-ROMAN THEORIES ON THE PRIMITIVE RECKONING OF TIME

In their efforts to develop a way of synchronizing Babylonian and Egyptian antiquities, Christian chroniclers were aided by a tradition of Greek scepticism about the accuracy of the more grandiose claims of the oriental chronicles. This scepticism generally centered on two questions: 1) whether primitive men could have enjoyed the longevity customarily supposed of them; and 2) whether the Orientals had a record of their past extending as far back into the remote past as they claimed. A clear expression of such incredulity appears in a scholium to Proclus' commentary on the *Timaeus* (22AB). To Iamblichus' claim that the chronicles of the Assyrians spanned whole "Great Years," the scholiast responds: If you (Iamblichus) mean by a Great Year "a cycle from Aries to Aries (ἀπὸ κριοῦ εἰς κριὸν περίοδον), who would believe you? This is what I would say to Iamblichus."[15]

To confirm these suspicions, chroniclers had recourse to various explanations which foreshortened the duration of Egyptian and Babylonian chronology. One explanation that enjoyed extended popularity, both among Christian and pagan commentators, theorized that accurate reckoning of time in years, months, and days was not known to primitive mankind, and that the regnal years of the primordial kings of Babylon and Egypt represented some smaller interval of time, variously reckoned as a year, a month or a day. This explanation, which Proclus attributes to Eudoxus (fourth century B.C.E.), appears in a vast array of sources, most often in connection with primordial Egyptian chronology. "Among the Egyptians," wrote the chronicler Varro, "months are accounted as years,

[13] Cf. Sync. 17.19–27.
[14] Ibid., 41.30–42.23 (trans. Waddell, fr. 2.4–5.).
[15] Ed. E. Diehl, 1. 462.22–25.

so that the circuit of the sun through the twelve signs of the Zodiac does not make a year, but rather the moon, which traverses that sign-bearing circle in the space of thirty days."[16] Significantly, even Egyptian priests and chroniclers were sometimes prepared to accept this explanation as a rationalistic way of accounting for some of the more incredible claims of their chronicles. Thus, Diodorus (first century B.C.E.) states that Egyptian priests, recognizing that the length of the rules of the first Egyptian kings was not believable, resort to the supposition that the year was first equated with a month, and subsequently with a "season" of three months:

> Hence, they argue that, if the year consisted only of 30 days, it would be possible for a man to live 1,200 of these years; being equivalent to 100 years, according to the ordinary mode of reckoning: a term of life which many people exceeded. With regard to the reigns of later date, they suppose the year to have consisted of four months, according to a division into three seasons of spring, summer and winter: which gives a similar result for a reign of 300 years; and it is for this reason that among some of the Greeks the years are called "seasons (ὥρας)" and that their yearly records are called horographs.[17]

Africanus too would later refer to Egyptian priests and astrologers who identified the primordial Egyptian year as "lunar (σεληνιαίους)" (years of 30 days). In this case, its purpose was synchronistic—to harmonize (συμπίπτουσι) their own native chronicles with the "eight or nine thousand" years of Egyptian history recorded in the *Timaeus*.[18]

Reducing the Egyptian year to a month or a season had an obvious application for Christian chronography as well. But while recognizing the appeal of this explanation, few Christian chroniclers were prepared to accept it without reservation. Some, like Africanus, rejected it out of hand. Equating the Egyptian year with a month was simply a contrivance, he writes, its proponents "leaning no less than others to the mythical (οὐδὲν ἔλλατον ἐπὶ τὸ μυθῶδες ἀπονενευκότες)."[19] Such techniques could not conceal the fact that the Egyptian "cycles and myriads (περιόδους καὶ

---

[16] In Lactantius *Div. Inst.* 2.13; see also Pliny *NH* 7.48.155. For Proclus' tracing of this theory to Eudoxus, see Proclus *Comm. Tim.* 22B (ed. Diehl, 1. 102.25–28): "But if Eudoxus is speaking the truth, that the Egyptians used to call a month a year, then the numbering of these many years would not be something remarkable." For a list of other classical authors who were familiar with this method, see Böckh, *Hundsternperiode*, 63.

[17] Diodorus 1.26.1–5.

[18] In Sync. 17.32–18.3.

[19] Ibid., 18.1–2.

μυϱιάδας)" were little more than ethnic boasting.[20] Augustine later would echo the same sentiment. Even if one accepts the proposition, he says, that the Egyptians had in former times "years so short that a year ended every four months," it would still far exceed the more restrained chronology of the Greeks.[21]

While far more accommodating than either Africanus or Augustine to the possibilities of reducing the primitive Egyptian or Chaldean year to some smaller interval of time, Eusebius by no means considered it a wholly persuasive solution. As for the 432,000 years of Berossus' pre-flood chronology, Eusebius proposes only that the year of the Babylonian sar, like the primitive Egyptian year, might represent some "smaller interval."[22] The inspiration for this idea came from his application of a similar method to Egyptian antiquities. Since the Egyptians, he writes, "claim by a sort of prerogative of antiquity that they have before the flood a line of Gods, Demigods and Spirits of the Dead, who reigned for more than 20,000 years, it clearly follows that these years should be reckoned as the same number of months as the years recorded by the Hebrews; that is, that all the months contained in the Hebrew record of years should be reckoned as so many lunar years of the Egyptian calendar. . . ."[23]

"What we now call a month," Eusebius suggests, "the Egyptians used formerly to style a year."[24] When Eusebius applied this principle to the 24,900 "lunar years" of the reigns of the primordial supernatural kings of Egypt before Menes, the result he obtained was 2,206 "solar years," a number that could be comfortably fitted into the 2,242 years from Adam to the flood. But Eusebius did not expect this method to yield a fully satisfactory result; for he qualified this explanation with the condition that "if the number of years is still in excess," some other solution might have to be investigated (such as the idea of collateral dynasties).[25]

---

[20] Ibid., 17.30.

[21] Augustine *City of God* 12.11. Augustine knows as well of certain chronologers who, on the authority of Pliny, sought to apply this same idea of a "short year" to the archaic chronology of Genesis, maintaining that the period of time "then called a year was so brief that ten of those years were equal to one of ours." The "utter falsity" of this view can be easily demonstrated, he says, since, if true, it would mean that the antediluvian patriarchs were still children when they begat offspring (*City of God* 15.12).

[22] *Chronica* 9.31–32.

[23] Ibid., 64.16–21 (trans. Waddell, fr. 1.5–6).

[24] Ibid., 63.29–30 (trans. Waddell, fr. 1.1).

[25] Ibid., 63.31–64.25 (trans. Waddell, fr. 1.7). Since the reduced total of 2,206 years is, in fact, not in excess of the period of time from Adam to the flood, Sirinelli conjectures that Eusebius was referring here to the whole span of Egyptian history, and not just the mythic period; see *Les vues historiques*, 71–72. The theory of "collateral dynasties" had great influence

Eusebius, as we have seen, was persuaded that archaic chronology was
largely indeterminate. Ostensibly for this reason, he felt little need to for-
mulate a fully synchronized chronology of antediluvian biblical, Egyptian,
and Babylonian history. But his equivocations on primitive Babylonian
and Egyptian chronology were destined to draw vigorous criticisms from
his Alexandrian successors. Both of them, Syncellus writes, indict him for
failing both to "allegorize" the profane histories of the Chaldeans and the
Egyptians and thus recognize their chronological compatibility with the
chronology of Genesis. In the course of Syncellus' protracted refutation
of them, he furnishes a fairly detailed account of their treatment of this
problem, especially Panodorus'.

PANODORUS ON THE EGYPTIAN AND CHALDEAN "SHORT YEAR"

Despite his sharp criticisms of Eusebius, it is clear that what Panodorus
would term his "allegorical" solution to the antiquities of the Babylonians
and Egyptians found its inspiration in the very technique that Eusebius
had earlier proposed, however inconclusively—namely, that the year of
the Chaldeans and Egyptians was anciently reckoned as some smaller interval. Syncellus later observed that Panodorus' explanation assumed that
the year of the primitive Chaldean sar was only one day of the solar year:
"He says that that which is called by them (the Chaldeans) a sar is 3,600
days . . . and the sar of 3,600 years, divided (ἀναλυόμενος) by the 365 days
of the year, makes 9 years and 10 months and a half . . . 120 sars make
432,000 days. This reduced to individual solar years yields 1,183 years, 6
months and a half. These years added to the 1,058 (prior) during which
there were no kings complete from Adam up to the flood a period of 2,242
years, in harmony with our scriptures (συμφώνως τῇ ἡμετέρᾳ γραφῇ)."[26]

Manetho's chronology of the archaic reigns of Egyptian gods and demigods admitted a similar solution. In this case, the 11,985 years of the reigns
of the Egyptian god/kings from Hephaestus to Typhon were to be under-

---

on subsequent chronography; cf. Anthony T. Grafton, "Joseph Scaliger and Historical Chronology," 175–76. Eusebius' use of this method was reserved: "It must be supposed that perhaps several Egyptian kings ruled at one and the same time. . . . It seems, moreover, that
different kings held sway in different regions, and that each dynasty was confined to its own
nome: thus it was not a succession of kings occupying the throne one after the other, but
several kings reigning at the same time" (trans. Waddell, *Manetho*, fr. 1.7). In his discussion
of Chaldean chronology (*Chronica* 9.24–28), Eusebius offers a third solution, namely that the
primitive year of the Egyptians represented a season of three months.
  [26] Sync. 33.8–16.

stood as "so many lunar months (μένων σεληνιακῶν)," hence 969 solar years.[27] In a later passage, Syncellus states that his Alexandrian predecessors had considered the regnal years of the demigods who succeeded the gods as ὧραι—that is, periods of three months.[28] These 969 "solar years" of the reigns of the gods, added to the 214 years of the reigns of the demigods, yield a total of 1,183 ½ years. When added to the 1,058 years from the time of Adam up to the reigns of the gods, "it completes a total of 2,242 years down to the flood."[29] In this way, Panodorus had, or so he held, succeeded in accomplishing two things. Panodorus, Syncellus writes, "exerts himself to show that the Egyptian writings against God (κατὰ θεοῦ) and against our divinely inspired Scriptures are really in agreement with them."[30] Not only that; Panodorus had claimed as well to have demonstrated that Chaldean and Egyptian civilization began in the same year of the world—1,183 years before the flood.

Panodorus himself was evidently quite impressed with the result of his work; Syncellus says he considered it "rather novel (καινότερόν τι)."[31] Nor had his evident success in achieving that which Eusebius before him had only intimated was possible escaped the attention of Syncellus himself; he acknowledges in several places Panodorus' skill as a chronicler. But despite his vigorous criticisms of Panodorus' attempt to "pit a ludicrous falsehood against truth," he never doubted that his Alexandrian predecessors used anything but authentic sources. If there was any chronological compatibility between Genesis, Berossus and Manetho, he argues, it was only because Manetho had written in "imitation of Berossus," and Berossus had pirated many of his ideas from Scripture.[32]

Modern scholarship has assessed the whole situation rather differently, especially concerning the integrity of Panodorus' sources for early Egyptian history. It should first be noted that the unreduced reigns of the Egyptian gods and demigods are attested in no other witness to Manetho; moreover, Panodorus' source for Manetho's primordial chronology was not the *Aegyptiaca*, but the pseudepigraphic *Book of Sothis*. These consid-

---

[27] Ibid., 18.25–33.
[28] Ibid., 42.15–17. Since the reign of the demigods in Panodorus' canon of Egyptian kings begins with Horus (Ὧρος) (cf. Sync. 19.9), Panodorus evidently drew some connection between the onset of his reign and the beginning of reckoning in "seasons (ὧραι)."
[29] Ibid., 42.18–19.
[30] Ibid., 42.20–21.
[31] Ibid., 42.2; cf. 18.29.
[32] Ibid., 17.1–4; τὰ περὶ τῶν Αἰγυπτιακῶν δυναστειῶν ὑπὸ Μανεθῶ τοῦ Σεβεννύτου πρὸς Πτολεμαῖον τὸν Φιλάδελφον συγγεγραμμένα πλήρη ψεύδους καὶ κατὰ μίμησιν Βηρώσσου πεπλασμένα. . . .

erations, together with the fact that Manetho's chronology was so easily reconcilable with Berossus and Genesis, make it reasonably certain that, at the least, Panodorus had manipulated the chronology of his sources for Egyptian history in order to achieve the desired result.[33]

In general, it may be said that Panodorus' whole method is largely a Christianizing of a technique that goes back well before the fifth century. As we have seen, already in the first century B.C.E., Diodorus knows of Egyptian priests who, in order to explain away the implausible longevity of the earliest Egyptian kings, had appealed to the explanation that the reigns of the gods and demigods were not solar years, but some other duration. Due to ignorance of chronology, they said, the earliest Egyptians first reckoned a year as a month; later, beginning with Horus, they began to reckon time in seasons. This explanation is virtually identical to Panodorus', only antedating him by over 400 years.[34] Indeed, what distinguishes Panodorus' achievement is not so much the formulation of the technique, but rather his assimilation of it to Christian chronography. Probably the most original and distinctive aspect of his reconstruction of the primordial calendar is his wide-ranging appeal to the Jewish pseudepigrapha of the Second Temple Period.

THE JEWISH PSEUDEPIGRAPHA IN ALEXANDRIAN CHRONOGRAPHY

In the period between the closing of the Old Testament canon and the emergence of Rabbinic Judaism, Jews of both Palestine and the diaspora produced a large corpus of religious literature, often classified today, somewhat infelicitously, as "intertestamental literature," or "Jewish pseudepigrapha."[35] For reasons that have never been fully appreciated, this literature owes its survival mainly to Christian scribes, who, in appropriating it, reworked and added to this literature with their own productions.

One of the richest collections of excerpts and traditions from Jewish pseudepigrapha is to be found in the Christian chroniclers after Eusebius. One need only consult Fabricius' still valuable *Codex pseudepigraphus* to

[33] For discussion, see below, Chap. 6, pp. 172–73.

[34] Diodorus 1.26.

[35] An earlier and still valuable English edition of the Jewish pseudepigrapha and apocrypha was edited by R. H. Charles, *The Apocrypha and Pseudepigrapha of the Old Testament*, 2 vols. (Oxford, 1912); a more recent edition, which includes several additional works, has been edited by James H. Charlesworth, *The Old Testament Pseudepigrapha* (Garden City, N.Y., 1983). For a discussion of this corpus, and related literature of the period, see George W. E. Nickelsburg, *Jewish Literature between the Bible and the Mishnah* (Philadelphia, 1981).

find confirmation for this.[36] References to and extracts from a variety of these sources are diffused throughout Syriac, Byzantine, and Arabic world chronicles. For some of the pseudepigrapha, the chroniclers are among the most important, if not the only, witnesses. Up until the discovery of the Ethiopic witnesses to *1 Enoch,* Syncellus' three excerpts from the *Book of the Watchers* were the single most important testimony to this work. The Greek version of the *Testament of Adam* is known only in Syncellus and the more expanded version preserved by Cedrenus. Were it not for the Byzantine chroniclers, some of these works would now be unknown. Syncellus, for example, is the only witness to a work called the *Life of Adam,* from which he gives a highly compressed excerpt.

Over a century ago, Gelzer surmised that few, if any, of the Byzantine chroniclers knew these sources directly, depending instead on earlier collections of excerpts. Even Syncellus, according to Gelzer the "richest collection of Jewish apocrypha" and the source of pseudepigrapha for several subsequent Byzantine chroniclers, knew these works only from his Alexandrian authorities, principally Panodorus.[37]

Gelzer's tracing of the pseudepigrapha in Syncellus to intermediaries formed only one part of a larger theory of literary dependence. The precise nature of Syncellus' dependence on the Alexandrian chroniclers for these sources was never fully addressed. Nor did he spend much time trying to explain why chronographers would have consulted sources, which as Syncellus would say on more than one occasion "do not appear to be authoritative." As for Panodorus' use of *1 Enoch,* for example, Gelzer's only explanation was that the work was "highly esteemed in the Alexandrian church."[38] This may be true, but it does not explain what the specific attraction of these works was.

There is, broadly speaking, a congruity of interests between Christian chronography and the Jewish literature of the Second Temple Period, especially the Jewish apocalypses. Christian chronography was originally conceived as a highly specialized form of Jewish/Christian apocalypticism. Both the Christian universal chronicle and the Jewish apocalypse characteristically encompassed the whole course of human history, and both were known to periodize human history according to some artificial scheme.[39] For both, matters of precise reckoning of time figured impor-

---

[36] Cf. J. A. Fabricius, *Codex pseudepigraphus Veteris Testamenti* 1, 2nd ed., (Hamburg, Leipzig, 1722).

[37] *SJA,* 2. 249–97.

[38] Ibid., 1. 84.

[39] For a general summary of historical periodization in the Jewish apocalypses, see, for

tantly, especially insofar as this involved the dating of feasts and commemorations, and eschatological speculation. To be sure, the mythological
vocabulary of the apocalypses could and did disturb the chronographers
who consulted these sources. But one need only examine Syncellus' excerpts from the Enochic *Book of the Watchers* to see how readily chronography, either through the insertion of chronological detail or the histori-
cization of mythic figures, could rationalize even this fabulous legend.[40]

In their treatment of primordial history, neither Josephus nor the Christian chronographers hesitated to appeal to extra-biblical sources, provided
these sources answered a few requirements. One of these conditions was a
certifiable antiquity. There can be little doubt that the fascination with the
pseudepigraphic *Book of Sothis* and the *Babyloniaca* arose largely from the
presumed antiquity of these works—one claiming to be a pre-flood revelation by Hermes Trismegistus, the other a compilation of native records
extending the whole span of Chaldean civilization. For the chronographers, the Jewish pseudepigrapha satisfied the same demands. Characteristically, these works claimed authorship from a biblical worthy, not infrequently one of the antediluvian patriarchs. It was in the nature of such
claims that proponents of their authenticity went to great pains to validate
their antiquity and authorship—temples, rocks, or monuments were typical media of preservation. When, for example, Tertullian advanced the
case for the canonical acceptance of *1 Enoch,* he was aware that its detractors had doubted that such a work could have survived the flood; to these
sceptics, Tertullian responded that the work had been entrusted to Noah,
or alternately, like the Jewish scriptures restored by Ezra after the Exile,
had been miraculously reconstituted afterward.[41] Byzantine chronography
had its own theory of transmission, including the well-known tradition
that Enoch's teachings had survived the flood by being inscribed on stelae.

---

example, D. S. Russell, *The Method and Message of Jewish Apocalyptic* (Philadelphia, 1964),
224–29. The Christian chronographers, starting with Africanus, used many of the same
schemes, especially the 7,000-year millennial "week" and Daniel's "seventy weeks of years"
(Dan. 9:24–26). Africanus makes a contrived attempt to prove that Daniel's prophecy referred to the birth of Christ; see Sync. 299.25–26; 392.1–393.30; see also Eusebius *Demonstratio
Evangelica* 8.2.46–54 (ed. Ivar A. Heikel, GCS 23, *Eusebius Werke* 6 [Leipzig, 1913]); for detailed discussion of Daniel 9 in Christian chronography, see Franz Fraidl, *Die Exegese der
siebzig Wochen Daniels in der alten und mittleren Zeit* (Graz, 1883), 45–50, 58–68. Schemes like
these were subject to penetrating criticism by the Muslim chronographer al-Bīrūnī, *The Chronology of Ancient Nations,* 21–22 (trans. Sachau).

[40] On Annianus' euhemeristic interpretation of the legend of the Watchers, see below,
Chap. 4, pp. 117–25; for the insertion of chronological detail into the text of *1 Enoch,* see
Chap. 6, p. 180.

[41] Tertullian *On the Apparel of Women* 3.

One has only to compare the conditions of the presumed preservation of *1 Enoch* with the pseudepigraphic *Book of Sothis* to see that both works had the same appeal—an account of primordial history recorded and preserved for later generations by an antediluvian sage. As in the case of the oriental chronicle, the putative antiquity of *1 Enoch* ensured its continued popularity among writers on primordial history. Though the *Book of Enoch,* wrote the British chronicler John Jackson in the eighteenth century, "was justly thought Apocryphal and to be mixed with fables, yet it contains many things of note and of the highest antiquity, and was esteemed by the primitive Christian Writers."[42]

Self-described antiquity alone, however, could not guarantee the validity of these works. Any amplification of Genesis by an extra-biblical source was delimited by its perceived value in corroborating or complementing the biblical narrative. Granted, complete unanimity as to the proper application of this principle did not always reign. But there was a general consensus that where some parallelism could not be established the extra-biblical source was considered suspect. Few chroniclers, for example, could refer to the Babylonian cosmogony and the story of Oannes without, at the same time, subjecting them to ridicule.

Use of the Jewish pseudepigrapha was governed by the same axiom. Syncellus might see fit to include several portions from *1 Enoch* in his chronicle, but not without first advising his readers about the proper way to read the book. Readers should be satisfied only with excerpts from *1 Enoch,* he warns, because it contains much that is "apocryphal, questionable in places," and "contaminated by Jews and heretics."[43] Yet he is prepared to grant that the value of this apocalypse in attesting to the accuracy of Genesis often outweighs the occasional lapses into heresy. Indeed, in his view, a work such as *1 Enoch* is even more to be preferred than the "lies of Berossus and Manetho," if only because it is "more akin to our Scriptures (συγγενεστέρα ταῖς ἡμετέραις γραφαῖς)."[44]

Syncellus' assessment was essentially correct, for it required less strain to validate Genesis with the Jewish pseudepigrapha than with the ethnic histories of the Babylonians and Egyptians. Although many factors must have stood behind the writing of the pseudepigrapha, one motive was simply to enlarge upon cryptic or inconclusive portions of the biblical narrative. The Enochic *Book of the Watchers,* from which Syncellus quotes

[42] John Jackson, *Chronological Antiquities* (London, 1752), 59 (note 100).
[43] Cf. Sync. 24.6–9; 27.11.
[44] Ibid., 24.7–8.

at length, is mainly an extended extrapolation upon the mysterious legend of the sons of God of Genesis 6, and it is for this reason that Syncellus quotes from it; in order to forestall doubts about the historicity of this legend, he says, it is necessary to quote from corroborative works, among which he names *1 Enoch*.[45] The *Book of Jubilees,* aptly called by the Greek chronographers Λεπτὴ Γένεσις, performed much the same function—that of fleshing out the details of portions of antediluvian history left unexplained by Genesis.

Jubilees *on the "Prehistoric"* Life of Adam

᾽Απορίαι in Genesis' account of Adam's life in Paradise were in fact the principal reason why chronographers turned to these sources. In, for example, *Jubilees'* narrative of Abraham's burning of the temple of idols in Ur, Syncellus found what he considered the solution to a perennial dilemma for interpreters of Genesis—namely, the apparent inconsistency in Moses' ordering of events between Abraham and Terah's flight from Ur and the migration to Canaan.[46] An equally renowned problem, for which *Jubilees* proved helpful, was the one that Eusebius had turned into a cause célèbre. This was the exact period of time spent by Adam and Eve in Paradise, a matter that Eusebius was prepared to leave unsettled.

Since dating of events from the origin of the universe was a virtual axiom of Byzantine chronography, the problem appears to have precipitated great interest among Eusebius' successors. Syncellus was still speculating about it in the ninth century. "Moses," he acknowledges, obliquely deferring to Eusebius, "leaves unaccounted for (ἀτράνωτον) the duration of time spent by the Protoplasts in Paradise."[47] Confronted by this silence, "certain chronographers," he writes, "spurred on either by vainglory or by an illusory desire for learning (εἴτε ἐκ δοκουμένης φιλομαθίας εἴτε καὶ κενοδοξίᾳ νυττόμενοι)" had also been investigating the subject of Adam's stay in Paradise.[48] Amid what appears to have been considerable speculation on this subject, these unnamed chronographers had concluded that the chronology proposed by John Chrysostom—that the creation of Adam, his transgression, and expulsion had all occurred on one day—was impossible; given the limitations of "human frailty," the simple act of nam-

---

[45] Ibid., II.II–14.
[46] For discussion, see below, Chap. 6, pp. 188–91.
[47] Ibid., 3.24–25: τὴν μὲν ποσότητα τοῦ χρόνου τῆς ἐν τῷ παραδείσῳ διαγωγῆς τῶν πρωτοπλάστων ἀτράνωτον ἡμῖν ὁ θεόπτης Μωϋσῆς καταλέλοιπε.
[48] Ibid., 4.3–4.

ing the beasts must have consumed more than one day.[49] Instead, they leaned to the view that a 40-day interval had elapsed between Adam's creation and his admission into Paradise, during which time he assigned names to the animals. Confirmation for this particular chronology of events came from two works, both of which, Syncellus writes, "do not appear to be authoritative."[50] These were the pseudepigraphic *Book of Jubilees* and "the so-called *Life of Adam* (τοῦ λεγομένου βίου 'Αδάμ)."[51] This latter work survives only in Syncellus' chronicle, but from the citation furnished by him it appears to be an enlarged and modified form of *Jub.* 3:1–9, adhering closely to the sequence of events that *Jubilees* gives for the period from Adam's creation to his expulsion. Why Syncellus' predecessors had consulted these works is clear from Syncellus' own account of the contents of the *Life of Adam:* a chronology of the "number of days for the naming of the beasts, and the creation of the woman, and the entrance of Adam into Paradise, and the edict of God regarding the eating from the tree, and the entrance of Eve into Paradise, the affairs relating to the transgression, and what happened afterwards."[52]

Although it is at once clear that Syncellus did not know the *Life of Adam* or *Jubilees* directly, he does not name as his source the Alexandrian chroniclers explicitly, using instead what proves to be a characteristically elliptical way of identifying them: "other historians (ἄλλοις ἱστορικοῖς)."[53] Presumably, these unnamed intermediaries included the Alexandrian monks Panodorus and Annianus. Syncellus' knowledge of his Jewish sources for primordial history has at least been partially mediated to him through his Alexandrian sources. Moreover, as we shall see, the Jewish

---

[49] Ibid., 4.7–8. The problem seems to have elicited a variety of responses. Cedrenus, for example, says that according to some chroniclers, Adam had spent 100 years in Paradise; others, that Adam was created in the third hour of the sixth day, and was expelled in the ninth hour (1. 12.1–5, ed. I. Bekker, CSHB [Bonn, 1838–39]); cf. *T. Sanhedrin* 38b, where on the authority of R. Johanan b. Ḥanina, Adam is said to have named the beasts in the sixth hour, transgressed on the tenth hour and been expelled in the twelfth hour. For discussion of the various chronological schemes, see Louis Ginzberg, *Die Haggada bei den Kirchenvätern und in der apokryphischen Litteratur* (Berlin, 1900), 48–49. See also below, Chap. 6, pp. 165–68.

[50] Sync. 4.22.

[51] Ibid., 4.21–22.

[52] Ibid., 4.23–28.

[53] Ibid., 4.20. In justifying his own excerpts from these two works, Syncellus gives the following explanation: "Necessarily (ἀναγκαίως), I too am forced to explain this subject in part, which has been discussed also by other historians who have composed Jewish Antiquities and Christian histories from the "Little Genesis" and the so-called "Life of Adam," even if it does not appear to be authoritative, lest those who investigate these matters fall into more absurd ideas" (Sync. 4.19–23).

pseudepigrapha, principally *1 Enoch,* were crucial to Panodorus' solution to the chronology of Berossus and Manetho, and his speculations about the evolution of the primitive calendar.

The Book of Enoch *and the Formulation of the Solar Year*

Proponents of the theory that the primitive Chaldeans and Egyptians mistook a year for some smaller interval of time did so on the assumption that earliest mankind was confused about the motion of the sun and the moon through the zodiac. When, for example, the Egyptian priests mentioned by Diodorus sought to explain the implausibly long reigns of their primordial kings, they attributed this to "ignorance of the motion of the sun." According to Pliny, the putative longevity of the early peoples was an exaggeration, "due to ignorance of chronology, because some people made the year coincide with the summer, the winter being a second year, others marked it by the periods of the four seasons (*quadripertitis temporibus*)—for example the Arcadians, whose years were three months long, and some by the waning of the moon (*lunae senio*), as do the Egyptians. Consequently, with them even individuals are recorded to have lived a thousand years."[54]

As Syncellus was later to recognize, Panodorus also premised his synchronization of Berossus, Manetho and Genesis on the hypothesis that when these civilizations began there did not yet exist the capacity to distinguish between years, months, and seasons. Panodorus regularly alludes to this. When Chaldean civilization began, in the 1,059th year of the world, "neither a month, nor a season, nor the measures of them were known to mankind." It was not until the year A.M. 1286 that mankind learned how to distinguish units of time accurately. In that year, which Panodorus had calculated as the 165th year of Enoch, the archangel Uriel "stationed among the stars, at the behest of God who is over all things, revealed to Enoch what a month is, and a season, and a year, as it is recorded in the book of this same Enoch (ἐν τῇ βίβλῳ αὐτοῦ Ἐνώχ), and that a year has 52 weeks, and that 1,286 years are 469,390 days and 67,056 weeks during which time men did not know what a month was, nor seasons, nor years, nor the measures of them."[55]

As Milik has observed, Panodorus appears to be summarizing from the *Book of the Heavenly Luminaries* (= *1 Enoch* 72–82). In this section of *1*

[54] Pliny *NH* 7.48.155 (trans. Rackham).
[55] Sync. 34.16–22.

Enoch, the archangel Uriel reveals to Enoch the "courses of the luminaries of the heavens, the relations of each, according to their classes, their dominion, and their seasons."[56]

Enoch's reputation as the prototypical sage, "the first man born on earth who learned writing and knowledge and wisdom, and who wrote down the signs of heaven, according to the order of the months," is a well-attested tradition, especially among the Christian chroniclers, who credit both him and Seth with numerous discoveries.[57] In particular, Enoch was thought to surpass even the Chaldeans and the Egyptians in the knowledge of astronomy. Already in the early second century B.C.E., an anonymous writer, probably of Samaritan origin but incorrectly identified as "Eupolemus" by Alexander Polyhistor, asserted that Enoch was the first to learn astrology, and that Abraham, a descendant of the Giants of Genesis 6, taught this science to the Chaldeans and later to the Egyptians.[58] Panodorus understood the tradition about Enoch's knowledge of astronomy in a similar way; before Uriel's revelation to him, the Chaldeans and the Egyptians did not know how to calculate accurately the duration of the year, month, or season.

Although Enoch was the first to learn to reckon time accurately, Panodorus knew from this same work that mankind had also received revelations about celestial phenomena before his birth. Described at great length in the Enochic *Book of the Watchers,* these teachings, including all manner of esoteric lore, were imparted by the Watchers to the daughters of men. What intrigued Panodorus most about this account was its tracing of primitive astronomy to these fallen Watchers. Although Syncellus does not tell us all we would like to know about Panodorus' interpretation of this story, he does provide us with a few important excerpts, enough to enable us to see how Panodorus treated this matter. In a lengthy excerpt from his chronicle, Syncellus recapitulates Panodorus' derivation of the origins of Egyptian astronomy:

> Eusebius, "son" of Pamphilus, gives the following account [of Manetho's history of the first Egyptian kings] in his *Chronica:* "Con-

---

[56] Cf. *1 Enoch* 72. See J. T. Milik, *The Books of Enoch: Aramaic Fragments of Qumrān Cave 4* (Oxford, 1976), 19–20.

[57] See *Jub.* 4:17. For this tradition in the chronographers, see, for example, Michael Glycas (ed. Bekker, CSHB [Bonn, 1836]), 228.7–13.

[58] Quoted by Eusebius in *PE* 9.17.8–9 (419c). For discussion of (ps-)Eupolemus see Ben Zion Wacholder, "Pseudo-Eupolemus' Two Greek Fragments on the Life of Abraham," *HUCA* 34 (1963), 83–113, esp. 95–98; Carl R. Holladay, *Fragments from Hellenistic Jewish Authors* 1 (Chico, 1983), 157–65.

cerning Gods, Demigods, Spirits of the Dead, and mortal kings,
the Egyptians have a long series of foolish myths. The most ancient Egyptians, indeed, alleged that their years were lunar years
(σεληναίους ... ἐνιαυτούς) consisting of 30 days, whereas the
Demigods who succeeded them gave the name "hōrai" to years,
which were three months long (τριμηνιαίους)." So Eusebius wrote
with good reason, criticizing the Egyptians for their foolish talk; and
in my [Syncellus'] opinion, Panodorus is wrong in finding fault (μέμφεται) with Eusebius here, on the ground that Eusebius failed to
explain the meaning of the historians, while Panodorus himself thinks
he succeeds by a somewhat novel method, as follows: "From the creation, indeed, down to Enoch ... the number of days was known in
neither month nor year, *but the Watchers* (ἐγρήγοροι), *who had descended to earth in the year 1000, held converse with men, and taught them
that the orbits of the two luminaries, being marked by the twelve signs of
the zodiac, are composed of 360 parts. Observing the moon's orbit, which is
nearer the earth, smaller, and more conspicuous, as it has a period of 30
days, men decided that it should be reckoned as a year, since the orbit of
the sun also was filled by the same twelve signs of the Zodiac with an equal
number of parts, 360.* So it came to pass that the reigns of the Egyptian
gods who ruled among them for six generations in six dynasties were
reckoned in years each consisting of a lunar cycle of thirty days. The
total in lunar years is 11,985, or 969 solar years. By adding these to the
1,058 solar years of the period before their reign, they reach the sum
total of 2,027 years." Similarly, in the two dynasties of nine Demigods—these being regarded as real, although they never existed—
Panodorus strives to make up 214 ½ years out of 858 hōrai (periods
of three months) or seasonal changes (τροπαί), so that with the 969
years they make, he says, 1,183 ½ years, and these when added to the
1,058 years from the time of Adam to the reign of the Gods, complete
a total of 2,242 years down to the Flood.[59]

One of the excerpts from *1 Enoch* that Syncellus preserves in his chronicle, ostensibly via Panodorus, describes the fall of the Watchers and their
revelations to women.[60] The above excerpt illustrates how Panodorus interpreted the legend. In line with the traditional dating of the fall of the

[59] Sync. 41.23–42.19 (trans. Waddell, fr. 2.1–4).
[60] Cf. Sync. 11.20–13.19 (= *1 Enoch* 6:1–9:5).

Watchers, Panodorus set the date of the event in the year A.M. 1000.[61] The revelations imparted to women included Chochabiel's teachings about the orbits of the "two luminaries," the sun and the moon. However, people living in the year 1000 misunderstood his teaching, confusing the orbit of the moon with the orbit of the sun; as a result, when they began to record the reigns of the first Egyptian kings some 59 years later, they reckoned in "lunar" years of 29 ½ days. Still later, beginning with the reign of Horus, the first demigod king, the year came to be equated with a "season (ὥρα)" consisting of three months.

In his lengthy and at times tortured refutation of Panodorus' account of the origins of primitive time reckoning, Syncellus provides an analogous description of Panodorus' application of the same legend to the chronology of the *Babyloniaca:*

> Therefore I [Syncellus] assert that their [Berossus, Alexander Polyhistor and Abydenus] discussion of the endless years [of Chaldean antediluvian history] and the ten kings who ruled before the flood and whatever other ridiculous things are in it are not true. Nor do I accept the division or reduction [of archaic Chaldean years]. And I reject those who "allegorize" these years, contending that people before the flood reckoned a year as a day (εἰπόντας τὸν ἐνιαυτὸν ἡμέραν λογίζεσθαι τοὺς πρὸ τοῦ κατακλυσμοῦ), having learned from the fourth leader of the Watchers, Chorabiel, that the period encompassed by the orbit of the sun is in the twelve signs of the zodiac, and equals 360 degrees. . . . But people of that time, he [Panodorus] claims, did not know what the length of a year is, because its measure was not yet known to mankind. So how was it possible for men to know that the annual period of the sun is encompassed in the twelve signs of the zodiac, when they did not realize that a year is made up of twelve parts and months? . . . The 120 sars make up 432,000 days. These reduced to the individual year make 1,183 years and six months and a third. These years added to the 1,058 kingless years yield from Adam up to the flood 2,242 years in harmony with our Scripture.[62]

Panodorus' line of reasoning is more difficult to follow in this extract, principally because Syncellus has poorly excerpted from his chronicle. But

[61] Syncellus gives two different datings for the fall of the Watchers: A.M. 1000 (11.8) and 1058 (17.7); the second date comes from misunderstanding Panodorus' distinction between the descent of the Watchers and the subsequent establishment of the kingdoms of the Chaldeans and Egyptians.
[62] Ibid., 32.29–33.16. On the name "Chorabiel," see below, Chap. 6, p. 178, note 67.

the outlines of the argument are clear. When "Chorabiel" (= Eth. Koka-b'el) instructed some people (the first Chaldeans) about the course of the sun through the 360 degrees of the Zodiac, the 360-degree orbit was confused with the daily orbit of the sun. The year of the primitive Chaldean sar was thus one day of the solar year. In order to determine the length of the reigns of the ten antediluvian Chaldean kings from Alorus to Xisuthrus, it was necessary to divide the 432,000 years by 365. When this is done, the result—1183 ½ years—demonstrates that 59 years after the fall of the Watchers (A.M. 1000), the first Chaldean king began to rule, in the same year as Hephaestus began to rule in Egypt.

Panodorus could hardly have been unaware of the fact that even after Uriel's revelation to Enoch, the *Babyloniaca* continued to assign implausibly long reigns to the postdiluvian kings of Chaldea. According to Eusebius' extracts from Alexander Polyhistor, Berossus ascribed long reigns up to the conquest of the Medes, reckoning the duration of the postdiluvian kings Euechsius and Chomasbelus alone as four ners and four ners, five soses, respectively. In all, Berossus assigns to the eighty-six Chaldean and Median kings who reigned before the conquest of the Medes a total of 33,091 regnal years—ostensibly inconsistent with biblical chronology.[63] If the true length of the solar year had already been known in the time of Enoch, why did the Chaldeans continue to use the archaic calendar?

Syncellus informs us that Panodorus solved this inconsistency in the following way:

> Alexander Polyhistor, from the 2,405th year of the world, endeavored to renew his account of the Chaldean kingdom after the flood, recording his fables in sars, ners, and soses, and reporting that the 86 kings of the Chaldeans and Medes ruled 34,090 years, that is nine sars, two ners, and eight soses. *Some of our church historians unwisely* (οὐ καλῶς) again consider these 94 solar years and 8 months, which as they say corresponds with the cosmic year 2499. From the time of the 86 kings (both the two Chaldean kings Euechius and Chomasbelus, and the 84 kings of the Medes) this same Polyhistor introduced Zoroaster and the seven Chaldean kings after him, ruling 190 years, no longer in sars, ners, and soses and other irrational mythic history, but in solar years. For believing that their ancestors were gods or demigods, . . . they recorded that they really ruled enormous years,

---

[63] *Chronica* 12.24–25; Syncellus, probably on the authority of Panodorus, assigns 34,090 years to the reign of these kings (88.16–17); for discussion see below, Chap. 6, pp. 173–74.

thinking, contrary to divine Scriptures, that the world is eternal. . . . And it seems to Panodorus and to some others (τῷ Πανοδώρῳ . . . καὶ ἑτέροις τισί) that Zoroaster finally began to reckon the years of kings in solar years, even though solar years had been known by those descended from Enoch.[64]

Panodorus is claiming here that since the Chaldeans continued to reckon in sars, ners, and soses until the "time of Zoroaster," he was justified in reducing the 34,090 years of the rule of Euechsius, Chomasbelus, and the 84 Median kings to 94 "solar years," that is, from the year A.M. 2405 to 2499.[65] It was not until the year 2499 that Zoroaster, a man widely regarded in the ancient world for his wisdom, began to apply to the Chaldean and Persian calendar the wisdom that Enoch and his generation had learned about the true length of the solar year. This would explain, Panodorus argued, why the Babylonians continued to use an archaic mode of reckoning time.[66]

Syncellus includes a puzzling tradition, which may also form part of Panodorus' theory about the origins of reckoning. In the year 2585, "Cainan, when he was walking in a field, found the writing of the Giants (τὴν γραφὴν τῶν γιγάντων), and he hid this work for himself."[67] Although the contents of this work, which had once been thought to refer somehow to the Manichean *Book of the Giants,* are not specified, there is a very close parallel to the same legend in *Jubilees.*[68] *Jub.* 8:3 reports that

---

[64] Sync. 88.13–89.6.

[65] Something is not right with the calculation here, since 34,090 divided by 365 yields 93.4, not 94 years. Gelzer (*SJA*, 2. 201) believed that Panodorus was using 360-day years here, which hardly seems appropriate, since Panodorus reduced the 432,000 years of the antediluvian Chaldean kings by a factor of 365.

[66] Later, Syncellus asserts that according to a tradition (ὡς ὁ λόγος), the Greeks learned about the 365-day year from the Egyptians, who received it from the Chaldeans through Abraham (377.20–22; see also III.11–12). Since this notice comes in the context of a technical discussion of Panodorus' use of the Ptolemaic canons in the reckoning of Christ's birth (376.26–378.18), we may assume that the Alexandrian monk had extended his discussion of the origins of the solar calendar to include the Egyptians and Greeks. Here again Panodorus appears to have enlarged upon an older Jewish tradition, according to which Abraham introduced the Egyptians to the science of astronomy first revealed to Enoch; cf. (ps-)Eupolemus, in Eusebius *PE* 9.17.8 (419c); Josephus *Antiquities* 1.167–68.

[67] Ibid., 90.11–12.

[68] It is conceivable that this notice does imply the existence of some work circulating in the name of the Giants. Unlike the *Jub.* tradition upon which this report is based, Syncellus refers to a "book," not stelae. Further, Panodorus, the probable source of this tradition, seems to know material from the Enochic *Book of the Giants;* see below, Chap. 6, pp. 181–82. On the connection of this tradition with the Manichean work of the same name, see Isaac de Beausobre, *Histoire critique de Manichée et du Manichéisme* 1 (Amsterdam, 1734), 429. P. Alfaric (*Les écritures manichéenes* 2 [Paris, 1919], 32) identified the Γραφὴ τῶν Γιγάντων mentioned by

when Cainan was seeking for a place to build a city "he found a writing which former (generations) had carved on the rock, and he read what was thereon, and he transcribed it and sinned owing to it; for it contained the teaching of the Watchers in accordance with which they used to observe the omens of the sun and moon and stars in all the signs of heaven. And he wrote it down and said nothing regarding it."[69]

The passage from *Jubilees* describes antediluvian stelae containing revelations about the sun and the moon—a motif which, as we have seen, appears also in connection with Hermes, Seth, and Enoch. The *Jubilees* account is given a distinctly unfavorable cast, since Cainan was led astray because of his discovery. The legend is an implicit polemic against the wisdom of the Chaldeans, since Cainan was thought to have been the ancestor of the Chaldeans.[70] Cainan's discovery of antediluvian stelae is a story told repeatedly in Byzantine and Syriac chronography, with a startling number of variations, of which the chronographers themselves are aware. But despite its several forms, one theme persists. This is the belief that with Cainan's discovery came the discovery of Chaldaism and astrology.[71]

Syncellus with the work anathematized in the Gelasian decree: "Liber de Ogia nomine gigante qui post diluvium cum dracone ab hereticis pugnasse perhibetur apocryphus." See also W. Speyer, "Gigant," *RAC,* 10. 1263–64. On the Manichean *Book of the Giants,* see in particular, W. B. Henning, "The Book of the Giants," *BSOAS* 11 (1943/46), 52–74; for Aramaic fragments of this book found at Qumran along with other portions of the Enoch corpus, see Milik, *The Books of Enoch,* 55–58; 298–339.

[69] *Jub.* 8:3 (trans. Charles, *APOT* 2).

[70] See M. Hengel, *Judaism and Hellenism,* 242–43; for Cainan as forefather of the race of Chaldeans, cf. Josephus *Ant.* 1.144. According to this passage in Josephus, Arpachshad, Cainan's father, was the founder of the Chaldeans.

[71] Cedrenus includes the same version of the legend, adding: "He (Cainan) sinned in these things, and he taught others the same nonsense. But others say that Sala found this work" (1. 27.11–15). Other variations of the legend are numerous. One account appears to be a blending of the *Jubilees* story with a parallel one in Josephus' *Antiquities* 1.68–71; this blending was facilitated by the fact that the Watchers and the Sethites were often equated (see below, Chap. 4, pp. 113–17). For examples of this conflation, see the anonymous chronicler included in the CSHB edition of John Malalas, 6.1–5 (ed. L. Dindorf [Bonn, 1831]); Joel *Chronographia Compendaria* 3.14–4.17 (ed. I. Bekker; CSHB [Bonn, 1836]); Michael Glycas, 242.23–243.12 (ed. I. Bekker). Traditions about Cainan's discovery of antediluvian stelae and the origins of Chaldaism have a rich history in Syriac chronography. The Syriac *Chronicon anonymum ad annum Christi 1234 pertinens,* a work that makes extensive use of *Jubilees,* reports that "Cainan discovered a book which the ancients had written on stone, and he read it, because on it was written the teaching of the ancients for examining the omens in the sun, in the moon, in the stars, and in all the signs of the heavens. And he revealed this to no one, because he was afraid lest by chance Noah might be angry with him"; for Syriac text and translation, see Eugene Tisserant, "Fragments syriaques du Livre des Jubilés," *Recueil Cardinal Eugène Tisserant* 1 (Louvain, 1955), 57–58 (repr. from *RB* 30 [1921]). A puzzling legend in Syriac that appears to have evolved from this holds that Cainan introduced Chaldaism and that the temple

The rough synchronization of Cainan's discovery with Zoroaster's re-discovery of the solar year can hardly be coincidental, first because both revelations pertain to the knowledge of astronomy, and secondly because Panodorus has had to manipulate the chronology of Berossus to achieve it.[72] Presumably, the story of Cainan's discovery of antediluvian stelae left by the demonic offspring of the Watchers at about the same time that Zoroaster was rediscovering the revelations of Enoch formed part of a more ambitious undertaking on Panodorus' part, aimed at tracing the origins of astronomy and astrology back to the antediluvian period. Zoroaster, who here is represented as the heir to Enoch's revelation, is sometimes said by the chronographers to have passed on true reckoning of time to the Babylonians and then to the Egyptians, from whom it was then trans-mitted to the Greeks.[73] Given the background of the tradition about the stelae of the Watchers, it is probable that Panodorus included this variant of the *Jubilees* legend in order to contrast Zoroaster's discoveries of true reckoning with the demonic astrological lore discovered by Cainan, a body of false wisdom that lay at the root of Chaldaism and idolatry.

Panodorus was not the first Egyptian chronographer to have known and used *1 Enoch*, particularly the *Astronomical Book*. In the third century, An-atolius, a native of Alexandria and bishop of Laodicea, had cited *1 Enoch* in his treatise Περὶ τοῦ Πάσχα, in order to show that "with the Hebrews the first month lies around the equinox."[74] Later, and probably through Alexandrian chronography, the *Astronomical Book* exercised a profound in-fluence on Ethiopic chronography, both in eschatological speculation and in the computation of feasts. "No man, may he come from East or West, from North or South, from all the four corners of the world, can compute the time of Fast, of Easter and its feasts, or of the stars, without Enoch."[75]

The chronographers' esteem for the astronomy of *1 Enoch* often man-aged to override the obvious deficiencies of its 364-day year calendar. Ethiopian chronographers, as Neugebauer observed, tried, often awk-

---

of idols destroyed by Abraham in Ur was erected to him; see Bar Hebraeus, 9 (Budge trans.); Michael Syrus, 2.5,6 (trans. Chabot, 25). For further discussion, see below, Chap. 6, pp. 196–98, 215–16.

[72] Cf. Gelzer, *SJA*, 2. 201.

[73] So see Cedrenus, 1. 73.6–8.

[74] In Eusebius *Ecclesiastical History* 7.32.19.

[75] From Zar'a Ya'qob (15th century), quoted by Otto Neugebauer, in *Ethiopic Astronomy*, 110. For the use of *1 Enoch* in Abyssinian chronography, see ibid., 109–13, 172–75, 179–82; also H. Weld Blundell (trans.), *The Royal Chronicle of Abyssinia* (Cambridge, 1922), 496 (note 1).

wardly, to bring the 364-day year up to 365 days.[76] And in the *Astronomical Book* itself, a later interpolator has attempted, again without success, somehow to merge Alexandrian years with Enoch years.[77] Panodorus himself does not seem to have been aware of or even troubled by the problem, since his summary of that book makes it plain that, as far as he was concerned, Uriel revealed to Enoch a 365-day solar year. The oversight is especially striking in light of Syncellus' own report that Panodorus was highly skilled in chronography. It is thus conceivable that Panodorus did not know the *Astronomical Book* directly; indeed, what Syncellus reports of this portion of *1 Enoch* is only a highly abbreviated summary, similar to *Jub.* 4:17, and this may be all that he found in Panodorus' chronicle.

Syncellus, of course, did not recognize this as a flaw in Panodorus' reasoning. What he found most objectionable in Panodorus' reconstruction of the evolution of the primordial calendar was his claim, often repeated, that before Uriel's revelation no one, not even the biblical patriarchs, knew how to reckon time accurately in units greater than weeks. This was bound to be one of the more controversial features of Panodorus' reconstruction, since it presupposed that ignorance of chronology extended to Adam and his generation as well. Few other writers on the primordial calendar seem to have shared this view. Only a little before the publication of Panodorus' chronicle, Ephrem, in his *Commentary on Genesis,* had concluded that not only was Adam able to compute the duration of the year accurately, he was even able to intercalate days into the luni-solar calendar.[78] Syncellus would later identify this as one of Panodorus' most dubious claims: "It is

---

[76] Neugebauer, *Ethiopic Astronomy,* 114–15. According to Neugebauer, "somehow the change of the length of daylight and night is made responsible for the addition of one day to bring the 364-day year of Enoch at least up to 365 days."

[77] See Otto Neugebauer, *The 'Astronomical' Chapters of the Ethiopic Book of Enoch (72 to 82),* The Royal Danish Academy of Sciences and Letters 40.10 (Copenhagen, 1981), 18–19. Neugebauer thinks the interpolation was inserted under the "influence of some computus treatise, where a mix-up of Alexandrian and Enoch years is quite common." What the interpolator tries to do is describe an *octaeteris* using Enoch, not Alexandrian years.

[78] Like Panodorus, Ephrem was given to speculation about the chronographic skills of the early Chaldeans and Egyptians. While acknowledging that the Chaldeans anciently knew how to "arrange the times and years," he wants to trace the origins of exact reckoning to Adam: "So the Chaldeans did not institute the chronology which was already instituted before Adam" (*CGen* 22.12 f.). Adam knew how to intercalate, he argues, because when the moon was placed into the heavens on the 4th day, it was already 11 days old. "Those eleven days by which the moon was older than the sun and which were added to the moon that first year are the selfsame which those who use the calendar every year add to it. The first year of Adam and Eve was not incomplete because at the creation of the moon the missing part of its measure was supplemented. From that year until now Adam and Eve learnt that they were to add every year 11 days to it" (trans. T. Jansma, "Investigations into the Early Syrian Fathers on Genesis," *Studies on the Book of Genesis,* OS 12 [Leiden, 1958], 124). Ephrem later makes a similar claim about Noah on the basis of Gen. 8:3, again in the context of Egyptian and

absurd for him to suggest that . . . Moses did not mention measures of time except for the day and the night and the week. For Scripture everywhere makes mention of years, such as Adam lived 930 years and died, and likewise for all the generations—unless someone is convinced, which I am not, that from him, that is, Adam, they used to reckon time in weeks until the 165th year of Enoch."[79]

Despite Syncellus' criticism, this supposition must have figured importantly in Panodorus' speculations about the early calendar, for in the excerpts from him, Panodorus often alludes to the fact that before Enoch the only reckoning of time was in the "week, month, and day." "Starting with him—that is, Adam—" he writes, "they used to reckon time in weeks, up to the 165th year of Enoch (δι᾽ ἑβδομάδων τοὺς χρόνους ἠρίθμουν, ἕως τοῦ ϱξε´ ἔτους Ἐνώχ)."[80] During that time, neither "a month, nor years, nor the measures of them were known by men (ἐν ᾇς οὔτε μὴν οὔτε τροπαὶ οὔτε ἐνιαυτοὶ οὔτε τὰ τούτων μέτρα τοῖς ἀνθρώποις ἐγνώσθησαν)."[81]

Commentators have noted the claim without offering any explanation as to its meaning.[82] We are on more precarious grounds here, since Syncellus does not state explicitly how Panodorus reached this conclusion. But a conclusion like this would have been a reasonable inference from two other works that Panodorus appears to have consulted. These are the *Life of Adam* and *Jubilees,* both of which use calendrical systems based on a hebdomadal system. As is well known, the primary purpose of the calendar of *Jubilees,* and works related to it, is to ensure that the day of the

---

Chaldean chronography: "Observe that even the Noachic generation was used to this computation of a year for 365 days. Why hold that the Chaldeans and Egyptians are those that have arranged and invented this computation?" (*CGen* 61; trans. Tryggve Kronholm, *Motifs from Genesis 1–11 in the Genuine Hymns of Ephrem the Syrian,* ConBOT 11 [Lund, 1978], 200–201.

[79] Sync. 34.9–16.

[80] Ibid., 34.14–16.

[81] Ibid., 34.21–22; cf. 34.9–11. Panodorus clearly applies this reasoning to the chronology of archaic Babylonia and Egypt: "The measurement of the 1,058 years (before the founding of Chaldea) used to be in weeks (δι᾽ ἑβδομάδων) (Sync., 33.16–17); see also Syncellus' quotation from Panodorus on Egyptian chronology (42.2–4): "From the creation of Adam up to Enoch, that is A.M. 1282 (read 1286), the numbering of neither the year nor month was known."

[82] In commenting on the supposed reckoning of time in weeks by primordial generations, Scaliger observed (*Thesaurus Temporum,* 2. 246): "quarum Hebdomadum vestigia extant in computo Aethiopico." Scaliger's knowledge of Ethiopian chronography was limited, and there is no suggestion of this sort of hebdomadal reckoning in the preserved Ethiopic mss. The only hebdomads are the 7-year periods used in the computation of the 532-year Easter cycle. I owe this information to a private communication from Prof. Neugebauer.

week and the day of the month will always coincide—this in order that festivals and commemorations will always be observed on the same day of the week. To achieve this, *Jubilees* adheres to a calendar which is essentially hebdomadal—based on weekly cycles. According to the calendar of *Jubilees*, the year is 364 days in length, consisting of four three-month periods, each of 91 days. Presumably because the "great lights" were placed in the sky on the fourth day, the calendrical year begins on Wednesday and the fourth day appears to hold special significance in the dating of events, including the events of primordial history. Adam's entrance into Paradise, his transgression and expulsion are all made to occur on a Wednesday.[83]

The 364-day year of *Jubilees* is an idealized calendar, of liturgical value only, and not corresponding to the observable motions of the sun and moon. For Panodorus, a chronographer who according to Syncellus kept accurate "tables of the motion of the sun and the moon,"[84] it would follow from the deficiencies of this calendar that in this period of world history there had not yet evolved the means for reckoning in years, months, and seasons. Such confusions as those which arose when Chaldean civilization began could thus be attributed to the fact that during this period, "measurement of time was only in hebdomads."[85]

The same motive would appear to account for another work that Gelzer believed came from the chronicle of Panodorus. This is the so-called *Testament of Adam*, for which Syncellus is one of two Greek witnesses. In Syncellus' description of this pseudepigraphon, Adam, "after having repented," learns through a revelation about the "Watchers and the flood, and about repentance, the divine incarnation, and the prayers according to the hour of the day and night sent to God by the created things through Uriel. . . ."[86] A Syriac recension of that work describes these revelations to Adam as a "chronicle,"[87] but of the various elements of that work, the

[83] For a good summary of the calendrical principles underlying the *Book of Jubilees*, see Jack Finegan, *Handbook of Biblical Chronology* (Princeton, 1964), 49–57. For a more extensive account, see A. Jaubert, "Le calendrier des Jubilés et les jours liturgiques de la semaine," *VT* 7 (1957), 35–61.

[84] Sync. 35.33–34.

[85] As will be seen below (Chap. 6, pp. 183–88), an editor of Syncellus' excerpts from *Jubilees* has mostly translated this hebdomadal scheme into Alexandrian years; but traces of it still survive in Syncellus. Thus Syncellus (8.17–18) states that Adam and Eve "grieved for Abel four hebdomads (ἑβδομαδικούς), that is 28 years." See G. L. Huxley, "On the Erudition of George the Synkellos," *Proceedings of the Royal Irish Academy* 81.C.6 (1980), 213.

[86] For a recent study and translation of the various recensions of this work see Stephen Robinson, *The Testament of Adam*, SBLDS 52 (Chico, 1982).

[87] Ibid., 69.

only part with the clearest chronographic application is the so-called *hor-arium*—the prayers for the individual hours of the day and night.[88]

Although Gelzer concluded that this work, like the other pseudepigra-pha in Syncellus' chronicle, was taken from Panodorus, he argued this only on the basis of a general theory of literary dependence.[89] Syncellus simply quotes from the work without commenting on its meaning or applications to chronography. However, judging from the contents of the *Testament of Adam*, it is possible to place this work within the framework of Panodo-rus' theory about the origin of the "day and the night." In the explanation of the *horarium* in one of the Syriac versions, Adam describes to Seth how he had learned "about the hours of the day and night" and their mean-ing.[90] Panodorus, it will be recalled, had claimed that the division of the day and the night, and the calculation of the week, were the only measures of time known to Adam and to the generations before Enoch. It was from the hebdomadal calendar of *Jubilees* and the *Life of Adam*, and the *horarium* of the *Testament of Adam* that Panodorus had made this argument.

PANODORUS AS A PRODUCT OF ALEXANDRIAN CHRISTIANITY

For Panodorus, primitive reckoning of time evolved incrementally, in a series of successive revelations, finally culminating in Uriel's teachings to Enoch. "Scientific (ἀποδεικτικός)" is how he describes his imaginative fusion of Genesis, Jewish apocrypha, and oriental antiquities.[91] The word embodies the high expectations that Panodorus brought to the discipline and the principles that guided his work, namely, to give to Christian chronography a degree of precision that would both conform to the stan-dards of contemporary Alexandrian scholarship and surpass his predeces-sors, notably Eusebius. Indeed, Panodorus' rebuke of Eusebius' handling of his Babylonian and Egyptian sources constitutes only part of what must have been a more comprehensive set of criticisms, including Eusebius' failure to mention the second Cainan, his 290-year error in calculating

---

[88] In the text of Syncellus, the actual prayers of the *horarium* are lacking, but these can be reconstructed from other recensions of the same work, including the chronicle of George Cedrenus (1. 17.18–18.17)

[89] Gelzer, *SJA,* 2. 267.

[90] Robinson, *Testament of Adam,* 87.

[91] Sync. 33.19.

Christ's birth, and his neglect of the interregnal period of foreign kings in the time of the judges.[92]

In light of their conflicting conceptions of chronography, it is understandable that Panodorus should have objected most vigorously to Eusebius' handling of archaic chronology. The conflict originated in a fundamentally different view as to how much could be known about events in the remote past. As is well known, Panodorus dated events from the first day of creation, which he had reckoned confidently as the first day of the first month of the Egyptian calendar—1 Thoth (= August 29).[93] This represented an important departure from his predecessors. Although Christian chronography had experimented with the possibility of establishing a chronology of events from the creation, neither of its two major representatives had applied it. Africanus' era was *ab Adam;* Eusebius', even more conservative, was *ab Abraham.* Eusebius had, moreover, expressly ruled out the whole idea of dating events from the creation. In the course of seeking to develop an absolute chronology *ab origine mundi,* it followed that Eusebius' own hesitations about the primordial period should have served both as Panodorus' principal object of censure and as his point of departure.

The vigorous criticisms of Eusebius reveal an independence and scholarly temperament that is largely responsible for the enduring respect accorded Panodorus' work by modern scholars. Unger called him "the most learned (*kenntnissreichen*) successor of Africanus and Eusebius."[94] These qualities appear even more sharply in his evidently keen interest in reconciling pagan sources and pagan scholarship with biblical chronology. Indeed, when Syncellus later came to assess his work, no single feature of Panodorus' chronicle disturbed him more than this. Panodorus, he complains, "exerts himself to show that the Egyptian writings against God and against our divinely inspired scriptures are really in agreement with them. In this he criticizes Eusebius, not understanding that these arguments of his, which are incapable of proof or reasoning, have been proved against

---

[92] For a useful discussion of Panodorus' reorganization and adaptation of Eusebius' chronicle, as well as his use of Africanus, see most recently A. Mosshammer, *The Chronicle of Eusebius,* 77–78, 81, 147.

[93] Although Panodorus' world era is a more controversial matter, it was apparently derived from the widely used era of Diocletian (August 29th 276 C.E. = 284). Since Syncellus states (397.9) that Panodorus calculated Augustus' death in A.M. 5506 (= 19 August 14 C.E.), his world era would then work out to be 5493 B.C.E.; cf. F. K. Ginzel, *Handbuch der mathematischen und technischen Chronologie* (Leipzig, 1914), 3. 289.

[94] Unger, *Manetho,* 41; cited approvingly by Gelzer, *SJA,* 2. 189.

himself and against truth."[95] "What is this compulsion to reconcile the lie (of Berossus and Manetho) with the truth (ἀνάγκην . . . συμβιβάζειν τὸ ψεῦδος τῇ ἀληθείᾳ)"?[96]

Even harsher judgment was reserved for Panodorus' embrace of what Syncellus later described slightingly as "outside wisdom (τοῖς ἔξω σοφοῖς)." By this, he meant the Alexandrian astronomers—in Serruys' words, "les maîtres et les modèles de Panodore."[97] As is clear from his ruminations on the origins of the solar year, Panodorus had an abiding interest in astronomy; his work, Syncellus writes, "contained not only chronographic theory, but tables of lunar and solar motion."[98] The influence of Alexandrian astronomy extended even to the calculation of Christ's birth and resurrection. Syncellus, who accuses Panodorus of erring by seven years in calculating this date, leaves no doubt as to what caused this error; it was because he "followed the 'astronomical canon'," that is, the *Handy Tables* of Claudius Ptolemy.[99] Insofar as one of the expressed aims of his own chronicle was to uphold the traditional date of Christ's birth (A.M. 5500/5501,) Syncellus adjudged this a serious failing, an enormity of sufficient proportions to negate whatever else was valuable in his predecessor's work. In the estimation of Syncellus, his predecessor's zeal for pagan wisdom had caused him to stray dangerously "from apostolic and patristic tradition."[100]

Modern treatments of Christian chronography tend to represent Panodorus in much the same way (although not with the same opprobrium as Syncellus). In many studies, Panodorus emerges almost as a prototypical Scaliger—that is, as a chronographer whose independence, wide-ranging literary interests, and critical acumen often overrode what he had inherited

---

[95] Sync. 42.20–24.

[96] Ibid., 17.26–27.

[97] Ibid., 378.7; see D. Serruys, "Les transformations de l'aera alexandrina minor," *Revue de philologie* n.s. 31 (1907), 253.

[98] Ibid., 35.31–33.

[99] The canon Syncellus refers to is probably not the whole *Handy Tables,* but rather the canon of kings found with it in Theon's recension. I owe this observation to Prof. Anthony Grafton. For Syncellus' summary of how Panodorus determined this date using Ptolemy's *Handy Tables,* see Sync. 396.12–397.10. In his own chronicle, Syncellus retains a portion of an "astronomical canon" which also appears to be based on Theon's recension of Ptolemy's work (see Sync. 243.25–246.18).

[100] After rebuking Panodorus for his 7-year error, Syncellus defends his own dating strictly on grounds of its greater conformity to orthodoxy. Panodorus, he says, too "zealous to conform to pagan wisdom regarding celestial motion, deviated by 7 years from the year 5500, dating (the birth of Christ) in the year 5493 instead of 5500, even though he was esteemed among many in other things" (378.7–10).

as "traditional."[101] Unger suggested, for example, that Panodorus' "predilection (*Vorliebe*)" for heathen sources showed he was a chronicler relatively unencumbered by the constraints of orthodoxy.[102] Gelzer, noting
Panodorus' originality and his appetite for esoteric literature, saw Panodorus as the product of the intellectually permissive society of fifth-century
Alexandria. The environment in which Panodorus wrote, he maintained,
was that of "Theophilus, the destroyer of idols, but also of Synesius." For
Gelzer, Panodorus would have found more in common with Synesius.
Like Synesius, he had not foresworn his interest in Hermetism or Chal-
dean wisdom.[103]

It is important, however, not to let Syncellus' judgment of Panodorus
some 400 years later color our perception of Panodorus' own conception
of his task as a Christian chronographer. Syncellus' harsh judgments notwithstanding, Panodorus sees himself a champion of orthodoxy. Indeed,
in an excerpt from his chronicle preserved in Syncellus, the Alexandrian
monk claims that one of the reasons why he undertook to write a continuous chronology from the creation was to prove "scientifically" that the
heretics (that is, the Arians) and pagans entertained false views about the
age of the world.[104]

Syncellus, impressed by the orthodox self-consciousness of the author
of the quotation, expressed open amazement why a self-professing opponent of paganism would take such pains to accommodate himself to it.
His complaint reveals the extent to which the goals and interests of Christian chronography had evolved in 400 years. For Syncellus, in ninth-
century Constantinople, the task of reconciling pagan sources with Scripture no longer commanded any urgency; hence, the repeated demand of
his Alexandrian predecessor to justify his zeal to accommodate the "lie of
Berossus and Manetho with the truth of Scripture." A far different situation prevailed in Alexandria in the early fifth century. The emperor Julian
had died only shortly before, and paganism in Alexandria, especially in its

---

[101] Scaliger, normally abstemious in his praise of other chronographers, did, however, have
a very high regard for him. In the notes to the miscellaneous Greek witnesses to Eusebius,
Scaliger referred to Panodorus and Annianus as "doctissimi suorum temporum . . . Aegyptii
monachi" (*Thesaurus Temporum* 2. 141).

[102] Unger, *Manetho*, 39.

[103] Gelzer, *SJA*, 2. 192–93. Gelzer found Panodorus more to be preferred than Syncellus;
the latter's censure of Panodorus reveals "den feinen Spürsinn des inquisitorischen Hier-
archen." "I regard," he writes, "Panodorus as one of the many neo-Platonists going over to
Christianity at that time, but who, in the garb of a monk, has not also surrendered his love
for the old wisdom of Egypt and Chaldea" (*SJA*, 2. 192; English translation by the author).

[104] In Sync. 33.27–33; for discussion, see below, Chap. 5, pp. 149–51.

Greco-oriental form, was enjoying a small revival. And from what we can surmise from other sources about the intellectual atmosphere in Alexandria of the fifth and sixth centuries, the question of "creationism" was one of the most hotly contended issues in the pagan/Christian dispute. In this discussion, the appeal and the dangers of the Chaldean and Hermetic literature could hardly have been lost on a Christian chronographer, especially one apprised of the use of these sources in supporting opposing conceptions about the age and duration of the universe.[105]

One could, as Africanus had done and as Syncellus would urge, avoid the question by rejecting these sources altogether; but the response more in line with the temperament of the learned fifth-century monk was to find a way to defuse them. What Panodorus terms an "allegorical" interpretation of his sources is mainly a Christian adaptation of a method that was widely known and applied in Antiquity. Syncellus would later represent this as a dangerous capitulation to paganism; Panodorus himself believed he had undermined his ethnic sources by showing "scientifically" that their long duration arose from a defect in the very science in which the Egyptians and Chaldeans were believed to excel: astronomy.

PANODORUS AND HIS SUCCESSORS

In modern studies of chronography, Panodorus is often represented as the most influential of all the chronographers to succeed Eusebius. Traces of this influence are thought to be evident in a broad range of subsequent sources, ranging from the Syriac universal chroniclers to the Ethiopic computus. Gelzer even maintained that Syncellus' own chronicle was almost entirely derivative of Panodorus'—this in spite of the fact that Syncellus' assessment of his Alexandrian predecessor was far from enthusiastic.[106]

The influence imputed to Panodorus is largely through inference; were his reputation to be measured strictly on the basis of subsequent references to him by ancient authors he would have to be adjudged a minor figure. The Syriac chronicles acknowledge only Annianus as an authority. And although the Ethiopian chronographers applied the same era from creation (1 Maskaram = 1 Thoth, 5493 B.C.E.), they do not credit Panodorus with having formulated it. Panodorus' name is never even mentioned by

---

[105] For general discussion of the Christian appropriation and adaptation of the Hermetic tradition in Alexandria, see most recently Garth Fowden, *The Egyptian Hermes,* 179–82.

[106] See below, Chap. 5, pp. 142–45; Chap. 6, pp. 161–63.

them.[107] In fact, were it not for Syncellus, Panodorus would today be entirely unknown.

Panodorus' influence on subsequent chronographers can be measured only imperfectly from Syncellus' witness. When Syncellus refers to Panodorus, he sometimes places him in the company of unnamed "others." This would suggest that, at least in Syncellus' estimation, Panodorus was the most important of several Christian chronographers, and that his views either influenced or were shared by other chroniclers. In other places, however, Syncellus treats Panodorus as a relative unknown, rarely presupposing of his readers any degree of familiarity with either Panodorus or Annianus. Eusebius and Africanus are mentioned without elaboration. But when he first introduces his Alexandrian authorities, he furnishes fairly detailed biographical information about them: when and where they lived, under which bishop, etc.[108] His vague way of referring to Panodorus in other places—"some historians," a "certain Panodorus"—strongly implies that in Syncellus' day Panodorus was a relatively obscure figure.

It is important, therefore, to be clear about the extent and manner in which Panodorus' impact on his successors can be established. In the first place, any hypothesized influence must mainly be limited to archaic history; with the exception of his calculation of Christ's birth, this is all we can know about his work with certainty. Traces of views similar to Panodorus', but not attributed to him directly, appear in a broad range of later sources. But in few of these sources can direct dependence be demonstrated. Panodorus' influence here has been attenuated through intermediaries, the blending of traditions from other sources, and sometimes deliberate editing, intended to bring Panodorus' chronology more into conformity with orthodoxy and tradition. Rather than speaking of a direct influence from Panodorus, it is perhaps more accurate to view these later sources as part of a continuum with him, fixed points in a dynamic and evolving process.

The process began almost immediately after the appearance of Panodorus' chronicle, when Annianus emended the more prolix work of his colleague. Ostensibly because of its greater conformity with orthodoxy and its more condensed form, Annianus' chronicle seems to have exerted a far larger influence on a subsequent generation of chronographers than Panodorus. Highly regarded among the Syriac chronographers, Annianus

---

[107] Cf. H. Weld Blundell, *The Royal Chronicle of Abyssinia*, 494.
[108] Ibid., 35.4–9.

is cited as an authority equal in stature to Eusebius, especially for archaic history.[109] And although the extent of influence is more difficult to trace in Byzantine chronography, it is clear that the Alexandrian chronographers stimulated further research into the same questions they had raised.

One of the chronographers who followed in the footsteps of the Alexandrians was an obscure author named Pyrrho, writing sometime before the seventh century. In his *Anagoge,* Anastasius of Sinai (seventh century) referred to "certain historians," among whom he names Pyrrho, who had, like the Alexandrians, asserted that forty days had elapsed between Adam's creation and his entrance into Paradise. To support this chronology, Pyrrho had consulted a pseudepigraphon, similar to *Jubilees* and the *Life of Adam,* which Anastasius knows as the *Testament of the Protoplasts.*[110]

The Alexandrians' synchronization of Chaldean and Egyptian chronology, Genesis, and *1 Enoch* was destined to exert a considerable impact upon the Syriac and Byzantine chronographers and, mainly through Syncellus, even in European chronography. The problem of Chaldean and Egyptian chronology was a perennial one in Christian chronography, especially after Scaliger published the fragments of Berossus and Manetho which he knew from Syncellus and other earlier chronicles. Several suggestions had been offered, ranging from the notion of collateral dynasties to Scaliger's claim that these works should be treated as independent of biblical chronology. In his *Thesaurus Temporum,* Scaliger had simply commented on Panodorus' method without passing judgment on it. But chronographers were extremely impressed by Panodorus' suggestion as well, and it is not uncommon to see his solution to the problem included among many of the other widely discussed solutions.[111]

---

[109] Thus, in the prologue, the author of the anonymous Syriac *Chronicon ad annum Christi 1234 pertinens* names among his authorities Eusebius, Andronicus and Annianus "an Egyptian monk," adding as well that "many from our fathers adhere to them" (18.2–5; Latin trans. I.-B. Chabot, CSCO 109, Scriptores Syri 56). For Michael Syrus' and Bar Hebraeus' use of Annianus, see below, Chap. 4, pp. 118–26.

[110] "Whence," Anastasius writes, "the Hebrews on the basis of a book which is not received into the Canon, say that on the 40th day Adam entered Paradise. And so it also seems to a certain chronographer Pyrrho, as well as certain other expositors" (*Anagoge contemplationum in Hexaemeron* 7.895 (PG, 89. 967D).

[111] After Scaliger, John Marsham, in the *Prokataskeue* to his *Chronicus canon Aegyptiacus, Ebraicus, Graecus et disquisitiones* (London, 1672) had the following to say about this technique: "After Eusebius, Panodorus an Egyptian monk under Arcadius Augustus, supposing that the years of the Gods were lunar and were broken down into 30 lunar cycles, contends that he has proved that these commentaries were sufficiently harmonious with sacred Scripture. From Adam he holds that kingless years were 1,058 years: in that year of the world the Watchers descended. Then he says that the lunar years which are attributed to the Gods are 11,985 and yield 969 solar years and the 858 seasons of the semi-gods, or trimester years, make

The Byzantine chronographers, in general, reacted less favorably than their Syriac counterparts to the Alexandrian chronographers' appeal to extra-biblical works. Syncellus was not the only Byzantine chronographer to polemicize against them. The *Jubilees'* chronology of Adam's stay in Paradise found few supporters in Byzantine chronology. In his day, Cedrenus knew that chronographers had proposed several solutions to this question. "Some say Adam spent," he writes, "100 years in Paradise. Others that he was created in the third hour, transgressed on the sixth, and was expelled in the ninth."[112] But, he, like Syncellus, preferred Chrysostom's chronology.[113] Later, Michael Glycas, commenting on the supposed 40-day interval that was alleged to have passed before Adam entered Paradise, states: "I do not know where Adam was previously spending time during this period. . . . So pay no attention to Pyrrho, but rather to Chrysostom, for he is truly moved by the holy spirit."[114] As for the source of the tradition, Michael says: "The so-called Little Genesis—I do not know whence and how it was written—states that Adam was forty days before he entered Paradise, and Eve was eighty days."[115]

With his fusion of various sources—Genesis, Jewish pseudepigrapha, and Babylonian and Egyptian antiquities—Panodorus also contributed to what later eventuated in a bewildering tangle of sometimes conflicting traditions. Chronographers after him, who rarely knew these sources firsthand, were often far less prudent than Panodorus in distinguishing among them. Thus, the Arabic Christian chronicler Agapius (tenth century), who might have known some garbled material ultimately derived from Panodorus, states that Manetho himself wrote that Enoch was the first to learn about the motion of the planets and reckoning of time, recording this in the *Astronomical Book*.[116] Even more widespread was the blending and conflation of Enoch traditions with similar ones about Seth.

---

214 solar years and a half. In that way, the number of years makes 2,242: evidently as many years as there were, according to the Greek version of the Bible, from the beginning of things to the flood" (11).

[112] Cedrenus, I. 12.1–5.

[113] Ibid., I. 12.20–13.2.

[114] Michael Glycas *Annales* 156.12–157.4 (ed. I. Bekker).

[115] Ibid., 392.18–393.3; "and for this reason," he adds, echoing Syncellus, "they introduce into the temple the male and female child in as many days, perhaps conformably to Adam and Eve. But put away this book. For the genuine history of Moses shows that on the sixth day, God created Adam, and placed him immediately in Paradise". See also Theodore Metochites (14th century), *Historiae Romanae liber,* in Hermann Rönsch, *Das Buch der Jubiläen oder die Kleine Genesis* (Lepizig, 1874), 321; Rönsch's work is still a very valuable collection of citations from *Jubilees* in later sources.

[116] Agapius, *Kitab al-ʿUnvan* (ed. and trans. A. Vasiliev, PO 5.4 [1910], 591–92).

According to an old Jewish tradition attested as early as Josephus, Seth, having learned from Adam about the coming deluge, had carved all the antediluvian knowledge on stelae, including astronomy and geometry. This tradition, very widespread in the Byzantine chronicles, became the basis for the attribution to Seth of numerous revelations and discoveries, many of them precisely parallel to those imputed to Enoch.[117] R. H. Charles has quite correctly observed that many of the discoveries attributed to Seth in the Byzantine chroniclers reflect a transfer of "Enoch's greatness to Seth."[118] Implicit in this transference might have been a criticism of those chronographers, including Panodorus, who had traced the beginnings of accurate measurement of time to Enoch; Seth had learned these things earlier. The Byzantine chronographers, heirs to all these traditions, would make some token efforts to reconcile and harmonize them; but, in the main, what survives in these later chronicles is a web of largely unassimilated legends about the discoveries and contributions of antediluvian heroes to culture and wisdom.[119]

[117] Cf. Leo Grammaticus, 9.22 (ed. I. Bekker, CSHB, [Bonn, 1842]); Michael Glycas, 228.7–13; Joel, 3.6–13; Cedrenus, I. 16.10–11. For other sources, see Suidas, s.v. Σήθ; Agapius (citing Africanus), *Kitab al-ʿUnvan*, 587 (ed. Vasiliev); also Manuel Comnenus in CCAG 5. 118.10; Stephanus in CCAG 2. 182.26. For discussion, see A. F. J. Klijn, *Seth in Jewish, Christian and Gnostic Literature* (Leiden, 1977), 48–61.

[118] Note to *Jub.* 4:15 (*APOT,* 2. 18).

[119] Thus, Michael Glycas writes of two successive revelations of the same heavenly phenomena. "It is said," he writes (228.7–13), "that the angel stationed among the stars, that is the divine Uriel, descended to Seth and then to Enoch and taught them the distinctions between hours, months, seasons, and years"; but he adds that according to George, Seth was the first to "discover Hebrew letters, the signs of heaven, the seasons of the years, and the months and weeks, and gave names to the stars and the five planets so that they could be identified."

CHAPTER FOUR

Civilization before the Flood: Euhemeristic Historiography in Alexandrian Chronography

The discrepancies between Genesis and the ethnic histories of the Egyptians and Babylonians did not, as Syncellus was to note, extend only to chronology. Even in the archaic period of history, Berossus had described highly evolved social and political institutions in Babylon, possessing "everything which is connected with the civilized life (συνόλως πάντα τὰ πρὸς ἡμέρωσιν ἀνήκοντα βίου)."[1] From reading Genesis, the same conclusion was hardly forthcoming. A most conspicuous area of disagreement was in Berossus' and Genesis' respective descriptions of antediluvian political institutions. The *Babyloniaca* was unmistakable in its account of a succession of kings before the flood. Genesis was at best noncommittal on the subject. Finding in this last point a convenient argument against Panodorus and Annianus, Syncellus harks back to it again and again. It is necessary to recognize, he writes, "that in divinely inspired Scripture, there is no mention of a kingdom before the flood. . . . (So) neither Babylon nor Chaldea was ruled by kings before the flood, nor Egypt before Mestrem. And in my opinion, it was not even inhabited before that time (οὔτε Βαβυλὼν ἢ Χαλδαϊκὴ πρὸ τοῦ κατακλυσμοῦ οὔτε ἡ Αἴγυπτος πρὸ τοῦ Μεστρὲμ ἐβασιλεύθη, οἶμαι δ' ὅτι οὐδ' ᾠκίσθη)."[2]

Syncellus does not explain clearly how his Alexandrian predecessors established the existence of a pre-flood monarchy in the face of Genesis' silence on this question. We know, however, from other sources that Panodorus and Annianus, and numerous subsequent chroniclers as well, derived the institution of monarchy before the flood from the sons of God of Genesis 6 and their giant offspring. The connection seems at first far-

---

[1] In Sync. 29.15–16; cf. *Chronica* 7.5–28.
[2] Sync. 42.24–26.

fetched, and it is not easy to penetrate the subject without first examining the background of the issue in Hellenistic historiography.

THE ORIGINS OF CIVILIZATION IN HELLENISTIC HISTORIOGRAPHY

Primitive Society and the Boundaries of Historical Knowledge

In the third book of Plato's *Laws,* an Athenian stranger discourses on the kind of society that must have existed in the wake of the destruction of civilization caused by a flood. People then "must necessarily have been unskilled in the arts (ἀπείρους ... τεχνῶν) generally."[3] "Those born in that age of the world's history did not as yet possess the art of writing (οὐδὲ γὰρ γράμματά ἐστί πω τοῖς ἐν τούτῳ τῷ μέρει τῆς περιόδου γεγονόσιν), but lived by following custom and what is called patriarchal law (πατρίοις νόμοις)."[4] Everybody "gives the name of 'headship (δυναστείαν)' to the government which then existed."[5] Although men living in such primitive societies might have been "more brave and temperate and in all ways more righteous" than their more civilized successors,[6] it was not until a society had evolved beyond its primitive stage that it began to enter into meaningful social behaviour, both good and bad, for example, writing, the arts of war by land and sea, enactment of laws, building of cities, and planting of seeds.[7] Along with this cultural evolution came political change as well—from hereditary patriarchy (δυναστεία) to kingship.[8]

In his highly schematized account of the rise and fall of states, the Athenian had expressly ruled out the possibility of ascertaining the duration of time that had "passed since cities came into existence and men lived under civic rule."[9] This was so, he claimed, because of the rise and fall of numerous states during this time, and the endless succession of floods and plagues that had contributed to their destruction.[10] But reasoning from

[3] *Laws* 677B (trans. Bury).
[4] Ibid., 680A.
[5] Ibid., 680B.
[6] Ibid., 679E.
[7] Ibid., 679DE; 681AB.
[8] Ibid., 681D. Although this form of government was considered the most primitive, there were those who believed it was a more blessed state than monarchy, since mankind was also not subject to the oppression of tyrants. For a general discussion of this theme in Antiquity, see A. O. Lovejoy and G. Boas, *Primitivism and Related Ideas in Antiquity* (Baltimore, 1935), 162 ff., 269.
[9] *Laws* 676B.
[10] Ibid., 676BC.

the same premises, Hellenistic world historians had attempted to determine a suitable starting point from which to commence a historical and
chronological narrative.

Greek antiquarians liked to speculate about the progress of civilization
and the identities of the earliest culture-heroes.[11] The period before the
transition from primitivism to civilization was likely to be dismissed as
historically insignificant and even unknowable. Historians had assumed,
for example, that as a consequence of the flood at the time of the autoch-
thonous Ogygus, memories of pre-flood Greece had been lost; presumably for that reason, Varro had elected to relegate this period to the category of "indeterminate."[12] It had been supposed as well that Attica had,
for a time, reverted to a state of cultural and political primitivism. For all
of their supposed virtue, people living after the flood produced at that
time nothing of note; and even if they had, they lacked the means to
record it. "After Ogygus," writes Africanus, "because of the vast destruction caused by the flood, the present land of Attica remained without a
king (ἀβασίλευτος) up to Cecrops, a period of 189 years."[13] For Africanus, this interlude between barbarism and the rediscovery of culture
after the flood meant a hiatus in his own narrative. The 94 years immediately after the flood of Ogygus should be passed over, he says, "as no
remarkable event is recorded during it among the Greeks. But after 94
years, as some say, came Prometheus, who was said in the legend to have
formed men; for being a wise man, he tried to reform them out of their
extreme uncouthness into an educated condition."[14]

A continuous historical narrative, then, was impossible because Greek
civilization, often ravaged by cataclysms, had been periodically reduced to
primitivism, during which time nothing historically remarkable had occurred; and even if there had, the means did not exist for recording it. The
past affairs of non-Greek cultures had to be treated differently, however,
because they had, or so it was claimed, been far less vulnerable to such
catastrophes. Already in the *Timaeus,* the Egyptian priest, after reminding

---

[11] On the role of the discovery of the arts and the culture-hero in Hellenistic universal
history, see A. Momigliano, "The Origins of Universal History," 83–85; for the importance
of this theme in Antiquity, see K. Thraede, "Erfinder" (2), *RAC* 5 (1962), 1191–1278.

[12] Varro, in Censorinus *De die natali* 21.1–2. Hellanicus' *Atthis* also began with Ogygus'
flood, which he dated 1,120 years before the first Olympiad. For dating of this flood, see
Drews, "Assyria in Classical Universal Histories," 131–32 (note 14).

[13] In Sync. 173.25–27.

[14] Excerpt in *PE* 10.10.23 (491b) (trans. Gifford). Prometheus as a bringer of culture is
already intimated in Aeschylus' *Prometheus* 454–505. For the survival of this motif in Christian
chronography, see Eusebius' *Canons* 35b (ed. Helm); Sync. 174.22–24.

Solon of the continuity of Egyptian culture, boasted that their sacred writings preserved virtually all of the entire 9,000-year sweep of Egyptian civilization. Even for the 1,000 years that were omitted, the Egyptian claimed to be able to recount, albeit only briefly, "certain of their laws and the noblest of the deeds they performed."[15] Since their past was undisrupted, the question was not determining when their civilizations had been restored after periodic catastrophes, but rather the point at which their civilizations first evolved from primitivism.

Diodorus takes up the theoretical aspects of the problem in the prologue to his history.[16] Noting here that primitive peoples were non-literate and thus incapable of bequeathing a record of their affairs for their posterity, he insists that any treatment of this period in world history must necessarily be highly generalized, not, he says, to exceed "due proportion (τῆς συμμετρίας)."[17] Diodorus also observes that there were other historians, himself not included, who had gone so far as to claim that the historical period began precisely with the first king. These historians, Diodorus states, maintain moreover that it is their cultures whose founders were the "first of all men to discover the things which are of use in life (εὑρετὰς . . . τῶν ἐν τῷ βίῳ χρησίμων), and that it was the events in their own history which were the earliest to have been held worthy of record."[18]

Diodorus was personally not disposed to accept this view; for him, the competing claims of different nations precluded the possibility of determining which civilization was the oldest. And even granting that "the discovery of writing was of so early a date as to have been contemporary with the first kings," this was no grounds for assuming that the recording of events commenced at that time. Historians, he says, are as a "class a quite recent appearance in the life of mankind."[19] But he acknowledged that it was a view held by many historians of his day. The belief that the discoveries of things "worthy of note," and thus historical consciousness, were coterminous with the beginnings of monarchy must have informed the historians of Orosius' day as well. In his critique of his contemporaries, Orosius had observed that when pagan historians had elected to consign the period before Ninus, the supposed first king, to prehistory, they had done so on the assumption that nothing significant or worthy of recount-

---

[15] *Timaeus* 23E. In Book 2 of the *Laws* (656E), Egyptian civilization is said to have lasted 10,000 years "exactly."

[16] For Diodorus' discussion of primitive society, see 1.8.1–9.

[17] Ibid., 1.8.10.

[18] Ibid., 1.9.3.

[19] Ibid., 1.9.2 (trans. Oldfather).

ing had occurred before that time. They "definitely state that kingdoms and wars began with Ninus," writes Orosius, "as if forsooth the human race had existed up to that time in the manner of beasts and then, as though shaken and aroused, it arose for the first time to a wisdom previously unknown to it."[20]

Berossus on the Evolution of Babylonian Culture

Another notable application of the same idea was the *Babyloniaca,* a work clearly written with these principles in mind. Berossus claimed to have reproduced a continuous and unbroken historical narrative from the beginning of civilization, undisrupted by natural catastrophes; care in preservation ensured this continuity.[21] But, conformably to the conventions of Hellenistic historiography, what had preceded the inception of civilization in Babylonia was set outside the scope of his narrative. It is true that in the first book of the *Babyloniaca* Berossus had included a cosmogony and brief history of primitive Babylonia. But the cosmogony was dehistoricized, here presented only as an allegory told to the early Babylonians by Oannes. And Berossus' description of the primitive Babylonians was a highly generalized one, not unlike Diodorus'. Berossus says only that they were a "great crowd, and they lived without laws (ἀτάκτως) just as wild animals."[22] When, however, Babylonian civilization arose, it was not the product of a long or incremental development. Instead, it was the outcome of one giant leap forward, that is, Oannes' revelations "how to found cities, establish temples, introduce laws and measure land."[23] For

---

[20] Orosius 1.3 (trans. Irving W. Raymond, *Seven Books of History against the Pagans* [New York, 1936]).

[21] According to Berossus, Cronus had in a dream revealed that on the "15th day of the month Diasios mankind would be destroyed by a flood. Therefore, he ordered Xisuthrus to bury the beginnings and the middles and the ends of all writings in Sippar, the City of the Sun" (Sync. 30.28–31.1; trans. Burstein, fr. C.2.1, 20).

[22] Trans. Burstein, fr. B.1.4, 13.

[23] *Chronica* 7.15–17; Sync. 29.13–15 (trans. Burstein, fr. B.1.5, 13–14). This is not to suggest that the *interpretatio Graeca* has completely eclipsed Berossus' Mesopotamian sources. As Komoróczy has shown, elements of Berossus' story of Oannes bear the imprint of Sumerian mythology (see his "Berosos and the Mesopotamian Literature," 142–51). But these parallels are often very attenuated; in many cases, Berossus' narrative can be far better explained by Hellenistic parallels. Thus, Komoróczy finds only faint resonances in the Sumerian sources with Oannes' revelations about "land-measuring" (Komoróczy, 147). But parallels from Greek sources are numerous; surveying means the establishment of cities and property, thereby marking man's transition to civilization. Josephus, in fact, does much the same kind of thing in his *Antiquities* 1.61–62. Josephus says Cain was the first to introduce surveying and boundaries, thereby bringing greed into the world. This was clearly a Hellenizing adaptation of Gen. 5:17, which credits Cain with building a city in the name of his son Enoch. For surveying and the marking off of boundaries as signalizing mankind's advance from primitivism, see Lovejoy and Boas, *Primitivism and Related Ideas in Antiquity,* 47–48, 257–58. For further discussion, see below, Chap. 5, p. 137.

Berossus, this pivotal moment in Babylonian history marked not only the boundaries between "primitive" and "civilized." It delimited as well the frontier between history and prehistory. Indeed, Berossus does not commence his actual chronology of events until Alorus, the first king of Chaldea, to the first year of whose reign he traces Oannes' revelations.

The value of the *Babyloniaca* in documenting the *gesta* of mankind in this very early period of world history assured the continued appeal of this work for the Christian chronographers. Granted, they could find a few passing references in Genesis to the early onset of civilization; Cain's building of a city in the name of his son Enoch (Gen. 4:17), and the discovery of metallurgy and musical instruments by his offspring (Gen. 4:21–22) were themes that Josephus and the chronographers elaborated on freely.[24] But Moses wrote about the social and cultural progress of the antediluvians, in the words of the seventeenth-century chronographer Wilhelm Lange, "breviter saltem et aliud agens." It was, Lange admits, possible to gain more secure knowledge of the period from the fragments of the *Babyloniaca* that had been preserved by Alexander Polyhistor and Eusebius. "On the basis of the archives of the Chaldeans, a race most zealous in recording events," he writes, "Berossus and Abydenus have written more diligently (than Moses) about the wisdom and the inventions of these men."[25]

Here, however, the value of the *Babyloniaca* was mitigated for reasons not unlike those created by the great duration of Berossus' antediluvian chronology—namely, Berossus' implausibility and the difficulty of squaring Genesis with the story of Oannes, a being, writes Syncellus, "who never existed, nor was ever seen by anybody, nor had any reality, just as there are neither 'whosits (σκίνδαψοι)' and 'thingamijigs (τραγέλαφοι)'."[26] Even the idea of antediluvian monarchy stirred controversy. Although Eusebius, like Josephus before him, had pointed to parallels be-

---

[24] Theophilus writes, for example, that the founding of the city of Enoch dispels the idea that cities were a later institution. "From that time on," he says, "there was made a beginning of cities, and this before the flood; not, as Homer says, 'Not yet had men a city built'" (*To Autolycus* 2.30).

[25] Wilhelm Lange, *De annis Christi libri duo* (Leiden, 1649), 2.252. The superiority of the benefactions of the Chaldean and Egyptian culture-heroes was something that pagan controversialists could also point to. In his treatise *Against the Galileans,* Julian seized on this as proof that the Jews and Christians had in their heritage no one who contributed anything considerable or of great value; but "the Egyptians . . . can boast that they possess many successors of Hermes . . . (and) the Chaldeans and Assyrians can boast of the successors of Oannes and Belos" (176AB).

[26] Sync. 32.13–14. Christian chronographers were not the only ones to lampoon Berossus' legend of Oannes; for the Egyptian Chaeremon's parody of Oannes, see above, Chap. 2, pp. 60–61.

tween the ten pre-flood Biblical patriarchs and Berossus' succession of ten Chaldean kings, the comparison had nothing to do with a supposed symmetry in the form of government described; it was rather based on a numerical correspondence and the obvious similarity between Noah and Xisuthrus. Indeed, Christian writers on antediluvian history, including Syncellus, quite often had concluded from Moses' silence on the issue that the form of government before the flood was not monarchy, but its supposed antecedent, hereditary patriarchy.[27] The magnitude of the discrepancy could hardly go unnoticed; "as for the beginning," writes the Armenian historian Moses of Chorene, "sometimes they [Berossus and his successors] tell the truth, sometimes they lie. For example, just as they call the first created not the first man, but [the first] king, so they give him a barbaric name, attributing to him 36,000 years; whereas in the number of the patriarchs and the mention of the Flood, they concur and agree with Moses."[28]

It may be said that a Christian chronicler seeking to harmonize Berossus with Genesis confronted a problem not unlike that which Hellenistic universal historians had faced in their initial confrontation with the older oriental histories. Greek historians recognized quite soon that the older oriental civilizations recorded a succession of human kings in a segment of their history that the Greeks considered "mythic"—the period of the gods. To overcome this asymmetry, they resorted to a well-known expedient—euhemerism. For it was Euhemerus who had supposedly discovered that the Greek gods were not gods at all, but simply primordial kings who were later divinized for their heroic deeds and benefactions.

A well-known example of the application of this technique, attested in several different forms, had cast Zeus and Cronus as mortal kings and contemporaries of Ninus' father Bel.[29] In this way, the chronological frontier of Greek history was made coterminous with a civilization widely assumed to be, as Drews has observed, "the pioneer of civilization in Asia."[30] The Christian chronographers of Alexandria were to follow the same approach, only for them the principal figures were not the Titans of

---

[27] In Josephus' *Antiquities,* for example, antediluvian rule was hereditary patriarchy, transmitted from father to son (1.83–88); see also the pseudepigraphic *Cave of Treasures:* "And Seth became the governor of the children of his people, and he ruled them in purity. . . . And Anosh (after Seth's death) rose up to minister before God in the cave of treasures. And he became the governor of the children of his people" (trans. Budge, 74,77).

[28] *History of the Armenians* 6 (trans. Thomson).

[29] See, for example, Diodorus (6.1.10), who attributes this to Euhemerus himself.

[30] Drews, "Assyria," 133.

Hesiod and the kings of Assyria; rather they were the antediluvian kings of Berossus' *Babyloniaca* and the sons of God of Genesis 6 and their off-spring, the Giants and Nephilim.

JEWISH AND CHRISTIAN EXEGESIS OF GENESIS 6

The antecedents for this euhemerizing interpretation of Genesis 6 appear already in early Hellenistic Jewish historiography. In the early second century B.C.E., an anonymous writer (identified by Polyhistor as Eupolemus) had traced the building of Babylon after the flood to the antediluvian Giants.[31] "The city of Babylon was first founded by those who were saved from the flood . . . they were the Giants, and built the tower renowned in history."[32]

(Ps-)Eupolemus' euhemeristic fusion of Genesis, Chaldean history, and Hesiod contained the seeds for a long subsequent tradition. Versions of the same legend appear in a wide range of texts, including Polyhistor's own rendition of the *Babyloniaca,* as it had been interpolated by a Jewish scribe.[33] Equally important, however, was (ps-)Eupolemus' tracing of the lineage of the post-flood founders of Babylon to Genesis 6.

The reasons for this identification of the founders of Babylon with the offspring of the "sons of God" and "daughters of men" are not difficult to ascertain. In Hellenistic world histories, Bel, the reputed founder of Babylon, was often said to have aided Cronus and the Titans in their war against the gods."[34] (Ps-)Eupolemus, in fact, identifies Bel with Cronus, as well as Nimrod, the founder of Babylon according to Genesis.[35] It would not have taken a great leap to have traced Nimrod, whom the Septuagint calls a γίγας, to the antediluvian Giants who survived the flood. Already implicit in this identification was the idea that the pre-flood Giants and sons of God of Genesis 6 were themselves to be understood euhemeristically—not as supernatural beings, but simply as an exalted race of men who were to establish a civilization and the first monarchy.

---

[31] Polyhistor's excerpt from (ps-)Eupolemus is preserved in Eusebius *PE* 9.17.1–9 (418c–419d). For text, translation and commentary, see most recently Holladay, *Fragments,* 157–87.

[32] In Eusebius *PE* 9.17.2 (418c).

[33] *Chronica* 12.10–15.

[34] For the fusion of the Babylonian Bel with the legend of the war between the Olympians and the Titans, see Thallus, *FrGH* 2B, 256 F 2; also Castor of Rhodes, *FrGH* 2B, 250 F 1. For discussion, see Drews, "Assyria," 133 (note 20).

[35] In other Christian sources Nimrod is identified with Ninus, thereby establishing him as the first king of the Assyrians; cf. the *Paschal Chronicle* 50.15–51.3 (quoting the Pseudo-Clementine *Recognitions* 4.29.)

The second stage in this evolution would occur not long afterwards. Although the legend of "fallen angels" exerted a great fascination in Judaism and Christianity, exegesis of Genesis 6 soon reflected a certain uneasiness about the plausibility of intercourse between angels and women. Already in the first century, Philo of Alexandria had tendered as one interpretation of the "sons of God" the view that they were "good and excellent men . . . while wicked and evil men [Moses calls] bodies."[36] And although Christian writers of the first and second centuries continued to cling to the older "supernaturalistic" understanding of Genesis 6, it soon gave way to a rationalistic interpretation of the sons of God as merely one of the antediluvian generations, the descendants of Seth.

A chronographer was, in fact, the first Christian writer to urge this interpretation. In an excerpt from his chronicle preserved by Syncellus, Julius Africanus observed that in the versions of the Greek Bible that he had consulted he found two conflicting Greek renderings of the Hebrew "benē elohim" at Genesis 6:2. "In certain copies (ἐν ἐνίοις ἀντιγράφοις)," he found the words οἱ υἱοὶ θεοῦ, whereas other versions preserved the reading ἄγγελοι τοῦ θεοῦ.[37] Africanus believed that the difference was more than a matter of words. If one preferred the reading ἄγγελοι τοῦ θεοῦ, then it would be necessary to conclude, he says, that non-corporeal beings descended to earth and taught mankind magic (μαγείας), sorcery (γοητείας), and the motion of astronomical bodies (τῶν μετεώρων), thereby inducing God to destroy the world in a flood.[38] If, on the other hand, one accepted the alternate reading (υἱοὶ τοῦ θεοῦ), this would refer to the descendants of Seth, whose illicit intercourse with the daughters of men (the Cainites) aroused God to take the punitive action which he did.[39]

[36] Philo *Questions and Answers on Genesis* 1.92 (trans. Ralph Marcus, LCL, Philo Supplement 1 [Cambridge, 1971]). But Philo does not rule out the identification of the "sons of God" as "incorporeal essences," who imitate the "forms of men and for immediate purposes, as in respect of knowing women for the sake of begetting Haiks" (trans. by Marcus; see also *de gigantibus* 2.6–11, 13.58–61). A similarly variegated picture is presented in the (ps-)Clementines. According to the *Recognitions* (1.29), the "sons of God" were "righteous men who had lived the life of angels (*qui angelorum vixerant vitam*), [and] being allured by the beauty of women fell into promiscuity and illicit connection with these." In the *Homilies*, however, incorporeal angels descended from heaven and metamorphosed themselves into various inanimate objects, finally changing themselves into the "nature of men (εἰς τὴν ἀνθρώπων φύσιν)" (*Homilies* 8.12–13 [ed. Rehm; GCS 42]); cf. also *Recognitions* 4.26 [ed. Rehm; GCS 51]). For the Rabbinic naturalistic interpretation of Genesis 6, see Philip S. Alexander, "The Targumim and Early Exegesis of 'Sons of God' in Gen. 6," *JJS* 23 (1972), 60–71.

[37] In Sync. 19.25–26.

[38] Ibid., 19.31–20.4.

[39] Ibid., 19.26–19.31. For discussion of the "Sethite" interpretation of Gen. 6, see especially A. F. J. Klijn, *Seth*, 41–80; also L. R. Wickham, "The Sons of God and the Daughters of

Although Africanus did not entirely rule out the older view that the sons of God of Genesis 6 were incorporeal, opposition to this interpretation increased steadily after him; by the fourth century, adherence to the belief that spiritual, incorporeal beings had once had intercourse with women was condemned as heresy. Thus, Augustine, while not rejecting out of hand the existence of corporeal angels, or the legends of "incubi" having intercourse with women, denies that the sons of God in Genesis 6 were angels of God "in the sense that they were not also human beings."[40]

At the same time that Christian commentators were rejecting the supernaturalistic interpretation of Genesis 6, they were developing techniques for explaining several features of the legend that seemed to stand in a way of a naturalistic understanding of it. The two biggest stumbling blocks were the fact that, regardless of the reading preferred, Genesis 6 referred to angels or sons of God, not of Seth. Moreover, the description of their offspring as "Giants (γίγαντες; Heb. nephilim)" clearly implied supernatural parentage.[41]

One way to overcome the first problem was to hold that the expression "sons of God" did not refer to physical incorporeality, but only to moral conduct. For this interpretation, Christian exegetes were able to draw on Jewish traditions that clearly distinguished the impious Cainite line from the righteous descendants of Seth. Josephus, for example, while falling short of the identification of the Sethites with the "sons of God," characterizes them as prosperous, wise and devoted to God.[42] It would not have taken a big step for Christian commentators to have equated these righteous descendants of Seth with the "sons of God" of Genesis 6: the Sethites were sons of God by "adoption."[43] The same principles could even be applied to the less popular designations "angels of God" and "Watchers."

Men: Genesis VI 2 in Early Christian Exegesis," *OS* 19 (1974), 135–47. The idea that Seth was the forefather of a line of mankind whose righteousness earned them the title "sons of God" seems to grow out of the earlier view that Seth was the first link in a chain of piety. Traces of this idea are already discernible in *Sirach* 49:16; *Jub.* 19:24; *1 Enoch* 85:8–9; Philo *The Posterity and Exile of Cain* 40, 43, 48, 172; and especially Josephus *Antiquities* 1.68–71, where the pious Sethites are set off against Cain and his progeny.

[40] Augustine *City of God* 15.23.

[41] Cf. Gen. 6:4. The belief that the birth of the Giants was proof of supernatural parentage was often attacked in Christian literature: cf. Augustine *City of God* 15.23; Philaster *On the Heresies* 108.1: "Alia est heresis quae de gigantibus adserit quod angeli miscuerint se cum feminis ante diluvium, et inde esse natas gigantas suspicantur" (ed. F. Heylen, CC Series Latina 9, 272 [Turnholt, 1957]). See also the Syriac *Cave of Treasures*: the Giants are not proof that angels had intercourse with human beings, "for it is not in the nature of beings of the spirit to beget" (trans. Budge [London, 1927], 102).

[42] Josephus *Ant.* 1.68–71.

[43] For the development of this interpretation in the 3rd and 4th centuries, see L. R. Wickham, "The Sons of God," 135–47.

Thus, the *Paschal Chronicle* (seventh century) states that because of their righteousness the Sethites became "like angels of God."[44] And a later anonymous Syriac chronicle holds that the title of "Watchers" was applied to the Sethites because of their vigilance in safeguarding chastity.[45]

From about the fifth century, a genealogical element was introduced into the discussion of Genesis 6. While not entirely precluding the former belief that the Sethites were sons of God by adoption, Christian commentators began to suggest that the term "sons of god" was not to be taken literally; rather it referred only to the fact that the Sethites were descended from a man whose beauty and stature earned him the title of "god." Because of the glory which shone in Seth's face, says Anastasius Sinaita (seventh century c.e.), the people of his time called him "god," for which reason his descendants were called sons of the god Seth.[46] This interpretation had the added advantage of explaining why Giants were born out of the intercourse of the Cainites and Sethites; their size simply reflected the great beauty and god-like stature which they had inherited from their forefathers, Seth and Enosh in particular.[47]

---

[44] *Chronicon paschale*, 38.11–18 (ed. Dindorf, CSHB [Bonn, 1832]).

[45] *Chronicon anonymum ad annum Christi 1234 pertinens*, 34; Latin trans. by Chabot in CSCO 109, 24.8–9.

[46] Anastasius Sinaita (7th cent.), *Viae Dux* 13.8.55–74 (ed. K.-H. Uthemann, CC Series Graeca 8 [Turnholt, 1981]):

> In the beginning when God created Adam after his image and likeness, he breathed into his face grace and illumination (ἔλλαμψιν) and a ray of the Holy Spirit. But when through disobedience and sin the grace was extinguished from his face . . .[Adam] begat a son in his likeness and image, that is the image and brilliance which Adam had in the beginning, as he was created by God . . . and he called his name Seth, that is resurrection, because in his face he saw renewed in him the resurrection of the original and wonderful form and the grace and brilliance of the Holy Spirit. And all those living at that time, when they saw the face of Seth, immediately called him "god"; for this reason, Scripture says about his sons, 'The sons of God,' that is, the sons of Seth, 'seeing the daughters of men'. . . ." (for the interpretation of the name Seth as "resurrection," see also George Cedrenus, 1. 16.6–7; Augustine *City of God* 15.18).

It is difficult to determine the extent to which the introduction of a genealogical element into the interpretation of Gen. 6:2 precluded the idea that the Sethites were sons of God by "grace." That is, the view that the sons of God were sons of the god Seth carries an entirely different sense than the idea that they received this name because of righteousness. Wickham ("The Sons of God," 147) has already commented on the problem, and it will suffice here to say only that writers such as Cyril of Alexandria (*Glaphyra* 2.23, 29 [PG 69. 47AB, 53CD]) and John Chrysostom (*In Psalmum* 49 [PG 55. 241]) do not appear to draw a clear distinction between the two interpretations.

[47] See, for example, Sync. 15.19–20 (quoting from Ephrem): "His (Cain's) offspring were low to the ground (χθαμαλοί) in stature, on account of the curse of Cain. But the offspring of Seth were Giants (γίγαντες) and like angels of God, [dwelling] in the elevated region." In some cases, the expression "sons of God" was taken to refer to the sons of Seth and Enosh, both of whom could be identified as gods. The source of this interpretation apparently arises

The "Sons of God" and the Primordial
Kings of Babylonia

This naturalistic "Sethite" interpretation of the fall of the "sons of God" found a variety of applications in Christian exegesis of Genesis. Anti-Manichean polemicists, such as Ephrem Syrus, emphatically supported this interpretation in order to rebut the Manichean cosmology, of which the supernaturalist interpretation of Genesis 6 formed a central part.[48] Byzantine chronographers, who are virtually unanimous in endorsing this interpretation, had their own reasons for seizing upon it. When, for example, Africanus first suggested the identification, it was ostensibly to avoid what would, in Africanus' opinion, invite an unacceptable view of divine justice: why would God have destroyed the whole world for the failings of a few rebellious angels?[49] Syncellus himself had urged this naturalistic interpretation upon his readers in order to allay doubts about the historical plausibility of Genesis 6, an event, he says, that "some people dispute (τινες ἀντιλέγουσι)."[50] But for Syncellus' Alexandrian predecessors, the principal application of this interpretation lay in its demonstrating the existence of a kingdom and a developed civilization even before the flood. The "sons of God" were none other than the first kings of Chaldea.

Probably the best witness to their reconstruction of archaic society is

---

from an ambiguity in the Septuagint text of Gen. 4:26; it reads "καὶ τῷ Σὴθ ἐγένετο υἱός, ἐπωνόμασεν δὲ τὸ ὄνομα αὐτοῦ Ἐνώς. οὗτος ἤλπισεν ἐπικαλεῖσθαι τὸ ὄνομα κυρίου τοῦ θεοῦ" (ed. J. W. Wevers [Göttingen, 1974]). The ambiguity lies in the meaning of the word ἐπικαλεῖσθαι, which could be translated in either the middle or passive voice (i.e., "hoped to be called the name of the Lord God"). If the latter intepretation were chosen, then Gen. 4:26 could be taken to show that Enosh, like his father Seth, was a "god" and that their descendants were sons of the "gods Seth and Enosh." To support this interpretation, Christian exegetes sometimes turned to Aquila's translation of the Hebrew "benē elohim" as υἱοὶ τῶν θεῶν; cf. Cyril of Alexandria Glaphyra 2.29 (PG 69. 53CD); Suidas (s.v. Σήθ). Augustine also knows Aquila's translation (City of God 15.23), accepting the possibility that the Hebrew is "translatable either as sons of God or as sons of gods"; "either expression is correct," he says, and one is therefore justified in regarding them as sons of God by grace, or sons of gods by being descended from god-like men. For Christian interpretations of Gen. 4:26 in connection with Gen. 6, see Procopius of Gaza Comm. in Gen 6 (PG 87.1. 265–67); Theodoret Quaest. in Gen. 6 47.60 (PG 80. 148D). For detailed discussion, see Steven D. Fraade, Enosh and his Generation, SBLMS 30 (Chico, 1984), 47–107.

[48] For discussion, see Tryggve Kronholm, Motifs from Genesis 1–11 in the Genuine Hymns of Ephrem the Syrian, ConBibOT 11 (Lund, 1978), 166–67.

[49] See Wickham, "The Sons of God," 144–45. Wickham also suggests that the Sethite interpretation of Gen. 6 may have figured in 4th-century christological discussions about the existence of sons of God by grace in Old Testament times (Wickham, "Sons of God," 147).

[50] Sync. 11.11–12.

the twelfth-century chronicle of Michael Syrus, a chronicler heavily indebted to Annianus' treatment of archaic history.[51] Following him, Michael describes the first 1,058 years of world history as "years without a king." "During this time," he writes, "there did not exist a king, and one cannot speak of royalty, since Adam, the first man and father of the human race, created in the image of God, governed all those who were born from him and their children."[52] During the rule of Seth, however, his offspring divided into two lines: 1) those who married and lived "in a lower region"; and 2) their brethren who "pursued the prosperous life of Paradise, and they longed to please God by their purity; they ascended to Mt. Hermon and they dwelt there in holy works, avoiding marriage. That is why they were called 'benē elohim' and angels."[53] They continued to live chaste lives until the fortieth year of Jared:

> In that year, the "benē elohim" came down from the Mountain Hermon, being in number 200. For seeing that they had not returned to Paradise, they were discouraged, and so abandoned their angelic way of life, and they were smitten ⟨with a desire for marriage⟩. And they set up a king for themselves, whose name was Semiazos. Concerning these Annianus relates that they came down from the Mountain Hermon to their brethren, the children of Seth and Enosh, but they were unwilling to give them any wives, on the grounds that they had transgressed their promise. And so they went to the children of Cain, and took wives; and they gave birth to great Giants, that is plunderers, mighty and renowned assassins, and audacious bandits.[54]

When the "sons of God" descended from the top of Mt. Hermon and had intercourse with the Cainite women they established a kingdom, ruled over by the chief Watcher Semiazos. "Having broken their promise, they descended and mixed with the daughters of Cain; they committed acts of impiety. They established an empire of which the first king was Semiazos;

---

[51] Syriac text and translation of Michael's chronicle by I.-B. Chabot, *Chronique de Michel le Syrien, Patriarche jacobite d'Antioche 1166–1199*, 3 vols. (Paris, 1899–1924; reprinted in 4 vols., Brussels, 1963). Unless otherwise specified, translations are based on Chabot's French translation. All references are to the reprint. In the preface of his chronicle, Michael names "Annianus the monk of Alexandria" as an authority for the period from Adam to Constantine (trans. Chabot, 2). For Michael's sources, see Chabot's introduction, xxiv–xxxvii.

[52] Ibid., 1.3 (trans. Chabot, 4).

[53] Ibid., 1.3 (trans. Chabot, 4).

[54] Ibid., 1.3. Translation of Syriac text is by Sebastian Brock, "A Fragment of Enoch in Syriac," *JTS* 19 (1968), 627.

this empire lasted up to the flood, in which they all perished."[55] Not long after the fall of the Watchers, the remaining Sethites began to imitate the corrupt kingdom of their brethren. "They also chose for themselves a first king Alorus, in imitation of Semiazos. From that time on, there were ten kingdoms."[56]

For the period before the fall of the sons of God, Michael's description of their polity adheres closely to other pseudepigraphic Christian legends, many of monastic provenience, narrating the same event. In the Syriac *Cave of Treasures*, for example, the Sethites, before their fall, are also said to have lived sexually abstinent lives under patriarchal rule on a mountain near Paradise. What distinguishes Michael's narrative from this and other legends based on Genesis 6 is the author's deliberate blending of motifs from other sources. The reference to the Chaldean empire from Alorus to Xisuthrus obviously owes its origin to Berossus; Michael's enumeration of these ten kings is precisely the same list of Chaldean antediluvian kings that survives from Syncellus' and Eusebius' extracts from the *Babyloniaca*. Equally clear is the intrusion of themes from *1 Enoch*, from which Michael quotes directly.[57] According to the *Cave of Treasures*, before their fall the sons of God, numbering 100, lived on the outskirts of Paradise on a mountain called the "Mountain of Victories." Michael's account, while similar, bears the unmistakable imprint of *The Book of the Watchers;* the sons of God, he says, lived on Mt. Hermon, were ruled by Semiazos, and numbered 200 in all.

As Gelzer recognized years ago, Michael's segmentation of antediluvian history into kingless and regnal years is taken from his Alexandrian source, Annianus.[58] In describing the succession of Chaldean kings from Alorus to Xisuthrus, Michael asserts that the total length of their rule came to approximately 1,183½ years. "1,183 years and 203 days," he says, "added to the 1,058 years during which there did not exist a king, and during which Adam and Seth governed, complete the interval of time which elapsed from Adam up to the flood and form a total of 2,242 years, according to Scripture."[59] This is precisely how Syncellus characterizes the method of Panodorus and Annianus. According to them, 1,183½ years added to the

[55] Ibid., 1.8 (trans. Chabot, 13).
[56] Ibid., 1.4 (trans. Chabot, 5).
[57] For discussion of Michael's excerpt from *1 Enoch*, see Brock, "A Fragment of Enoch," 626–31.
[58] See Gelzer, "Die vorflutigen Chaldäerfürsten des Annianos," *BZ* 3 (1894), 391–93.
[59] Michael, 1.4 (trans. Chabot, 8).

1,058 kingless (ἀβασίλευτοι) years "complete a period of 2,242 years from Adam up to the flood in accordance with our Scripture."[60] Gelzer was also able to recognize the hand of the Alexandrian chronographers in Michael's appeal to *1 Enoch*, from which he even a cites a small passage. In Gelzer's view, Annianus merged the *Book of the Watchers* with Sethite traditions from another source, which he identified as the *Life of Adam*, a work mentioned by Syncellus and evidently bearing some features in common with the *Cave of Treasures*.[61]

Annianus' blending of these sources invited some sharp criticisms from later commentators. Syncellus failed to see how his Alexandrian predecessors could have appealed to the *Babyloniaca* when Genesis says nothing about the existence of kingdoms before the flood.[62] More modern commentators wondered about the mixing of the two conflicting exegeses of Genesis 6. Of all the sources that patristic writers found to contradict the Sethite interpretation of Genesis 6, *1 Enoch* was the one normally singled out for special censure.[63] Yet Annianus and his Syriac successors seem unaware of, or at least untroubled by, any conflict. "L'auteur cite, confusément," observes Chabot of Michael, "les deux légendes, d'après l'une, les Benê Elohim étaient des descendants de Seth, d'après l'autre, des anges."[64]

What lies beneath this seemingly random merging of sources is a coherent attempt to reconstruct, on the basis of the available sources, a picture of antediluvian civilization that will conform both to the prevailing norms of Christian exegesis of Genesis and Hellenistic historiography. By tracing the Watchers to one of the antediluvian lines, Michael could show that the corruption that afflicted the earth encompassed both antediluvian families. From the standpoint of Christian exegesis, this demythologizing interpre-

---

[60] Basing himself only on the rather corrupt Armenian recensions of Michael for the reigns of the individual Chaldean kings, Gelzer attempted to restore what he believed were the original "reduced" reigns of the ten antediluvian Chaldean kings, as Michael knew them from Annianus. His restorations have been almost entirely confirmed by Chabot's publication of the textually superior Syriac version; cf. Gelzer, "Die vorflutigen Chaldäerfürsten," 393. Gelzer's reconstructions agree with the Syriac text for the reigns of all but one of the pre-flood Chaldean kings—Amemsinus; see also *SJA*, 2. 440–41.

[61] *SJA*, 2. 264–73; 440–41.

[62] See, for example, Sync. 14.15–17 (for discussion, see below, Chap. 6, pp. 140–41).

[63] See, for example, Augustine (*City of God* 15.23), who, while attacking the "angelic" interpretation of Gen. 6 on the grounds that such a mixing of opposites is unthinkable, also calls into doubt the *Book of Enoch* for espousing such a view. When Jerome denounces as "Manichean" the idea that spirits had descended into bodily form in order to mingle with women, he too questions a "certain apocryphal book (*quendam librum apocryphum*)," which the Manichees use, he says, to confirm the heretical belief that "souls desired human bodies to be united in pleasure" (*Homily on Psalm 132* [CC 78, Series Latina, 280.137–281.150]).

[64] See Chabot's note to his French translation, 11 (note 3).

tation of the *Book of the Watchers* was intended to forestall the theological objections typically made against that work, namely, that the *Book of the Watchers* presupposed an impossible union of spirit and flesh, and that it attributed God's destruction of the entire world to the rebellion of only 200 angels.

Michael's characterization of the material advances and moral degeneration of antediluvian society conforms as well to Hellenistic views of primitive social development. During the first 1,058 years Adam and Seth "ruled over the people" as family governors, by which Michael intends to distinguish their rule from formal kingship, the second stage in human development. In this reconstruction of the primitive polity of the Sethites we may assume that Michael was following a source related to the *Cave of Treasures*. The formation of kingdoms marks an end to the pure and prosperous state in which the Sethites lived, introducing corruption on earth. In its detailed account of a succession of pre-flood kings, the *Babyloniaca* offered the best evidence for the existence of a developed political constitution before the flood. And with his euhemeristic intepretation of Genesis 6, Michael, following the Alexandrian chronographers, has integrated Berossus' account securely into the Genesis narrative.

In his treatment of pre-flood history, Berossus had also described the onset of culture, but his tracing of its origins to revelations from the sea monster Oannes was impossible to assimilate to Genesis. A far more amenable source for this purpose was the *Book of the Watchers*. The *Book of the Watchers* describes what may be broadly construed as the beginning of τέχναι. To be sure, the author(s) of that work, in tracing these arts and sciences to a betrayal of heavenly secrets by fallen angels, wanted readers to recognize in these revelations the beginning of a depravity that led ultimately to the flood.[65] But Michael's (that is, Annianus') adaptation has fit the fall of the Watchers into a different interpretive framework. By introducing monarchy and civilization into the world, the Watchers inaugurate a new era in human history. The complex and evolved societies that they created as a result should, Michael says, challenge the prevailing view that in this remote period of world history mankind, as yet unevolved culturally and politically, had produced nothing of note. He writes,

> From the beginning of the life of Adam up to the deluge which occurred at the time of Noah, the sum of the years is 2,242, during

---

[65] See most recently Ryszard Rubinkiewicz, *Die Eschatologie von Hen 9–11 und das Neue Testament*, Oesterreichische Biblische Studien 6 (Klosterneuburg, 1984), 60–68; see also Rüdiger Bartelmus, *Heroentum in Israel und seiner Umwelt*, AThANT 65 (Zurich, 1979), 160–66.

which time there were ten patriarchs, whose names are recorded. We find as well the names of 10 kings who had reigned one after the other. We find likewise the mention of three cities. Those who invented the arts, astrology, fabrication of arms, and instruments of combat, the cithar and musical instruments, are also briefly mentioned in a short expression. It is easy, for men of wisdom, to *comprehend that events very considerable and very important, frequent and numerous, must have transpired during this long period of time. They have not been mentioned in Scripture, doubtless because these things were not useful for the listeners.* For this purpose, the Holy Spirit did not want them to be recorded.[66]

Κλίματα in the Antediluvian Cosmography of Annianus

One final feature of Annianus' reconstruction of primitive societies is his attempt to rationalize the geography of Genesis and *1 Enoch*. Although the first several chapters of Genesis reveal an interest in the geography of Paradise and its environs, the few geographical references found there are far from complete. The *Book of the Watchers* and the *Astronomical Book* of the Enoch corpus, on the other hand, have elaborate cosmographies, perhaps adapted from Babylonian sources; but the accounts of Enoch's journeys to the various corners of the earth are described in mainly mythic terms, in the words of Neugebauer "too mythological to allow accurate identifications."[67] Attempts to give more specificity to the cosmography of *1 Enoch* are already found in the *Astronomical Book* (= *1 En.* 77:3), where a later redactor has evidently inserted some fairly detailed information about the location of Paradise.[68] From Michael's account, we can suppose that Annianus' rationalizing of the mythology of Genesis 6 and *1 Enoch* extended as well to matter of cosmography. Specifically, this involved the use of the Greek theory of "climate" zones. Although the origins of κλίματα are uncertain and the conventions for determining them were not uniform, the term as it was used by ancient geographers normally referred to seven latitudinal zones, limited only to the οἰκουμένη, and calculated

---

[66] Michael, 1.7 (trans. Chabot, 11).

[67] Otto Neugebauer, "The 'Astronomical' Chapters," 27; for the Babylonian origin of the geography of *1 Enoch*, see in particular, P. Grelot, "La géographie mythique d'Hénoch et ses sources orientales," *RB* 65 (1958), 33–69; Milik, *The Books of Enoch*, 15–18, 33–41.

[68] See Milik, *The Books of Enoch*, 16. The mythical geography of *1 Enoch* contrasts with the more realistic geography of *Jubilees*, whose exposition of the table of nations seems to presuppose an actual world map; for discussion, see Philip S. Alexander, "Notes on the 'Imago Mundi' of the Book of Jubilees," *JJS* 33 (1982), 197–213.

by maximum hours of sunshine.[69] Claudius Ptolemy used such climate zones in his *Geography,* and it is not surprising, therefore, to find Christian chronographers of Alexandrian provenience employing them as well.

One of the principal applications of κλίματα by the chronographers was in the account of the διαμερισμός, the distribution of the world's races after Noah, recounted in Genesis 10. In, for example, the *Paschal Chronicle,* there appear tables, presumably of Alexandrian origin, describing the locations of the πόλεις ἐπίσημοι after the division of the world, devised according to Ptolemy's theory of κλίματα.[70] Agapius, a tenth-century Arabic-speaking Christian chronographer of Alexandria, would later present, in a long digression on the division of the world among Noah's sons, a fairly elaborate anthropology based on a theory of the seven κλίματα, the source of which he identifies as Ptolemy and Eratosthenes.[71] Of the third climate (which, he says, includes Alexandria) he writes, for example, that its inhabitants are interested in matters of the physical and natural world: "they are zealous in their work; they study the 'belles lettres,' and sciences with more zeal than the inhabitants of the first climate and those of the second, because this κλίμα is fairer than the preceding two." The inhabitants of the fourth κλίμα, which includes the cities of Harran, Edessa, and Nisibis, are, he says, the most culturally advanced of all. Because of the moderate temperatures in this region, the inhabitants are scholars, philosophers, learned men, astronomers, physicians, and writers, whose research extends to the ten sciences, among them astronomy, astrology, geometry, arithmetic, music, medicine, alchemy, mechanics, and the "categories."[72]

Understandably, Christian universal chronographers were similarly motivated to furnish as much geographic specificity as was possible for the primordial generations. In various Christian chronicles and apocryphal legends of the dwelling places of primordial generations, it was widely believed that the Sethites, before their fall, inhabited a high mountainous region, the Cainites a low land. Syncellus states, for example that Cain, "separated from Seth at Adam's command," lived with his offspring in the low land that quakes. "Seth's offspring, called by some the sons of God and Watchers, lived in the more elevated land of Eden, near Paradise. . . .

---

[69] For discussion, see in particular E. Honigmann, *Die sieben Klimata and die* ΠΟΛΕΙΣ ΕΠΙΣΗΜΟΙ (Heidelberg, 1929).

[70] 1. 62.6–64.8 (ed. Dindorf). For discussion, see Honigmann, *Die sieben Klimata,* 61–72; A. von Gutschmid, "Zur Kritik des Διαμερισμὸς τῆς γῆς," *Kleine Schriften* 5, ed. Franz Rühl (Leipzig, 1894), 263–73.

[71] *Kitab al-ʿUnvan* (ed. and trans. A. Vasiliev), 604–17, esp. 605.

[72] Ibid., 611–13 (ed. Vasiliev).

At Adam's behest, they (the Sethites) inhabited the more elevated land of Eden, opposite Paradise, living as angels do, until the 1,000th year of the world."[73] Gelzer believed, not unreasonably, that Syncellus knew this account from one of the apocryphal Adam books; similar accounts are, to be sure, found in Syriac Christian apocrypha.[74] In the Syriac *Cave of Treasures,* for example, the Sethites are said to inhabit the skirts of a mountain, to the top of which they would ascend each morning to worship and glorify God.[75] Paradise is described as being located somewhere nearby. Subsequently, the mountain is identified as the "Mountain of Victories" where only three patriarchs, Methuselah, Lamech, and Noah remained after the other descendants went over to the Sethite camp. A "Mountain of Victories" is also found in the *Chronicle* of (ps-)Dionysus.[76] According to it, the mountain, at the top of which was situated the "Cave of Treasures," was located in the remote Orient, to the east of the region of Sir, which is also described as a mountain or a region.[77]

Many of the same elements are found in Michael's Annianus-based account of the dwelling places of the antediluvian generations. What is distinctive to it, however, is the influence of both the Enochic *Book of the Watchers* and the theory of κλίματα. Both Michael and, following him, Bar Hebraeus refer to the elevated region as Mt. Hermon, here reflecting the influence of *1 Enoch*.[78] But Michael adds to this cosmography several further details about the location of the antediluvian generations. After the "sons of God" descended from Mt. Hermon, the remaining Sethites, "who lived to the North, in the *third climate, which is called the 'lower region',*" followed the example of their straying brethren.[79] A similar description appears in an anonymous Greek chronicle, also dependent on Annianus. In that work, the author states that the "descendants of Seth, the

[73] Sync. 9.15–18; 9.27–30.

[74] *SJA*, 2. 265.

[75] *Cave of Treasures,* 72–75 (trans. Budge). Cf. *SJA*, 2. 267–72.

[76] For "Mountain of Victories" as the dwelling place of the antediluvian Sethites, see *Cave of Treasures,* 96 (trans. Budge); *Chronicle of (ps-)Dionysus* 59 (ed. I.-B. Chabot, CSCO 91, Scriptores Syri 43); Latin trans. by Chabot [CSCO 121, Scriptores Syri 66] 46.28–31). See also *Opus Imperfectum in Matthaeum* 2 (PG 56. 637).

[77] The land of Sir is "the most remote part of all the Orient in the land inhabited by men, opposite the great Ocean, the great sea which is around the earth to the East of the Land of Nod" (trans. Chabot, 45.32–35). On the location of Sir, see G. J. Reinink, "Das Land 'Seiris'," 72–85.

[78] According to Bar Hebraeus, "In the time of Seth, when his sons remembered the blessed life in Paradise, they went up into the mountain of Hermon, and there they led a chaste and holy life" (trans. Budge, 3).

[79] Michael, 1.4 (trans. Chabot, 5).

Chaldeans, in the year 1058, in the *northern klima* (ἐν τῷ βορείῳ κλίματι), *the so-called 'lower region'* (τῇ καλουμένῃ κάτω χώρᾳ), established for themselves a Chaldean kingdom from Babylon." Gelzer believed that the reference here to the so-called lower region where the antediluvian kingdom of the Chaldeans was established, contrasts with the ὑψηλὴ χώρα in which the corrupted Sethites lived.[80] But the term is not meant in the modern geographical sense of a lower altitude. The "lower region" refers instead to the east-west band that Alexandrian geographers had determined ran through lower Egypt, lower Babylonia, and, by extension, Paradise.[81] We have here one more example of the attempt by Christian chronographers of Alexandria to rationalize the mythical geography of Paradise and its environs according to the contemporary standards of Alexandrian science.

EUHEMERISTIC INTERPRETATIONS OF GENESIS 6 AFTER ANNIANUS

What we have been describing thus far is a process that corresponds closely to attempts by the Greek historians of the early Hellenistic period to rationalize Hesiod. From the third century B.C.E., chronographers and universal historians interpreted the stories of Zeus and the Titans euhemeristically as referring only to mighty kings and heroes of old, believed by other men to be gods because of their benefactions to mankind. Once understood in this way, the dates of these ancient notables were synchronized and sometimes even identified with oriental kings. In Annianus' interpretation of Genesis 6, Berossus, and *1 Enoch,* the same thing has happened. The "sons of God" of Genesis 6 are first understood naturalistically as only a distinguished class of antediluvians, venerated as gods because of the wisdom and stature that they had inherited from Seth and the revelations that they had imparted to mankind. The beginning of their kingdom is then synchronized with the onset of Babylonian civilization, with whose kings the Sethites are identified. Annianus' fusion of sources is not simply casual eclecticism, but represents instead a characteristic interest of Hellen-

[80] *SJA,* 2. 199 (note 2).
[81] The same designation is also reflected in Latin writers. Isidore of Seville (3.42.4) refers to "tertius Catachoras (id est Africa)." As Honigmann points out, "die Glosse zu Catochoras ... ist natürlich unsinnig, da vielmehr Unterägypten gemeint ist"; cf. *Die sieben Klimata,* 54 (note 3). Pliny (*NH* 6.39.212) places Alexandria in "Aegypti inferiora quae Chora vocatur." It is less clear why Michael refers to Chaldea as "the northern κλίμα"; possibly this is a result of a transference from "northern Egypt." I owe this information to personal correspondence with Profs. Otto Neugebauer and O. A. W. Dilke.

istic historiography in the culture-hero, the beginnings of civilization and political organization, and in this case the onset of corruption. Genesis' acknowledged insufficiencies here furnish the warrant for the use and domestication of other sources.

More abbreviated forms of Annianus' reconstruction of primordial civilization appear in several later chronicles. The Syriac chronicler Bar Hebraeus would in his chronicle preserve a version of the same legend, mediated to him from Annianus through Michael.[82] Another Syriac work, the anonymous chronicle *ad annum Christi 1234*, also gives a condensed form of the same legend. But the version that this latter chronicler knows is very secondary; he names as its source only "some of the elders," and does not include in his account any reference to Berossus' succession of antediluvian kings.[83] There is also a fragment from an anonymous Byzantine Greek chronicle that narrates the fall of the sons of God in much the same way as Michael does, while at the same time omitting any reference to *1 Enoch*:

> Men who are well known for their learning, Alexander Polyhistor, Berossus, Abydenus, and Apollodorus, record the first kingdom of the Chaldeans; they write that there were at first 1,058 years without a king (ἀβασίλευτα ἔτη). For they say that Adam the first man ruled as a governor (ἡγήσασθαι) for the period of his life and that after this Seth his son ruled 930 years, so that there are in all 1,058 without a king, during which time an empire (βασίλειον) was not yet referred to by name in Scripture. In the 1,058th year, first in the northern latitude, in the so-called lower region, the descendants of Seth, the Chaldeans, established for themselves a Chaldean kingdom from Babylon.[84]

Syncellus himself, while rejecting any attempt to trace the origins of Babylonian or Egyptian kingdoms before the time of Nimrod (in Babylon) and Mestrem/Menes in Egypt, had preserved enough material from his Alexandrian authorities to enable European chronographers after Sca-

---

[82] Text and English translation of Bar Hebraeus by E. A. W. Budge, 2 vols. (London, 1932) 3.

[83] Latin trans. of text in CSCO 109 (Scriptores Syri 56), 25.32–26.7.

[84] This anonymous Greek chronicle was edited by A. Mai (*Scriptorum veterum nova collectio,* 10 vols. [Rome, 1825–31], 1.2, 40). It is perhaps significant that although this fragment traces the first Chaldean king to the Sethite line and dates the establishment of their kingdom to the year 1058 (pace Michael), there is no reference to the fall of the Watchers or other legends from *1 Enoch*. It is conceivable that this particular chronicler elected to suppress material from *1 Enoch,* owing to its questionable status.

liger to adopt the whole scheme. Learned discussions in the seventeenth century about the origins of culture sometimes appealed to the division between kingless and regnal years as proof that antediluvian society was sufficiently evolved to pass a record of events on to posterity. Along with the other sources of primordial origin, writes the German philologist D. G. Morhof in the early eighteenth century, Berossus' account of antediluvian kingdoms proves that before the flood "there was some method for conserving the memory of events. . . . *And that whole antediluvian period is divided into a period without kings and a period of kings* (εἰς χρόνον ἀβασίλευτον καὶ εἰς χρόνον βασιλέων), that is, that time in which there were no kings, when rule had as yet remained among families, and that time in which there was monarchy. . . . It is therefore not likely that through such a period of time and duration of years, men were without memory of deeds."[85]

It is in the nature of euhemeristic treatments of mythic history that as they are transplanted from one culture to another they tend to assimilate local traditions. The same process is clearly documentable here as well. Since Syncellus says that Panodorus, Annianus' elder colleague and an aficionado of Egyptian antiquities, had traced the beginning of Egyptian civilization to the same year as the onset of the Chaldean kingdom, we must assume that the reigns of Manetho's primordial Egyptian gods and demigods also figured somehow in his reconstruction.[86] Some of the most interesting and unexplored subsequent developments of Annianus' interpretation of Genesis 6 occur in the elaborations of the tradition in Islamic Iran, probably through the mediation of Syriac Christian chronographers. Here we need only comment on one of these later witnesses. In Guzgani's *Tabaqat-i Nasiri*, the author states that during the time of Jared the children of Cain and the Watchers "began to use violence and tyranny and they opened their hands for oppression and corruption, and they appointed for themselves a man from their own people, and that one was Semyaza. . . . But the children of Seth . . . and those who were obedient to him assembled themselves and chose the kings of the Chaldeans. . . . And the first of the king reformers who was chosen to combat the tyrants took the name of 'Ailurus in Greek, and *the name (Alorus) signifies that*

[85] D. G. Morhof, *Polyhistor Literarius philosophicus et practicus* (Lübeck, 1714), 1.6.16. Among the other sources that Morhof adduces as evidence for the same thing are the *Book of Enoch* and the antediluvian stelae of Seth.

[86] Since one of the Sethite lines founded the kingdom of the Chaldeans, Gelzer (*SJA*, 2. 200) suggested that the rival kingdom of the Watchers and Cainites was identified by Panodorus as the Egyptian gods and demigods.

which the non-Arabs and the Persians name Gayumart."[87] To Annianus' euhemerizing interpretation of Berossus, *1 Enoch,* and Genesis 6, the author
has introduced an additional element, namely, the native Persian legend of
Gayomart, a figure conceived of in Persian mythology not only as the
primal man, but as the first world ruler as well.[88]

Like their Syriac counterparts, the Byzantine chronographers contributed their own adaptations. One notable variant seeks to identify the first
kings of Chaldea, not with the Watchers, but with their offspring, the
Giants and Nephilim. The earliest attestation for this is the seventh-
century *Paschal Chronicle.* The Sethites, the author says here:

> begat children, of very great stature. Hear what Genesis says, "The
> Giants were on the earth in those days. For when the sons of God
> were going into the daughters of men, and they bore children for
> themselves, these were the Giants of old, men of renown." . . . And
> when these angels were called by some Gods, and worshipped, Alorus
> was the first to rule among the Chaldeans, and after him Alaparus,
> and the remaining rulers of them. And Scripture hints at them, when
> it says, "these were the Giants of old, men of renown." And this is
> what Berossus and his successors, those who described their deeds,
> have taught.[89]

The tradition evidently reached the *Paschal Chronicle* in a garbled form,
since the author does not appear to make a sharp differentiation between
the Giants and their progenitors. What is clear is that the identification of
the Giants, not the Watchers, with Alorus and his successors differs from
Annianus', at least as it can be inferred from the Syriac witnesses.[90] Although the reasons behind this are obscure, the association seems to have
evolved from the earlier tradition that the first kings of Babylon after the
flood were descendants of the pre-flood Giants. Evidently in order to improve the symmetry between the post-flood kings of Chaldea and the pre-
flood rulers, chroniclers had determined that it was the Giants, not their
progenitors, who had ruled in Chaldea before the flood. Syncellus himself
seems to know the tradition, for in several places he suggests that the

---

[87] French translation of text in Sven S. Hartman, *Gayōmart* (Uppsala, 1953), 151–56.
[88] For Gayomart as the first world king, see Arthur Christensen, *Les Kayanides,* Det Kgl.
Danske Videnskabernes Selskab, Historisk-filologiske Meddelelser 19.2 (Copenhagen, 1931),
42. According to Hartman, the same conflation of sources appears in Biruni's *Al-Qanun al-
masʿudi;* cf. *Gayōmart,* 151 (note 3).
[89] I. 38.21–39.13 (ed. Dindorf).
[90] Cf. Gelzer *SJA,* 2. 152.

Giants were believed to be antediluvian despots, and that Nimrod, the giant and post-flood founder of Babylon, was their heir.[91] European chronographers, who knew both the *Paschal Chronicle* and Syncellus through Scaliger's publications of them, gravitated to the same conclusion. "There are learned men . . . ," writes the German theologian Johann Heidegger in his *Historia Patriarchum* (seventeenth century), "for whom the ten kings of the Chaldeans, whose names are described in the fragments of Abydenus and Berossus in Eusebius, are thought to be these same renowned Nephilim. That opinion was once accepted by some, as the *Paschal Chronicle* states. . . . The period of their rule according to Berossus and Abydenus makes 120 sars, that is 1,180 years according to some. The remaining period of time, which preceded this, they make out to be kingless."[92]

Probably one of the most palpable illustrations of the way in which Annianus' theory of antediluvian political evolution was reshaped for varying purposes is the introduction of his reconstruction in discussions of the legitimacy and origins of monarchy. When Scaliger made Syncellus and the *Paschal Chronicle* available in Europe, chronographers and world historians were embroiled in a controversy about the origins of monarchy, particularly whether it could be traced back to Adam or arose only later in the course of political development.[93] From his own investigations, Sca-

[91] See, for example, 14.15–21, where Syncellus, while denying that kingdoms existed before the flood, asserts that after the rule of Adam, Seth, and Enosh, the Giants "ruled over weaker men." Elsewhere (23.35–36), he says that Berossus appears "to agree partly with divinely inspired Scripture regarding the flood, and the Giants and Noah himself, who is called Xisuthrus by them." Finally, in likening Nimrod to the pre-flood Giants, he says that he "ruled tyrannically in imitation of the antediluvian Giants. . . . For this reason, Scripture says the words, 'he began to be a giant on the earth,' that is, after the destruction of the previous Giants, he began to be a giant after them, foremost in evil over the earth" (38.6–11).

[92] Johann Heidegger, *Historia Patriarchum*, Exerc. XI de Nephilim seu gigantibus antediluvianis 28 (Amsterdam, 1688–89), 311–12. Heidegger himself had rejected this identification, on the grounds that it would imply that Noah (i.e., Xisuthrus) was himself one of the Nephilim. The chronicler Wilhelm Lange, here too reflecting the influence of Byzantine chronography, states that the antediluvian kings of Chaldea were "without doubt, the Nephilim, who were ancient 'viri nominis,' that is famous men, as Moses says" (*De Annis Christi*, 2.3, 252). Curiously, Annius of Viterbo's spurious but influential forgeries had given more confirmation to this identification. In the name of Berossus, Annius had stated that before the flood the Giants of Gen. 6, "contemptores religionis et deorum," had ruled over the whole world "ab occasu solis ad ortum" (from his *Berosi et aliorum authorum Antiquitates* [Antwerp, 1552], 44). For discussion of the Annian forgeries and their influence, see Anthony Grafton, "Josephus Scaliger and Historical Chronology," 164–67.

[93] If pressed to conjecture on this matter, Walter Raleigh surmised in his *History of the World* (1.9.2) that the world was "not without kings in that first age . . . (it being) very likely, that the cruel oppressions in that age proceeded from some tyranny in government, or from some rougher form of rule, than the paternal." But this was only conjecture, and based, as he acknowledges, on Annius' (ps-)Berossus.

liger concluded that the theory of the divine right of kings was without merit, since monarchy came about only as the result of human effort.[94] Other European chronographers tended to the view, also well represented in Byzantine sources, that the first unmistakable evidence for kingship in Genesis was the postdiluvian Nimrod, the first to rule Babylon after the flood. The institution of monarchy, therefore, far from being divinely ordained, reflected the predatory instincts of a "mighty hunter before the Lord." Chronographers seeking to trace the origins of the institution even earlier could find in the Byzantine chronographers more support that the first world rulers were a race of usurpers and tyrants. By tracing the origins of despotism to the "men of renown," a bastard and mixed race, whose excesses presaged the flood, chronographers had further proof that the first kings were only tyrants whose size and boldness allowed them to usurp power and rule violently over men of lesser stature. "Moses," acknowledges the English chronographer John Jackson, "does not directly tell us that there was any Kingdom set up before the Flood:

> but in the sixth chapter of Genesis he intimates, that after the Earth was grown populous, great Alterations happened in the Manners and State of Men. That a gigantic or warlike Race of Men were born, whose Daughters marrying with the Descendants of Seth, bare another Race of robust and mighty, whom he calls Men of Renown, viz. for their martial exploits. These Giants are called in the Hebrew Naphilim, probably from their great Size, as being able to oppress with Violence and Force, all who resisted them or refused to be subject to them. Hence Symmachus interpreted the Word by violent [Βίαιοι], or Invaders. *So that the Antediluvian Kingdom or Tyranny was an Innovation on the patriarchal Government, under which the Descendants of Adam had lived under the several Heads of Families, till an absolute Monarchy was erected by the Naphilim, over both the Cainites and Sethites, by Marriage united into one People.*[95]

[94] For Scaliger's views, see James William Johnson, "Chronological Writing," 143. Of the earliest dynasty of the Egyptian kings, Scaliger asserts: "et profecto illa vetustissima regna fuerunt instar latrociniorum, ubi vis, non lex, aut successio, aut suffragia populi reges in solio regni collocabant" (*Thesaurus Temporum*, 2 (*Animadversiones*, 57 [an. MXXV]).

[95] John Jackson, *Chronological Antiquities*, 203. Also: "The Patriarchal Government, invested in the several Heads of Families, was dissolved; and an ambitious and warlike Leader of the Cainites set up an absolute Monarchy over all Descendants of Adam. Under this Kingdom, set up and supported by Violence and Tyranny, Men grew more wicked and irreligious" (204).

Jackson has not hesitated to take some liberties with the tradition, but its Byzantine sources are clear. Through Syncellus, Jackson knows of the work of the Alexandrian chronographers Panodorus and Annianus. The identification of the "Naphilim" as the first tyrants is a legacy of the *Paschal Chronicle*. This latter work, he writes, "relates that the first Chaldean Kings mentioned by Berosus were the Giants who are called mighty Men and Men of Renown, and these are said to be born of the Descendants of Seth."[96]

It is a testimony to the influence of Byzantine chronography that this influential chronicle, published in the eighteenth century, would still be endorsing the same identification. A modern writer on chronography, struck by the symmetry in their views about the origins of kingship, has gone so far as to suggest that Byzantium "opened the way for a series of attacks on royal rights in later centuries."[97] When, however, Annianus and Panodorus, in Alexandria, first derived the institution of monarchy in Babylon from the fall of the Watchers, the issue at stake was not the legitimacy of kingship; their concern was to link the available sources together in such a way as to satisfy an abstract conception of primitive social evolution. That a later generation of chronographers could adapt this picture to discussions of a more overtly political character shows only that different ages extract from their sources different meanings.

[96] Jackson, *Chronological Antiquities,* 203–4. For his use of Panodorus and Annianus, see 61–64, 201–2.

[97] See Johnson, "Chronological Writing," 134–35, 143–45.

CHAPTER FIVE

George Syncellus and His Predecessors

SYNCELLUS AND HIS CRITICS

In the proemium to his continuation of Syncellus' chronicle, Theophanes gives what was, among George's Byzantine successors, a characteristically enthusiastic assessment of his abilities as a chronicler:

> The most blessed elder George, who was also the syncellus of Tarasius, the most holy patriarch of Constantinople, was a highly esteemed and very learned man (ἐλλόγιμος ἀνὴρ καὶ πολυμαθέστατος). Having read (ἀναγνούς) many chronographies and histories, and having examined them critically (ἀκριβῶς τούτους διερευνησάμενος), he composed a concise (σύντομον) chronological record from Adam to Diocletian, emperor of the Romans and persecutor of Christians. And he made a record of the governments of the ancient kings of every people, and their dates, having accurately ascertained the chronology through close scrutiny (τούς τε χρόνους ἐν πολλῇ ἐξετάσει ἀκριβολογησάμενος), reconciled their contradictions (τὰς τούτων διαφωνίας συμβιβάσας), and arranged them into a more correct order than anyone else before him (ὡς οὐδεὶς ἄλλος τῶν πρὸ αὐτοῦ).[1]

Modern assessments of Syncellus' ability as a chronicler have never been as favorable as that of Theophanes.[2] It is perhaps a measure of their temperaments and the distance that separated them that Scaliger, the sixteenth-century savant, should have reached conclusions about Syncellus' chronicle precisely opposite to those of Theophanes. If Theophanes had

---

[1] Theophanes *Praef.* 1. 3.9–17 (ed. de Boor, 2 vols. [Leipzig, 1883]).

[2] Theophanes' testimony, Gelzer would observe later, with some contempt, might have carried more authority if Theophanes himself had not been a complete "homo rudis" (*SJA*, 2. 184).

regarded the chronicle as the concise and accurate ἐϰλογή of a highly
learned man, Scaliger condemned it as the "silly (*inanum*)," nonsensical,
and needlessly repetitive work of a very poor chronicler.[3] The most significant feature of Scaliger's critique was his evaluation of Syncellus' debt to
his authorities. Scaliger held that the chronicle was neither a careful comparison of various sources, nor an advance beyond his predecessors. To the
contrary, it was simply a very inferior copy of Eusebius' chronicle, differing from it only to the extent of committing more errors in chronology.
While noting that Syncellus did not hesitate to rebuke Eusebius for various lapses, Scaliger dismissed these as carping and petty criticisms, and
further proof of Syncellus' incompetence as a chronicler. In Scaliger's estimation, Syncellus had "transcribed in his own work the whole chronology of Eusebius without any alteration of words (*universam Eusebii chron-
ologiam sine ulla verborum immutatione in suum volumen transtulisse*)."[4]
Indeed, it was on the basis of this presumed dependence on Eusebius that
Scaliger felt justified in using Syncellus as the principal source for reconstructing the first book of Eusebius' chronicle, as yet unknown in Europe.

Scaliger's attack against Syncellus was written well before the discovery
of the Armenian translation of the *Chronica,* and a measure of Syncellus'
impugned integrity was restored when the text revealed that his chronicle
was far more than a flawed transcription of Eusebius.[5] Even before that
discovery, however, both Goar and Bredow, in separate essays, had chal-
lenged Scaliger's conclusions on the basis of internal evidence in Syncellus'
chronicle.[6] Specifically, Goar and Bredow sought to demonstrate that various features of the chronicle militated decisively against the thesis that it
was dependent only on one source.

There was first the fact that Syncellus named Christian chroniclers other

---

[3] A sampling of Scaliger's often intemperate invective against Syncellus can be found in
Leo Allacci, "De Georgiis et eorum scriptis diatriba," 10. 633–34. Among the more memorable of Scaliger's insults collected by Allacci: "Insignis hallucinatio, vel potius deliratio.
Insigne delirium. Quae sunt stultissima. Non pauca vomit, quae non referam. . . . Plane pue-
rile est" (634).

[4] *Thesaurus Temporum,* 2. 241 Unless otherwise specified, references to Scaliger are from
his "Notae in Graeca Παντοδαπῆς Ἱστορίας Eusebii, quae supersunt" (vol. 2 of *Thesaurus
Temporum*).

[5] For a clear and useful discussion of the textual history of Eusebius' chronicle, see A.
Mosshammer's *The Chronicle of Eusebius,* 37–83.

[6] Both essays are included in vol. 2 of Dindorf's edition of Syncellus. Goar's essay was
originally a preface to his 1652 editio princeps of Syncellus (52–73 in vol. 2 of Dindorf's
edition). Bredow's was originally in response to a topic suggested by the literary society of
Paris on the "sources and authority of George Syncellus (Dissertatio de Georgii Syncelli
fontibus et auctoritate)"; reprinted in Dindorf's edition of Syncellus, 2. 3–49. For Bredow's
assessment of the importance of Syncellus, see especially pp. 10–11.

than Eusebius as authorities, notably Julius Africanus, Eusebius, Panodorus, and Annianus, the latter two *succeeding* Eusebius (a point recognized
by Scaliger himself).[7] This use of different sources was further suggested
by the title of the chronicle (ἐκλογή = collection of excerpts) and the
testimony of Theophanes, who explicitly praises Syncellus for reading several histories and chronicles before him. As Goar argued, "the diversity of
style, the complex structure of composition, and the varied modes of reckoning time" clearly indicated "equally diverse sources, not a unified work
extracted from the hand of Eusebius, but diversified written records."[8]

It should be stressed that although Goar and Bredow were less stringent
in their assessments of Syncellus than Scaliger, they were not unaware of
his shortcomings. Bredow acknowledged that Syncellus' chronicle bore all
the faults of those Christian historians who "virtually despise the craft of
historiography, pursuing instead an excessively arid style of historical composition."[9] Syncellus, he claimed, was repetitious, unduly critical of his
predecessors, his chronicle containing numerous errors and contradictions.[10] Moreover, precisely those arguments that Goar had adduced to
prove that Syncellus used more than one source could also be construed
as a criticism of him; "the diversity of style, the complexity of its arrangement, and the various modes of reckoning time" meant that, as far as Goar
was concerned, Syncellus had failed to do precisely what Theophanes had
praised him for—reconciling and correcting chronological discrepancies
in earlier sources. Even granting this, however, it is clear that for both
Goar and Bredow Syncellus had, in composing his chronicle, examined
many different sources; he was not simply "Eusebius redivivus."[11]

This contention that Syncellus had access to a variety of different
sources in the writing of his chronicle did not hold sway for very long,
however. Largely due to the work of Heinrich Gelzer, it is now almost
universally taken as a given that Syncellus' chronicle was not a rough transcription of Eusebius, as Scaliger had claimed, but rather of Eusebius'
successors, the early fifth-century Alexandrian monks Annianus and Panodorus. It was the latter chronicler, in particular, from which Syncellus'
"Profangeschichte" was "in Grossen und Ganzen" derived.[12]

<hr/>

[7] Goar, *Praefatio* (in Dindorf's edition, 2. 59–60); cf. Scaliger, *Thesaurus Temporum*, 2. 247.
[8] Goar, *Praefatio*, 61.
[9] Bredow, *Dissertatio* (ed. Dindorf, 2. 11).
[10] Ibid., 11: "Georgius inprimis nimius est in iisdem iterum iterumque repetendis, maxime
in vituperationibus aliorum Chronographorum, atque in perturbatis annorum numeris er-
roribusque librariorum. . . ."
[11] So Bredow concludes (11): "Scaliger quidem nimius est et in Eusebio laudando et in
Georgio vituperando."
[12] *SJA*, 2. 185.

Gelzer was not the first to have called attention to the ostensible influence of these Alexandrian chroniclers on Syncellus. Unger, Gutschmid, and others had already remarked upon this.[13] But Gelzer was the first to mount a systematic case for literary dependence. It may be said that Gelzer's source analysis was of such scope as effectively to deprive Syncellus of any truly original contribution to Christian chronography; virtually all that appeared to be new or different from Eusebius and Africanus was, Gelzer argued, simply taken over from his Alexandrian predecessors.[14]

Whereas the abundance of sources cited by Syncellus created the impression of a vast erudition, Gelzer was persuaded that most of this learning was derivative. While he granted that Syncellus might have examined other sources, the sources that Syncellus had "actually (*wirklich*)" used were only three—the Bible, Panodorus and Annianus.[15] He thought it improbable that, writing in Constantinople in the early ninth century, Syncellus should have access to such a wide spectrum of source material. The more permissive intellectual environment of fifth-century Alexandria was another matter, however, and access to a diverse body of reading material was fairly unrestrained for Syncellus' two Alexandrian predecessors.[16] That Syncellus did not acknowledge the full measure of his indebtedness to the Alexandrians counted for little, Gelzer maintained, since Syncellus regularly failed to name intermediary sources.[17] Excerpts, for example, from Castor, Alexander Polyhistor, Diodorus, and Abydenus were cited as if they were taken from the original works; but a comparison of them with the same material in Eusebius revealed their true origins— from Eusebius' *Chronica* via his Alexandrian intermediaries. Syncellus might not have been a swindler, Gelzer claimed, but he knew how to cloak himself in an aura of learning that was more feigned than real.[18]

In one of the few systematic critiques of Gelzer's reconstruction of Syncellus' sources, R. Laqueur called attention to aspects of the composition of Syncellus' chronicle that he believed proved that it was not a copy, even a flawed copy, of one or two earlier sources.[19] As he pointed out, especially

---

[13] Wrote Unger: "Panodor ist überhaupt für profane Chronologie der Hauptgewährsmann Syncells, inbesondere auch in methodischer Beziehung" (*Chronologie des Manetho,* 35); see also A. von Gutschmid, "Die Sothis," 226–43, esp. pp. 230–35.

[14] Cf. *SJA,* 2. 185–89.

[15] Ibid., 2. 189: "Wirkliche Quellen seines Werkes kann man nur die heilige Schrift und die beiden alexandrinischen Chronisten nennen."

[16] Ibid., 2. 192.

[17] Ibid., 2. 184–89.

[18] Ibid., 2. 263.

[19] R. Laqueur, "Synkellos," 1388–1410. For a more recent assessment of the question, see G. Huxley, "On the Erudition of George the Synkellos," 207–17, esp. 217 (note 78); see also preface to Mosshammer's edition of Syncellus, xxv–xxx.

the antediluvian portion of the chronicle was full of inconsistencies, contradictions, and fragmentary arguments. This, while far from a complimentary assessment of the chronicle, vindicated Syncellus of the charge that he had simply transcribed the work of forerunners. To be sure, Laqueur misrepresented Gelzer somewhat, since Gelzer granted that Syncellus did not follow Panodorus and Annianus "slavishly" in all cases.[20] But Laqueur was correct in criticizing Gelzer for taking insufficient notice of aspects of the composition of Syncellus' chronicle that pointed to his independence from his authorities. Laqueur's criticisms recall the sorts of objections mounted earlier by Goar against Scaliger—that Syncellus' convoluted style and the varying chronological schemes in his ἐκλογή showed that he had used a number of different chronographies, not succeeding, however, in reconciling them. Goar saw this as a refutation of Scaliger's representation of Syncellus as "Eusebius redivivus"; as Laqueur had argued, it could also be applied to Gelzer's "Panodorus/Annianus" source theory.

The term that Gelzer typically used to characterize Syncellus' relationship to his Alexandrian predecessors was "Abhängigkeit"—a word that presumably referred to Syncellus' sources.[21] Indeed, as has been seen, Syncellus does include in the antediluvian segment of his chronicle many sources that he as much as acknowledges were borrowed from predecessors. But the word "dependence" conceals the complexity of the problem. Where did Syncellus copy, where did he abridge, and where did he depart from the Alexandrian chroniclers? Did Syncellus' dependence on them apply only to the sources used, or did it extend to other areas of the chronicle as well? The specific question to be addressed here is: How does he treat the same sources as his Alexandrian predecessors, while at the same time diverging so widely in his use and interpretation of them? Analysis of the literary structure of Syncellus' chronicle for at least one segment of his treatment of primordial history suggests that there is a fairly consistent pattern of borrowing and adaptation of material from his Alexandrian authorities.

The relevant material for this analysis begins with the chronology of events after the expulsion of Adam from Paradise and the death of Abel.

---

[20] So see Gelzer's remark apropos of Syncellus' canon of Egyptian kings (*SJA*, 2. 185): "Damit soll natürlich nicht gesagt sein, dass er in seinen Königslisten überall sclavisch dem Panodoros gefolgt sei."

[21] Cf., for example, *SJA*, 2. 191.

Syncellus draws a sharp distinction between the characters and dwelling places of the respective races. Cain and his generation were, he states, "small in stature (χθαμαλός)" and lived in the "low (χαμηλή) land that quakes"— Nod.[22] After his condemnation, Syncellus says, Cain became "rapacious and very greedy (ἅρπαξ καὶ πλεονέκτης)," having been the first to invent "measures and weights and surveying (μέτρα καὶ σταθμία καὶ ὅρους γῆς)" and having taught his descendants to "engage in wars (ἐν πολέμοις ἀσχολεῖσθαι)."[23] The idea that property, boundaries and civilization signalize an end to mankind's "state of nature" was widespread in Antiquity.[24] Applied to Cain, the tradition has its earliest attestation in Josephus. In his *Antiquities*, Josephus remarks that Cain, far from being chastened by his punishment by God, used it to "increase his vice (ἐπ᾽ αὐξήσει τῆς κακίας)." By introducing surveying and boundaries, Cain brought greed into the world, thus ending the "guiltless and generous existence" that people had enjoyed in ignorance of these things.[25] Syncellus contrasts the depravity of Cain and his offspring with the comeliness of Seth and his descendants, who were "devout and beautiful (εὐσεβεῖς καὶ ὡραῖοι)."[26] At the behest of Adam, they remain apart from the Cainites, living in the "more elevated region of Eden, opposite Paradise (τὴν ὑψηλοτέραν γῆν . . . τῆς ᾽Εδέμ, κατέναντι τοῦ παραδείσου)."[27]

In distinguishing the two antediluvian races so clearly, Syncellus seeks to demonstrate the historical veracity of the fall of the "sons of God" of Genesis 6 in the year 1000—an event, he says, that "some people dispute (τινες ἀντιλέγουσι)."[28] His narrative shows pervasive influence of pseudepigraphic legends about Seth and his descendants, similar in content to the Syriac *Cave of Treasures*.[29] "Until the year 1000 (that is, the fall of the sons of God)," he says, "the Sethites lived as angels do (ἀγγελικῶς βιοῦντες)."[30] In that year, however, "the descendants of Seth, having been led astray, descended and took for themselves wives from the daughters of men."[31] The idea expressed here, analogues of which appear in numerous

---

[22] Sync. 9.14–15.
[23] Ibid., 9.11–14.
[24] For the idea that surveying was part of the general corruption of the world, see for example Ovid *Amores* 3.8.35–56; Cicero *De officiis* 1.7.21. For general discussion of this theme in Antiquity, see A. O. Lovejoy and G. Boas, *Primitivism*, 47–48, 257–58.
[25] Josephus *Antiquities* 1.60–63.
[26] Sync. 9.27.
[27] Ibid., 9.28–29.
[28] Ibid., 11.11–12.
[29] See Gelzer, *SJA*, 2. 260–72.
[30] Sync. 9.29.
[31] Ibid., 11.9–10.

other works, is that the Sethites bore the name "sons of God" and "Watchers" because of the piety and physical stature that they inherited from Seth.[32] In this way, Syncellus explains not only the significance of the expression "sons of God" or "angels of God," but the fact that the offspring of the Watchers were Giants—they inherited the physical size of the Sethites.[33]

SYNCELLUS' CRITIQUE OF HIS ALEXANDRIAN PREDECESSORS

Having established the historical veracity of the fall of the sons of God of Genesis, Syncellus introduces quite abruptly a second theme. "This being so concerning the Watchers, it is necessary to recognize that in divinely inspired Scripture there is no mention of a kingdom of this type (οἰασοῦν)."[34] Indeed, the only reason why he feels it necessary even to broach the subject is that Berossus suggested that there was:

> But Berossus, the author of the Chaldean ancient history, who flourished, as he says, during the period of Alexander of Macedon, found carefully preserved in Babylonia the records of many [writers], records which encompassed about 150,000 years and a little more; he wrote down, with a certain boastfulness, certain stories about heaven

[32] Seth, says Syncellus, was "pious and exceedingly well formed, and all those descended from him were pious and beautiful" (9.26–27). Syncellus also writes that Seth, in Adam's 270th year, was taken up into heaven for forty days and received a revelation about the "transgression of the Watchers, the coming cataclysm and the advent of the Savior" (9.22–25). With the exception of the *horarium*, Seth's apocalypse parallels Uriel's revelation to Adam in his 600th year (cf. Sync. 10.14–24). Revelations to Seth are found in other chronicles as well. In the chronicle of (ps-)Dionysus, Seth had received a heavenly book of secrets, which was passed down from generation to generation, ultimately placed in the Cave of Treasures under the custody of the Magi (58–59, ed. I.-B. Chabot; Latin trans. Chabot, 46–47).

[33] Possibly in connection with this interpretation of Gen. 6, Syncellus (10.8–11) includes a curious quotation from Julius Africanus concerning the birth of Enosh: "'Enosh was the first to hope to call upon (be called[?]; ἐπικαλεῖσθαι) the name of the Lord God (ἐπικαλεῖσθαι τὸ ὄνομα κυρίου τοῦ θεοῦ; cf. Gen. 4:26),' that is, to be addressed as God by name (προσαγορεύεσθαι ὀνόματι θεοῦ). Thus also the Saviour is the son of the real man, according to Africanus' natural history (τὸν φυσικὸν λόγον)." Africanus' understanding of Enosh as a type of Christ is not altogether clear. However, since Gen. 4:26 was often used in connection with the Sethite interpretation of Gen. 6, and since Africanus himself endorsed this explanation (cf. Sync. 19.24–20.4), it is possible that Africanus too saw this verse as proving that the sons of God referred to the sons of Seth and Enosh. In this respect, Syncellus probably understands the verbs ἐπικαλεῖσθαι and προσαγορεύεσθαι passively; cf. Sync. 14.17–19, where Syncellus identifies the Watchers as sons of Seth and Enosh. For discussion of this difficult passage, see Gelzer, *SJA*, I. 62; see also above, Chap. 4, p. 116, note 47.

[34] Sync. 14.15–18. The term οἰασοῦν is unclear here, since up to that time Syncellus has not yet discussed the question.

and earth and the sea and the oldest of the kings and their deeds, and the settlement of the region of Babylonia and its fertility, and certain creatures appearing from the Red Sea, unnatural in form, all of which, according to an accurate account, appear to be figments of demons. Therefore, I think it necessary to set out the sequence of things in order from the 1,059th year of the world, although I am convinced that Berossus and those who follow him (I mean Alexander, who is called Polyhistor, and Abydenus) wrote these things, wanting to glorify the Chaldean race and to show that it was older than all other peoples.[35]

Although Syncellus implies here that he is directly objecting to Berossus and Manetho, it is clear that he intends his Alexandrian predecessors as well. The whole program for his subsequent narrative begins from the date that they had calculated (A.M. 1059) as the beginning of the pre-flood Babylonian and Chaldean empires. "To think," Syncellus writes, "that the world in which we live, in which the lands of the Babylonians and Egypt are situated, was, rather, uninhabited before the deluge, seems to correspond better to divine Scriptures and the testimonies of certain early authorities, and the natural sequence of things."[36]
There are, Syncellus owns, certain similarities between Berossus and Manetho, on the one hand, and Genesis on the other, but these similarities do not count as independent corroboration. Although "simple-minded" and "inexperienced" readers might be impressed by apparent parallels between Berossus, Manetho, and Genesis, these similarities can be attributed to the fact that the Babylonians and Egyptians stole from Moses, distorting his doctrines in the process. Those "who have composed these histories have taken every worthwhile idea (πᾶν νόημα χρηστόν)" from divinely inspired Scriptures.[37] Specifically, Syncellus cautions his readers against being seduced by these superficial similarities into believing the many distortions that the Egyptians and Babylonians have introduced into the doctrines that they have stolen from Moses. "Having purloined from divinely inspired Scriptures, they appropriate as their own certain things about the flood and the ark, by means of which the more simple-minded, and those devoted to other nonsense are led astray."[38]
Such similarities, Syncellus writes, the result of plagiarism, cannot con-

---

[35] Ibid., 14.22–15.3.
[36] Ibid., 15.3–6.
[37] Ibid., 24.1–2.
[38] Ibid., 16.19–20. For Syncellus, the two most insidious aspects of the *Babyloniaca* are the legend of Oannes and the reckoning of time in sars, ners, and soses.

ceal what are, on their face, the manifest contradictions between Genesis and these sources. If, he says, Egyptian and Babylonian kingdoms did exist before the flood, one might reasonably assume that Manetho would know Berossus' account of antediluvian monarchy in Babylon and vice versa. Instead, neither mentions the other: "It can be shown . . . that Manetho's history of events and the dynasties of the Egyptians before the flood is a lie, first of all from the fact that each of them, i.e., the authors of the *Chaldaica* and *Aegyptiaca,* confirms himself, but the other is not mentioned; neither the author of the *Aegyptiaca* confirms the *Chaldaica,* nor the author of the *Chaldaica* the *Aegyptiaca,* accusing each other of lying about his past; each glorifies his own nation and country and weaves a web of lies."[39]

Nor is it possible to find any confirmation for the existence of preflood kingdoms in Genesis. Instead, Syncellus asserts, Scripture expressly states that neither Babylon nor Egypt came into existence until well after the flood. The critical passage for him is Genesis 10:8–12: "Cush fathered Nimrod. He began to be a giant on the earth. He was a mighty hunter. . . . And the beginning of his kingdom was Babylon, Orech and Archad, and Chalane in the land of Senaar." "It is clear from these things," Syncellus says, "that the kingdom of the Babylonians, or of the Chaldeans, was begun by Nimrod, who flourished in the 630th year after the deluge."[40] Syncellus applies a similar argument against Panodorus' synchronization of Manetho's chronology with Genesis. After describing Panodorus' novel technique, Syncellus concludes with the following criticisms:

> Thus Panodorus exerts himself to show that the Egyptian writings against God and against our divinely inspired Scriptures are really in agreement with them. In this he criticizes Eusebius, not understanding that these arguments of his, which are incapable of proof or of reasoning (ἀναπόδεικτά τε καὶ ἀσυλλόγιστα), have been proved against himself and against truth, since indeed, just as we demonstrated above from Genesis, neither Babylon nor Chaldea was ruled by kings before the flood, nor was Egypt before Mestrem. And in my opinion, it was not even inhabited before that time. . . .[41]

Syncellus has apparently formulated this from the table of nations of Genesis 10, according to which Mestrem, Noah's grandson, settled Egypt. Syncellus fixes Mestrem's founding of Egypt to the year 2776, or 534 years

[39] Ibid., 38.15–21.
[40] Ibid., 16.13–15.
[41] Ibid., 42.20–26 (fr. 2, trans. Waddell).

after the flood. As Syncellus maintains later, this Mestrem is the same as the first mortal king of Manetho's chronology of Egypt—Menes.[42]

As we have seen, a fundamental part of Syncellus' predecessors' reconstruction of antediluvian civilization was that Paradise, Egypt, and Babylon lay in the same κλίμα and all three regions formed part of the presently inhabited world. Syncellus questions their geography. The "world in which we live, in which the lands of the Babylonians and Egypt are situated, was . . . uninhabited before the flood." This view, he says, "seems to correspond better to divine Scripture and the testimonies of certain early authorities and the natural order of things (τῆς φυσικῆς τῶν πραγμάτων ἀκολουθίας)."[43] To support his case, Syncellus quotes, from among other authorities, Ephrem Syrus:

> Paradise is higher than all the high beautiful places. The deluge reached to its base. The people who lived before the deluge dwelt between the Ocean and Paradise, the offspring of Cain in the land called Od, which is translated "trembling," the descendants of Seth in the higher land, having been ordered by Adam not to mingle with the race of Cain, the fratricide. His [Cain's] offspring were low to the ground in stature, on account of the curse of Cain. But the offspring of Seth were Giants and like angels of God, [dwelling] in the elevated region. But the daughters of Cain, coming [to them] with wind and stringed instruments, led them down to their own land, and the sons of God married them. When their lawlessness was rampant, the flood came. And God led the ark of Noah away to Mt. Ararat. And from that time, people came to dwell in this land. This illustrates that the land now inhabited was then uninhabited. For on account of the compassion of God, the people who lived before the deluge dwelt near Paradise between the Ocean and Paradise. Now the "outer Paradise," about which Christ spoke, comes from within Paradise. And Paradise, together with the Ocean, encircles the World. Eden is toward the East, and the lights of the sun and the moon rise from within Paradise, but they set outside, having passed through it . . . and so on.[44]

The reference is evidently a highly glossed Greek translation from Ephrem's Syriac *Hymns on Paradise*.[45] Although it is not entirely clear why

---

[42] Ibid., 58.14–15: "from the first ruler of Egypt Mestraim, also called Menes by Manetho."

[43] Ibid., 15.5–6.

[44] Ibid., 15.13–31.

[45] I.10–11 (ed. E. Beck; CSCO 174, Scriptores Syri 78); see also Ephrem's *Commentary on Genesis* 6:5 (ed. and Latin trans. R.-M. Tonneau, CSCO 152, 153; Scriptores Syri 71, 72 [Louvain, 1955]).

Syncellus considers this passage a refutation of his Alexandrian predecessors' views about the existence of Babylon and Egypt before the flood, he appears to see in it confirmation for his own "two world" geography, a view very prevalent in later patristic sources. According to it, the world now inhabited is surrounded on all sides by a great ocean. This ocean is itself encompassed by another world, in the eastern corner of which is situated Paradise and the abode of the antediluvian generations.[46] Since Babylon and Egypt are located in the world now inhabited, it follows that before the flood "neither did Babylon exist on the earth, nor the kingdom of the Chaldeans, as is held by Berossus and his successors in a way that undermines divine Scripture (πρὸς ἀνατροπὴν τῶν θείων γραφῶν); nor was there an Egyptian dynasty, as Manetho, the liar and glorifier of the Egyptian race, saw fit to write."[47]

The criticisms described above are for the most part not directed expressly at Panodorus or Annianus. Rather they form general objections to the belief that Babylon and Egypt existed before the flood. Later in his discussion, however, Syncellus begins his refutation of the actual method which his predecessors, specifically Panodorus, applied to demonstrate the harmony of Berossus and Manetho with Genesis. In the main, these consisted of pleas against adopting a conciliatory attitude toward works that encouraged heresy. Here Syncellus expresses amazement that any chronographer, recognizing their insidiousness and their numerous absurdities (πλεῖστα πολλῆς ἀδολεσχίας γέμοντα), would seek to include these sources, "unworthy of any mention at all (ἀνάξια πάσης . . . μνήμης)," into their own reckoning of events.[48] "It is not necessary to accommodate to our faith their antediluvian testimonies, nor anything else of their demonic history. For from this narrative, as if from some filthy spring . . . almost every mythic and false doctrine of the Greeks and Manicheans has sprung forth, and not a few of our heresies take their point of departure from deceptive writings of this kind."[49]

When it comes to specific criticisms of his predecessors, particularly Panodorus, Syncellus displays only modest abilities. He does recognize

---

[46] On the existence of two worlds, see in particular the extensive and polemical discussion in the *Topography* of Cosmas Indicopleustes (6th century). Greek text of Cosmas with introduction and notes, ed. E. O. Winstedt (Cambridge, 1909); more recently by Wanda Wolska-Conus, 3 vols., SC 141, 159, 197 (Paris, 1968–73.) See also G. L. Huxley, "On the Erudition of George the Synkellos," 212.

[47] Sync. 16.3–6.

[48] Ibid., 16.30–31.

[49] Ibid., 34.33–34.4.

that the cornerstone of Panodorus' reconstruction of primitive calendars is the claim that before Uriel's revelation to Enoch in the year 1286, mankind did not know how to reckon time in "months, years and seasons." Syncellus can find little to recommend this view:

> . . . before the flood, neither was there a kingdom of the Babylonians nor a Babylonian race, nor did Babylon exist, which it (Scripture) says was founded after the flood. And it is absurd for him to suggest that in the beginning, in the six-day cosmogony, the first book given to us by Moses did not mention measures of time except for the day, the night and the week. For Scripture everywhere makes mention of years, such as Adam lived 930 years and died, and likewise for all the [remaining] generations, unless someone is convinced, which I am not, that, as they say, people after him, i.e. Adam, used to reckon time in weeks, up to the 165th year of Enoch.[50]

Besides, Syncellus argues, even granting that "in the 956th year before the flood, Enoch and his successors learned about the yearly cycle, and its four-part seasons, and its twelve lunations, then the antediluvian generations in around the year 1000, that is in the year 1058, also knew how to measure regnal years in solar years and months."[51]

Syncellus' apology for Eusebius' handling of Babylonian and Egyptian antiquities is especially weak. It is unfortunate here that he apparently did not take the time to consult Eusebius directly, depending instead on his predecessors' very one-sided treatment of him. Eusebius, he says, "being a polymath knew that the Chaldeans introduce endless eons for the creation of the universe, and that the Greeks and the Egyptians say that there is a cosmic revolution in 25 periods of 1,461 years, that is in 36,525 years . . . for which reason, he considered it superfluous to allegorize their strange ideas, as is fitting."[52] Eusebius nowhere discusses such cycles; the reference to 36,525 years is derived rather from the *Ancient Chronicle*, one of Panodorus' sources for Egyptian chronology. Moreover, it is not altogether true that Eusebius rejected the "allegorical" interpretation of Egyptian chronology, since, as we have seen, he does mention it as a possible solution to the problem.[53] In both cases we may assume that Syncellus was defend-

---

[50] Ibid., 34.7–16.
[51] Ibid., 34.25–30.
[52] Ibid., 36.10–16.
[53] See above, Chap. 3, pp. 77–78.

ing Eusebius only on the basis of what he was able to infer about him from Panodorus' own references and criticisms.

If, in fact, Syncellus had known Eusebius firsthand, he might have mounted a far stronger case against Panodorus than he had. While boasting about having succeeded where Eusebius before him had failed, Panodorus conveniently suppressed the fact that his source for Manetho (the *Book of Sothis*) was far better suited for the purposes of synchronization than Eusebius' epitome of the *Aegyptiaca;* indeed, it is now generally recognized that Panodorus had subjected archaic Egyptian chronology to very comprehensive adjustments in order to achieve the desired result.[54] Syncellus was certainly capable of recognizing tendentious manipulation of sources; he elsewhere accuses Eusebius of doing just that.[55] But in his critique, he never points out that Eusebius' list of Egyptian kings was far different from Panodorus'; his only way of explaining the success of Panodorus' technique is to suggest that Manetho had copied from Berossus.[56]

In the whole discussion, Syncellus, otherwise an admirer of his Alexandrian authorities, displays an uncharacteristic animus against both of them, even to the extent of doubting their orthodoxy. The acerbity of his criticisms, often more polemical than substantive, must have puzzled chronographers after him. George Cedrenus, who followed Syncellus for much of antediluvian history, apparently regarded the whole exercise as largely superfluous, since he excised most of Syncellus' account here.[57] Scaliger, himself hardly an admirer of Syncellus, could scarcely contain his contempt for Syncellus' adamant refusal to accept Panodorus' discussion of this matter. The existence of a Babylonian kingdom before the flood, "appears absurd to Syncellus. Nor is he able, however, to substantiate his opinion with any valid argument, except obstinacy, which is familiar to him."[58]

Although Syncellus' motives must remain partly obscure to us, the central issue dividing him from his Alexandrian predecessors here concerned the sufficiency of Genesis and the proper use of sources meant to supplement it. If for Scaliger the practical value of sources like Berossus and

---

[54] For discussion, see below, Chap. 6, pp. 172–73.

[55] See Sync. 65.18–20, 69.1–7.

[56] Whether Syncellus knew Eusebius' chronicle firsthand or only through intermediaries is uncertain. Although not certain that Syncellus had before him a copy of Eusebius' chronicle, Gelzer considered it virtually assured that Syncellus at least knew Eusebius' *Ecclesiastical History;* see *SJA,* 2. 189 (note 2).

[57] Cedrenus (1. 20.2–8) gives a short, but not wholly coherent summary of Syncellus' arguments against the existence of Babylonia and Egypt before the flood.

[58] *Thesaurus Temporum,* 2. 246.

Manetho was to be assessed by their intrinsic worth, Syncellus' Alexandrian authorities found in these sources a useful amplification of Genesis, and a means for rapprochement with paganism. Syncellus was hardly of a mind to let these sources stand on their own merit. Nor could he, in ninth-century Constantinople, understand how the few parallels between these sources and Genesis could justify the extensive appeal to these sources by his predecessors. "What is," he asks, "this compulsion to reconcile the lie with truth?"[59] In his view, whatever objective benefits were to be reaped by this approach were entirely outweighed by the dangers inherent in it.

The question posed here, however, extends to the sources that Syncellus has apparently taken over from his Alexandrian predecessors. If Syncellus depended on Panodorus and Annianus to the extent that Gelzer assumed, he must have had reasons for citing these sources which are in some cases diametrically opposed to theirs. For most of his treatment of antediluvian history is an extended polemic against the Alexandrian monks. How, then, does Syncellus justify quoting from sources that he considers either false or incorrectly interpreted?

SYNCELLUS' ADAPTATION OF BORROWED SOURCES

There can be little doubt that much of Syncellus' primordial chronology consists mainly of transcribing source material from earlier chronicles and adapting it for his own purposes, sometimes in a very superficial way. At the same time, however, one sees little evidence that Syncellus sought deliberately to cloak this dependence in a veil of false erudition. In, for example, his discussion of Babylonian and Egyptian antediluvian chronology, he freely acknowledges the use of intermediaries. "I am amazed," he says, "how they (his predecessors) agree at all to include in their chronological tables things not worthy of mention. Out of respect for these men, I deem it unnecessary to mention them by name. But *because of them I too feel obliged to use the same tables.*"[60] After this acknowledgment of dependence, what Syncellus then offers as his own reason for quoting from these same sources will come as a disappointment. It is simple pedantry; even though he has no use for non-biblical chronologies, he says, he will include these sources anyway, "lest my work seem to be incomplete (ἀτελές)."[61]

Desire for completeness also appears to be the motive behind Syncellus'

---

[59] Sync. 17.26–27.
[60] Ibid., 16.30–33.
[61] Ibid., 16.33.

initial citations from *Jubilees* and the *Life of Adam*. We may wonder, for example, why, if Syncellus opposed the chronology of Adam's life in Paradise proposed in *Jubilees* and the *Life of Adam*, and if he recognized that both works were non-authoritative, he felt it necessary to quote at length from both works. The shallowness of his explanation exposes his own uncertainties about the proper way of incorporating "suspect" material:

> And it is necessary that the less mature among us not investigate and overwork questions about which Scripture is silent. Whatever happens to be useful and beneficial to mankind, these things have been given to us through the holy spirit, and it is not necessary for orthodox readers to overstep divine boundaries, lest in exchange for a small gain they might incur a great penalty. But some have boldly investigated this question, either from an illusory curiosity or spurred on by vainglory. And taking divine Scriptures in hand they attempt to show that our forefather Adam was not immediately introduced into Paradise by God, or else entering before the creation of woman gave names to the wild beasts and the birds of heaven. But this is not a work of one day for human weakness and frailty, as they argue, because Scripture says that God "also planted Paradise in Eden toward the East, and set there the man whom he fashioned, and God made to grow from the ground every tree pleasant to the sight and good for food, the tree of life also in the midst of the garden, and the tree of the knowledge of good and evil. And out of the ground God formed every beast of the field and every bird of the air." And after similar things, it adds, "for Adam there was not found a helper similar to him, so the Lord cast a deep sleep on Adam, and as he slept, the Lord took one of his ribs, and filled up flesh around it, and so forth." So necessarily I am also compelled to make clear in part (ἀναγκαίως προήχθην καὶ . . . δηλῶσαι ἐν μέρει) what is said regarding this by *Jubilees* and the so-called *Life of Adam* . . . lest those investigating these matters fall into more absurd ideas.[62]

Syncellus' predecessors, as we have seen, appealed to these two apocryphal works in order to prove that the protoplasts had after their creation spent some time outside of Paradise.[63] Syncellus has strangely vacillating views on the matter, which, as will be seen later, probably are due to the

---

[62] Ibid., 3.26–4.23.
[63] See above, Chap. 3, pp. 84–86.

character of the source upon which he has depended.[64] Although Syncellus begins by saying that he accepts Chrysostom's suggestions on the question,[65] he soon reverses himself by warning that Genesis' silence on the matter should deter all speculation about it. Then, however, Syncellus reverses himself again by saying that he must consider the subject because others have concluded, on the basis of Genesis 2:8–9 and 2:19, that the naming of the beasts must have exceeded one day. In order to "prevent readers from falling into more absurd views," he says he must quote from the same sources that they have consulted: the *Life of Adam* and *Jubilees*. From this justification, one expects to find a refutation of the chronology proposed by these two works, but all he ends up doing is citing from the two works. After his excerpt from the *Life of Adam*, Syncellus concludes only by saying that he has furnished the quotation "for the sake of curiosity (φιλομαθίας χάριν)."[66] Moreover, despite his initially very limited reasons for using these two works, Syncellus continues quoting them for the period well after Adam's expulsion from Paradise.[67] His equivocations reveal two dimensions of Syncellus' personality—the Byzantine *eclogarius*, fond of displaying his learning, and the champion of orthodoxy.

Nor does Syncellus display much independence in his strange selection of proof texts for the "Sethite" interpretation of Genesis 6. As we have seen, this demythologizing interpretation is a standard piece of Christian exegesis, attested in a wide range of sources, some of which Syncellus mentions for other reasons—Chrysostom and Ephrem, for example. In the light of this, one is surprised to see what weak evidence he offers in defense of his interpretation. Along with 2 Peter, he cites the Enochic *Book of the Watchers* and Zosimus the alchemist as corroboration for the historical veracity of the fall of the sons of God.[68] In fact, neither Zosimus nor *1 Enoch* can with any certainty be counted as corroboration for the naturalistic interpretation of Genesis 6. *1 Enoch*, as we have seen, was often repudiated for not conforming to this interpretation.

One can easily surmise why the eclectic Panodorus would have gravitated to such sources as confirmation for Genesis 6. Because *1 Enoch* was to play a vital part in Panodorus' reconstruction of primordial history, he was keen to establish the groundwork for its use by reconciling the apoc-

[64] See below, Chap. 6, pp. 165–68.
[65] Sync. 3.19–22. For further discussion of Syncellus' appeal to Chrysostom, see below, Chap. 6, pp. 165–66.
[66] Ibid., 5.26.
[67] See below, Chap. 6, pp. 182–93.
[68] Ibid., 11.11–14.4.

alypse with the naturalistic interpretation of Genesis 6, even to the extent of adducing it as a proof-text for the Sethite interpretation of Genesis 6. The quotation from Zosimus, tracing the origins of alchemy to the Watchers, had its own value: independent confirmation from the Hermetic literature for the fall of the Watchers.[69] None of these reasons, however, would have had any cogency for Syncellus; certainly, if he had thought more originally about the question, he could have come up with far less controversial witnesses for the historicity of Genesis 6 than a fourth-century Egyptian alchemist and what was by the ninth century a discredited Jewish apocalypse. Here we must assume that Syncellus was simply transcribing excerpts from his source, evidently not fully understanding where Panodorus' use and interpretation of these sources were tending.

As his narrative progressed and as his dispute with Panodorus and Annianus became more heated, Syncellus stepped up his polemic against both of them and the sources that they used. The main thrust of his arguments, however, was against Panodorus. From the acerbity and occasional incoherence of his prose style, Laqueur argued that Syncellus could not have been simply transcribing from a source with which he had so little in common. Syncellus represents himself as a resolute opponent of the "lies of the gentiles," contrasting himself with Panodorus' accommo-

---

[69] Ibid., 14.4–14. The quotation from Zosimus, the 4th-century alchemist from Panopolis (or, according to Suidas, the Thebaid) is from an alchemical treatise addressed to his "sister" Theosebeia. Reitzenstein suggests that Theosebeia was not an actual sister, but simply a colleague (*Poimandres*, 266 (note 2); Georg Luck thinks Theosebeia was a "wealthy lady interested in Zosimus' alchemic researches"; see his *Arcana Mundi* (Baltimore, 1985), 370. The treatise from which this excerpt comes is one of twenty-eight composed by Zosimus, arranged, says Suidas, κατὰ στοιχεῖον, that is, according to the letters of the Greek alphabet. The significance of the passage lies mainly in its attesting to the wide dissemination of the legend of the Watchers, extending to Egyptian Hermetism:

> The holy Scriptures, that is the Bible, say, O woman, that there is a race of demons (τι δαιμόνων γένος) which becomes involved with women. And Hermes mentioned this in his *Physica*, and virtually every treatise, whether public or hidden, made mention of this. Thus, the ancient and divine scriptures said this, that certain angels lusted after women, and having descended, taught them all the works of nature. Having stumbled on account of these women, he says, they remained outside of heaven, because they taught mankind everything wicked and nothing befitting the spirit. The same scriptures say also that from them the Giants were born. And so the first teaching of Chemes concerning these arts is theirs. He called this the book of Chemes, whence the art is called alchemy.

For the association of the fall of the Watchers with the origins of alchemy in Egyptian Hermetism, see also the letter of Isis to her son Horus, describing how, after considerable delay and the swearing of an oath of secrecy, a Watcher named "Amnael" agreed to reveal to her alchemical secrets (cf. A.-J. Festugière, *La Révélation d'Hermès Trismégiste*, 1. 254–60).

dating attitude toward non-biblical sources. As Laqueur maintained, Syncellus' spirited criticisms of his Alexandrian predecessor, and the often disorganized arrangement of his arguments, would on the face of it preclude the possibility that Syncellus had simply transcribed from a work with which he held so little in common.[70]

This characterization of Panodorus is accurate insofar as it applies to his and Syncellus' conflicting views about resolving chronological discrepancies among various sources. Upon closer examination, however, it becomes clear that the differences between the two chroniclers are narrower than might first appear. One should not conclude from Syncellus' representation of him that Panodorus was an uncritical devotee of pagan literature. He shared with Syncellus a characteristic suspicion of these sources, if incorrectly interpreted. Indeed, Syncellus himself expresses amazement that Panodorus should have accepted profane sources into his primordial chronology when he, like Syncellus, was aware that these works promoted heresy. The comment appears in the midst of an extended attack against one of his Alexandrian predecessors, in the course of which Syncellus preserves a direct citation from him:

> So, he (i.e., Panodorus) says, having solved scientifically (ἀποδεικτικῶς) the questionable meaning of the Chaldeans, *I think it necessary first to interpret the events before the transgression (of the Watchers) up to the 165th year of Enoch in the year 1286,* and then to arrange in chronological order the events from Adam up to the 20th year of Constantine, so that by naming the kings of each race of people, I will give a continuous account of 5,816 years.
>
> Moreover, on the basis of the men whose genealogies have been traced in divine Scriptures from Adam up to the praiseworthy twenty-second Archbishop Theophilus, destroyer of idols, archbishop of Alexandria, Egypt and the two Libyas, I will compute the chronology, and set forth the total number of years as 5,904—this, so that the heresiarchs, wise in their conceit, and the pagans might find no point of departure in our divine Scriptures. For the pagans, wise in their conceit, believed that the universe was many thousands of years old, and the *heresiarchs conversely confess that Christ the creator of time was subject to time, saying, "there was a time when he was not."* But let all of them withdraw from before the Catholic church when they

---

[70] Laqueur, "Synkellos," 1403–5.

hear, "Friend, how did you get in here, without wearing a wedding-garment?" (cf. Mt. 22:12).[71]

The above citation is embedded in an extended attack by Syncellus against its author; the transition from Syncellus' own criticisms to the actual quotation is barely perceptible. Although the source of the excerpt is not explicitly identified, it belongs to a larger description of the chronographic technique for reducing a Chaldean year to a day—precisely parallel, even in small details, to the technique for reducing the Egyptian year to a month and a season, which Syncellus subsequently expressly attributes to Panodorus. This, and the reference to the archbishop Theophilus of Alexandria, suggest that the origin of this citation is Panodorus' chronicle.

The orthodox self-consciousness of the author, which first led Unger to argue unconvincingly that Annianus was the source of this quotation, reveals a hitherto unrecognized dimension of Panodorus' self-understanding as a chronicler.[72] Modern writers on Panodorus tend to see him both as an enthusiastic proponent of pagan wisdom and afficionado of esoteric literature, with only a slender attachment to orthodoxy.[73] But although Syncellus would later rebuke him for being too hasty to accommodate "pagan wisdom," Panodorus represents himself here as a champion of orthodoxy—clearly evident in his denunciation of gentile wisdom and heresy (that is, Arianism). His "scientific" reduction of the primitive Chaldean and Egyptian year strengthens the case for the orthodox calculation of the age of the world; by demonstrating the actual harmony of Babylonian and Egyptian chronology with Genesis, Panodorus hopes to forestall pagan and Arian conceptions about the age of the universe.

Panodorus composed his chronicle in Alexandria in the fifth century, at a time when orthodoxy was still in the process of defining itself internally and over against its environment. He describes his approach to sources that might promote the interests of heresy and paganism as "scientific" and "allegorical." Syncellus, writing in Constantinople some four hundred years later, would characterize it another way—as a vain attempt to accommodate a lie with the truth of Scripture. At the same time, however, he recognizes that in their respective assessments of the dangers of ethnic

---

[71] Sync. 33.18–33.

[72] Unger, *Manetho*, 39.

[73] Ibid., 39. Unger states that Panodorus' "great predilection for heathen chroniclers (*grosse Vorliebe für die heidnischen Chronologen*)" would have made it impossible for him to express such sentiments; on the other hand, he states that Annianus was not guilty of this. Given the fact that, according to Syncellus, both Panodorus and Annianus agreed in their approach to these pagan sources, Unger's comment makes little sense.

chronicles they are not far removed. In fact, Syncellus uses their agreement on this question as one of his arguments against his predecessor's work. After giving this excerpt from Panodorus' chronicle dealing with the pagan and heretical use of the ethnic chronicle, Syncellus makes this observation: If Panodorus himself understood that ethnic chronicles entertained false and dangerous notions about the age of the world, why did he not reject them altogether rather than try to accommodate them? It would be better, he says, to "spit upon their opinion (διαπτύσαι τὴν δόξαν)" rather than develop artificial means to accommodate them.[74]

Syncellus' bitter polemic against Panodorus' accommodating attitude toward pagan chronicles should not overshadow the fact that he had more common ground with the Alexandrian monk than might first appear. This insight may enable us better to understand Syncellus' use and interpretation of two blocks of material originating in Panodorus' chronicle, the second excerpt from *1 Enoch* and Alexander Polyhistor's excerpt from the *Babyloniaca*. Laqueur has already commented on the ungainly way in which Syncellus introduces his second excerpt from *1 Enoch*. He begins first by introducing not *1 Enoch*, but rather the early histories of the Babylonians and the Egyptians; then he abruptly reverses himself and introduces *1 Enoch*:

> It would be superfluous for those who steadfastly believe that the flood occurred at the time of Noah in A.M. 2242 to accept the histories of the Chaldeans and the Egyptians. For they introduce endless myriads of years, and arrange everything for the subversion of truth, even if they appear in part to agree with the divinely inspired Scripture concerning the flood and the Giants and Noah himself, also called Xisuthros by them, from which those who have written these things have stolen every useful idea. But since destructive things not understood often work to bring death to those not familiar with them, I think it is necessary to set out a few passages side by side with those available to us from divine Scriptures, not so they might be believed—not at all!—, but rather for the refutation of their falsehood. *But before this, the corresponding account about the Watchers from the first book of Enoch will be cited, since it is more akin with our Scriptures— even if it is apocryphal and doubtful in places.* . . .[75]

---

[74] Sync. 34.2–5.

[75] Ibid., 23.31–24.9. This same explanation appears regularly. He will set out some "little fragments" from the authors of Babylonian and Egyptian histories, through which "their lack of harmony with one another and with divine Scripture will be clear to the faithful" (28.12–15). See also 32.4–8.

This case is developed in the context of seeking to discredit the opinions of those who believe that the lies of profane histories can be reconciled with Scripture. Here the excerpting of material from non-biblical sources is justified on the grounds that readers who are properly informed about their content will resist efforts to seek points of intersection between them and Scripture. At 28.12, after furnishing his second citation from *1 Enoch*, as well as a lengthy disclaimer on the use of apocrypha, Syncellus returns to Chaldean and Egyptian histories: "It remains after this, just as we promised (ἐπηγγειλάμεθα), to cite a few passages from those who wrote Chaldean and Egyptian histories, through which their disagreement with each other and divine Scripture will be clear to the faithful."[76]

On the basis of the verbal parallels, Laqueur has perceptively suggested that the material from *1 Enoch* and the apology for the use of the apocrypha (24.10–28.11) were a later insertion by Syncellus.[77] The motive for this insertion here is clear from Syncellus' own justification for quoting from the work. Even if "apocryphal and doubtful in places," it is worth quoting from *1 Enoch* because it is "more akin to Scripture" than the lies of Berossus and Manetho—here again an implicit refutation of Panodorus. This and the fact that the excerpt seems to have been detached from its original context suggest that Syncellus has wrenched it from its original location and placed it in a context more appropriate for his own purposes.

We gain a sharper understanding of Syncellus' adaptation of Panodorus from the conclusion of his second excerpt from the *Book of the Watchers*. Here Syncellus gives an interesting and erudite discourse on the legitimate use of apocrypha. Worth quoting in extenso, it is noticeably different in tone from his explanation for the first *Enoch* excerpt, which he cites, without apology, along with 2 Peter and Genesis 6:

> And this passage is taken from the first book of Enoch concerning the Watchers, even if it is necessary that especially the more simple-minded not embrace apocrypha whole-heartedly, because they contain some strange material and material that is alien to ecclesiastical teaching, and because they have been adulterated by Jews and heretics. Nevertheless, blessed Paul on occasion used passages from apocrypha, as when he says in the first letter to the Corinthians, "what the eye hath not seen . . ." and other things from the *Apocrypha of Elijah*. And again in the letter to the Galatians, he quotes from the *Apocalypse*

---

[76] Ibid., 28.12–16.
[77] Laqueur, "Synkellos," 1399.

of Moses, "there is neither circumcision, nor uncircumcision, but a new creation." And in the letter to the Ephesians, from the work called the *Apocrypha of Jeremiah,* "Awake, O sleeper, and arise from the dead, and Christ shall give you light." We say this, not to give license to those who want to read apocrypha indiscriminately—not at all! For many people have gone astray because they have believed in all of it, for which reason the blessed church of God and the chorus of our divinely inspired fathers have prevented us from reading them as if they were other divine writing. But we have set out the preceding excerpts in order to demonstrate only the transgression of the Watchers and the impiety of the Giants, concerning which divine Moses also makes mention, and that because of them, the universal flood occurred; *and to make it unnecessary for Christians to suppose that those who have written Chaldean and Egyptian antiquities have from canonical* (ἐνδιαθέτων) *or apocryphal books any kind of basis for their own false talk, and to write a refutation of their endless years and the kingdoms and dynasties reported by them;* but also in order that the person who investigates these apocryphal books concerning such matters may be satisfied with the foregoing excerpts from them, lest thoughtlessly reading these works wholesale he might lapse from the true and orthodox view. For it is reported in the so-called *Apocalypse of Moses* regarding them (περὶ αὐτῶν = the Giants), that after the flood in the universal year 2582, they, moved by envy after death, led astray the sons of Noah. And when Noah prayed that they withdraw from them, the Lord ordered the archangel Michael to cast them into the abyss until the day of judgment. But the devil asked to receive a portion of them to test men, and at the behest of God, a tenth of them was given to him, so as to test mankind to prove each person's devotion to God. And the remaining nine-tenths were cast into the abyss. This seems incongruous to us, that a living man is tested by the spirit of someone who has died. Therefore, we too urge those who read apocrypha either there or elsewhere not to follow entirely the ideas expressed in them.[78]

Syncellus has simply transcribed and augmented a long apologia for the use of apocrypha from Panodorus. It is clear that the three segments of *1 Enoch* preceding this passage were carefully preselected by an editor with a very circumscribed purpose in mind; they describe the further impieties

[78] Sync. 27.8–28.11.

of the Watchers, God's judgment upon them, the savagery of the Giants, and the burning of Mt. Hermon. Why these passages were selected is stated in the above passage: *1 Enoch,* he says, corroborates and enlarges upon Moses' account of the flood. But the author (Panodorus) warns his readers that they must be satisfied only with excerpts; other material from the same work has been contaminated by Jews and heretics. Presumably by heretics Panodorus means Manichees, for whom the activities of the Giants figured prominently in their own cosmology.[79] Indeed, one of the examples adduced as evidence of the questionable status of apocrypha is the account in *Jubilees* of the tormenting of Noah's offspring by the post-diluvian spirits of the Giants. Passages like these, he says, show that apocryphal books are not altogether credible.

Panodorus' reasons for citing this second excerpt from *1 Enoch* had nothing to do with Chaldean and Egyptian antiquities; this was the purpose for which he had cited the *first* excerpt. Here his motive in adducing *1 Enoch* as a witness is simply to amplify Genesis, while at the same time warning his readers against indiscriminate reading of it. Syncellus, fully in support of Panodorus' orthodox scruples about apocrypha, appropriates this justification as his own, contributing along the way his own rather contrived one. Among the reasons he names for citing from *1 Enoch* is that it will make it unnecessary for anyone to accept Chaldean or Egyptian antiquities. This additional justification, far from self-evident from the excerpt itself, all but destroys the sense of the passage. One must assume, for example, that the words περὶ αὐτῶν refer to the Giants already mentioned, but the long insertion by Syncellus has left the antecedent to αὐτῶν ambiguous.

What follows this lengthy interlude on the legitimate and illegitimate applications of apocrypha is a long excerpt from Alexander Polyhistor's adaptation of the *Babyloniaca,* transcribed from Panodorus, who in turn knows it from Eusebius. There ensues an extended tirade by Syncellus against the dangers of Chaldean history:

> These passages are set forth from Alexander Polyhistor, quoting from Berossus who made up the fictitious *Chaldaica.* But for those who want things properly it is fitting to juxtapose the divine Scripture of Genesis with the preceding marvelous Chaldean fable, to see how much they disagree with one another and how it also conflicts with

---

[79] On Manichean use of *1 Enoch,* especially the so-called *Book of the Giants,* see W. B. Henning, "The Book of the Giants," *BSOAS* 11 (1943/46), 52–74.

divine writings in most things. . . . But it(?) avoids acknowledging
that it stole the whole basis of its account from the writings of Moses
and invents Oannes, the sea-creature, who never existed nor was seen
by anyone, nor has any reality, just as there are neither "skindapses"
nor "tragelophs." And it says that this monster recounted to mankind
that there was a time in which all was darkness and water. But since
it did not have the courage to proclaim openly the words of the man
who saw God—"and darkness was over the abyss"—it changed the
words. But it has by no means deceived those of sharp mind, even if
it adds in imaginary beings and other things, eager to confuse its
audience; and in addition to the water and darkness before the creation of the heaven and earth, it proposes a most idolatrous belief in
the existence of unreal beings. Images of these beings, it says, are
maintained in the Temple of Bel. Similarly, by veiling in myth the
remaining narrative about the heaven and the earth . . . , it introduces, according to divine Gregory, the error of polytheism to those
it wins over, and from preexistent matter it endeavors to prove the
existence of beings of a moist nature.[80]

The passage is initially confusing, since it is unclear what the subject
of the sentence is. But the numerous feminine participles (λαβοῦσα,
φεγοῦσα) probably refer to the Chaldean τερατολόγια. Aside from this,
however, the argument is very clear and straightforward.

At 32.29, the quality of the prose deteriorates dramatically. Suddenly and
without notice, Syncellus is debating one of his Alexandrian sources on
the question of the Chaldean year. The very awkward transition contrasts
sharply with Syncellus' usual method of citing from sources. Although he
occasionally is not precise in naming the exact origin of citations, he is, as
a rule, careful to delimit the extent of the excerpt, normally under some
identifying rubric such as ἐκ τῶν λεπτῶν Γενέσεως, ἐκ τοῦ πρώτου Βιβλίου Ἐνώχ, or ἐκ τοῦ Ἀλεξάνδρου τοῦ Πολυίστορος. He rigorously
observes this practice in his citations from the two well-known Christian
chronographers: for example, "From Africanus concerning the Watchers,"
"Africanus says," "Eusebius says." By contrast, this passage, although
extending several lines, remains anonymous, and is not clearly delimited. Syncellus slurs together material from the Chaldean "fable
(τερατολόγια)" of Berossus/Polyhistor with this excerpt from his source.

[80] Sync. 32.4–28.

Only the change of gender and person, and the occasional φησί here and there enable the reader to know that Syncellus is citing from a source.[81]

The whole section from 32.4 to 35.5 should be seen as a rough transcription from Panodorus, with an occasional gloss from Syncellus himself. In his own chronicle, Panodorus had begun the discussion of Chaldean chronology with his excerpt from Polyhistor via Eusebius. Two features of this excerpt required explanation: the τερατολόγια of Oannes, and the long reigns of the Chaldean kings. The tale of Oannes is rejected *tout court* as a dangerous and idolatrous fantasy—hence the strongly worded caveat about the absurdities of the myth and the distortions of Genesis. In support of this argument the author cites Gregory of Nazianzus, from his second dialogue on theology. Panodorus' appeal to Gregory here is understandable; the passage from which he cites deals with the dangers of idolatry, a favorite concern in Alexandria under Theophilus ὁ εἰδωλοκτόνος.[82] Indeed, in the title that Panodorus has assigned this extract from Polyhistor, he already makes it clear that he considers the narrative about Oannes a far-fetched myth—"From Alexander Polyhistor concerning the 10 kings of the Chaldeans who ruled before the flood, and the flood itself, and concerning Noah and the ark, *in the midst of which he also says some fantastic things* (τινα . . . τερατώδη), as they were written by Berossus."[83]

Up to this point, Syncellus is in full sympathy with Panodorus' observations, appropriating them as his own. Following this, however, Panodorus turns to the second matter—the long reigns of the ten pre-flood Chaldean kings. Outlining here his proof that Berossus' chronology of this period can be explained "scientifically," and appealing to the *Book of the Watchers* and the *Astronomical Book,* he claims that with his interpretation he has confuted Arianism and pagan wisdom. Because Syncellus rejects this method, he is no longer directing his criticisms against Chaldaism, but against Panodorus himself. From this point, Syncellus begins his refutation of Panodorus, continuing to cite from him, but interspersing his own editorial opinions and objections. The liberties that Syncellus takes with his Alexandrian source often make the text extremely difficult to understand, at times creating the impression of a dialogue instead of a quotation. Indeed, the ensuing passage dealing with Panodorus' interpre-

---

[81] Of this section, Laqueur writes: ". . . so kommt man zu einer vollkommenen Konfusion," ("Synkellos," 1403).

[82] Gregory Nazianzus *Oratio Theol.* 2.14.

[83] Sync. 28.17–20.

tation of the astronomical portion of *1 Enoch* is a mass of confusion, filled with parenthetical statements and unfinished sentences.[84]

The foregoing analysis would tend to add support to some of the main features of Gelzer's theory of sources. Generally, scholars who have pressed for Syncellus' originality have pointed to literary infelicities in his work as evidence of his independence from earlier authorities. At least in the passages examined above, however, these infelicities are largely attributable to Syncellus' apparent lack of skill in adapting material from his sources—a deficiency which, as Laqueur has suggested, may be due to the fact that the work was an unfinished first draft.[85] Indeed, Gelzer himself was unaware of the extent of dependence, since his conclusions were often based on general impressions rather than detailed literary analysis. For the sections examined here, the bulk of Syncellus' literary activity consists mainly of excerpting, adapting, and reshaping material from earlier chronicles, and this, ironically, in order to disprove those very authorities upon whom he is so dependent.

It should be stressed, however, that the portion of Syncellus' chronicle examined here represents only that part in which Syncellus is in self-conscious dialogue with his predecessors. It is far from clear that the same degree of adaptation characterizes his whole chronicle; indeed, there are good reasons to doubt this. Even for his treatment of primordial history, Syncellus will occasionally cite from works that he could not conceivably have known from his Alexandrian authorities. And although Gelzer's theory of literary dependence was formulated mainly on his analysis of Syncellus' primordial chronology, the same extent of self-conscious borrowing can hardly be said to characterize the rest of Syncellus' chronicle. For postdiluvian history, Syncellus in fact rarely refers explicitly to Annianus and only infrequently to Panodorus.

In the preceding discussion we have discovered a fairly consistent pattern of adaptation of material from his Alexandrian predecessors, especially Panodorus. But Syncellus himself is extremely vague in acknowledging where he knew his extra-biblical sources, often using terminology like "some historians." How Syncellus' sources for primordial history were mediated to him raises numerous related questions, not the least of which is the issue of the textual history of these sources. On the basis of Syncellus'

---

[84] Laqueur's ("Synkellos," 1404) characterization of this section as "Zusammenhanglosigkeit und Zerrüttung" is apt.
[85] Laqueur, "Synkellos," 1404–5.

presumed dependence on the Alexandrian monks, Gelzer proposed an in-
genious and very influential theory about the textual history of Syncellus'
sources. According to this theory, the heterogeneous corpus of sources
first collected and then edited by Panodorus had been further redacted by
Annianus. Syncellus knew and incorporated into his own chronicle source
material from both works; as a consequence, editorial reworkings in Syncellus' sources reflect redactional activity in at least two earlier stages. Reasoning from this hypothesis, Gelzer went on to propose a very sweeping
reconstruction of the textual history of Jewish pseudepigrapha and Chaldean and Egyptian antiquities in Byzantine and Syriac chronography. In
the next and final chapter, we shall attempt to see if Gelzer's reconstruction
fully accounts for the character of the preserved sources.

CHAPTER SIX

Text and Redaction in Byzantine Chronography

After citing from the apocryphal *Life of Adam*, Syncellus acknowledges to his readers that he has given them only an abridgment (ἐν συντόμῳ) of portions of the original work. Like other Byzantine chronographers, Syncellus counted conciseness a virtue.[1] This practice was, to be sure, only observed irregularly, and when it was it often produced incoherence—a lamentable quality of some of the later chronographers. But the very scope of the universal chronicle required some degree of selectivity, and chronographers exercised this function freely.

Byzantine chronographers had various motives for epitomizing their sources. One reason was simply to offer a smattering of obscure texts. The "appropriate" matter that he has gleaned from earlier works, writes George Cedrenus in the introduction to his Σύνοψις Ἱστοριῶν, will at the least serve as a guide for those readers who might never be able to read the originals.[2] By editing his sources, the chronographer was also acting as censor; readers, Syncellus warns, will have to settle for excerpts from Jewish apocrypha because, while useful in places, "doubtful" works read wholesale might lead astray the unsophisticated.[3]

Textual editing could sometimes be more extreme. Christian chronography operated on what must be considered now very dubious principles, often requiring its practitioners to exercise considerable latitude with non-biblical sources. Chronographers were always looking for ways to assimilate one source with another, either through synchronization or syncretism. Sometimes this amounted to the simple insertion of chronological

---

[1] For conciseness as a desirable quality in chronography, see, for example, Theophanes' praise, not altogether warranted, of Syncellus' work as a "concise chronography (σύντομος χρονογραφία)" (1. 1.13, ed. C. de Boor). Syncellus himself praises Annianus for being concise, at the same time castigating his elder colleague for being long-winded and repetitive (cf. Sync. 35.20–32).

[2] Ced. 1. 6.11–12.

[3] Sync. 27.30–33.

detail or the reworking of a calendrical system. At other times, it might assume a grosser character, as, for example, in the extensive, and sometimes deliberate, interpolation of Josephus' *Antiquities* with material from *Jubilees*.[4] The Byzantine, Syriac, and Arabic chronographers, standing at the end of a long chain of textual transmission, have inherited what is in many cases an amazingly conflated set of traditions, the result of inevitably occurring accidental corruptions and deliberate editing.

It is impossible to understand fully the character of these reworkings without attempting first to piece together the history of the transmission that produced them. Here we are not always on firm ground. Far from scrupulous in citing authorities, the chronographers frequently leave their sources unattested or falsely attributed. A work that has been filtered through several intermediaries is often cited as if it were known firsthand. Even when chronographers name predecessors, they tend to telescope the textual history of their sources, excluding intermediate agents. Tracing the transmission of these sources is further aggravated by the fact that earlier chronographers often thought to be sources for later chroniclers do not survive independently. Julius Africanus, Panodorus, Annianus, and (at least in Syriac) Jacob of Edessa are authors who, while revered by later chronographers, are known almost entirely on the basis of what these later historians have elected to preserve from them.

GELZER'S RECONSTRUCTION OF THE TEXTUAL HISTORY OF SYNCELLUS' SOURCES

Much of the uncertainty as to the extent to which Syncellus and the other Byzantine chronographers depended on Eusebius for primordial history has been removed by the discovery of the first book of Eusebius' chronicle. The influence of Africanus and the Alexandrian chronographers is far more difficult to document, however. The most systematic and thoroughgoing attempt to resolve this latter question was undertaken by Heinrich Gelzer, whose views on this matter have already been discussed in the previous chapter.[5] Our discussion here will be mainly limited to Gelzer's reconstruction as it extends to the textual transmission of nonbiblical sources for primordial history, notably the Jewish pseudepigrapha and Egyptian and Chaldean antiquities.

Expanding on a conjecture proposed earlier by Unger, Gelzer main-

[4] See below, pp. 188–93.
[5] See above, Chap. 5, pp. 134–35.

tained that virtually all of Syncellus' non-biblical sources originated in the chronicle of Panodorus, but that many of these works had undergone a second reworking by Annianus, his younger colleague.[6] Gelzer was led to this conclusion from Syncellus' own observations about the relationship of Annianus to Panodorus. As has already been noted, Annianus' knowledge and use of Panodorus can be inferred both from the striking similarities between the two works and the likely priority and originality of Panodorus. But Annianus was not merely a slavish transcriber. From Syncellus' own observations about the composition of the two works, Gelzer was persuaded that Annianus functioned as an ecclesiastical redactor.

In his highly qualified praise of his Alexandrian predecessor, Syncellus remarks that whatever commended Panodorus—for example, his skill in "precise chronology" and his theoretical knowledge—was undermined by repetitiousness and "zeal for pagan sages."[7] Syncellus especially faults him for following the "astronomical canon" and the "mathematical tables," meaning by this the "Handy Tables" of Claudius Ptolemy, astronomical charts used in the dating of the reigns of kings.[8] By applying these tables to his own chronology, Panodorus had erred in computing the birth and resurrection of Christ seven years earlier than the traditional date. Although Syncellus does not say so expressly, implicit in his description of Panodorus' chronicle is the latter's formulation of the world era from 1 Thoth (= August 29th), in conformity with the Egyptian calendar.[9]

Since Syncellus had set as the goal of his own work the vindication of the "traditional" dating of Christ's incarnation in the year A.M. 5500, this seven-year error was a serious failing, sufficient to mitigate whatever else was laudable about Panodorus' work. But Annianus did not share the same reproach. Of the two aforementioned historians, Syncellus writes, "it should be recognized that the exposition of Annianus is more concise and more accurate, and in line with apostolic and patristic tradition; in it he assigns the divine incarnation to the end of the 5,500th year and the beginning of the year 5501, the holy and luminescent day of the resurrection in the 25th of the Roman month March, the 29th of the Egyptian month Phamenoth, which, in the 532-year Paschal tables compiled by him,

---

[6] Cf. Unger, *Manetho*, 40. For Gelzer's analysis of particular sources preserved by Syncellus, see *SJA*, 2. 185–93; 198–217 (Chaldean and Egyptian antiquities); 2. 247–49 (Annianus' correction of Panodorus' dating of Christ's birth); 2. 249–80 (Jewish pseudepigrapha).

[7] Sync. 378.7–8.

[8] Ibid., 397.7–10.

[9] 1 Thoth, the first day of the Alexandrian year, was also the basis for Ptolemy's *Handy Tables*. On the world era of Panodorus, see D. Serruys, "Les transformations," 251–60.

he also shows with the aid of learned investigations was the first-formed day."[10]

What Syncellus says about Annianus reveals the interests of a monk more narrowly governed by ecclesiastical concerns than his Alexandrian colleague. To Syncellus' approval, the birth and resurrection of Christ were determined not, as in the case of Panodorus, by "pagan wisdom." Theology and tradition were the determinants: namely, the establishment of a mystical relationship between the first day of creation, the resurrection, and the incarnation, all occurring on March 25th.[11] The same concern is revealed as well in the 532-year Paschal cycle, a cycle thought to have been first formulated by Annianus. This cycle, based on the lowest common multiple of 19, 7, and 4, served mainly to fix the dates of Easter, a perennial problem that had divided the Church and consumed the energies of Christian chronographers.[12] In Gelzer's opinion, Annianus used these Easter tables as the organizational principle for condensing portions of what Syncellus would later describe as Panodorus' "multi-faceted (πολυμερῆ)" and repetitious work.[13] The structure of Annianus' chronicle, Syncellus observed, took the form of "11 Paschal cycles of 532 years along with accurate scholia (σχολίοις ἀκριβέσι)." By the term "scholia," Syncellus probably means historical notices set in the margins, examples of which still survive in the Ethiopic computus.[14]

Little more than a "handwerksmässigen Passacalculator," said Unger of Annianus, who had, he claimed, transcribed from Panodorus whatever historical scholia he had inserted into these Easter tables.[15] As for Syncel-

---

[10] Sync. 35.20–27.

[11] For discussion of the eras used by the Alexandrian chronographers, see in particular, Unger, *Manetho*, 34–43; D. Serruys, "Les transformations," 251–64; idem, "De quelques ères usitées chez les chroniqueurs byzantins," *Revue de philologie* n.s. 31 (1907), 151–53; Gelzer, *SJA* 2. 247–49; V. Grumel, *La chronologie: Traité d'études byzantines 1*, Bibliothèque byzantine (Paris, 1958), 84–97; Marius Chaîne, *La chronologie des temps chrétiens de l'Egypte et de l'Ethiopie* (Paris, 1925), 8–12.

[12] On this cycle and its influence on Ethiopic chronography, see Neugebauer, *Ethiopic Astronomy*, 8, 56–67.

[13] Syncellus describes Panodorus' chronicle as ἐν πολλοῖς δε ταυτολογοῦσαν (35.35).

[14] Ibid., 382.1–2: Ἀννιανοῦ τε τοῦ ὁσιωτάτου μοναχοῦ τοῦ συντάξαντος κύκλον ια' πασχουάλια φλβ' ἐτῶν ἅμα σχολίοις ἀκριβέσι. According to Neugebauer (*Ethiopic Astronomy*, 67), many of the 532-year Easter tables of the Ethiopic computus include a column in the left hand margin called *tārik*, containing brief historical notices.

[15] Unger, *Manetho*, 40. Unger likened Annianus to the "unwissende Osterrechner Hippolyt." Hippolytus' relationship to the "learned Africanus" was similar to Annianus' relationship to Panodorus, the latter in Unger's words the "most knowledgeable successor to Africanus and Eusebius" (41). For other unflattering assessments of Annianus' capacities, see Gelzer, *SJA*, 2. 190–191, 249; D. Serruys, "Les transformations," 256–58.

lus, Panodorus was "für profane Chronologie der Hauptgewährsmann."[16] In the uniquely "ecclesiastical parts of his chronology," however, Syncellus preferred Annianus' dating of the first day of creation and Christ's birth and resurrection.[17] Proceeding from the same premise, Gelzer ventured a sweeping theory about the textual history of Syncellus' sources. Although virtually all of Syncellus' extra-biblical sources originated in Panodorus, he knew as well Annianus' redaction of them, retaining, however sporadically, traces of these reworkings in his own chronicle.[18] This reconstruction of the textual transmission of Syncellus' sources would furnish the groundwork for Gelzer's analysis of the use of the Alexandrian chronographers by other chronicles, both in Syriac and Greek. Since Syriac chronographers frequently name "Annianus the monk" as an authority, Gelzer reasoned that in those instances where they cited the same sources as Syncellus they must have, like him, known these works through the Annianan redaction.[19] On the basis of parallels between Syncellus and other Byzantine chronographies, Gelzer believed it possible, moreover, to discern evidence of the Panodorus/Annianus source, even where neither chronicler was even named.[20]

Presumably because of its systematic character, Gelzer's assessment of the textual history of Syncellus' sources has found widespread and largely uncritical approval in most subsequent studies of the subject, where it is common to see references to Syncellus' "Panodorus/Annianus" source. Yet as D. Serruys, one of the few scholars to subject the thesis to detailed scrutiny, was later able to conclude: "La reconstruction était méthodique mais les formulations étaient trop caduques."[21] Gelzer himself could iden-

---

[16] Unger, *Manetho*, 35.

[17] Ibid., 40; see also Gelzer, *SJA*, 2. 248.

[18] For Gelzer's discussion of Syncellus' dependence on Panodorus for "Profanhistorie," see *SJA*, 2. 191. In Gelzer's estimation, the ἐκκλησιαστικὴ στοιχείωσις or ἐκκλησιαστικὴ κανών referred to by Syncellus in his list of Chaldeo-Persian kings was formulated by Annianus; see *SJA*, 2. 226–29. For Annianus' redaction of Panodorus and Syncellus' use of source material from both chronicles, see *SJA* 2. 211–14 (on Annianus' improvements of Panodorus' Egyptian sources); 2. 226–29 (on Annianus' redaction of Panodorus' list of Chaldean kings); and 2. 249–51 (on Syncellus' use of apocryphal sources from Panodorus and Annianus).

[19] See Gelzer, *SJA*, 2. 401–10; 430–58 (on Bar Hebraeus and Michael Syrus).

[20] Cf. *SJA*, 2. 152 (*Paschal Chronicle*); 280–97, 298 ff. (Ἐκλογὴ ἱστοριῶν); 360 ff. (Paris ms. 1712). Gelzer's views have inspired other attempts to locate the influence of Panodorus and Annianus in other chronicles. See, for example, A. Bauer and J. Strzygowski, *Eine alexandrinische Weltchronik*, DenkAkWien 51 (Vienna, 1905); A Bauer, *Die Chronik des Hippolytos*, TU 29.1 N.F. 14 (1905–6), 169–94, 222–31 (on Panodorus' and Annianus' supposed role in transmitting Hippolytus' chronicle to later chronographers).

[21] "Les canons d'Eusèbe, d'Annianos, et d'Andronicos d'après Élie de Nisibe," *BZ* 22 (1913), 17; see also Laqueur, "Synkellos," 1402.

tify unambiguously very little evidence in Syncellus' sources of traces of
Annianus' corrections which Syncellus had incorporated into his own
work.[22] And in his own examination, Serruys demonstrated that where his
theory could be tested empirically it proved wanting. After comparing
Annianus' Chaldeo-Assyrian kings list (as it is found in Elias of Nisibis)
with the parallel material in Syncellus, Serruys was able to challenge the
whole view. Not only was Annianus far less servilely attached to Panodorus than Gelzer had claimed; Syncellus himself "a certes fait des emprunts
considérables à Annianos mais il ne lui doit ni l'armature de sa chronologie
sacrée ni partant les listes profanes qui étaient incompatibles avec son
propre système. *Si le Syncelle n'est qu'un imitateur d'Annianos, du moins
peut-on prétendre qu'il a imité jusqu'à la liberté de son modèle.*"[23]

Gelzer's study of Byzantine chronicles was predicated on the assumption that there circulated in Byzantium *complete* copies of Africanus, Panodorus, Annianus, or Eusebius, and that their successors operated mainly
by transcribing from one or two of these earlier works. At least as it applied to Syncellus, this reconstruction presupposed a very improbable
view of his literary habits, namely, that he had before him two related
works (one a synopsis of the other), transcribing from both of them, but
in no obviously systematic or predictable way. One might better begin to
approach the question of Syncellus' use of the Alexandrian chroniclers by
first taking account of two characteristic features of many Byzantine
chronographers—their "eclecticism," and their habit of epitomizing and
distilling earlier chronicles. Syncellus' chronicle was called an ἐκλογή, and
numerous other chronicles bear the same or similar titles.[24] We need not
assume from such nomenclature that any of these highly derivative works
represented firsthand knowledge of the works cited in them, but we
should at least take seriously the chronographers' own conception of what
it was they thought they were doing—compiling and condensing the
views of many different authors. Although we can never know precisely in
what form they knew all of these sources, we are better served by the
assumption that, as in the case of his other sources, Syncellus did not have

[22] Some of his conjectures are very implausible. See, for example, his emendation of Syncellus at 58.7 (= Dind. ed., 97.21); *SJA,* 2. 212.

[23] Text of Elias of Nisibis, edited and translated by E. W. Brooks and I.-B. Chabot, CSCO
62, 63; Scriptores Syri 21–24 (Louvain, 1954). Specifically, Serruys ("Les canons," 16–28) chal-
lenged the contention that the "ecclesiastical canon" mentioned by Syncellus (246.19–20) was
taken from Annianus.

[24] See, for example, the superscriptions to the various chronicles collected by J. A. Cramer
in vol. 2 of his *Anecdota Graeca* (Oxford, 1839): Ἐκλογὴ Ἱστοριῶν; Ἐκλογὴ τῶν Χρονικῶν;
Ἐκλογαὶ Ἱστοριῶν.

at his disposal complete and independent copies of Panodorus or Annianus. What he consulted instead was a collection, which included among other things only extended extracts from the chronicles of his Alexandrian predecessors.

Syncellus' Indirect Knowledge of His Alexandrian Authorities

In his analysis of Syncellus' sources, Gelzer recognized that several of the patristic writers adduced by him could not have been transcribed directly from his Alexandrian authorities.[25] This is so because Syncellus regularly appeals to the church fathers to refute them. One illustration of this occurs in the context of his discussion of "those historians" who had consulted apocryphal works to establish their own chronology of Adam's life in Paradise. Before turning directly to this matter, Syncellus first warns his readers against any speculation about it, cautioning them that χρὴ τοὺς καθ᾽ ἡμᾶς ἀτελεῖς μὴ ζητεῖν καὶ περιεργάζεσθαι τὰ σεσιγημένα τῇ θεοπνεύστῳ γραφῇ.[26] Although Syncellus does not identify the source, the warning is virtually identical to Anastasius Sinaita's (seventh century) prohibitions against the same sort of speculation, and is probably derived from it. In his account of Adam's stay in Paradise, Anastasius writes: οὐ γὰρ δεῖ ἡμᾶς περιεργάζεσθαι τὰ σεσιωπημένα τῇ θεία γραφῇ. λέγω δὴ τὰ περὶ παραδείσου καὶ τοῦ ξύλου καὶ τῆς γυμνώσεως καὶ τῶν χιτώνων καὶ ἑτέρων τινῶν τοιούτων μὴ σαφῶς δεδηλωμένων ἡμῖν ἐν ταῖς βίβλοις ταῖς ἱεραῖς.[27]

As has been noted, Syncellus himself, although discouraging inquiry on the matter, expressed a personal preference for Chrysostom's chronology of Adam's early life. The passage in question is John Chrysostom's *Homilies on the Gospel according to Matthew:*[28] "'The blessed John, and Chrysostom great in teachings (καὶ μέγας ἐν διδασκάλοις Χρυσόστομος), says in his commentary on the gospel of Matthew that on the 6th day of the 1st week, that is on the same day of his creation, Adam was expelled from Paradise, as well as Eve, with whom (?) we also agree (ᾧ καὶ ἡμεῖς πειθόμεθα)."[29]

---

[25] *SJA*, 2. 188–89.
[26] Sync. 3.25–27.
[27] *Viae Dux* 4.32–36 (ed. Karl-Heinz Uthemann, CC Series Graeca 8 [Turnholt, 1981]); in the same work, Anastasius employs the same formula elsewhere (1.1.15–17) as a general guideline.
[28] Hom. 59 on Mt. 18.7 (ed. F. Field [Cambridge, 1839]).
[29] Sync. 3.19–22.

Where did Syncellus know this passage? It is extremely unlikely that the quotation from Chrysostom's *Homilies on Matthew* was taken from one of his Alexandrian sources. The epithet applied here to John—"Chrysostom"—is not attested before the seventh century, and the Alexandrian chronographers, writing during the time of Theophilus, would probably have avoided citing from Chrysostom, in the words of Gelzer "on dogmatic and chronological grounds."[30] Simply the fact that Syncellus appeals to him against their views would preclude the possibility that he found him quoted in their work.

For this reason, Gelzer believed that Chrysostom was one of the few non-biblical sources that Syncellus had consulted directly.[31] The question arises, however, as to whether Syncellus knew this citation from Chrysostom directly or through some intermediary. Syncellus never cites either one of them thereafter. And if Syncellus consulted Chrysostom with the express purpose of overturning the views of his Alexandrian sources, he has done a very poor job of integrating the citation into his argument. When he first cites the passage, he initially gives no reason as to its purpose or significance. Moreover, the actual reference shows evidence of the hand of an editor. As Bredow noticed, the expression καὶ τὴν Εὖαν, lacking in the original passage from Chrysostom, appears to have been inserted by someone as an afterthought; the motive here might have been to improve upon Chrysostom's testimony by making it fit more precisely the question that occasioned it.[32] What is most striking is what a weak argument it makes against the chronographers with whom Syncellus disagrees. Chrysostom does indeed refer to Adam's life in Paradise in his commentary on Matthew. But the comment is made in an offhand way, Chrysostom only venturing a guess that "perhaps (τάχα) Adam lived not so much as a whole day in Paradise." It is in all an extremely thin thread with which to weave an argument against the cogent case presented by these as yet unnamed "Christian historians."[33]

---

[30] *SJA*, 2. 188. The epithet καὶ μέγας ἐν διδασκάλοις Χρυσόστομος is unusual. Bredow (*Dissertatio de Georgii Syncelli Chronographia*, 13) has already commented on the highly irregular use of the anarthrous epithet Chrysostom, proposing that the cognomen was originally in the margin of the manuscript and was later inadvertently inserted into the text. Bredow suggests (13) that the more appropriate designation would be either ὁ Χρυσόστομος or καὶ διδάσκαλος Χρυσόστομος.

[31] *SJA*, 2. 188–189.

[32] Cf. Bredow, *Dissertatio*, 14.

[33] In the Homily, Chrysostom says (595A): "And if you want, look at the first man. If having lived in Paradise only a short time, perhaps not a whole day (τάχα δὲ οὐδὲ ἡμέραν ὅλην ἐν παραδείσῳ), and having enjoyed its delights, he advanced to such a level of evil that

I propose that Syncellus neither referred to Chrysostom's original work, nor did he know the complete works of these unidentified "Christian historians." Instead, he has consulted here an anthology of views on one major question confronting the chronographer. Presumably in response to the dilemma first posed by Eusebius, an epitomator has compiled a list of witnesses on the ἀπορία of Adam's stay in Paradise—including Chrysostom, *Jubilees,* and the *Life of Adam,* as well as "some Christian historians."

Collections such as these are well attested, both in Syriac and Greek sources. Moses Bar Cepha, for example, in his *De Paradiso,* also knows a variety of views on the same subject, some attributed to Ephrem, Philoxenus, and Jacob of Serug, others only to unnamed commentators.[34] Cedrenus also records a more extensive collection of opinions of various chroniclers on the subject.[35] What Syncellus must have found in his reference work was simply a collation of varying views, compiled by a neutral epitomator. Thus, after referring to Chrysostom's views on this issue, Syncellus himself awkwardly glosses the words: ᾧ καὶ ἡμεῖς πειθόμεθα. These words make little sense in this context. We cannot ascertain from the context with what or whom Syncellus is concurring.[36] The words con-

---

he even fancied himself equal with God, and to consider the deceiver a doer of good, and not to keep one commandment; if he had lived the rest of his life without affliction, what would he not have done?"

[34] Moses bar Cepha 1.38 (PG, 111. 581–82): "So now, let us also solve this question: How much time did Adam spend in Paradise? On this matter, some believe that he was there 30 years, because this was how much time our Lord spent in the world for expiating its sin. . . . Others think that Adam remained there 40 days . . . But the master Ephrem, Philoxenus, and Jacob of Serug say that Adam remained in Paradise not more than six hours. . . ." See also Isho'dad of Merv's *Commentary on Genesis,* on Gen. 3:24 (ed. and trans. C. van den Eynde and J. M. Vostè, CSCO 126, 156, Scriptores Syri 67, 75 [Louvain, 1955]): "(On the question of knowing) how much time (mankind) had remained in Paradise, some answer stupidly: for thirty years, in order to harmonize, in their opinion, these (years) with those of Christ, so much more because he was called the second Adam. Others say: for forty years, by reason of the youth of our Lord, who was, in their view, young in compensation for the time of the enjoyments of Paradise. According to others, the formation of Adam and his companion, the conferring of names on the animals, the entry into Paradise, and the expulsion (of the man) could not have occurred in a half-day. But we answer that this was possible, seeing that it was done by God."

[35] See below, pp. 208–9.

[36] Concerning these words, Bredow (14) writes: "I do not see what then is meant by the words, ᾧ καὶ ἡμεῖς πειθόμεθα. If . . . you relate them to John, what follows immediately contradicts it, for he is not Ἰωάννῃ πείθεται; rather, he warns us not to investigate matters that are shrouded in secrecy by the holy spirit. If in fact you want to refer these words to the Gospel of Matthew, they would be absurdly placed." The same epitomator may be responsible for some of the other patristic excerpts in Syncellus. The quotation from Ephrem, referred to above (see Chap. 5, pp. 141–42) forms part of a refutation of his Alexandrian sources. Syncellus only refers to Ephrem on this one occasion, and the passage is full of interpolations and highly paraphrased.

tradict Syncellus' own warning, issued shortly thereafter, against all speculation on matters about which the Scriptures are silent. And it is not until the succeeding passage that we realize that he is expressing his views against an opposing chronology of events.

The function of such a collection was essentially to compile the opinions of many chronographers on individual questions, naturally tending to group together chronographers who were likeminded on any given subject—the problem of Chaldean antiquities, Christ's death, Adam's life in Paradise, or the faults of Eusebius. As such, it did not always specify by name the proponents of any given view, preferring instead more general categories. When, for example, Cedrenus wants to catalogue differing opinions on any particular issue, he will frequently speak of "some," "certain of the elders," or "others."[37] Syncellus, too, often refers to his predecessors in this way. In his discussion of those historians who espoused opposing views about Paradise, he, like Cedrenus, identifies them simply as "other historians who composed Jewish *Antiquities* and Christian histories." Although this terminology would have embraced his Alexandrian predecessors, we need not conclude from Syncellus that these were the only chronographers to hold similar views on these questions. As we have seen, the appeal to works like *Jubilees* for this purpose was not confined to Panodorus and Annianus; moreover, Syncellus' allusion to "the author of Jewish *Antiquities*" shows that he believed, wrongly as it turns out, that Josephus fell into this same category as well.[38] Here it is likely that what Syncellus found in his collection was a reference to the proponents of this opinion under a general rubric, not unlike the expression "certain of the elders" employed by Cedrenus.

The same thing occurs when Syncellus comes to discuss a second ἀπορία—the problem of Chaldean and Egyptian antiquities. At least initially, Syncellus refers to his opponents as "certain historians," only later naming Panodorus and Annianus. Syncellus, to be sure, justifies the use of the expression out of respect for his predecessors. But even after identifying them by name he will at times continue to use only generic categories. "It seems to Panodorus and certain others (ἑτέροις τισί)," he writes, that Zoroaster first learned how to reckon the solar year.[39] Gelzer inclined to the view that the "others" mentioned here numbered only one, Annianus.[40]

---

[37] See below, pp. 209–11.
[38] Syncellus here knows a text of the *Antiquities* that has been interpolated by material from *Jubilees*. For discussion of this interpolated Josephus, see below, pp. 188–93.
[39] Sync. 89.3–4; also, 88.17–18; τινὲς τῶν ἐκκλησιαστικῶν ἡμῶν ἱστορικῶν.
[40] *SJA*, 2. 203.

But there are no grounds for assuming this, apart from Gelzer's own conviction that these were the only two chronicles that Syncellus knew. Taking Syncellus at face value, we can assume that his reference work had alluded to several chronographers who held these views under the general heading "certain historians." In this case, Panodorus was presented as simply one of the more learned expositors of a solution to a chronological problem that had many other adherents.

We see further indications of Syncellus' indirect knowledge of his predecessors' work in his treatment of the actual contents of their chronicles. In discussing their criticisms of Eusebius, for example, Syncellus remarks: "This is exactly what Annianus says when he criticizes Eusebius justifiably concerning the omission of the 290 years. Panodorus also says these things in agreement with him, from whom we consider it unnecessary to set out excerpts regarding this matter."[41] Now the expression τὰς χρήσεις . . . παραθέσθαι is precisely the way Syncellus introduces other of his excerpts, and it would not be unreasonable to think that Syncellus here knew Panodorus and Annianus in much the same way that he knew the *Babyloniaca* or any of his other sources, that is, as χρήσεις that had been collected in an earlier reference work.[42]

With his very vague descriptions of the actual contents of their work, Syncellus himself betrays his own limited and indirect knowledge of Panodorus and Annianus. Apart from a few repeated statements, Syncellus in fact furnishes very little precise information about the nature of the relationship of these two works to one another. And although Syncellus often treats them together, thereby producing the impression that the one work was largely an "orthodox reworking" of the other, Annianus, as Serruys has shown, was both more independent from his elder contemporary and less traditional than Syncellus intimates.[43]

The reason for Syncellus' lack of precision is again traceable to the character of his source. If Syncellus treats Annianus largely as an orthodox digest of Panodorus, he has reached this judgment only on the basis of what limited information he has been able to glean about them from preselected excerpts. What distinctions existed between the two works would have been washed out by an earlier compiler, whose purpose after all was

---

[41] Sync. 37.12–15.

[42] For the use of similar formulae in introducing other excerpts that he knows only through intermediaries, see Sync. 28.12–13: μικρὰς χρήσεις . . . παραθέσθαι; 24.4–5: ἀναγκαῖον ἡγοῦμαι μικρὰς χρήσεις παραθέσθαι.

[43] Cf. D. Serruys, "Les canons," 16–28, esp. p. 26.

only to present selected features of their work. The same reason explains Syncellus' very inexact way of specifying the origins of sources like *1 Enoch* and the *Babyloniaca*. Even while acknowledging dependence on his Alexandrian predecessors for several of his sources for archaic history, Syncellus is quite often ambiguous as to how he knew these sources. From Panodorus or Annianus or both works? We need not fault Syncellus for dissembling here. The ambiguity goes back to his reference work, a collection of excerpts which had not in every case identified precisely the chronicle from which each one of them originated.[44]

For a chronicler who, as Gelzer alleges, relied throughout almost exclusively on two Alexandrian sources, Syncellus knows surprisingly little about the actual content of their works. To be sure, he does quote and extensively adapt from Panodorus in his handling of primordial history. But such use need not require direct familiarity on his part with their chronicles. It is worthwhile to recognize that an anthologizer would have been most impressed with Panodorus' and Annianus' achievements in the treatment of archaic history. Their establishment of an era from the creation of the world, their imaginative interpretation of non-biblical sources, and their criticisms of Eusebius, if only because of their novelty, would have earned the attention, even the admiration, of subsequent laborers in the field.

After that, however, the compiler's interest in explicitly excerpting from them declined, and, as a result, so did Syncellus'. Indeed, for postdiluvian history, Syncellus' discussion of Panodorus and Annianus trails off dramatically. Following his heated controversy with them about the existence of Babylonia and Egypt before the flood, Syncellus alludes only once more to Annianus and mentions Panodorus only sporadically. Contributing only marginally to what Syncellus had remarked about Panodorus in his treatment of the antediluvian period, these references are largely elaborations of criticisms and observations that Syncellus makes at the very outset of his work—that his speculations about the origins of the primitive year were wrong, that he was unduly influenced by pagan wisdom, and that this influence led him to miscalculate the age of Christ's birth.[45] In one of

---

[44] So, for example, Syncellus (4.19–20) says that *Jubilees* and the *Life of Adam* were used by "Christian historians," but he cannot specify exactly which of these historians was the source of his excerpt.

[45] Cf. Sync. 89.2–6; 378.7–18; 396.12–397.10. In Syncellus' one explicit reference to Annianus he repeats his earlier observation about the structure of his predecessor's chronicle, namely that it was arranged in the form of 532-year cycles with "accurate scholia" (Sync. 382.1–2).

the few allusions to his Alexandrian authority, toward the end of his chronicle, Syncellus gives no indication whatsoever that he has been adhering to Panodorus throughout. In the context of a discussion of the dating of Christ's birth, Syncellus here refers only to a "certain Panodorus":

> So Africanus, in harmony with apostolic tradition, reckons the divine incarnation in the 5,500th year, but concerning the passion and the salvific resurrection he erred by two years, calculating this event in the 5,531st year of the world.

> Eusebius, "son" of Pamphilus, records the affairs from Adam up to the birth of Abraham, which he affirms was in the time of Ninus and Semiramis, the rulers of the Assyrians; but in concert with the Hebrew chronology, he cut short the years and counted 3,184 years; and did not reckon the second Cainan, who lived 130 years before fathering a child. . . .

> A *certain Panodorus* (Πανόδωρος . . . τις), one of the monks in Egypt, was a historian not inexperienced in the precise reckoning of time. He flourished in the time of Emperor Arcadius and Theophilus, the archbishop of Alexandria, confirming the truth in many things, but erring by seven years, and when he reached the saving incarnation, he calculated this in the year 5493. [There follows an explanation of the reasons for this error.][46]

If, as Gelzer maintains, Syncellus was mainly transcribing from him, one scarcely expects to find in this quotation not only the impersonal reference to "a certain Panodorus," but biographical information supplied about him as well, as if to imply that the monk was unfamiliar to his readers.[47] Possibly Syncellus was deliberately attempting to conceal the extent of his dependence on him. We need not impute to him, however, such sinister motives. What Syncellus found collected in his source were the views of several chronographers on the subject of the dating of Christ's birth. One of them, Panodorus, enjoyed less notoriety than his more illustrious predecessors Eusebius and Africanus and required, therefore, a brief biographical introduction.

Finally, the existence of such an intermediate source enables us to gain

---

[46] Ibid., 395.19–396.16.
[47] See above, Chap. 3, p. 102; cf. Laqueur, "Synkellos," 1405.

a clearer perspective on the textual history of many of his sources. Gelzer, as I have suggested, was persuaded that Syncellus' work consisted mainly in reproducing source material that had already been collected and edited, first by Panodorus and later by Annianus, the latter an ecclesiastical redactor of the former. Scholars following him tend, therefore, to ascribe textual emendation to Panodorus, Annianus, or Syncellus, although rarely does one find more precision than that. As will be seen in the ensuing discussion, however, appeals to Gelzer's reconstruction of their textual history do not adequately account for the text of even those sources that have been mediated at some stage through his Alexandrian predecessors.

TEXT AND REDACTION IN SYNCELLUS' SOURCES FOR PRIMORDIAL HISTORY

In the case of Syncellus' chronology of archaic Egyptian and Chaldean history, it is virtually certain that Syncellus knew all of his sources through intermediaries. He identifies explicitly the source of the epitomes of Manetho's *Aegyptiaca* as Africanus and Eusebius respectively, and the excerpts from the *Babyloniaca* are almost identical to those preserved in the Armenian recension of Eusebius' *Chronicle*. Gelzer was probably correct in recognizing Syncellus' indebtedness to Panodorus for his knowledge of his sources; apart from what Panodorus himself says, Syncellus does not appear to show direct knowledge of Eusebius' treatment of Berossus and Manetho.

Several of these works bear the imprint of an Alexandrian redaction. This is especially true of Syncellus' sources for archaic Egyptian history. Although Syncellus uncritically accepted the authenticity of the chronology of the *Book of Sothis* of (ps-)Manetho, Panodorus must have subjected this work to considerable reworking in order to achieve the desired goal of harmonizing this source with the *Babyloniaca*. Such harmony could not fail to arouse suspicion about the integrity of Panodorus' sources. "Die divinatorischen Leistungen," observed Unger later, ". . . welche Panodor hier an den Tag legt, sind allzuglänzend um nicht Verdacht zu erregen."[48] Any attempt, however, to reconstruct the original contents of the *Book of Sothis,* which is unattested outside of Syncellus, or the later reworkings of it, is fruitless.[49] It is generally assumed that apart from Syncellus' epitomes

---

[48] Unger, *Manetho,* 31.
[49] Among the numerous attempts made to reconstruct the original contents of this work in the 19th century, see the following, A. von Gutschmid, "Die Sothis, die alte Chronik und

of the *Aegyptiaca* from Eusebius and Africanus, all allusions to "Manetho" by Syncellus refer to Panodorus' *Book of Sothis*.[50] But even this is far from clear. Syncellus only identifies the *Book of Sothis* by name once. And what he knows under the name of "Manetho" is an extremely heterogeneous and inconsistent corpus of material, sometimes arranged dynastically, at other times according to the reigns of individual rulers. It is difficult, in fact, to see how all of this can be traced back to a single work. In one place, for example, Syncellus says that Manetho's entire history comprised 3,555 years, beginning with the year A.M. 1586. This is entirely inconsistent with the chronology of Manetho that Syncellus knew from Panodorus' recension of the *Book of Sothis;* the *Book of Sothis* assigned 11,985 years to the reigns of the gods alone.[51]

Although Syncellus' excerpts from Polyhistor's and Abydenus' recensions of the *Babyloniaca* are textually very close to the citations from these same works in the Armenian text of Eusebius' chronicle, the editorial intervention of the Alexandrian chronographers is implied in the existence of some notable variants in chronology. Syncellus does not preserve enough from his chronicle to know Panodorus' motives precisely. But there is the suspicion here of a tendentious emendation. As we have seen, Syncellus notes that "some church historians," among whom he numbers Panodorus, had calculated that Babylon was reestablished after the flood in the year A.M. 2405. In his attempt to harmonize Berossus/Polyhistor's chronology of postdiluvian Chaldean kings with Genesis, Panodorus reasoned that the 34,090 years of the reigns of the 86 Chaldean and Median kings must have been only days, reducible therefore to 94 solar years.[52] This would mean that their reigns ended in the year 2499. Panodorus

---

die Pandorischen 3555 Jahre von Hephaestos bis Nektanebos II," *Kleine Schriften,* 1. 227–43; C. Frick, "Kritische Untersuchungen über das alte Chronikon, die ägyptische Königsliste des Eratosthenes und Apollodoros, das Sothisbuch und die ägyptische Königsliste des Synkellos," *RhMus* N.F. 29 (1874), 272–81; R. Lepsius, *Die Chronologie der Aegypter 1* (Berlin, 1849), 413–45; Unger, *Manetho,* 29–43; Gelzer, *SJA,* 2. 206–14.

[50]Cf. Gelzer, *SJA,* 2. 206–14; Unger, *Manetho,* 29–43; R. Lepsius, *Die Chronologie der Aegypter,* 1. 413–45.

[51]Sync. 58.1–9 (on the 3,555-year duration of Manetho's history); cf. Sync. 18.21–19.17, which assigns 12,841 years to the reigns of the gods and demigods. Even if the 3,555 years assume Panodorus' reduction of archaic Egyptian years to months and seasons, the two chronologies are still inconsistent. Syncellus says that the 3,555 years of Egyptian history began in the year A.M. 1586 and continued without interruption up until Nektanebo 1. Panodorus' chronology traced the beginning of Egyptian civilization to the year A.M. 1059.

[52]The calculation only works if a 360-day year is assumed here; but this would hardly seem appropriate, since Panodorus used 365-day years in his reduction of the antediluvian kings (cf. Gelzer, *SJA,* 2. 201).

recognized that reckoning of regnal years after their reigns was no longer calculated in "sars, ners, and sosses." From this, he inferred that in the year A.M. 2499 some important astronomical discovery had occurred, which he regarded as Zoroaster's rediscovery of the revelation of the solar year earlier shown to Enoch.[53]

The chronology of Polyhistor upon which this is based differs from Eusebius' text of the same work. In his own chronicle, Eusebius reports, also on the authority of Alexander Polyhistor, that "after the Flood Euechsios ruled over the land of the Chaldeans four ners. And after him his son Chomasbelos took over the kingship, four ners and five sosses. Polyhistor counts in all 86 kings from Xisuthrus and from the flood until the Medes took Babylon. He mentions each of them by name on the authority of the book of Berossus. He sums up the whole period as containing *33,091* years."[54] Syncellus' report that "from the 2,405th year of the world . . . the 86 kinds of the Chaldeans and Medes ruled 34,090 years" is derived from an "arbitrary rewritten version of Eusebius' text" by Panodorus, whose motives here were probably the same as those for his more extensive reworking of the chronology of the *Book of Sothis*.[55]

While rejecting any attempts to establish the existence of Chaldea or Egypt before the flood or even before Nimrod, Syncellus has dutifully preserved this material from his Alexandrian sources, all the while regarding it as the genuine chronology of Berossus/Polyhistor. It is notable, however, that Syncellus himself formulates a chronology of the earliest Babylonian kings entirely different from theirs. In discussing his opposition to his predecessor's dating of the origin of Babylon and Egypt, Syncellus maintains that Babylon and Egypt came into existence after the flood in the same year, A.M. 2776:

> Therefore, we are persuaded by divine Scriptures that these things too are false and that there was no kingdom upon the earth until Nimrod, who, as was also demonstrated above, was a rebellious king and imitator of the Giants, ruling during the building of the tower; but that after the flood, up to the dispersion, three men alone governed the masses dutifully, I mean righteous Noah, the remaining 350 years of his life, and his son Shem, the remaining 150 years of his life,

[53] Sync. 88.13–24.
[54] Fr. C.4.2. (trans. Burstein, 21).
[55] Burstein, 21 (note 63). See also Drews, "Assyria," 141.

and even after him, his son Arphaxad the remaining 34 years; that is, 534 years together with the 2,242 years at the time of the flood are 2,776 years. . . .[56]

Now one could assume that Syncellus simply formulated his own views independently of his Alexandrian sources. But an identical sequence of Chaldean kings is attested in another chronicle, the so-called Χρονογραφ-εῖον συντόμον:[57]

Χρ. Συν.		Syncellus
Nimrod	[70 years]	Nimrod (Euechios)
Chomasbelos	[15 years]	Chomasbelos
Puros	[20 years]	Poros
Nechoubes	[25 years]	Nechoubes
Nablios	[30 years]	Nabios
Onibalos	[35 years]	Oniballos
Zinzeros	[21 years]	Zinzeros

Although some of these kings are the same as those found in the *Babyloniaca,* the reworking is arbitrary and quite extensive. The striking similarities in the two lists strongly suggest that both Syncellus and the Χρονογραφεῖον συντόμον consulted the same work.[58] What is clear in any case is that Syncellus here knows some intermediate and independent source that served as the basis of his own reconstruction of Egyptian and Babylonian history.

Syncellus' sources from the Jewish pseudepigrapha furnish the best case for testing Gelzer's reconstruction of their textual history, since, with the exception of the *Life of Adam,* all of these works are attested, often in more complete form, elsewhere. Two works of special relevance are Syncellus' citations from *1 Enoch* and *Jubilees.*

Textual Emendation in Syncellus' Enoch Excerpts

For this Jewish apocalypse, we are fairly well equipped to examine the extent and nature of emendation in Syncellus' extracts. In addition to his citation, we have the several Ethiopic witnesses, the Aramaic fragments

---

[56] Ibid. 89.6–14.
[57] Ed. A. Schoene, *Eusebi Chronicorum Libri Duo,* 1. 83; cf. Sync. 101.22–102.8.
[58] This was recognized by Gelzer (cf. *SJA,* 2. 202–3).

from Qumran, the Akhmim Greek text, as well as the small excerpt in
Syriac from Michael the Great; this last excerpt is of particular importance,
since Michael's source for it is Annianus.

Textual emendation in Syncellus' two long citations "from the first book
of Enoch concerning the Watchers ('Εκ τοῦ πρώτου βιβλίου 'Ενώχ περὶ
τῶν ἐγρηγόρων)" is fairly extensive.[59] In his edition of the Ethiopic recension of this Jewish apocalypse, R. H. Charles professed a high regard for
the textual value of Syncellus' version.[60] More recent assessments have
been far less favorable. "A free paraphrastic type," wrote Matthew Black,
"suggesting at times a very drastic recension or even rewriting of the basic
Greek text."[61] Following Gelzer, modern commentators are inclined to
attribute these emendations either to Syncellus or one or both of his Alexandrian sources, although rarely with any more precision than this.[62]

It is extremely unlikely that Syncellus is responsible for either the selection or the editing of these excerpts. Unlike his Alexandrian predecessors,
for whom *1 Enoch* figured importantly in their reconstruction of primordial history, Syncellus had very narrow reasons for citing from the work;
and these reasons would hardly justify the extensive reworkings that characterize his excerpts from that book. Studies of these excerpts generally

[59] In modern parlance, the book is often called *1 Enoch* to differentiate it from the Slavonic
("Second") and the Hebrew ("Third") Enoch. Syncellus is the only ancient author to employ
this same terminology, thus implying that he knew other works also attributed to the patriarch. What books these were are unknown. It is not likely that by this title he intended to
distinguish the *Book of the Watchers* from the other books of the Enoch corpus, since he does
not appear to divide the work in this way. When, for example, Syncellus refers to the astronomical section of *1 Enoch*, he says only that it is found in the "book of the same Enoch"
(34.18). Milik maintains, without much evidence, that Panodorus had introduced this term
in order to distinguish the original Enoch corpus from the *Similitudes*, which, according to
Milik, Panodorus recognized was a later Christian composition and did not "belong to the
original Pentateuch." See his *Books of Enoch*, 78. But it is possible that the chronicler who gave
the book this title inferred the existence of multiple books from a statement in *1 Enoch* itself
(cf. *1 En.* 108.1).

[60] See *The Ethiopic Version of the Book of Enoch*, Anecdota Oxoniensia, Semitic Series 11
(Oxford, 1906), xiii–xiv; idem, *The Book of Enoch* (Oxford, 1912), xvii–xviii. This positive
assessment is most recently maintained by A.-M. Denis, *Introduction aux pseudépigraphes grecs
d'Ancien Testament*, SVTP 1 (Leiden, 1970), 20 (but cf. Denis, p. 17).

[61] See Matthew Black (ed.), *Apocalypsis Henochi Graece*, PVTG iii (Leiden, 1970), 8. Some
of the textual variants need not reveal the hand of a self-conscious editor. The names of the
chief Watchers, which deviate widely from the other witnesses, are largely traceable to understandable textual corruptions. For only one name can we assume deliberate emendation. The
Aramaic text of Enoch names the 11th Watcher as HARMONI, i.e., the one from Hermon
(= Ethiopic 'Armaros). The name of this angel in Syncellus' text—Φάρμαρος—is an inten-
tional correction, intended to link the name of the Watcher with his revelations—φαρμακεία; cf. Sync. 12.5.

[62] Cf. M. Knibb, *The Ethiopic Book of Enoch*, 2 vols. (Oxford, 1978), 2. 20; also Milik, *Books
of Enoch*, 76–78, 240.

follow Gelzer in tracing the origins of Syncellus' excerpts from these works to Panodorus "via Annianus." Sebastian Brock, for example, on the basis of his comparison of Syncellus' first citation from *1 Enoch* with the parallel material in a Syriac citation from the *Book of the Watchers* in Michael Syrus, claims to have found corroboration for Gelzer's theory.[63] Following Gelzer, Brock writes that Syncellus, like Michael, "derived his Enoch quotations from Annianos."[64] Since Michael, who names Annianus as his authority for antediluvian history, also excerpts from *1 Enoch,* it would follow that Michael's and Syncellus' excerpts should be textually allied. After examining the two texts, Brock concluded that "Synkellos and Michael are in all probability simply two independent witnesses to the text of Enoch as excerpted by the Alexandrian monk Annianos at the beginning of the fifth century."[65]

Now admittedly, the two excerpts tend to agree with each other more often than not against either the Akhmim Greek text or the Ethiopic (although these affinities should not be overstated). This is to be expected, since the provenience of both excerpts is Alexandria. But the very marked differences should not be ignored. In the first place, Michael's excerpt encompasses only seven verses (= *1 En.* 6:1–7), compared to the far more extensive citations in Syncellus. When the Syriac differs both from Syncellus and the other texts of *1 Enoch,* it is characteristically due to omissions or condensations.[66] One very striking example of this concerns the names of the Watchers. After describing the swearing of the oath by the Watchers on Mt. Hermon, the text in Syncellus records the names of all the dekarchs and what they taught the women. In Michael's excerpt from the *Book of the Watchers,* only two of them are named. After what appears to be a corrupt reference to Semiazos, the excerpt omits the names of all the remaining dekarchs, with the exception of one—Chochabiel. Chochabiel, "the fourth head, taught men astronomy, that is the revolutions of the sun,

[63] Sebastian Brock, "A Fragment of Enoch in Syriac," *JTS* 19 (1963), 626–31.

[64] Brock, "Fragment," 628. To be sure, Brock is slightly misrepresenting Gelzer here, since Gelzer never explicitly says this. But the fact that Brock interprets him in this way underlines the ambiguities in Gelzer's discussion of sources.

[65] Brock, "Fragment," 629.

[66] Syriac text omits or shortens the following:

   Sync. 11.22 (= *1 En.* 6:2): ὀπίσω αὐτῶν.
   Sync. 11.24 (= *1 En.* 6:3): πρὸς αὐτούς.
   Sync. 11.26 (= *1 En.* 6:4): πάντες.
   Sync. 11.26 (= *1 En.* 6:4): καὶ εἶπον.
   Sync. 11.27 (= *1 En.* 6:4): ἀλλήλους.
   Sync. 11.27–28 (= *1 En.* 6:4): μέχρις οὗ ἀποτελέσωμεν αὐτήν.
   Sync. 11.28 (= *1 En.* 6:5): ἀλλήλους.

360 zodia being numbered." Of Chochabiel, Syncellus' text states only that "he taught astrology."[67]

The reasons for the editorial excision of the names and functions of all but two of the chief Watchers (Chochabiel and Semiazos) can be inferred from Michael's summary of Annianus' interpretation of *1 Enoch*. Semiazos was the first to establish a kingdom on earth. And it was the revelations of Chochabiel, the Watcher who taught "that the period encompassed in the orbit of the sun is in the twelve signs of zodiac, and 360 degrees," which explained the origins of the Chaldean and Egyptian calendar. As has been already noted, Annianus' historical notices, adapted from Panodorus, took the form of scholia, probably embedded in the margins of Easter tables. Because this structure required the condensation of longer excerpts, Annianus edited out of Panodorus' excerpt whatever he considered extraneous. What is clear above all is that Syncellus' text of *1 Enoch* does not reflect any of these emendations.

In the preceding chapter, I proposed that Syncellus' entire section on Genesis 6 and the fall of the Watchers is mainly a reworking of a portion of Panodorus' chronicle.[68] It is not difficult to understand the motives behind his editing of *1 Enoch*. The very episode that attracted the chronographers to the work—the story of fallen angels and the birth of the Giants—was also the one that excited the most controversy. Indeed, when Syncellus wanted to exemplify his own reservations about apocryphal books, he adduced a legend recounted of the Giants in *Jub.* 10:1–10. The story describes the temptation of the offspring of Noah by the disembodied spirits of these Giants. "This seems inconsistent to us, that a living man is tested by a dead spirit."[69]

"For this reason," Syncellus warns, "we admonish those reading apocryphal books either here or elsewhere not to accept altogether the opinions reported in them."[70] It is this warning that underlies the decision to present χρήσεις only. By reading apocryphal books wholesale (καθόλου), the unsuspecting might lapse from the "right and true perspective (τοῦ ὀρθοῦ καὶ ἀληθοῦς σκοποῦ)."[71] Although useful in places, apocryphal

---

[67] The unintelligible Syriac text reads "'yd' dsmz" (cf. Brock, "Fragment," 631 [note 1]). Milik corrects this to "qdmy smz," i.e., "first Sem(ya)z(as)"; see *The Books of Enoch*, 82 (note 1). Syncellus refers to Chochabiel (= "star of God") by the names Chobabiel (12.4) and Chorabiel (33.2). Both names are corrupt.

[68] See above, Chap. 5, pp. 151–57.

[69] Sync. 28.8–9

[70] Ibid., 28.9–11.

[71] Ibid., 27.33–34.

books contain some "fabulous material (περιττά τινα)" and material opposed to ecclesiastical tradition, which has been "corrupted by Jews and
heretics (διὰ τὸ νενοθεῦσθαι αὐτὰ ὑπὸ ᾽Ιουδαίων καὶ αἱρετικῶν)."[72]
In this context, the term νενοθεῦσθαι bears the meaning of "textual corruption" by the insertion of spurious material, added to the original words
of the prophet Enoch.

This warning, which Syncellus has adapted from Panodorus, must have
served as the justification for removing or censoring what in his view were
adulterations of the original text. Because of such adulterations, less sophisticated readers should not embrace apocryphal works indiscriminately,
remaining satisfied with preselected excerpts only—that is, those that amplify and attest to the truth of Genesis.[73] The principles of preselection are
fairly obvious in the second body of excerpts from *1 Enoch*, under the
heading "From the Book of Enoch. The remaining material about the
Watchers (᾽Εκ του λόγου ᾽Ενώχ. Τὰ λοιπὰ περὶ ἐγρηγόρων)."[74] For reasons that have already been discussed in the preceding chapter, I have
suggested that the selection of citations under this heading was done by
Panodorus.[75] Consisting of three segments, this material treats mainly the
judgment against the straying Watchers and their demonic offspring, and
God's judgment upon them. Although these three small citations appear
under the rubric "From the Book of the Watchers," several commentators
have noted that the final segment of this excerpt does not appear in the
other preserved witnesses to the *Book of the Watchers*. Set apart with the
words καὶ αὖθις, this quotation describes the burning of Mt. Hermon
and the limiting of man's age to 120 years. In noting the absence of this
material in the other witnesses, Charles first conjectured that it belonged
to the so-called "Book of Noah," a work which Charles believed was interwoven with *1 Enoch*.[76] More recently, Milik, on the basis of similarities
between this text and a Manichean fragment from *1 Enoch*, concluded that
the passage came from the *Book of the Giants*, a segment of *1 Enoch* that
does not appear in Ethiopic Enoch, but which survives in the Enoch fragments at Qumran and in the literature of the Manichees.[77]

Panodorus' reason for consulting *1 Enoch* was to document a particular
thesis about the origins of reckoning of time, as well as the euhemeristic

[72] Ibid., 27.11.
[73] Ibid., 27.8–9.
[74] Ibid., 24.10–11.
[75] See above, Chap. 5, pp. 152–54.
[76] See Charles' note to *1 En* 16.2 (*APOT*, 2. 198).
[77] Milik, *The Books of Enoch*, 318–20.

fusion of Genesis 6 with Berossus and Manetho. Syncellus himself offers as his own motive for citing from the work the fact that the work establishes the historical veracity of the mixing of the Sethites and Cainites. Understandably, many of the variants in Syncellus' first excerpt from *1 Enoch* reveal a corresponding concern to historicize the work and fix the dating according to some predetermined chronological scheme. Although chronology was a subject of interest for Jewish and Christian apocalypticists, the major events recorded in the Enochic *Book of the Watchers* were not dated. As a consequence, Christian chronographers undertook to date many of these events. A.M. 1000, for example, was widely accepted by Christian chronographers as the date of the descent (κατάβασις) of the Watchers. Since 1000 was the 40th year of Jared, one could establish a word-play between the meaning of Jared's name ("go down") and the descent of the Watchers.[78] In setting the date in the year 1000, there was as well the implication that the fall of the Watchers coincided with the beginning of corruption, that is, the close of the first millennium. Panodorus, as we have seen, attempted to fix chronologically other events associated with the *Book of the Watchers,* for example 1058 as the beginning of the kingdom of the Watchers and 1286 as the date of Uriel's revelations to Enoch. With an eye toward fixing the sequence of events chronologically, an editor has inserted into Syncellus' first excerpt the chronological detail A.M. 1170 as the date of the transgression (παράβασις) of the Watchers, that is, when they began to incur pollution by intercourse with women.[79] It is, however, not clear precisely how this date was arrived at, nor can we with certainty attribute it to one of Syncellus' Alexandrian authorities. Elsewhere, in fact, Syncellus dates the same event differently; in "the year A.M. 1177, the Watchers openly committed adultery (φανερῶς ἐμοίχευσαν)."[80]

One of the most prominent tendencies of the editor of these excerpts is his habit of removing or improving upon theologically offensive passages, especially those that encouraged a supernaturalist reading of Gen. 6. The term οἱ ἐγρήγοροι, for example, is consistently preferred to οἱ ἄγγελοι,

---

[78] Cf. *Jub.* 4:15. For the beginning of corruption in the time of Jared, see Epiphanius *Pan.* 1.3 (ed. K Holl, GCS 25.1, [Leipzig, 1915] 172.19–20), who associates with Jared the beginnings of φαρμακεία, μαγεία, ἀσέλγεια, μοιχεία and ἀδικία.

[79] For discussion see Gelzer, *SJA,* 2. 260.

[80] Sync. 19. 21–22. For discussion, see Gelzer, *SJA,* 2. 260, who attributes the difference of seven years to a scribal error. Mosshammer (note ad loc., p. 19) suggests that the difference of seven years may arise from Panodorus' dispute with other chronographers on the dating of Christ's birth. But this suggestion is not likely since, according to Syncellus, Panodorus' seven-year error in chronology began with his dating of the reign of Alexander's successors.

presumably because the former nomenclature squared better with the naturalistic interpretation of Gen. 6 favored by Syncellus and his Alexandrian predecessors.[81] For the same reason, the editor has also endeavored to tone down, where possible, language in *1 Enoch* tending to cast the Giants in mythic terms. At *1 En.* 15:9, the Akhmim Greek text refers to the spirits of the Giants as πνεύματα πονηρά . . . διότι ἀπὸ τῶν ἀνωτέρων ἐγένοντο. Syncellus' text, probably emended here for theological reasons, has substituted ἀνθρώπων for ἀνωτέρων.[82]

The most conclusive evidence of emendation for dogmatic purposes occurs in the passage describing the classes of offspring produced by the illicit intercourse between the Watchers and the daughters of men (= *1 Enoch* 7:1 ff.). Syncellus' text has the following:

> 1) These and all the other remaining Watchers took for themselves women in the 1,170th year of the world, and they began to be polluted with them up to the flood. And they [the women] bore to them three races. 2) First, the great Giants (γίγαντας μεγάλους). 3) The Giants begat Nephilim (Ναφηλείμ), and to the Nephilim were born Elioud ('Ελιούδ). 4) And they were increasing (ἦσαν αὐξανόμενοι) in accordance with their greatness, and they taught (ἐδίδαξαν) themselves and their wives the uses of potions and spells. 5) First, Azael, the tenth of the leaders, taught them to make swords and armor and all instruments of war. . . .[83]

The subject of the fourth verse is ambiguous. Although the syntax would lead us to believe that the antecedents of the verbs ἦσαν αὐξανόμενοι and ἐδίδαξαν are the same, the sense would not. First, the subject of the preceding sentence is γίγαντες; second, the idea of "increasing in accordance with their greatness" better characterizes the Giants than the Watchers, especially since the word μεγαλειότητα is elsewhere used to describe the Giants. The implied subject of the second verb, however, would appear to be the ἐγρήγοροι since, according to the well-known tradition, the Watchers instructed women in the various revealed sciences. Moreover, the following verse describes the teachings of the Watchers.

The legend about the three races of the Giants descended from the women and Watchers appears in none of the other extant witnesses to *1*

---

[81] See, for example, 11.21. Also 25.23 (=*1 En.* 10:7): καὶ ἴασαι τὴν γῆν ἥν ἠφάνισαν οἱ ἐγρήγοροι; cf. Akhm.: καὶ ἰαθήσεται ἡ γῆ ἥν ἠφάνισαν οἱ ἄγγελοι.

[82] Sync. 26.12. For the preferability of the Akhmim text here, see Knibb, ad loc. (2. 201).

[83] Sync. 12.8–14.

Enoch at these verses, including most recently, the Aramaic fragments from Qumran.[84] This, and the syntactical ambiguities of Syncellus' text at these verses, strongly suggest that this material was a later insertion.[85] In the other witnesses to *1 Enoch* at these verses, there appears here a lurid account of the demonic behavior of the Giants: their massive height, their unspeakable crimes against animals, and their drinking of blood.[86] The highly mythological account of the Giants, describing their superhuman and demonic character, was clearly at variance with the kind of interpretation that Christian chronographers wanted to impose on *1 Enoch*, and an editor has removed it. In its place, he has substituted a rather restrained account of the three classes of Giants, and at line 13.2 a very concise summary of the excised material: "After this the Giants began to devour the flesh of men."

Syncellus' Text of Jubilees

Of all the extra-biblical Jewish sources that Syncellus and the other Byzantine chronographers consulted in their treatment of primordial history, *Jubilees* is the most extensively used, and at the same time subject to some of the most thoroughgoing reworking.[87] When he first appeals to *Jubilees*, Syncellus, as we have seen, acknowledges dependence on intermediaries, whom he identifies as "some historians." Like other Byzantine chronographers, he appeals repeatedly to *Jubilees*, even though he initially warns his readers that the work does not appear to be authoritative. While typically referring to *Jubilees* by the name by which it was best known among

---

[84] In the other preserved witnesses to *1 Enoch* there appears a discussion of the cannibalism of the Giants. For discussion of Syncellus' text in comparison to the other witnesses to *1 Enoch* at these verses see, most recently, Knibb 2. 19–20, 77 ff.; also Milik, 240.

[85] The fact that the tradition about three classes of Giants is explicitly mentioned in *Jub.* 7:22 and is alluded to later at *1 Enoch* 66 ff. suggested to Milik that the inserted material about the three classes of Giants originated in the Enochic *Book of the Giants*, one of the books of the Enoch corpus which survives only in fragments from Qumran and from the literature of the Manichees (Milik, 240). The same source may have provided the source material for the third segment of Syncellus' second excerpt from *1 Enoch* (Sync. 26.26–27.7).

[86] The Ethiopic text reads: (7.2) "And they became pregnant and bore large Giants, and their height (was) three thousand cubits. (3) These devoured all the toil of men, until men were unable to sustain them. (4) And the Giants turned against them in order to devour men. (5) And they began to sin against birds, and against animals, and against reptiles and against fish, and they devoured one another's flesh and drank the blood from it. (6) Then the earth complained about the lawless ones. (8.1.) And Azael taught men to make swords, and daggers. . . ." (trans. Knibb, 2. 77–79.)

[87] For edition of the Ethiopic text, see R. H. Charles, *The Ethiopic Version of the Book of Jubilees* (Oxford, 1895); translation by the same author in *APOT*, 2. 1–82. More recent English translation by O. S. Wintermute, in J. H. Charlesworth, ed., *The Old Testament Pseudepigrapha*, 35–142.

the chronographers—ἡ λεπτὴ Γένεσις or some variant of it—, he is aware that the work also circulated under the name *Apocalypse of Moses,* and occasionally identifies it in this way.[88] In many other cases, excerpts are cited from that work without express attribution.

As in the case of the other Byzantine chronographers who cite from *Jubilees,* Syncellus never quotes verbatim from it. Unlike his fairly faithful Greek citations from *1 Enoch,* Syncellus' citations from *Jubilees* and the allied *Life of Adam* are, as he himself knows, epitomized forms of these works.[89] Some of the other emendations are readily understood. In his account of the hexamera, for example, Syncellus counts 22 individual works, adding, on the authority of *Jubilees,* the notice that these 22 works correspond to the 22 Hebrew letters and the 22 books of the Hebrew Bible. "Altogether the 22 works of creation are equal in number to the 22 Hebrew books and the 22 heads of mankind from Adam up to Jacob, as it is reported in the *Little Genesis.*"[90] But the enumeration of the individual acts of creation deviates from the account that survives in the Ethiopic text of *Jub.* 2:2. Part of the reason for this arises from theological grounds. Among the acts of the first day of creation, *Jubilees* lists the creation of the angelic powers. The Byzantine chronographers largely adhered to the Greek hexameral tradition in setting the creation of the angels before the creation of the universe. *Jubilees* was cast into doubt as result. "I know, to be sure," writes the chronographer John Zonaras (twelfth century), "that in the *Little Genesis* it is written that on the first day the heavenly powers were created before the other things by the creator of the universe. But because this *Little Genesis* is not numbered with the books of Hebrew wisdom recognized by the holy fathers, I consider none of the things written in it certain and do not agree with this work."[91] Syncellus, too, chooses to reject *Jubilees* on this point. He does not include the angelic powers as works of the first day, adding at the end of the account, and by way of an aside, that *Jubilees,* "which some know as the 'Apocalypse of Moses,'" says that "the heavenly powers (τὰς οὐρανίους δυνάμεις) were created on the first day."[92]

Predictably, the most extensive reworkings involve bringing *Jubilees'*

---

[88] See Sync. 3.16–18; 27.33.
[89] Ibid., 5.26–27.
[90] Ibid., 3.14–17.
[91] *Annales* 1. 18.4–10 (ed. M. Pinder, 2 vols. [Bonn, 1841]).
[92] Ibid., 3.17–18. The same notice is found in Cedrenus, 9.12–14; Theodosius Melitenus, 2.2–3 (ed. Tafel): Ἐν ταύτῃ οὖν τῇ ἡμέρᾳ λέγει Μωσῆς ἐν τῇ λεπτῇ γενέσει ἐκτίσθαι τὰς οὐρανίους δυνάμεις.

chronology into conformity with a system more in harmony with the tenets of Greek Christian chronography. Although vestiges of a systematic effort to conform *Jubilees* to the chronology of the Septuagint are discernible, whatever the principles were that once determined the redating of events are now obscure, if not completely arbitrary.[93] There still survive some very meagre traces in Syncellus of *Jubilees'* hebdomadal system for the dating of events; the protoplasts, for example, are said to have mourned for Abel "four periods of weeks, that is 28 years."[94] In general, however, Syncellus has, like most of the other chroniclers who use *Jubilees,* abandoned this cumbersome system of dating events in favor of straightforward counting in years.[95]

Much of the reworking of *Jubilees* has been designed mainly to bring its chronology into conformity with the Septuagint and a 365-day calendrical year. Evidence of this latter type of emendation appears already in Syncellus' first excerpt from *Jubilees,* concerning the length of Adam's stay in Paradise. According to the Ethiopic text of *Jubilees,* the transgression of Adam and Eve occurred precisely seven years after Adam's introduction into Paradise. 45 days later they were expelled. Assuming, as the author of *Jubilees* does, that Adam entered Paradise 46 days from the first day of creation, then the expulsion would have occurred after the completion of seven years and 91 days. By the reckoning of *Jubilees,* this would be the fourth day of the week, the first day of the fourth month, supposedly "on the new moon of the fourth month."

In the highly schematized calendar of *Jubilees* this date is supposed to signify important events, but the system of hebdomads upon which it is based bears no relationship to the observable motion of the sun and the moon. Cognizant of its deficiencies, an editor has sought to bring the chronology of *Jubilees* into harmony with the 365-day solar year. Thus, under the heading Ἐκ τῶν λεπτῶν Γενέσεως, he gives the following: "In the seventh year he (Adam) transgressed and in the eighth they were cast out of Paradise, as they say, 305 days after the transgression, with Pleiades rising. Adam spent in Paradise a week of 365 days. And he was cast out of Paradise with his wife Eve, on account of his sin, on the tenth day of the month of May."[96]

---

[93] For discussion, see Rönsch, *Das Buch der Jubiläen,* 284–302.

[94] Sync. 8.20–21.

[95] Another of the chronicles that preserves traces of the hebdomadal dating of *Jubilees* is the Syriac anonymous chronicle *ad annum Christi 1234,* which preserves fairly literal excerpts from *Jubilees.* In one place it dates the death of Adam in the "19th jubilee, in the seventh week," here following closely *Jub.* 4:29; see Tisserant, "Fragments syriaques," 71–72.

[96] Sync. 7.28–32.

The pattern of emendation is clear. The 45-day interval between the protoplasts' transgression and expulsion has been preserved, but the other aspects of *Jubilees'* chronology have been entirely reworked. Years are here reckoned as 365 days, and Adam's expulsion occurs precisely seven years after his entrance into Paradise, not, as in *Jubilees,* 45 days later. The system underlying this chronology can be inferred from the statement that this expulsion occurred on May 10. Working back from here would yield March 25 (= 1 Nisan) as the first day of creation.

A similar pattern of emendation marks the *Life of Adam,* a work known only in Syncellus:

> On the first day of the second week, which was the third day from the creation of Adam, on the eighth day of the first month of Nisan, on the first day of the month of April, and on the sixth day of the Egyptian month Pharmouthi, Adam named the wild beasts, by a divine gift of grace. On the second day of the second week, he gave names to the beasts. On the third day of the second week, he gave names to the birds. On the fourth day of the second week, he gave names to the reptiles. On the fifth day of the second week, he named the swimming things. On the sixth day of the second week, which according to the Romans was the sixth of April, according to the Egyptians the eleventh of Pharmouthi, God took a part of the rib of Adam and created the woman. On the forty-sixth day from the creation of the world, on the fourth day of the seventh week, the fourteenth of Pachon, the ninth of May, with the sun in Taurus and the moon in opposition in Scorpio, in the rising of the Pleiades, God introduced Adam into Paradise on the fortieth day from his creation. On the eighth day from the creation of the world, on the forty-fourth day from his creation of Adam, on the Lord's day, on the eighteenth day of Pachon, on the thirteenth day of May, three days after his entrance into Paradise, with the sun in Taurus and the moon in Capricorn, God ordered Adam to refrain from eating from the tree of knowledge.
>
> On the ninety-third day from creation, on the second day of the fourteenth week, during the summer Solstice, with the sun and moon in Cancer, in the twenty-fifth day of the month of June, in the first of Epiphi, Eve the helper of Adam was introduced by God into Paradise, on the eightieth day from her creation. When Adam received her, he called her Eve, which is translated as "Life." For this reason, that is on account of the days of their separation from Paradise after their

creation, God ordained through Moses in Leviticus that in giving
birth to a male, a woman is impure for forty days, in giving birth to
a female, for eighty days (cf. Lev. 12:1–5). For since Adam was introduced into Paradise on the fortieth day from his creation, for this
reason, they also introduce into the Temple according to the Law
male children that are born on the fortieth day. But as to the female,
she is impure for eighty days, because of her entrance into Paradise
on the eightieth day, and because of the impurity of the female in
comparison with the male. For being menstrual again, she does not
enter into the temple until the seventh day, in accordance with divine law.[97]

In the absence of other witnesses to this work, we can only guess about
the original form of what Syncellus acknowledges is only an abridgment
(ἐν συντόμῳ ἐστοιχείωσα).[98] The portion cited by Syncellus seems to be
mainly a more extensive exposition of the section of *Jubilees* dealing with
Adam = *Jub.* 3:1–9.[99] But the enlargements are worth noting. The passage
not only reckons events according to the day of the week; the text often
supplies as well the day of the month according to the Egyptian, Roman,
and Jewish calendar. In addition, for many events the excerpt gives the
zodiacal location of the moon and the sun. According to this chronology,
the sun and moon are created on the third day. Adam enters paradise one
lunation and a half later, at full moon (since the sun and moon were created at conjunction). Later, Eve enters at full moon, after another one and
a half lunations.[100] Again working back to the first day of creation, we
arrive at March 25. To summarize the general pattern of emendation,
therefore, it may be said that the editor has largely preserved the reckoning
of events according to weeks, but has modified the calculation of months,
years, and seasons.

Syncellus can hardly be considered the likely candidate to have made
these emendations; he rejects the whole chronology of events in Paradise
described in *Jubilees* and, in his own words, cites from it and the *Life of
Adam* only for the purposes of discrediting them. Nor can these reworkings be traced to Panodorus, since his era was the Egyptian era of 1 Thoth
(= August 29), not the ecclesiastical era of March 25. A more likely pros-

[97] Ibid., 4.29–5.25.
[98] Ibid., 5.26–27.
[99] Cf. Rönsch, *Das Buch der Jubiläen*, 281–82.
[100] The schematic structure of the chronology was pointed out to me by Prof. Anthony
Grafton.

pect would be his colleague Annianus, who, according to Syncellus, adhered to the more traditional day of creation = March 25. What we do know of Annianus' chronicle, however, shows that Syncellus has not here simply taken over Annianus' redaction of *Jubilees*. Michael Syrus preserves a quotation from Annianus that reflects a different chronology: "Annianus the monk adduces the witness of the *Book of Enoch* (sic) and says, 'After leaving Paradise, Adam, being 70 years of age, knew Eve, and she bore Cain, and after 7 years she bore Abel; and after 53 years Cain slew Abel, Adam and Eve wept 100 years, and then they begat Seth in their image and likeness.'"[101] Nothing like this survives in *1 Enoch,* and it is reasonable to assume that this chronology is derived from *Jubilees;* either Annianus or a later source misattributed it to *1 Enoch.*[102] What are most striking are the deviations of this chronology from the chronology of both Syncellus and the Ethiopic text of *Jubilees.* This can be illustrated in the following table:

	Annianus	*Syncellus*	*Eth. Jub.*
Cain born	70	70	64–70
Abel born	77	77	71–77
Abel's death	130	99	99–105
Adam and Eve cease mourning	230	127	99–127
Cain's marriage	***	135	190–196
Seth born	230	230 (no longer quoting *Jubilees*)	130

Annianus' and Syncellus' Adaptation of *Jubilees*

Like Syncellus, Annianus has undertaken to fuse the chronology of *Jubilees* with the Septuagint. Thus, according to Annianus, Adam and Eve stopped mourning and begat Seth in the year 230 (= chronology of the Septuagint). But Syncellus more clearly demarcates material from *Jubilees* from his chronology based on the Septuagint. Starting with the birth of Seth, he ceases to quote from *Jubilees,* whereas Annianus attributes to *1 Enoch* a chronology evidently revised according to the Septuagint. What is especially important to recognize is that up to the birth of Seth, Syncellus *adheres more closely* to Eth. *Jubilees* than Annianus. Syncellus' text of

---

[101] Michael Syrus 1.1 (trans. Chabot, 3).
[102] See Brock, "Fragment," 626–27.

Jubilees, here revealing the editorial hand of a chronicler other than either Panodorus or Annianus, leads us to assume that Syncellus has not transcribed from either one of them directly, but has used instead some intermediary collection of source material.

Jubilees *and the Interpolated Josephus*

As we have noted, among the factors that drew chronographers to this work was its value in resolving chronological ἀπορίαι in Genesis. We have already commented on the appeal to this work in order to establish a sequence of events for Adam's life in Paradise. Syncellus consults the same work in his discussion of a second, and very well-known problem in Christian chronology—the sequence of events preceding Abraham's departure to Canaan, and the dating of Terah's death. The manner in which he misattributes material from *Jubilees* here reflects the long and rather complex prior textual history of that work.

The controversy over Terah's death had been fueled both by an apparent contradiction in Genesis' ordering of events after Abraham and Terah migrated to Haran and ambiguity in Genesis about the time and setting of Abraham's call. By placing the death of Terah (Gen. 11:32) before the journey of Abraham to Canaan (Gen. 12:1 ff.), Genesis implied that his death preceded Abraham's migration. But this raised a chronological inconsistency. If Terah was 70 years of age when Abraham was born, and if Abraham left Haran at age 75, then Terah could have been no older than 145 when Abraham departed; Genesis, however, reported his age as 205. The problem took on a special urgency for Christian exegetes, because Stephen's speech in Acts 7 had stated explicitly that Terah's death occurred before Abraham's emigration to Canaan.[103]

Syncellus knows of some unnamed interpreters who had claimed that the reference in Genesis to the birth of Abraham when Terah was 60 years of age was a shorthand expression, stated for the "purpose of conciseness

---

[103] For other discussions of this famous problem in chronology, see Jerome's *Hebraicae Quaestiones in Libro Geneseos* 15–16 (CC Series Latina 72.1.1) (on Gen. 12:4). Also, Augustine *City of God* 16.15; Eusebius of Emesa, in *L'héritage littéraire d'Eusèbe d'Émèse,* ed. É. M. Buytaert, Bibliothèque du Muséon 24 (Louvain, 1949), fr. 16. Among the Syriac commentaries, see, for example, Isho'dad of Merv's *Commentary on Genesis,* 142 (Gen. 12:4) (trans. C. van den Eynde, 154.21–155.12); Bar Hebraeus, *Scholia on the Old Testament,* ed. Martin Sprengling and William Creighton Graham (Chicago, 1931), 48–49. For discussion of the whole question, especially as it relates to *Jubilees* and Syriac chronography, see S. P. Brock, "Abraham and the Ravens: A Syriac Counterpart to *Jubilees* 11–12 and its Implications," *JSJ* 9 (1978), 135–52; William Adler, "Abraham and the Burning of the Temple of Idols: Jubilees' Traditions in Christian Chronography," *JQR* 77 (1986–87), 95–117.

and not accuracy (συντομίας χάριν καὶ οὐκ ἀκριβείας)."[104] Actually, they maintained, Abraham was born sometime after that. After all, he and his brothers were certainly not triplets, so that they must have been born at different times. The expression "Terah begat Abram, Nachor and Haran" at age 70 must be understood as referring to the time when Terah *began* to beget, implying thereby that the whole process consumed more than one year.[105]

While acknowledging that these exegetes had been astute in recognizng the problem, Syncellus dismisses their solution as problematic (ἀπόρως).[106] His own explanation is allegorical. The description of Terah's death before Abraham's sojourn in Canaan should not be taken to mean that Terah had physically died before Abraham's departure. In the first place, Scripture, he says, regularly transposes (ὑπερβατικῶς λέγουσα) the order of events.[107] The reason why Moses placed the death of Terah before Abraham's departure from Haran should be clear to anyone who wants to investigate the γραφικὸν νοῦν of the passage. The probable explanation, he suggests, is that Terah had died a spiritual death (ψυχικὸς θάνατος) after Abraham's departure.[108]

Terah had, along with the rest of his family and when he was still in Ur, originally resolved to renounce idolatry; when, however, he reached Haran, he changed his mind and reverted to idolatry, since this had been his profession and the source of material gain for him. Proof that Terah had himself originally resolved to go to the land of Canaan with Abraham is, Syncellus asserts, suggested in Gen. 11:31, where it is stated that "Terah took Abraham and Nachor and Lot and Sarah and led them out from the region of the Chaldeans to go forth to the land of the Canaanites."[109]

---

[104] Sync. 106.17.

[105] Ibid., 106.18–20. Augustine also refers to this solution in his *Questions on the Heptateuch* 25.2, on Gen. 11:26 (CC Series Latina 33): "The problem can also be solved in the following way, since Scripture, when it states: 'when Terah was 70 years, he fathered Abraham, Nachor and Haran,' by no means intends this to be understood that he fathered all three in the 70th year of his life; rather Scripture recalls that year as the one from which he *began* to produce children. It is possible that Abraham was born later, but in reward for his virtue, for which he is strongly praised in Scripture, he was named first."

[106] Sync. 106.21–22.

[107] Ibid., 105.21–29. Among the other passages cited by Syncellus as examples of transpositions are the sequence in which Noah blesses his sons and the reference to the city of Babylon before the tower of Babel incident, when the city was "properly called Babylon because of the confusion of tongues" (105.26–27). The Syriac chronographer Bar Hebraeus observes the same thing: "Many earlier and later events," he writes, "are transposed in narrative" (*Scholia on the Old Testament*, 48–49).

[108] Sync. 106.28.

[109] Ibid., 106.31–107.2.

Because Terah reneged on this intention, Moses considers the events after Abraham's departure as years of spiritual death. Evidence for this, Syncellus states, is found in Genesis itself. For Scripture says that "all the days of Terah in Haran were 205 years and Terah died in Haran." This is not strictly accurate, and the conclusion to be drawn is that this is a shorthand expression, Moses having joined together in this notice the affairs in Terah's life before and after Abraham's departure to Canaan.[110]

In his speech to the Jews in Acts, Stephen had referred to a call to Abraham "when he was still in Mesopotamia." Genesis, moreover, hinted that Terah had also been party to the divine promise, since it was Terah who had led his family out of Ur, only to stop at Haran. But Syncellus adds to this another tradition that, in his view, proved that "Terah and the remaining members of his family (excluding Haran), having received the promise, went forth with Abraham to the land of Canaan, being admonished to do so by Abraham." Support for this, he writes, comes from a well-known tradition, according to which Abraham had rejected the cult of idols and set fire to the temple of idols when he was still in the land of the Chaldeans. According to this same tradition, when the temple of idols was set ablaze, Abraham's brother Haran was also consumed in the fire, because he was eager to worship the fire "before his father Terah."[111] The implication that Syncellus draws from the episode is that Terah had, after the conflagration, also renounced idolatry, and left from Ur;[112] but in Haran, greed and an obsession with idols had caused him to stray. "From all these things it can be shown," Syncellus concludes,

---

[110] Ibid., 107.5–11. A tradition recorded in *Bereshit Rabbah* 39.7–8 credits R. Isaac with a similar allegorical explanation. "From the point of view of chronology a period of 65 years is still required. *But first you must learn that the wicked, even during their lifetime, are called dead.* For Abraham was afraid, saying, 'Shall I go out and bring dishonour upon the Divine Name, as people will say, "He left his father in his old age and departed"?' Therefore, the Holy One, blessed be He, reassured him: 'I exempt you from the duty of honoring your parents, though I exempt no one else from this duty. Moreover, I will record his death before your departure.' Hence, 'And Terah died in Haran' is stated first, and then, 'Now the Lord said unto Abraham,' etc." The idea suggested here is that Terah was already "dead," even during his lifetime. This solution resolves the chronological problem at the same time as it frees Abraham of the charge of abandoning his father.

[111] Sync. 107.25. Here Syncellus wants to interpret Genesis 11:28—"Haran died before (ἐνώπιον) his father Terah"—not in the chronological sense, but in the sense that Haran died in the presence of Terah.

[112] Eusebius of Emesa (fr. 16, ed. Buytaert) also considers it likely that Terah and the rest of Abraham's family had received a first call in Mesopotamia; how else to explain why Terah went out to Haran with Abraham? But he too concludes that Terah changed his mind when he reached Haran. As evidence for this he adduces Jos. 24:2, which states that "your fathers, sojourned beyond the river, even Terah, the father of Abraham and the father of Nachor; and they served other gods."

that when Terah and all the remaining members of his family had received the promise along with Abraham, they went forth to the land of Canaan, as Scripture says, especially if we think that Abraham was admonishing them. But coming to Haran to that city which is even now idolatrous, they settled there because of greed and mania for idols. And thus Abraham, seeing that they had died in spirit and did not want to share in the inheritance of the divine promise to him, but were rather faithless to God, was resettled by God to the land of promise after the death of his father, that is, a spiritual death. In this way also, our Lord knew that the dead are those who do not believe in Him, even if they live a temporary life, as Scripture says somewhere, "Let the dead bury their own dead."[113]

Syncellus' reference to Abraham's episode in the temple recalls the same account in *Jub.* 12. As to the source of this tradition, Syncellus says only that it is "reported frequently (πολλαχοῦ ἱστορεῖται)."[114] Later, however, in summarizing the whole sequence of events in Abraham's life, Syncellus reports in tandem a collection of isolated traditions about Abraham, including the legend of the burning of the temple idols, and the death of Haran. What is distinctive about this material is that, although originating in *Jubilees,* Syncellus attributes much of it to Josephus.[115] In many other instances as well, he, like other Byzantine chronographers, assigns to the *Antiquities* traditions that are only attested in *Jubilees.*[116]

Indeed, in Syncellus' opinion, Josephus' *Antiquities* was a work directly influenced by *Jubilees. Jubilees* and the allied *Life of Adam* are, he says, works that have been consulted by authors of "Jewish archeologies and Christian histories." The words Ἰουδαϊκὰς ἀρχαιολογίας obviously refer here to Josephus' *Antiquities.*[117] Syncellus bases this conclusion in part on recognizable parallels between the two works, as, for example, the legend that the snake spoke the same language as the protoplasts before the transgression.[118] But his very regular pattern of misattributing citations from *Jubilees* to Josephus' *Antiquities* makes it clear that at a prior stage in the transmission of these two works, material from the two works had become confused.

[113] Sync. 107.26–108.5.
[114] Ibid., 107.22.
[115] Ibid., 111.6–17; 112.4–13.
[116] Cf., for example, Sync. 127.10–12, on Isaac's blessing of Judah and Levi (καθά φησιν Ἰώσηππος) = *Jub.* 31:15–20; Sync. 129.18–23 (ὡς Ἰώσηππος) = *Jub.* 31:15–20.
[117] Sync. 4.20.
[118] Ibid., 8.1–2; cf. *Ant.* 1.40–41, 1.50; *Jub.* 3:28.

Since the false attributions always proceed in the same direction—from *Jubilees* to Josephus and never the other way round—Gelzer concluded that (ps-)Josephus was deliberately manufactured by a single interpolator, who felt that the prestige of *Jubilees* would be enhanced by making the highly esteemed Josephus into a corroborating witness. This interpolator was either Panodorus himself, who had fashioned (ps-)Josephus out of whole cloth, or else it was an earlier chronicler, from whom Panodorus was delighted to incorporate into his chronicle a text of the *Antiquities* that agreed so extensively with the *Book of Jubilees*.[119]

Gelzer's explanation was entirely consistent with his own theory of sources. In his view, Syncellus knew only Panodorus and Annianus, and thus the interpolated Josephus must have been part of Panodorus' legacy to Byzantine chronography. Are we, however, dealing with an interpolated text of Josephus that can be recognizably traced to a single chronicle? Many of these false attributions appear to be inadvertent errors. In, for example, his discussion of Abraham's various accomplishments, Syncellus reports a collection of testimonia drawn mainly from Josephus' *Antiquities* and *Jubilees*. Some of these excerpts are correctly ascribed expressly to *Jubilees*. Others are incorrectly associated with Josephus, and authentic citations from both the *Antiquities* and *Jubilees* are left unidentified.[120] Under the rubric, 'Ιωσήππου, Syncellus provides a summary, based mainly on *Jub.* 35–37, of the war between Esau and Jacob. But at the conclusion of this same passage he states correctly that "this is reported in the little Genesis (ταῦτα ἐν λεπτῇ Γενέσει φέρεται)."[121] Similarly, under the heading "from divine Scripture concerning the race of Cain (τῆς θείας γραφῆς περὶ τοῦ γένους Κάιν)," he includes citations from the *Life of Adam*, *Jubilees*, Josephus, and Julius Africanus, a typological interpretation of the meaning of the names Cain and Abel, and a notice of the completion of the first 532-year Paschal cycle.[122] This piling up of citations creates the impression that what Syncellus consulted here was a compilation of various ancient witnesses concerning the descendants of Cain and Seth.

A comparison of Syncellus' citations from *Jubilees* with other Byzantine

[119]Cf. *SJA*, 2. 280. For additional discussion of the (ps-)Josephus passages in Syncellus and the other Byzantine chronographers, see Robert Eisler, ΙΗΣΟΥΣ ΒΑΣΙΛΕΥΣ ΟΥ ΒΑΣΙΛΕΥΣΑΣ (Heidelberg, 1929), 521–27 (Eisler considers these citations to be genuine); Heinz Schreckenberg, *Die Flavius-Josephus-Tradition in Antike und Mittelalter* (Leiden 1972), 110–12 (on Syncellus); 134–36 (on Cedrenus); 152–54 (on Michael Glycas). I am grateful to Prof. Louis Feldman for providing these references.
[120]Sync. III.6–17; 112.4–13. See below, pp. 217–18.
[121]Ibid., 124.1–15.
[122]Ibid., 8.25–11.18.

chronographers underscores the point. George the Monk regularly cites from Josephus and *Jubilees* in tandem, habitually conflating material from both works and sometimes, like Syncellus, misattributing *Jubilees* citations to Josephus.[123] Likewise in the chronicle of George Cedrenus, we find a pattern of mistaken references to Josephus, similar to but not identical to those in Syncellus. Here we may assume that George Cedrenus had access to a collection of excerpts akin to the one Syncellus used.[124] Confusions such as these would have been encouraged by the highly eclectic character of the reference work that Syncellus and the other chronographers used. This was, as has been proposed, not a continuous chronological narrative, but rather a collection of source material. In a work of this sort Josephus and *Jubilees* were regularly cited together, since, in the scope and nature of the material treated, the two works were parallel. Nor was the confusion always a result of accident. Those chronographers who held *Jubilees* in low regard had an added incentive for associating traditions from that work with some work other than *Jubilees* itself. Michael Glycas, for example, has nothing but reproach for *Jubilees,* a book which he regularly calls the "so-called Little Genesis." Thus, when he uses a tradition from that work for positive purposes, he usually suppresses its origins, either tracing it to Josephus, to an intermediary such as Syncellus, or leaving it unidentified altogether.[125] In any event, the (ps-)Josephus citations of the chronographers are a cumulative development, not the work of one interpolator.

JEWISH PSEUDEPIGRAPHA IN THE "LOGOTHETE" CHRONOGRAPHERS

The same systematizing spirit that encouraged Gelzer to classify all of Syncellus' pseudepigraphic excerpts as constitutive of an "Alexandrian" text type was at work in his analysis of other Byzantine chronographies. In his examination of the diverse pseudepigraphic citations in George Cedrenus, Gelzer perceptively recognized that many of these traditions originated in a chronicle not only independent of Syncellus, but arguably

---

[123] See below, pp. 213–16.

[124] See below, pp. 206–11.

[125] Michael attributes the following traditions from *Jubilees* to other sources: 221.6–10 (ed. I. Bekker), on Seth and Cain's wives (καθά φησι Γεώργιος); 243.1–2, on Cainan's discovery of stelae (ὥς φησι Γεώργιος); 246.12–19, on Abraham's knowledge of God at age 14 (ὁ δὲ Γεώργιος); 263.13–264.6, on the war between Esau and Jacob (ὁ δὲ Ἰώσηπος). Whenever Michael refers explicitly to *Jubilees,* it is always pejorative; cf. 198.1; 206.20–22; 392.18–22; see Rönsch, *Das Buch der Jubiläen,* 320. It should be noted, however, that Michael frequently criticizes Josephus with equally strong language.

earlier than the source or sources from which Syncellus had gotten them. In those cases where Cedrenus supplemented or conflated Syncellus' citations from Jewish pseudepigrapha with parallel material from an independent source, they regularly bore close textual resemblances to several other Byzantine chronographers, mainly the "Logothete" family (Symeon the Logothete, Leo the Grammarian, Theodosius Melitenus, and [ps-]Julius Pollux) and, to a lesser degree, George the Monk. Most notably, this family of chronographers, of which Gelzer regarded Leo as one of the purer representatives, preserved citations that often reproduced a text both independent of and, at least in the case of *Jubilees,* possibly from a source earlier than one used by Syncellus.[126]

On other grounds, Gelzer had concluded that Leo and the allied chronographers represented a fairly faithful rendition of the lost chronicle of Africanus. Indeed, Gelzer depended on these chronographers extensively for his reconstruction of Africanus from Adam up to the period of the Judges.[127] In his estimation, a chronicle was composed around the year 800 C.E. which "was generally based on Africanus." This source was "heavily used by George the Monk, Leo the Grammarian and the author of Paris 1712 (Cedrenus)," who supplemented it with pseudepigraphic source material from the Alexandrian chronographers (so, George the Monk, the Logothete chronographers, Cedrenus, and Paris ms. 1712) and Syncellus (so, Paris ms. 1712 and Cedrenus).[128] If correct, the particular value of Gelzer's hypothesis for text criticism of the Jewish pseudepigrapha is that the redaction of these Jewish works represented principally in the "Logothete" chronographers and Cedrenus originated in a very early stage in their transmission in Greek—the third century C.E.[129]

---

[126] *SJA,* 2. 281–96. The epithet "Logothete" originates in the superscription to one of the members of this family preserved fragmentarily in Paris ms. 1712: "συμεὼν μαγίστρου καὶ λογοθέτου." Fragments from this chronicle also survive in Vienna ms. 91 (cf. Gelzer, *SJA,* I. 57). The other representatives of this group of chronographers, all dating ca. 10th century, include: *a*) Leo the Grammarian (hereafter, LG) (ed. I. Bekker, CSHB [Bonn, 1842]); earlier edition by J. A. Cramer, *Anecdota Graeca* 2. 243–381; *b*) Theodosius Melitenus (hereafter, TM) (ed. T. L. F. Tafel; Monumenta Saecularia, Königlich Bayerischen Akademie der Wissenschaften 3.1 [Munich, 1859]); *c*) (ps-)Julius Pollux (hereafter, JP) (ed. I. Hardt [Munich and Leipzig, 1792]). The name of this latter work ('Ιστορία Φυσική) and its author have been shown to be the fabrications of a Greek copyist; for discussion, see Karl Krumbacher, *Geschichte der byzantinischen Litteratur,* Handbuch der klassischen Altertumswissenschaft 9.1, 2nd ed. (Munich, 1897), 363–64. Edition of George the Monk by C. de Boor, 2 vols. (Leipzig, 1904). Henceforth, all citations from George the Monk are from vol. 2 of de Boor's edition.

[127] Cf. *SJA,* I. 57.

[128] Ibid., 2. 297.

[129] These chronographers' use of *Jubilees* and, in Gelzer's terms, "ähnliche, meist kindisch einfältige jüdische Midraschim" (*SJA,* I. 60) is a subject deserving much greater scrutiny.

Some references to the Jewish pseudepigrapha in the Logothete chronographers probably can be traced, at least obliquely, to the chronicle of
Africanus:

The Fall of the Watchers

As has already been noted, Syncellus and virtually all of the other Byzantine chronographers identify the "sons of God" of Genesis 6 with the
descendants of Seth. The Logothete chronographers are the single exception to this pattern. In describing the moral contrast reflected in the translation of Enoch to Paradise and the fall of the Watchers, they write that in
this period of the world men such as Enoch were improving in character
just as angels were being corrupted. For the Watchers

> having had intercourse (ἐπιμιξίαν ποιησάμενοι) with the daughters
> of men begat Giants; and (the Watchers) introduced divination and
> black magic (μαντείας τε αὖ καὶ γοητείας) to men, teaching as well
> astronomy and astrology and the motion of every heavenly and celes-
> tial body, and they transmitted knowledge of all these things to the
> women, and caused mankind to reach the height of evil. It is said
> (λέγει) that the offspring of the Watchers were evil spirits, fond of
> pleasure and indulging the flesh (φιλήδονά τε καὶ φιλοσώματα; JP:
> om. λέγει . . . φιλοσώματα). For this reason, they aroused in God a
> great anger against them, and they were cast down to Tartarus, to the
> depths of the earth (LG 10.21–11.6; cf. Cramer 2. 248.3–11; TM 15.8–
> 16; JP 60.18–62.6).

The Logothetes do not identify the origin of this summary of the *Book
of the Watchers*. But the "angelic" interpretation of Genesis 6, which would
have been an anachronism after the fourth century, implies that this family
of chronographers preserves here vestiges of a very early chronicle (pre-
fourth century).[130] Resonances of the same account appearing in an ex-

---

Neither Rönsch nor Denis' collection (*Fragmenta pseudepigraphorum quae supersunt Graece,*
PVTG 3 [Leiden, 1970], 70–102) seem aware of the *Jubilees* material in the "Logothete"
chronographers. The omission is regrettable, because the *Jubilees* citations from Cedrenus
reprinted by Rönsch and Denis are often attested in better form in the Logothetes. For
discussion of the textual value of these excerpts in the light of Gelzer's analysis, see J. T. Milik,
"Recherches sur la version grecque du Livre de Jubilés," *RB* 78 (1971), 545–57.

[130] Notice, however, that (ps-)Pollux, after presenting this interpretation, corrects it with
the more acceptable one (62.7–22): "Others (ἄλλοι) have the following interpretation concerning this: the sons of God seeing the daughters of men, that they were beautiful, took for
themselves wives from among them, because there were at that time the race of Seth and the
race of Cain. And the race of Cain was accursed. And the race of Seth looked after piety.

cerpt in Syncellus expressly attributed to Julius Africanus identify the origin of this notice. In his discussion of the heavenly knowledge imparted by the Watchers to the women, Africanus writes: ". . . τῶν περὶ μαγείας καὶ γοητείας, ἔτι δε ἀριθμῶν κινήσεως τῶν μετεώρων ταῖς γυναιξὶ τὴν γνῶσιν παραδεδωκέναι" (in Sync. 19.31–20.2). This is closely approximated by the Logothetes' report: "μαντείας τε αὖ καὶ ἀστρολογίας καὶ πάσης ὑψηλῆς καὶ μετεώρου κινήσεως, καὶ ταῖς γυναιξὶ τούτων ἁπάντων παραδεδωκότες τὴν γνῶσιν."

The Postdiluvian Discovery of the Stelae of the Watchers

According to *Jub.* 8:2–5, Cainan, having learned from his father how to write, "went to seek for himself a place where he might seize for himself a city. And he found a writing which former (generations) had carved on the rock, and he read what was thereon, and he transcribed it and sinned owing to it; for it contained the teaching of the Watchers in accordance with which they used to observe the omens of the sun and moon and stars in all the signs of heaven. And he wrote it down and said nothing regarding it."

Syncellus, as we have seen, has his own unique form of the legend, most likely derived from his Alexandrian sources.[131] "In A.M. 2585," he writes (90.11–12), "Cainan, when he was traveling in the field found the book of the Giants, and hid it for himself (Τῷ ‚βφπε΄ ἔτει Καϊνᾶν διοδεύων ἐν τῷ πεδίῳ εὗρε τὴν γραφὴν τῶν γιγάντων, καὶ ἔκρυψε παρ' ἑαυτῷ)." The major variant from the preserved text of *Jubilees* concerns the stelae, here described only as a "book (γραφή)" and traced to the Giants, not their progenitors.

The Logothetes (LG 12.8–14; cf. Cramer, 2. 249.1–6; TM 16.15–20; JP 66.5–11) have a variant tradition. When Sala had grown up, they say, "his father taught him writing. And at that time Sala went forth to find for himself a foreign home (καὶ δήποτε ὁ Σάλα ἑαυτῷ πορευθεὶς ἀποικίαν κατασκέψασθαι) and coming to the ⟨land of the; sc. γῆν⟩ Chaldeans, he found writings carved on some rocks (γράμματα ἐπὶ τίνων εὑρίσκει διακεχαραγμένα πετρῶν). For these were the teachings of the Watchers

---

Enosh his son hoped to call upon the name of the Lord God.—'Concerning the sons born from Enosh.' Thence, those born from him took the name 'sons of God.' For this reason, they shunned intercourse with the race of Cain. But when many years had elapsed, the offspring of the pious, beholding the beautiful daughters [of Cain], were overcome by their beauty, and transgressing their ancestral law, they received them in marriage. And so intercourse introduced evil, whence the flood occurred."

[131] See above, Chap. 3, pp. 91–93.

(τῶν Ἐγρηγόρων αἱ παραδόσεις). After he transcribed these things, Sala sinned by them and taught others the wickedness in them."

The legend recorded in Leo and the allied chronographers bears all the evidence of originating in an early source. Leo's text is a fairly faithful translation from the Semitic original, implied both by the use of the paratactic καί and the preposition ἐν with αὐτοῖς instead of the simple dative of means to express instrumentality. Except for the substitution of Sala for Cainan, the text here is very close to the preserved Ethiopic text of *Jubilees*.

The significance of this variant cannot be fully appreciated unless one recognizes that the postdiluvian Cainan is found in the Septuagint and the Ethiopic text of *Jubilees*, but not in the Hebrew text of Genesis. In the latter it is Sala who is the offspring of Arphaxad. Presumably, then, the *Jubilees* tradition in Leo comes from a source that aligns more closely with the Hebrew tradition than does the preserved text of *Jubilees*. The source from which this legend is derived is probably early, possibly even earlier than the Greek exemplar of the Ethiopic text. Byzantine chronographers would hardly have emended the text of *Jubilees* from Cainan to Sala, since virtually all of the Greek chronographers after Eusebius accepted the genealogy of the Septuagint. Moreover, the legend of Sala's discovery of stelae is found in chronographers who themselves include the second Cainan, thereby implying that they have incorporated the tradition from a much earlier source.

Two of the better known chronographers who follow the Hebrew tradition in excluding the second Cainan were Africanus and Eusebius, both of whom Syncellus rebukes for failing to take account of this postdiluvian patriarch.[132] Since nothing like this tradition about postdiluvian stelae survives in Eusebius, Gelzer maintained that Leo's legend of Sala's discovery of the Watchers' stelae therefore originated in Africanus' chronicle and reflects an earlier form of *Jubilees* than the Greek text upon which the Ethiopic translation was made. In his view, removing the second Cainan from the succession of patriarchs produces a more consistent genealogical scheme.[133] Even accepting, however, that this text does reproduce a passage from Africanus, it cannot be automatically assumed that the reading

---

[132] See Sync. 132.18–20: "Instead of Cainan, Africanus and Eusebius say that Sala was born to Arphaxad . . . and they make no mention of the second Cainan at all." Although the Logothetes preserve unaltered Africanus' story about Sala's discovery of stelae, Leo (12.6–8) evidently amended Africanus by including the second Cainan in his own succession of postdiluvian patriarchs. Only Theodosius (16.14–15) and (ps-)Pollux (66.3–5) retain the original chronology of Africanus.

[133] *SJA*, 2. 275.

preserved by Leo reflects an earlier stage in the development of the text of *Jubilees* than the Ethiopic recension. As Gelzer acknowledges, in *Jubilees* Cainan, "kein Schatten," plays an important role in the rediscovery of the teachings of the Watchers.[134] Moreover, the inclusion of the second Cainan is necessary to preserve what for *Jubilees* is a striking arithmetic symmetry. After numbering the works of creation at 22, *Jub.* 2:23 likens this to the "22 heads of mankind from Adam to Jacob"; without the second Cainan, this would not be true. Conceivably, therefore, Africanus or another chronographer has emended the chronology to align with the Hebrew Bible. As is suggested by his letter to Origen on the matter of the Greek additions to Daniel, Africanus was not opposed to correcting the text of the Septuagint according to the Hebrew version.[135] The possibility of emendation is further suggested by a notice in the Ἐκλογὴ Ἱστοριῶν, a chronicle that preserves traces from Africanus' chronicle (ed. Cramer, 2. 171.14–16): "they say that he (Cainan) learned the science of astral movement. But the careful record of the Hebrews has not included him in the genealogy, saying rather that Arphaxad (fathered) Sala (τοῦτον ἡ Ἑβραίων παρατήρησις οὐκ ἐγενεαλόγησεν, ἀλλ' ὅτι Ἀρφαξὰδ τὸν Σάλα)."[136]

Abraham and the Temple of Idols

The Logothetes (LG 19.9–20.15; cf. Cramer 2. 253.17–254.9; TM 21.6–31; JP 82.19–86.10) preserve the following account of Abraham's conversion and his destruction of the temple of idols in Ur. The narrative is a digest of material from *Jub.* 11–13:

> Terah fathered Haran and Nachor besides. And Abraham received from his father Sarah as a wife. When people everywhere were sick with the deceit of (LG: περί; TM, JP: ἐπί) idols, he alone (Abraham) recognized the true God. And Haran took a wife and obtained a son Lot, and a daughter Melcha. Nachor took her as a wife. When he was sixty years of age, Abraham, when he saw that he was not persuading his father and the others in his family to turn from superstition for

[134] Ibid., 2. 275.

[135] A recent edition and French translation of Africanus' letter and Origen's reply are included in Nicholas de Lange's edition of Origen's *Philocalia, 1–20* (Paris, 1983), 514–21.

[136] Another Byzantine chronicle, the Ἐκλογὴ τῶν Χρονικῶν (ed. Cramer, 2. 233.16–27), associates Cainan's father Arphaxad with the discovery of the stelae, here too possibly reflecting evidence of emendation. For discussion of this question in the context of supposed revisions of *Jubilees* in accordance with the Septuagint, see James C. VanderKam, *Textual and Historical Studies in the Book of Jubilees*, HSM 14 (Missoula, 1977), 4–6, 107–16, and works cited there.

idols, secretly at night burned (LG: ἐμπρῆσαι; TM: ἐμπυρίσαι; JP: ἐμπυρίσας) the house of idols. Now as these idols were being destroyed (LG: ἐξ αὐτῶν ἀναλωθέντων; JP: ἐξαλουμένων; TM: ἐξαναλωμένων), his brothers, comprehending this (περινοήσαντες) jumped to their feet, hoping to pull the idols from the midst of the fire. But Haran, committing himself more zealously to the task (LG: προστάγματι; TM, JP: πράγματι), was killed in the midst of the fire. And after his father, who lived near (LG: ἐγγὺς ὤν; TM, JP: ἐν) the city of Ur, buried him, he emigrated, leading out his whole household (πάντας ἀποφερόμενος τοὺς οἰκείους) to Haran in Mesopotamia. After residing there with his father for fifteen years, Abraham one night stopped to consider the character (TM, JP: τὴν ποιότητα; LG: τὴν πιότητα) of the time to come from the movement of the stars. For his father's training in all such knowledge was not trivial. And then after he had learned to distinguish each of the things he had inquired into, he realized that all curiosity of this type was superfluous; and that God, if he were to desire it, would change according to his own will what had been predicted. And having foresworn all these things, and things like this with his whole heart and in all earnestness, and having furnished complete proof of his piety toward the divine, he heard from God, "Go out from your land, and from the house of your father." And going out together with his wife Sarah and his nephew Lot, he migrated to the portion of land assigned to his forefather Arphaxad, which the Canaanites possessed and called Canaan; he was seventy-five years of age.

There are very good grounds for supposing, pace Gelzer, that this material originated in the chronicle of Africanus. The most persuasive argument is the notice, appended to the above passage: "Altogether these are the years up to the migration of Abraham. The division of the world occurred in the beginning of the days of Phalek. From the division of the earth there are 1,006 years; from the flood 1,015 years; from Adam 3,277 years." This is a precise synopsis of Africanus' chronology, reckoned according to his era *ab Adam*. Africanus counted 2,262 years from Adam to the flood (3,277 − 1,015 = 2,262). And Syncellus reports that in his chronicle, Africanus reckoned that in the 3,277th year of the world, "Abraham went up to the promised land of Canaan."[137]

This excerpt from a third-century witness to *Jubilees* is not without in-

[137] Sync. 105.4–5. Syncellus himself rejects this reckoning out of hand (ὅπερ ἀδύνατον πέφυκε).

terest for the study of early Greek transmission of that work. Most notably, the arrangement of events preserved in the Logothete chronographers presents a more consistent chronology. According to the chronology of the Ethiopic text of *Jub.* 12:12–31, Abraham was sixty years old when he burned the temple, and seventy-seven years of age when he informed Terah that he was going to Canaan.[138] Unlike Eth. *Jubilees,* the Logothetes assign fifteen, not seventeen years, to the period from the episode in the temple to Abraham's departure from Haran. If this tradition does originate in Africanus, we have yet another example in which the Logothete chronographers have preserved a form of the chronology of *Jubilees* either earlier than that found in the Ethiopic version of the work or one that has detected and corrected an inconsistency in its chronology.[139]

While preserving vestiges from Africanus, this family of chroniclers should not be viewed, however, either as a direct transcript from him or as consistently representing an earlier stage in the history of the Greek transmission of the Jewish pseudepigrapha than Syncellus. The superscriptions to Symeon and Theodosius characterize themselves not as a synopsis of Africanus, but rather as "a collection (συναγωγή) arranged in order from Genesis and from other historians and different chronicles." There are very few direct allusions to Africanus in these chronicles, and some passages that directly contradict what we can know about Africanus from other sources. Even those citations that can be traced back to Africanus have been compromised by the Byzantine chronographers' penchant for paraphrasing and epitomizing their sources, and the existence of intermediate stages of transmission:

a) Unlike Syncellus, who preserves direct quotations from Africanus,

---

[138] The chronology according to Eth. *Jubilees:*

Jub. 12:12: burning of the house of idols at age 60 and flight to Ur (A.M. 1936).

Jub. 12:15: Abraham and Terah in Haran for 14 years (1950).

Jub. 12:16: Abraham watches stars at age 75 (1951).

Jub. 12:28: Abraham leaves for Canaan at age 77 (1953).

[139] Other chronicles order the events differently. According to Syncellus (112.7), Abraham was 61 years of age when he burned the temple. This cannot be a scribal corruption, since the same age is presupposed in the dating of this event *anno mundi*. Moreover, Abraham's departure from Haran is at age 75, meaning therefore a period of 14, not 17 years elapsed from the burning of the temple of idols to his departure to Canaan. Michael Syrus (2.6) reports that Abraham fled from Ur when he was 60 and dwelt in Haran for 14 years; see also Bar Hebraeus (trans. Budge, 10). For discussion, see Sebastian Brock, "Abraham and the Ravens," 147–49. Brock believes that the Syriac tradition is actually earlier than the composition of *Jubilees*. But the late date of the chronicles that witness to this tradition, and the fact that they know some of the same sources as the Byzantine chronographers (especially Annianus and Africanus) raises the likelihood either of a correction of *Jubilees* or of a text of *Jubilees* earlier than the preserved Ethiopic text.

the Logothetes never cite directly from him, furnishing only abstracts or epitomes of portions of his chronicle. As such, they display the characteristic habits of the epitomator.[140] The excerpts from Jewish sources have been subjected to the same kind of editing. Like the other Byzantine chronographers, the Logothetes tend in general to give only paraphrases of the pseudepigrapha, of a character quite different from, for example, the long and literal passages from *Jubilees* in the Syriac anonymous chronicle *ad annum Christi 1234*.[141]

These paraphrases were the product of an intermediary, not Africanus himself. Despite the abundance of references to Jewish writings in these chronicles (Josephus, *Jubilees*, *1 Enoch*), the Logothetes rarely identify these sources by name. Although they occasionally identify *Jubilees* by its full name (ἡ λεπτὴ γένεσις), the Logothetes are in general very lax in naming the source of *Jubilees* traditions, either not naming the source at all or using only the misleading shorthand expression "Moses says."[142] This casual and inconsistent practice is entirely at variance with Africanus himself, who, at least to the extent that it can be inferred from Syncellus, was more rigorous in naming his sources.

Nor has the epitomator done a wholly creditable job of representing Africanus' views on any given subject. The supernaturalistic interpretation of the legend of the fall of the Watchers is a good example. Although essentially reproducing a fragment from Africanus' chronicle, the epitomator has failed to capture Africanus' own sentiments on the matter. In the excerpt from him preserved by Syncellus, Africanus, while aware of the tradition that the Watchers were angels who introduced magic and divination to women, prefers the interpretation that was later to become a standard article of Christian exegesis: namely, that the sons of God were sons of Seth.[143] Indeed, Africanus is the first attested Christian writer to

---

[140] For a general discussion of the epitome as a literary genre in Antiquity, see I. Opelt, "Epitome," *RAC* 5 (1962), 944–73, esp. 966–72.

[141] See E. Tisserant, "Fragments syriaques," 55–86; 206–32.

[142] For the naming of the work as ἡ λεπτὴ γένεσις, see: TM 2.2; Leo 5.14–15 (cf. Cramer 2. 244.30) = TM 11.15–16. For the simple designation Μωυσῆς, see Leo 8.21–22 (cf. Cramer 2. 246.30); TM 14.1. The reference to "Moses" may simply be a shorthand way for an epitomator of sources to refer to *Jubilees;* Byzantine chronographers elsewhere, however, occasionally confuse *Jubilees* with Genesis. Thus, the Ἐκλογὴ ἱστοριῶν attributes to ἡ θεία γραφή the tradition, based on *Jub.* 4:10, about the 10 sons and 10 daughters of Adam (in Cramer, *Anecdota Graeca*, 2. 167.26–168.2).

[143] In Sync. 19.24–20.4. For discussion, see above, Chap. 4, pp. 114–15. Gelzer was ambiguous here. In the first volume of *SJA* he called this passage "entschieden unafricanisch" and argued that one could recognize here "traces of Panodorus, who followed the *Book of Enoch,* a highly regarded work in the Alexandrian church" (*SJA*, 1. 84). Later he completely reversed

question the very interpretation of Genesis 6 that the Logothetes propound. What seems to be the most probable explanation for the misrepresentation in the Logothetes is that an editor has preserved only a very fragmentary form of Africanus' chronicle, which succeeded in missing the point of his entire discussion of Genesis 6 and the *Book of the Watchers*.

b) Secondly, these citations have undergone considerable accretions and modernizings from later chronicles. One of these accretions is affixed to a narrative about Serug, whose birth, according to *Jub.* 11:2–9, was accompanied by a general decline in civilized behavior, marked by hostility, kingdoms, as well as idolatry and Chaldaism. The Logothetes' rendering of this legend cannot be a pure transcription from Africanus (LG 18.7–19.4; cf. Cramer, 2. 252.27–253.13; TM 20.13–21.2; JP 80.9–82.18):

> When he was 132 years of age, Ragau fathered Serug. In his time, men increased their deception against one another and established for themselves (LG: ἑαυτούς; TM: ἑαυτοῖς; JP: ἑαυτῶν) both generals and kings. And at that time they first [LG: πρῶτον; TM, JP: πρώτως] prepared engines of war, and began to war against one another. And immediately those descended from Canaan were subdued and were the first to be subjected to the yoke of servitude, according to the curse of Noah. [JP: + In the 115th year of Ragau, the kingdom of the Arabs began, holding power for 200 years.] When he was 130 years, Serug fathered Nachor. Serug lived in the land of the Chaldeans and in the city of Ur. And when Nachor was grown up, his father taught (LG, JP: ἐδίδαξεν; TM: ἐξεδίδαξεν) him the explanation of every omen (LG, TM: οἰωνῶν; JP: οἰωνοῦ), investigations both of signs (LG: καὶ σημείων; JP, TM: σημείων) in heaven and all things on earth (LG: τῆς γῆς; JP, TM: γῆς) and every Chaldean oracle.[144] [JP: + In the 36th year of Nachor, the kingdom of the Assyrians began, whose first king was Ninus, and holding sway for 1,500 years.

himself and claimed that the older interpretation of Genesis 6 attested in Leo and Cedrenus came from Africanus' chronicle (*SJA*, 2. 287, 293). The difference in interpretation between Africanus and the Logothetes is suggested as well by their respective treatment of Gen. 4:26. Figuring importantly as a proof-text for the Sethite interpretation of Gen. 6, many Christian exegetes interpreted the verb ἐπικαλεῖσθαι passively to mean that Enosh "was called god," hence his and Seth's offspring were called "sons of god or gods." The same understanding probably underlies Africanus' interpretation of the verse (see above, Chap. 5, p. 138, note 33). The Logothetes, however, interpret this verse only to mean that Enosh was the "first to call upon God (προσαγορεύειν) in the name of God" (LG 9.14–15).

[144] Cf. Charles' translation of *Jub.* 11:8: "And he (Nachor) grew and dwelt in Ur of the Chaldees, and his father taught him the researches of the Chaldees to divine and augur, according to the signs of heaven."

And in the 78th year of Nachor, the kingdom of the Sicyonians began, of which Aegisieus was the first king.] And when he was 79 years Nachor fathered Terah. When Ninus the first king of the Assyrians completed the 46th year of his reign, Abraham was born. This Ninus, having married his mother Semiramis, also called Rhea, built the city of Nineveh, and called it Ninus. From him there is a custom among the Persians to marry their own mothers and sisters, just as Zeus also married his own sister Hera. After him, his wife Semiramis ruled, who built embankments because of floods. During this same period, it was the 16th Egyptian dynasty, when the Thebans were ruling.

We have here a conflation of two sources, Africanus and Eusebius. Certain features of the passage in common with the account of Cainan's discovery of stelae indicate that the two reports have a common ancestor. The notice about Sala's education from Arphaxad (τοῦτον [sc. Σάλα] ὁ πατὴρ αὐξηθέντα γράμμαυιν ἐξεπαίδευσε) has verbal parallels with the account of Nachor's education in Chaldaism from Serug (αὐξηθέντα δὲ τὸν Ναχὼρ ἐξεδίδαξεν ὁ πατὴρ παντὸς ἐπίλυσιν). This would suggest that the *Jubilees*-based notice about Nachor's education of Serug in the art of divination also has its origins in the same source as the notice about the discovery of stelae by Sala, namely, Africanus. Presumably, Africanus had cited from both episodes (Sala's discovery of the stelae of the Watchers and Serug's education in divination) in order to describe the conditions in Chaldea on the eve of Abraham's conversions.[145] What is important to recognize, however, is that at least in the form in which the Logothetes know it, the text has been subjected to reworking. The narrative has been interwoven with the Ctesian legend of Semiramis and Ninus, with whose reign the Logothetes have synchronized the birth of Abraham. The synchronism of Abraham with the 46th year of Ninus and the 16th Theban dynasty originates in the *Canons* of Eusebius.[146]

c) The final observation has to do with the relationship of the Logothetes' excerpts from Jewish sources to those found in Syncellus. Although they in general are independent of Syncellus' citations, this is not uni-

---

[145] Notice also the presence of possible Semitic linguistic influence in the passage, i.e., the anarthrous noun in the expression ἐν γῇ Χαλδαίων and the repeated use of the conjunction καί.

[146] (Ps-)Pollux adds as well the synchronism with the rule of "Agisieus," the first king of the Sicyonians. This again is a borrowing from the chronological canons of Eusebius, who, following Castor of Rhodes, made Aegialeus the first Greek king and a contemporary of Ninus (*Canons* 20b, ed. Helm).

formly true. In, for example, Syncellus' and the Logothetes' discussions of
Cain's character we find two accounts that are in places virtually identical.
While based on Josephus' *Antiquities,* they cannot have been extracted
from Josephus independently:

LG 8.5–9: μετὰ γοῦν τὴν καταδίκην χειρόνως ἐβίω, ἅρπαξ καὶ
πλεονέκτης γενόμενος, καὶ πρῶτος μέτρα καὶ σταθμὰ καὶ γῆς
ὅρους ἐπενόησε, καὶ πόλιν κτίσας εἰς ἓν συνελθεῖν οἰκείους ἠνάγ-
κασε καὶ εἰς πολέμους ἀπασχολεῖσθαι.

Sync. 9.11–14: ὁ Κάιν μετὰ τὴν καταδίκην ἅρπαξ καὶ
πλεονέκτης μᾶλλον ἐγένετο μέτρα καὶ στάθμια καὶ ὅρους γῆς
πρῶτος ἐπινοήσας. τοὺς δὲ οἰκείους εἰς ἓν συναγαγὼν ἐν
πολέμοις ἀσχολεῖσθαι ἐδίδασκεν.

Josephus *Ant.* 1.62: ὅρους τε γῆς πρῶτος ἔθετο καὶ πόλιν ἐδεί-
ματο καὶ τείχεσιν ὠχύρεσεν εἰς ταὐτὸν συνελθεῖν τοὺς οἰκείους
καταναγκάσας.

Syncellus' and the Logothetes' references to *Jubilees* also occasionally
parallel each other:

1) In his discussion of the first day of creation, Theodosius Melitenus
(2.3) says that "on this day, then, Moses says in the Little Genesis that the
heavenly powers were created (λέγει Μωσῆς ἐν τῇ λεπτῇ γενέσει ἐκτίσθαι τὰς οὐρανίους δυνάμεις)." Later, he summarizes the significance
of the 22 acts of creation: "God, as Moses says, created 22 works in six
days. Therefore there are 22 letters and as many books among the Hebrews, and 22 patriarchs from Adam to Jacob (Εἴκοσι δύο ἔργα, ὡς λέγει
Μωσῆς, ἔκτισεν ὁ θεὸς ἐν ταῖς ἓξ ἡμέραις. Διὸ καὶ ἔικοσι δύο γράμματα καὶ βιβλία τοσαῦτα παρ' Ἑβραίοις, καὶ ἔικοσι δύο γενεαρχίαι
ἀπὸ Ἀδὰμ μέχρι Ἰακώβ) (4.24–26).[147]

Syncellus (3.14–18): "Altogether there are 22 works equal in number to
the 22 letters and the 22 Hebrew books and the 22 patriarchs from Adam
to Jacob, as is said in the *Little Genesis,* which some also call the *Apocalypse
of Moses* (ὁμοῦ τὰ πάντα ἔργα κβ' ἰσάριθμα τοῖς κβ' Ἑβραϊκοῖς γράμ-
μασι καὶ ταῖς κβ' Ἑβραϊκοῖς βίβλοις καὶ τοῖς ἀπὸ Ἀδὰμ ἕως Ἰακὼβ
εἴκοσι δύο γεναρχίαις, ὡς ἐν λεπτῇ φέρεται Γενέσει, ἣν καὶ Μωϋσέως
εἶναί φασί τινες ἀποκάλυψιν). This same work says that the heavenly

---

[147]The manuscripts of Leo and Symeon have lacunae here; (ps-)Pollux omits this passage.

powers were created on the first day (αὕτη τὰς οὐρανίους δυνάμεις τῇ πρώτῃ ἡμέρᾳ λέγει ἐκτίσθαι)."

2) Another example of the same thing appears in the *Jubilees*-based story (*Jub.* 35–38) of Rebecca's and Isaac's exhortation to their sons to avoid conflict, the subsequent contest between them, and the death of Esau. If Gelzer's theory of sources is correct, the source of these accounts can be derived from two distinct chronicles—one (Syncellus) an Alexandrian (that is, Panodorus') text of *Jubilees,* the other (Leo and the allied chronographers) from Africanus. But the affinities between the two militate decisively against the view that we confront here two independent witnesses to *Jubilees.* This is particularly true of the last several lines, where the readings are often virtually identical to one another (for translation, see below, pp. 225–26):

Sync. 124.9–14: Ἰακὼβ δὲ ἀποκλείσας τὰς πύλας τῆς βάρεως παρεκάλει τὸν Ἡσαῦ μνησθῆναι τῶν γονικῶν ἐντολῶν. τοῦ δὲ μὴ ἀνεχομένου, ἀλλ᾽ ὑβρίζοντος καὶ ὀνειδίζοντος, βιασθεὶς Ἰακὼβ ὑπὸ τοῦ Ἰούδα ἐνέτεινε τόξον καὶ πλήξας κατὰ τοῦ δεξιοῦ μαζοῦ τὸν Ἡσαῦ κατέβαλε. τοῦ δὲ θανόντος ἀνοίξαντες τὰς πύλας οἱ υἱοὶ Ἰακὼβ ἀνεῖλον τοὺς πλείστους.

LG 23.13–19 (cf. Cramer 2. 256.6–11; TM 23.29–24.2): ὁ δὲ ἀποκλείσας τὰς θύρας (TM: πύλας) τῆς πόλεως παρεκάλει τὸν Ἡσαῦ μνησθῆναι τῶν γονικῶν ἐντολῶν καὶ παραινέσεων. τοῦ δὲ μὴ ἀνεχομένου, ἀλλὰ μᾶλλον ὑβρίζοντος, τοῦ Ἰούδα παρακαλέσαντος ἐνέτεινε (TM: + τὸ) τόξον Ἰακώβ, καὶ πλήξας κατὰ τοῦ δεξιοῦ μαζοῦ τὸν Ἡσαῦ κατέβαλε. καὶ τούτου τελευτήσαντος ἐπεξῆλθον οἱ υἱοὶ Ἰακὼβ τὰς πύλας ἀνοίξαντες καὶ πάντας σχεδὸν ἀνεῖλον.

Even where the wording diverges, these passages have too much in common to assume independent origins. Not a continuous narrative from *Jubilees,* they both represent instead a paraphrastic composite of various verses from *Jub.* 35–38, the selection of which is identical. It would be beyond the improbable to suppose that Panodorus and Africanus, independently of one another, should have 1) agreed on which portions from *Jubilees* to select; and 2) paraphrased the relevant texts, often using the same choice of words.

To resolve these difficulties, Gelzer proposed, without real conviction, that Leo's text must have been a composite. Where it agreed with Syncellus, Leo was transcribing from Panodorus; where it departed, Leo was transcribing from Africanus.[148] This extremely unlikely explanation shows the extremes to which Gelzer was prepared to go to preserve his source theory. It would make no sense here for Leo suddenly and without notice to move from Africanus to Panodorus; and there is no indication of it in the text itself, which shows no signs of blending from different sources. Nor will it suffice to suggest that the explanation for the resemblances between Syncellus' excerpt and the one recorded by the Logothetes arises from the fact that Panodorus had earlier edited a portion from *Jubilees* that he knew from Africanus. The Logothete group does not uniformly represent an earlier textual form than Syncellus. The rendering τὰς πύλας τῆς βάρεως in Syncellus is probably closer to the original Hebrew reading in *Jubilees* than Leo's τὰς θύρας τῆς πόλεως. Moreover, the whole point of Gelzer's discussion is to demonstrate that Panodorus' knowledge of the pseudepigrapha was direct, and not mediated to him through predecessors. Why, in this one case, would Panodorus have reproduced an excerpt from Africanus? It seems far more likely that we are not dealing with a pure text mediated directly from Africanus. What we have instead is a collection of excerpts from *Jubilees* that cannot in every instance be traced directly to one chronicle.

SECONDARY COLLECTIONS OF PSEUDEPIGRAPHA: GEORGE CEDRENUS AND GEORGE THE MONK

The heterogeneity of the citations of Byzantine chronographers from Jewish sources is even more apparent in other chronicles, which often manifest overt evidence of conflations and secondary accretions. Two of the more notable examples of this are the chronicles of George Cedrenus (twelfth century) and George the Monk (ninth century).

The Σύνοψις Ἱστοριῶν of George Cedrenus, a chronicle that is, if nothing else, distinguished by its wealth of largely unassimilated citations, contains one of the most diverse collections of Jewish pseudepigrapha.[149] From a comparison of his primordial chronology with Syncellus (one of

---

[148] *SJA*, 2. 294.

[149] Scaliger contemptuously dismissed Cedrenus' chronicle as "quisquiliarum stabulum." As Gelzer notes (*SJA*, 2. 280), Cedrenus' chronicle is almost a transcription of one of the chronicles preserved in Paris ms. 1712. This chronicle should not be confused, however, with another chronicle also surviving in the same manuscript under the name "Συμεὼν μαγίστρου καὶ λογοθέτου." The latter is a member of the Logothete family of chronographers, concerning which see above, pp. 193–94. In his edition of Syncellus, Mosshammer has collated readings from Paris ms. 1712 under the name "(ps-)Symeon."

Cedrenus' named authorities)[150] it is clear that Cedrenus has in many cases either copied or abbreviated Syncellus' narrative, sometimes in a very clumsy and thoughtless way.[151] Dependence on Syncellus certainly characterizes many of his pseudepigraphic citations as well. Cedrenus gives what appears to be a highly condensed rendering of Syncellus' first excerpt from *1 Enoch*.[152] For the *Testament of Adam*, Cedrenus preserves a more complete text of the *horarium* than the existing manuscripts of Syncellus; whereas the Paris manuscript of Syncellus has a lacuna here, Cedrenus gives the prayers for all twelve hours.[153] Cedrenus' chronicle is, however, far from a simple transcription from Syncellus. Additional references to Symmachus and Josephus not found in Syncellus, citations from *Jubilees* culled from a variety of sources, and an extended disquisition on the symbolic meaning of the names of the antediluvian patriarchs, give his narrative of primordial history an even more eclectic and disjointed quality than Syncellus'.[154]

Conformably to his own theory of sources, Gelzer wanted to see in Cedrenus' excerpts from Jewish sources a pastiche of Syncellus, Panodorus, Annianus, and Africanus. His dissection of Cedrenus' chronicle presupposed of him almost irrational literary habits.[155] Where his pseudegraphic citations were identical to Syncellus, Cedrenus was transcribing directly from him. Where they preserved a more complete form of a text attested also in Syncellus, they were a transcription from the same intermediary (namely, Panodorus and Annianus) that Syncellus had used. Parallel citations with the Logothetes were taken from the same Africanus-based chronicle that they used.

As is clear from his treatment of pre-flood history, however, Cedrenus has only the remotest knowledge of Africanus and the Alexandrian chronographers. Virtually all of his allusions to Africanus are taken from Syncellus. And he never refers to Panodorus and Annianus by name; what he does know of them is not only entirely derivative of Syncellus, but very

---

[150] Ced. 1.2–3 (hereafter all citations from Cedrenus are from vol. 1 of the CSHB edition).

[151] Thus, his discussion of the language spoken by the snake before the transgression, while virtually an *ad verbum* transcription of Syncellus' treatment of the same subject, lacks the important phrase ὅπερ ἀδύνατον εἶναι δοκεῖ; it is unintelligible as a result (Ced. 9.22–10.10 = Sync. 8.1–10).

[152] *Ced.*, 19.12–20.2.

[153] Ibid., 17.18–18.7; cf. Sync. 10.14–24.

[154] Ced. 11.12–14 (Symmachus' rendering of Gen. 2:17); Ced. 16.11–16 (Josephus *Ant.* 1.68–70, on the stelae of Seth).

[155] See in particular *SJA*, 2. 288–93. I can hardly accept the idea that Cedrenus would have so capriciously moved between Syncellus, Annianus, Panodorus, and Africanus.

badly grasped as well.[156] We should not suppose, therefore, that Cedrenus has referred to complete copies of any of these earlier sources; he has consulted instead an anthology of excerpts from various chronicles, similar to the one used by Syncellus.

We see, in fact, clear evidence of Cedrenus' secondary knowledge of these chronographers in his treatment of Adam's stay in Paradise, a subject that preoccupied many of the chronographers. "Some (τινες) say on the basis of tradition," he writes,

> that Adam spent 100 years in Paradise. Others (ἄλλοι) that he was created in the third hour, transgressed in the sixth and was expelled in the ninth, adducing as proof the fact that Jesus was crucified in the sixth hour and died on behalf of us in the ninth. Possibly they are drawn to this conjecture because the Lord also came to them in the evening. But the three hour duration of our forefather in Paradise is quite meagre and extremely implausible, so as to be unworthy of the majesty of him who manages all things with incomprehensibly wise judgments. When did he have the time to give names in three hours to all the land animals and the birds? . . . For this reason, it is completely believable and trustworthy that on the sixth day and in the sixth hour those who disobeyed dared the transgression and in the ninth hour of the same day they fell from Paradise and their life in it, but that this occurred through a period of seven years, as some of the elders (τῶν πρεσβυτέρων τινές) have suggested. But John Chrysostom, great in his teachings, in his commentary on the Gospel according to Matthew, says that on the sixth day of the first week, that is on the same day of his creation, Adam was expelled from Paradise as well as Eve—which we too accept. And it is not necessary to be overly inquisitive about matters on which the Scripture, divinely inspired by the holy spirit, is silent, lest we incur a great punishment on behalf of a small reward.[157]

Cedrenus catalogues here a collection of views on the question of Adam's stay in Paradise, many taken from a source independent of Syncellus. These range from a period of 100 years to 7 years, in addition to

---

[156] Cedrenus (19.5–20.11) preserves, for example, portions of Syncellus' tirade against Panodorus' and Annianus' use of Babylonian and Egyptian sources, but he has only a very shallow understanding of the dimensions of the question.

[157] Ibid., 12.1–13.5.

the views of some chronographers who tried to fix the hours of Adam's
life in Paradise according to the hours of Jesus' passion.

What were the sources of these divergent chronologies? The discussion
of those "elders" who held the view that Adam was seven years in Paradise
recalls Syncellus' treatment of those "Christian historians" who used *Jubilees* and the *Life of Adam* to support the same chronology. By Gelzer's
theory, this would presumably be one of those cases in which Cedrenus
had consulted Panodorus directly. Yet Cedrenus never refers to him by
name, using only the very general expressions τινές, ἄλλοι, and τινὲς τῶν
πρεσβυτέρων to identify the proponents of the various viewpoints. One
could assume that this was simply a literary habit of Cedrenus. Judging
from his nomenclature, however, it is far more likely that what Cedrenus,
like Syncellus, relied on here was simply a collation or anthology of opinions on the question of Adam's stay in Paradise.

The compiler did not identify by name all those who held these views,
preferring instead general terms like "some," "others," or "certain of the
ancients." Moreover, the epitomator of these opinions must have preferred
the chronology that extends Adam's stay in Paradise to seven years, at the
same time fusing this with the attempt of others to see the chronology of
Adam's life in Paradise as a prefiguration of Christ's passion. Cedrenus
initially accepts the logic of the epitomator's argument. But he ultimately
allows Syncellus' judgment on the matter to prevail. A comparison of the
last few lines (beginning with the citation from Chrysostom) with Syncellus' treatment of the same question reveals that it is a verbatim transcription of Syncellus' discussion of this same subject.[158]

We have another example of Cedrenus' appeal to an anthology in his
handling of Genesis 6 and the Enochic legend of the fallen Watchers. The
whole passage illustrates clearly Cedrenus' fondness for collating different
opinions:

> After Adam, Seth ruled over mankind. In the 1,200th[159] year from the
> creation of the universe, the 40th year of Jared, and the 770th year of
> this Seth, the Watchers, from the Sethite race, were led astray and
> descended. And they took for themselves wives from among the

---

[158]Cf. Sync. 3.19–22; 3.28–4.2.

[159]Text: οἱ δὲ ἐκ γένους αὐτοῦ Ἐγρήγορες διακοσιοστῷ χιλιοστῷ τῆς κοσμογενείας
ἔτει . . . κατέβησαν. The date Cedrenus gives for the fall of the Watchers—A.M. 1200—is a
corruption of A.M. 1000 (i.e., the 40th year of Jared). According to *1 Enoch* 6:6 the fallen
Watchers were 200 in number. Emending διακοσιοστῷ to διακόσιοι produces the reading:
"The 200 Watchers from the race of Seth descended in A.M. 1000."

daughters of the sons of men, that is the daughters of Cain, and they fathered the famous Giants. Because of the righteous Seth these Giants were mighty and very great and exceedingly large in body and were both monstrous and abominable (whence they acquired their name); and through the corrupt Cain they were brave and very powerful in body and stubborn, and in their manner most murderous, impious, and wanton. Some (τινες) call them snake-footed (δραϰοντόποδας), either because they were feral in their habits and contemplated nothing good; or, as some narrate (τινες ἱστοροῦσιν), they were called snake-footed because, with their hands and feet and coils, they rose up against and made war with those dwelling in heaven. Many of them were shot at and killed by those from on high. The Most High, hurling missiles at them from heaven, destroyed not a few of them with balls of fire or thunderbolts. After this, God destroyed all the remaining ones who had not been mindful and remained incorrigible. These swore on the mountain Hermon to choose women from the sons of men, that is from the race of Cain, and they called the mountain Hermon, inasmuch as they swore and bound each other by an oath on it.[160]

In keeping with his eclecticism, Cedrenus has here blended Syncellus' treatment of this myth with a digest of other opinions. Following Syncellus he harmonizes the legend of the Watchers in *1 Enoch* with the Sethite interpretation of Genesis 6. The initial account of the descent of the Sethite Watchers has been excerpted from Syncellus; starting with the birth of the Giants, however, Cedrenus includes a long interlude on the character of the Giants. After this insertion, he resumes the narrative from Syncellus, with the story of the swearing of the oath by the Watchers on Mt. Hermon and a highly compressed form of Syncellus' first excerpt from the *Book of the Watchers*.[161]

Not found in Syncellus, this interpolation has been inserted by Cedrenus from one or more other sources. In the interpolated material, he speaks expressly of two differing groups. "Some chronographers (τινες)," he writes, had pressed for an allegorical interpretation of this legend, namely that the snakelike coils of the Giants referred only to their savage conduct. The ostensible reason for this interpretation is to reconcile this legend with the demythologizing "Sethite" interpretation of Genesis 6.

[160] Ced. 18.15–19.16.
[161] Ibid., 19.12–20.2.

Yet he acknowledges as well that another group preferred the straight, literal exegesis of Hesiod and Genesis 6, namely that these Giants were a mixed breed of monstrous creatures.[162] The salient feature of this interpolated material is its fusion of the legend of the Giants of Genesis 6 with an analogous myth recorded in Hesiod's *Theogony;* according to it, anguipede Giants, having risen up against the Olympians, were destroyed in battle by thunderbolts.

One need not assume that Cedrenus knew directly any of the proponents of this wide range of interpretation. What he had available to him was only an earlier compilation. Like his treatment of Adam's stay in Paradise, Cedrenus' collation of varying views on the subject reflects his use of an anthology of views on a single subject, which has been interwoven with material largely transcribed from Syncellus. Indeed, judging from his very imperfect understanding of Syncellus, it might not even be extreme to suppose that Cedrenus knew Syncellus himself only from an earlier collection of quotations from him.

The one pseudepigraphic work that Cedrenus accords the highest respect and from which he quotes most extensively is the *Book of Jubilees.* Explicitly listing it among his sources in the prologue to his chronicle, Cedrenus even gives the reader to believe that he knew the work firsthand. "We have culled not a few passsages from *Little Genesis,*" he reports, "as well as ecclesiastical historians, and other books, and have compiled them into one concise volume."[163] The heterogeneity of his citations from *Jubilees* suggests, however, that Cedrenus consulted several different intermediaries for his extracts from that work.

These extracts included either verbatim transcripts or very close approximations of *Jubilees* extracts in Syncellus. The deviations from Syncellus' excerpts from *Jubilees* that do occur can, moreover, sometimes be ascribed to inadvertent corruption. In the course of his discussion of the origins of the Sabbath, for example, Cedrenus writes: "For what reason did God bless the sixth day and not all the days, some say (φασί)? So we say that each of the other days had a blessing from the act of creation that took place on it. But this day alone was about to remain unhonored, since no act of creation took place on it; for this reason it was blessed and sanctified by God, and was called Sabbath as a rest, and as a type of the seventh millennium and the consummation of sinners, *as Josephus witnesses as well*

---

[162] Later, Cedrenus, referring to "those who were called Giants by the Greeks," describes them also as "anguipede" (61.19–20).

[163] Ibid., 6.2–4.

as the Little Genesis."[164] Neither *Jubilees* nor Josephus has anything to say on this subject. Immediately following this passage, however, Cedrenus writes that "the wild beasts and the four-footed animals and the reptiles spoke the same language as man before the transgression, for which reason, it says, the snake conversed with Eve in a human voice." This is identical to a notice in Syncellus, with the one notable exception that Syncellus assigns this tradition to Josephus and *Jubilees* (φησὶν ὁ Ἰώσηππος καὶ ἡ λεπτὴ Γένεσις). It is very probable that Cedrenus has simply miscopied something that he found either in Syncellus or in a collection of excerpts from his work.[165] Cedrenus' misattribution is a good illustration of the way in which citations from Josephus and *Jubilees* tended to become fused in the course of transmission.

Several of Cedrenus' excerpts from *Jubilees* were known to him independently of Syncellus. In his account of Moses' early life, for example, he reports, alongside excerpts from Artapanus and Eupolemus, the affairs of Moses' life culminating in the exodus out of Egypt; the whole narrative is absent from Syncellus.[166] It is of particular interest that Cedrenus will often quote excerpts from *Jubilees* that represent either a less corrupt or more complete form of a parallel citation found in Syncellus. Like Syncellus, Cedrenus reports the *Jubilees*-based story of the death of Cain. But although the report is identical to Syncellus', Cedrenus could not have transcribed it directly from him; for unlike Syncellus, Cedrenus expressly attributes the report to *Jubilees*.[167] Similarly, in his recitation of Abraham's wisdom, based here on *Jub.* 12–14, Cedrenus supplies a slightly more expanded account than does Syncellus.[168] Finally, Cedrenus' excerpts from *Jubilees* show less evidence of the (ps-)Josephus corruptions than do the parallel citations in Syncellus.[169]

Rönsch considered this proof that Cedrenus had available to him a copy of *Jubilees*—a view that seems to be disqualified by the highly derivative

---

[164] Ibid. 9.14–21.

[165] Cf. Sync. 8.1–3; Ced. 9.22–10.2.

[166] Ced., 85.19–87.20. For the citations paralleling those in the "Logothete" chronographers, see below, pp. 213 ff.

[167] Ced. 16.1–4; cf. Sync. 11.4–5. See Gelzer, *SJA*, 2. 288.

[168] Ced. 47.22–48.8 = Sync. 111.8–112.6; esp. Ced. 48.5–8 (= Sync. 112.4–6). See Gelzer, *SJA*, 2. 291.

[169] Syncellus, for example, preserves a cycle of legends concerning Jacob, which originate in *Jubilees*. One involves Jacob's celebration of first-fruits with Abraham at Beersheba (Sync. 120.4–8; cf. *Jub.* 22:1 ff.); the other recounts Jacob's sexual chastity until the age of 63, in accordance with the promise he had made to his mother (Sync. 120.16–17; cf. *Jub.* 25:4). Syncellus attributes both reports to Josephus; in the parallel accounts in Cedrenus they are left unattributed (Ced. 59.9; 59.15–17).

nature of the majority of his citations from *Jubilees* and other works.[170] Cedrenus' excerpts tend in general to be secondary versions of the same tradition attested in better form elsewhere. What is broadly characteristic of them is their tendency to conflate a story in *Jubilees* with a variant form of the same episode from *Jubilees* or another work recounting the same event. It is a characteristic that Cedrenus' chronicle shares with George the Monk, who, like him, knows a very corrupt form of traditions from *Jubilees,* generally blended with material from other sources, and habitually incorrectly identified.

The Death of Adam and Cain

According to *Jub.* 4:29–31, Adam is said to have "died at the close of the nineteenth jubilee . . . and all his sons buried him in the land of his creation, and he was the first to be buried in the earth. . . . At the close of this jubilee, Cain was killed after him in the same year; for his house fell upon him and he died in the midst of his house, and he was killed by its stones; for with a stone he had killed Abel, and by a stone was he killed in righteous judgment." The accounts of Adam's and Cain's deaths appear in several other chronographers, although attributed to a great variety of sources.

Syncellus refers to the legend without identifying its origins (11.4–5): "In the same 930th year, Cain also died, when his house fell on him (ἐμπεσόντος ἐπ' αὐτὸν τοῦ οἴκου), for he himself had killed Abel with stones." The "Logothetes" (LG 8.21–9.7; cf. Cramer, 2. 246.30–247.4; TM 14.1–7; JP 58.1–8) give a fuller summary of the same legend:

Cain, as Moses says (ὡς λέγει Μωϋσῆς), died when his house fell on him (τῆς οἰκίας πεσούσης ἐπ' αὐτόν; JP: om. ὡς . . . αὐτόν). And when he was 230 years of age, Adam fathered Seth. And having lived another 700 years, he died on the same day of his transgression. For since a day for God has a duration of 1,000 years, he died having lived only 900 years. He is said to have been buried in the land from which he was taken. *A certain Hebrew tradition records* (τις ἱστορεῖ παράδοσις) that his memorial was in the land of Jerusalem.

Characteristically, Cedrenus reports the legend of Cain's death twice:

(Ced. 16.1–4 = Paris ms. 1712 f. 22v): This Cain, as the *Little Genesis of Moses* states (ἡ λεπτὴ Μωσέως Γένεσις φησίν), died when his

---

[170] *Das Buch der Jubiläen,* 305, 309.

house fell in on him. For he killed his brother Abel with stones, and with stones he too died.

(Ced. 18.7–14): In the 930th year, Adam fell asleep on the same day of his transgression, and he went away to the land from which he was taken, leaving behind 93 sons and 27 daughters. He ruled over the race of men all of his life. And his grave was in the land of Jerusalem, *as Josephus records* (ὡς Ἰώσηπος ἱστορεῖ). Cain also died at the same time, when his house fell upon him, one year after the death of Adam.

Finally, a condensed account of Adam's burial appears in George the Monk (43.16–18):

(Adam) is said to be the first to have been buried in the ground from which he was taken, and *a certain Hebrew tradition, as Josephus says* (ὥς φησιν Ἰώσηπος), reports that there was a monument to him in the region of Jerusalem.

The earlier form of the story of Adam's death is the one found in the Logothetes, who assign the origin of the legend only to a "certain Hebrew tradition." Gelzer was probably correct in tracing the story of Adam's death to Africanus, who, it is known from an independent authority, treated the subject in his chronicle.[171] Both George the Monk and Cedrenus attribute the legend incorrectly to Josephus. The double attestation in George the Monk—to (ps-)Josephus and the anonymous Hebrew tradition—shows conflation from two different sources.

Cedrenus reports the story of Cain's death twice, indicating his dependence on two different sources for the same legend. Although these accounts are related to those found in Syncellus and the Logothetes, we cannot assume that Cedrenus is strictly derivative of either one of them. In his first notice of the event Cedrenus rehearses the same version as Syncellus, noting, however, that the source of the legend is ἡ λεπτὴ Μωσέως Γένεσις. Cedrenus must have had as his authority a chronicle independent of Syncellus, both because Syncellus leaves the legend unattested and because he never refers to *Jubilees* in this way.[172] Nor can the legend be traced directly to the Logothetes, who, as noted above, ascribe it only to "Moses." The complexity and several layers of the tradition and the varying forms of attestation strongly argue against the existence of a single chronicle that served as the source for these divergent witnesses.

[171] See Gelzer, *SJA*, 1. 60.
[172] Ibid., 2. 286.

Cainan's (Sala's) Discovery of Stelae

As noted above, the Logothetes and Syncellus report two rather different forms of the tradition, one assigning the discovery to Cainan, the
other to Sala. Both Cedrenus and George the Monk have secondary and
conflated versions of the same traditions. According to Cedrenus (27.11–15
= Paris ms. 1712, f. 26r.): "In A.M. 2585, Cainan, when he was travelling in
the field, found the writing of the Giants, and hid it for himself, and he
sinned because of them, and taught others the same wickedness in them.
Others say that Sala found this book (καὶ αὐτὸς μὲν ἐν αὐτοῖς ἐξημάρ-
τανε, καὶ τοὺς ἄλλους τὴν αὐτὴν ἀτοπίαν ἐξεπαίδευσεν. Οἱ δὲ τὸν
Σάλα φασὶ ταύτην εὑρηκέναι).

As is his custom, Cedrenus has fused the accounts found in Syncellus
and the Logothete family. On internal evidence alone we can discern here
the consultation of a second source. There is first his characteristic use of
οἱ to refer to unnamed sources of another tradition. Moreover, Cedrenus,
following Syncellus, first mentions Cainan's discovery of a "book of the
Giants." Then he says that Cainan stumbled because of "them (αὐτοῖς),"
presumably reflecting the tradition that identified these discoveries as
"stelae."

In George the Monk's narration of the event (10.12–25; see also Michael
Glycas 242.23–243.12), Cainan's discovery of antediluvian stelae has been
merged with Josephus' account (*Ant.* 1. 69–71) of the stelae of Seth:

> After the flood, Cainan, the son of Arphaxad, recorded astronomy,
> after he had discovered on a carved stone tablet the naming of the
> stars by Seth and his offspring (εὑρηκὼς τὴν τοῦ Σὴθ καὶ τῶν αὐτοῦ
> τέκνων ὀνομασίαν καὶ τῶν ἀστέρων ἐν πλακὶ λιθίνῃ γεγλυμμένη).
> For the descendants of Seth had been warned in advance from on
> high about the coming destruction of mankind, and made two stelae,
> one of stone, the other of brick; and they wrote on them all the celes-
> tial knowledge set forth from their forefather Seth, . . . as Josephus
> says.

The fusion of the *Jubilees* legend with the account in Josephus' *Antiquities* about the discovery of astronomy by Seth and his descendants is readily understood. Most of the chronographers held to the identification of
the Watchers with the descendants of Seth. Moreover, the story in the
Antiquities describes how Seth and his offspring, after having learned from
Adam about astronomy and geometry, preserved this learning from future

cataclysms by recording these discoveries on stone and brick tablets. That the similarity between the two accounts influenced George is seen by the fact that immediately after describing Cainan's discovery of these stelae he recounts the legend of the stelae of Seth, naming Josephus as its source (10.15–25). Here we see another example of chronographers blending together Josephus and *Jubilees*. Taken in connection with the recurring pattern of incorrect attributions to Josephus, this passage suggests that George used a source that often cited Josephus and *Jubilees* as parallel witnesses. A slight variant to George's notice links the discovery of the stelae of Seth to Arphaxad; here again, this may reflect a tradition that did not include the second Cainan.[173]

What is clear from this analysis is that there existed at least three separate traditions associated with the *Jubilees* legend of the discovery of the stelae of the Watchers: *a*) the earlier one reflected in the "Logothete family"; *b*) Syncellus' account based on Alexandrian sources, associating this with the Giants; *c*) the conflating of a story about Cainan's discovery of stelae with a parallel legend in Josephus (George the Monk and the Ἐκλογὴ τῶν Χρονικῶν).

Serug and the Origins of Idolatry

Cedrenus rehearses two versions of the birth of Serug and the onset of idolatry. One is very akin to the version found in the Logothetes, intended to describe the affairs in Chaldea on the eve of Abraham's conversion (47.7–15). In this passage, however, Cedrenus omits the discussion, found in the Logothetes, about the rise of idolatry in the times of Serug. Shortly thereafter he returns to the same subject (81.14–82.1), describing at the time of Serug the rise of "Hellenism." By this he means the origins of idolatry and the divinization of ancient heroes:

> In the period that has been described above, Serug, born from the tribe of Japhet, was the one who first began Hellenism and the custom of idolatry, just as Eusebius, "son" of Pamphilus, has recorded. This Serug, and those with him, honored with statues men of earlier times because, as warriors or leaders, they had performed something of manliness or virtue and worthy of being commemorated in their

---

[173] Cf. Ἐκλογὴ τῶν Χρονικῶν (ed. Cramer, *Anecdota Graeca*) 2. 233.16–19: "In the middle period (ἐν δὲ τῷ μέσῳ χρόνῳ) after the flood, Arphaxad recorded astronomy, having discovered, engraved on a stone tablet, the naming of the stars from Seth, the son of Adam, and his children (εὑρηκὼς τὴν τοῦ Σὴθ υἱοῦ Ἀδὰμ καὶ τῶν αὐτοῦ τέκνων τὴν ὀνομασίαν τῶν ἀστερῶν, ἐν λιθίνῃ πλακὶ γεγραμμένην)."

life, and because they were their ancestors. And they used to worship them as gods and make offerings to them. People after this, ignorant of the intention of their ancestors only to honor them with statues as being their forefathers and discoverers of good things, used to venerate them as heavenly deities and make offerings to them.

The passage, not attested in the so-called Logothetes, parallels a tradition found in John Malalas (53.15–54.12), who, like Cedrenus, incorrectly attributes it to Eusebius, in precisely the terms that Cedrenus uses: καθὼς Εὐσέβιος ὁ Παμφίλου συνεγράψατο (53.17–18). Variants of the same legend are also found in George the Monk (57.15–58.4); the Ἐκλογὴ ἱστοριῶν; 172.8–17); the *Paschal Chronicle* 87.6–13; and Suidas, s.v. Σερούχ (ed. Adler, 343). The idea that "Hellenism" began with Serug is already found in Epiphanius' *Panarion* (3.4).[174]

Abraham's Call and His Destruction of Idols

1) In summarizing the whole sequence of events in Abraham's life, Syncellus (111.6–17; cf. Michael Glycas 246.8–19) reports in tandem a collection of isolated traditions about Abraham, culled from *Jubilees* 11–13. Included among them is the story of Abraham in the temple of idols:

> *Little Genesis* says that the grandfather of Abraham on his mother's side was called Abraam, but his sister Sarah was of the same father as Abraham (cf. *Jub.* 11:14; 12:9).
>
> Abraham first proclaimed God as the creator of the universe (Πρῶτος Ἀβραὰμ δημιουργὸν τὸν τῶν ὅλων θεὸν ἀνεκήρυξε; cf. Jos. *Ant.* 1.155; πρῶτος οὖν τολμᾷ θεὸν ἀποφήνασθαι δημιουργὸν τῶν ὅλων ἕνα).
>
> Abraham first surrounded the altar with branches of date palms and olives (cf. *Jub.* 16:31).
>
> At the time of Abraham, an angel is first named in divine Scripture.
>
> From him the Egyptians first learned the placement and movement of the stars and knowledge of arithmetic (cf. Jos. *Ant.* 1.167).
>
> *In his fourteenth year, Abraham discovered the God of the universe, and worshipped him. And having destroyed the idols of his father, he burned them along with their house, and Haran was consumed along with them,*

---

[174] Ed. K. Holl, GCS 25.1 (Leipzig, 1915), 177.11–13: "Peleg fathered Ragau. Ragau begat Serug, which is translated as 'rebelliousness,' from which Hellenism and idolatry began among men." The chronographers elsewhere also supplement their excerpts from Jewish pseudepigrapha with related material from Epiphanius' *Panarion;* see below, p. 222.

when he was eager to worship the fire. He advised his father to turn away from idolatry and the making of idols, as Josephus says (cf. *Jub.* 11:16–17).

After a brief interlude dealing with Melchizedek (111.18–26), Syncellus furnishes a few additional references from *Jubilees* concerning the same events (112.4–12):

> The angel speaking to Moses said to him: "I have taught Abraham the Hebrew tongue according to the way that the fathers spoke it from the beginning of creation," as it is reported in *Little Genesis* (cf. *Jub.* 12:25–28).
>
> In the 3,373rd year of the world, the 61st year of Abraham, Abraham burned the idols of his father, and Haran, desiring to worship the fire at night, was consumed along with them. And Terah went out with Abraham in order to go to the land of Canaan. But he changed his mind in Haran, being crazed for idols up to his death. In the 3,387rd year of the world, which was the 75th year of Abraham, he (Abraham) departed from Haran by a divine oracle (cf. *Jub.* 12: 12–15).

2) As is his habit, Cedrenus (47.19–49.9 = Paris ms. 1712 30v.) gives a digest of the same material, which has been worked into a narrative paralleling that found in the Logothetes (see above, pp. 198–99):

> Terah fathered Haran and Nachor besides. And Abraham received from his father Sarah as a wife. When people everywhere were sick with the deceit of idols, he alone (Abraham) recognized the true God. . . . And he was the first to surround the altar with date palms and olives. And at his time an angel is first named in holy Scripture. And from him, the Egyptians learned the placement and creation of the stars and the knowledge of arithmetic. (That) in the 24th year (κδ′ ἔτει) of his youth, Abraham discovered the God of the universe and worshipped him. And an angel of the Lord taught him the Hebrew tongue, just as this very angel spoke to Moses, as it is reported in the *Little Genesis* . . . . When he was already 60 years of age, Abraham, when he saw that he was not persuading his father and the others in his family to turn from superstition for idols, slipped out secretly by night, having burned the house of idols. Now as these idols were being destroyed, his brothers, comprehending this, jumped to their feet, hoping to pull the idols from the midst of the fire. But Haran,

committing himself more zealously to the task, was killed in the midst of the fire. And his father, a maker of idols in Ur, buried him, and rose up and came to the city of Haran in Mesopotamia. After residing there with his father for fifteen years, Abraham one night stopped to consider the character of the time to come from the movement of the stars. For his father's training in all such knowledge was not trivial. And then after he had learned to distinguish each of the things he had inquired into, he realized that all curiosity of this type is superfluous; and that God, if he were to desire it, would change according to his own will what had been predicted. And having foresworn all these things, and things like this with his whole heart and in all earnestness, and having furnished complete proof of his piety toward the divine, he heard from God, "Go out from your land, and from the house of your father." And going out together with his wife Sarah and his nephew Lot, he migrated to the portion of land assigned to his forefather Arphaxad, which the Canaanites possessed and called Canaan; he was seventy-five years of age. This was the 3387th year of the world.

Like the account in the Logothetes, this narrative follows on the heels of Serug's introduction of idolatry. Most of this passage parallels the account of Abraham's conversion found in the Logothetes. It is not, however, strictly a simple digest from them.[175]

In the first place, Cedrenus has corrected the date of Abraham's migration to Canaan. The Logothetes, reproducing Africanus' chronology, date

---

[175] Some of the minor variants from the Logothetes are attributable to editorial omissions or abbreviations:

a) Cedrenus omits Leo 19.12–14 (on the marriages of Haran and Nachor).

b) Ced. 47.18: καὶ εἰς Χάρραν τῆς Μεσοποταμίας ἔρχεται; LG 19.23–20.1: πάντας ἀποφερόμενος τοὺς οἰκείους εἰς Χάρραν τῆς Μεσοποταμίας.

Among the other variants, Cedrenus deviates from Leo slightly more than from the other representatives of this family:

a) Ced. 47.19; 48.15: ᾿Αράμ; LG 19.9; 19.20; TM 21.6; 21.16: ῞Αρραν; JP 84.13: ῞Αραν.

b) Ced. 47.21: ἀπανταχοῦ; LG 19.11; TM 21.9; JP 84.2: πανταχῇ.

c) Ced. 48.11: περί; LG 19.16; JP 84.8; TM 21.12: πρός.

d) Ced. 48.12: ἐμπρήσας; LG 19.18: ἐμπρῆσαι; TM 21.13: ἐμπυρίσαι; JP 84.10: ἐπυρίσας.

e) Ced. 48.13; TM 21.14: ἐξαναλουμένων; LG 19.18: ἀναλωθέντων; JP 84.11: ἐξαλουμένων.

f) Ced. 48.13: νοήσαντες; LG 19.19; TM 21.14; JP 84.11: περινοήσαντες.

g) Ced. 48.15; TM 21.16; JP 84.13: πράγματι; LG 19.21: προστάγματι.

h) Ced. 48.16–17: ὁ ἀγαλματοποιὸς πατὴρ ἐν ῞Ωρ τῇ πόλει; LG 19.22: ὁ πατὴρ ἐγγὺς ὢν τῇ πόλει τῶν Χαλδαίων; TM 21.17; JP 84.15: ὁ πατὴρ ἐν ῞Ωρ τῇ πόλει.

i) Ced. 48.18: ἔνθα; LG 20.1; TM 21.19; JP 84.17: ἐνταῦθα.

j) Ced. 48.20; TM 21.21; JP 84.20: ποιότητα; Leo 20.14: πιότητα.

this event in the year A.M. 3277 which Cedrenus, following Syncellus (cf. Sync. 105.14), has amended to A.M. 3287.

Secondly, Cedrenus (49.9–13) appends to this account a notice about the derivation of the name Hebrew, which, as Gelzer saw, owes its origins to Africanus' chronicle:[176] "And Abraham, having come to Shechem by a divine oracle, established an altar between Bethel and Aggai. And having crossed (διαπεράσας) the Euphrates he received his surname (προσωνυμίαν). For the Hebrews are called 'Migrants (περάται).' But others say (οἱ λέγουσιν) that they are called Hebrews from Eber."

This is very close to a notice explicitly attributed to Africanus in Syncellus' chronicle (112.17–19): "[From Africanus concerning Abraham:] Whence the surname of the Hebrews has its origins. For 'Hebrews' mean the 'Migrants (Περάται),' when Abraham crossed (διαπεράσαντος) the Euphrates, and not as some think, from the aforementioned Eber."

The vestiges of Africanus' chronicle preserved by Cedrenus offer a good illustration of the way in which Cedrenus' reference work edited material from Africanus. Cedrenus is not even aware that he is rehearsing Africanus' opinions on this subject. He is dependent on an earlier compiler who has given no indication either of the source of this notice or that Africanus had favored one etymology over the other.[177] The derivation of Hebrew from Eber is simply offered here as a rival opinion, with the characteristic stamp of the compiler—"some say." The use of the same collection probably explains why the Logothetes produce a derivation of the name "Hebrew" that endorses the very one Africanus rejects. According to Leo (13.4–7; cf. Cramer 2. 249.18–21; TM 17.5–8), after the confusion of tongues at Babel, "it is said (φασί) that Eber alone preserved the ancient language. And when his offspring received this language, they called themselves by the patronymic 'Hebrew.' And they called the tongue Hebrew." Like Cedrenus, Leo simply found in his source a collection of views on the subject of the origin of the name "Hebrew."

Finally, Cedrenus has woven into the narrative a collection of testimonia about the "firsts" of Abraham, a more expanded collection of which is found in Syncellus, and gleaned mainly from *Jubilees* and Josephus' *Antiquities*.[178] Cedrenus gives here an epitome of the same testimonia, not

---

[176] For discussion, see Gelzer, *SJA*, 2. 291–92.

[177] On the meaning of "Hebrew" as "migrant," see Philo *The Migration of Abraham* 20: περάτης γὰρ ὁ Ἑβραῖος ἑρμηνεύεται.

[178] The reference in Cedrenus to Abraham's knowledge of God at age 14 refers to *Jub.* 11:16, at which age Abraham "separated himself from his father that he might not worship

necessarily taken, however, directly from Syncellus. The false attribution
to Josephus by Syncellus, regarding Abraham's advice to Terah to forswear
idols, is absent in Cedrenus.

3) George the Monk (92.18–95.3) also preserves a hybrid account of the
episode in the temple of idols:

> When he was 70 years of age, Terah fathered Abraham and Nachor
> and Haran the father of Lot, who also died before his father Terah.
> And after this Terah lived 135 years and he died having lived 205 years
> in all. And he was a sculptor, molding and selling gods from stone
> and wood (ἦν δὲ καὶ οὗτος ἀγαλματοποιὸς ἀπὸ λίθων καὶ ξύλων
> θεοὺς πλαστουργῶν καὶ πιπράσκων). But the period up to him in
> the 20th generation encompasses 3,332 years, and never in the previ-
> ous generations of men did it appear that a son died before his father,
> but rather the fathers died before the sons leaving them as successors
> to their affairs. And let this not be said of Abel, for he did not die on
> his own, but by a violent death. At that time, Terah set up a rival to
> God because, through his making of statues, he fashioned idols . . .
> and he was provoked to jealousy by his own son. For Haran died in
> the fire in which Abraham burned the idols of his father when Haran
> had gone in to rescue them (ἐν τῷ ἐμπυρισμῷ ᾧ ἐνεπύρισεν
> Ἀβραὰμ [καῦσαι] τὰ εἴδωλα τοῦ πατρὸς αὐτοῦ ἐν τῷ εἰσελθεῖν
> Ἄραν ἐξελέσθαι αὐτά). Therefore divine Scripture, wondering at
> this, takes note of it, saying: "Haran died before (ἐνώπιον) Terah his
> father." For Abraham being 14 years of age, and at that time deemed
> worthy of divine knowledge (ὁ γὰρ Ἀβραὰμ ὑπάρχων ἐτῶν ιδ' καὶ
> τότε θεογνωσίας ἀξιωθείς), admonished his father: "Why do you cause
> mankind to stray because of a pernicious greed? There is no other God
> except the one in the heavens, who even made the whole universe." In this
> way, he is reported to have been considered worthy of divine knowl-
> edge . . . (and) he went around each day laboring hard and with a
> heart that loved God sought out the God who really exists. And in
> this way, seeing the heaven at one time shining, at another time dark-
> ened, he said to himself: This is not a god. Similarly seeing the sun
> and the moon, the one often being hidden and becoming dark, the

---

idols with him. And he began to pray to the Creator of all things that He might save him
from the errors of the children of men." Nothing about Abraham's burning of the temple of
idols survives in Josephus' *Antiquities;* Cedrenus' lapse may be due to the juxtaposition of
material from both sources.

other waning and falling, he said: Nor are these gods. But inquiring closely into the course and movement of the stars (for he was an astronomer extremely well trained by his father) and not finding the creator either through these or some other phenomena he became extremely downcast and despairing. Having seen his desire and enthusiasm, the creator . . . appeared to him and urged him to make the journey to the land of promise saying: "Go forth from your land and your kin and from the house of your father, and go forth to the land which I will show to you." *And immediately taking the idols of his father, and having broken some, and burning others, he went out from the land of the Chaldeans with his father. And having gone forth to Haran his father died.*

The account contains a number of idiosyncratic features. There is first of all the very obvious conflation of *Jubilees* with other sources. The preliminary discussion of Terah and the death of Haran before his father Terah are based *ad verbum* on Epiphanius' *Panarion* 3.6.[179] According to Epiphanius, Haran was the first biblical patriarch to die before his father. Apparently, George has affixed the *Jubilees* story of Abraham's burning of the temple idols in order to explain how it came about that Haran died prematurely.[180] George has also emended the chronology according to Epiphanius' notice. Epiphanius' reckoning of 3,332 years after Adam up to Abraham is derived from the chronicle of Julius Africanus. As we have seen, Africanus assigned to the period from Adam to Abraham 3,202 years, but he did not include the postdiluvian Cainan in his calculations. Epiphanius, and following him, George the Monk, have simply counted in the 130 years that Africanus had left out. Here we see another example in which the chronographers have supplemented their pseudepigraphic citations with parallel material from Epiphanius.[181]

Abraham's rebuke of his father for trafficking in idols and his subsequent destruction of them is another conflation. It combines *Jub.* 12:1–13 with a related story also attested in John Malalas, the latter incorrectly attributing the story to Eusebius (57.1–9; cf. also Cramer 2. 240.12–19):

And Abraham attained knowledge of God, and determined that the statues which his father Terah was making were of mortal humans,

---

[179] Ed. K. Holl. 178.2–5.

[180] The tradition that Haran was the first one to die before his father is also found in the (ps-)Clementine *Recognitions* 1.31. This latter work, however, attributes Haran's death to the crime of incest.

[181] See above, pp. 216–17, on Serug.

and that it was not necessary to worship them as gods in heaven, since they were of earth and dust. And he criticized his own father Terah, saying, "Why do you lead astray men because of greed? There is no other god, except for the one who is in heaven, who created all things visible." And he took all the statues and broke them, and he departed from him and went out to Mesopotamia, as Eusebius "son" of Pamphilus, the wise chronographer, has recounted.

Unlike *Jub.* 12, Malalas reports that Abraham smashed the idols in Ur. This tradition, which is found in other Jewish and Christian sources, appears to have developed independently of the *Jubilees* story.[182] George the Monk has simply conflated the two traditions; Abraham, he writes, "broke some idols and burned others."

The sequence of events also does not follow that found in the other chronographers who recount this episode on the basis of *Jub.* 12. *Jub.* 12:1–8 says that Abraham did not admonish Terah for his idolatry until some 14 years after his experience of God at age 14. In the above account, his rebuking of Terah begins immediately after his encounter with God at age 14. In addition, according to *Jub.* 12:16–31 Abraham's star-gazing and the call by God to migrate to Canaan take place after his sojourn in Haran. George the Monk has set this whole episode in Ur.[183]

The Fall of Sodom and Gomorrah

1) Logothetes (LG 20.22–21.10; cf. Cramer, 2. 254.19–27; TM 22.5–18; JP 86.14–88.10):

Before Isaac was fathered by Abraham, Ishmael was born from Hagar, from whom come the race of the Ishmaelites, who are the same as the Hagarenes, also called Saracens. At this time (κατὰ τοῦτον . . . τὸν καιρόν), God rained down fire on the Pentapolis (πῦρ κατὰ τῆς Πενταπόλεως ὑετίζει) and he consumed the whole race of men from it (ἀναλίσκει μὲν ἐξ αὐτῆς ἅπαν τὸ γένος τῶν ἀνθρώπων) and he destroyed that which grew from the earth (LG: αὐτὸ ἀπὸ τῆς γῆς τὸ

---

[182] For other witnesses, see *Ber. Rab.* 38.7; Philaster *On the Heresies* 147.2 (CC Series Latina 9, 308): "et Abraham beatissimus frangens idola justificatus est." For Philaster, this tradition forms a series of arguments against heretics who, on the basis of the Septuagint text at Exod. 22:28, claim that it is improper to "revile foreign gods." Contrary to Rönsch's assertion (*Das Buch der Jubiläen*, 377), the origin of Philaster's report is probably independent of *Jubilees*. For discussion, see Louis Ginzberg, *Die Haggada*, 95.

[183] For a parallel account, see also Suidas, s.v. Ἀβραάμ; for discussion, see Rönsch, *Das Buch der Jubiläen*, 350–51.

ἀνάστημα; TM, JP: αὐτὸ ἄπαν τῆς γῆς τὸ ἀνάστημα) and he mortified the waters of the sea which was situated there. A little later Abraham arising from the oak at Mamre (LG: Μαμβρήν; TM, JP: Μαμβρή) settled at the well of the oath (ὁ ᾽Αβραὰμ ἐπὶ τὸ φρέαρ κατασκηνοῖ τοῦ ὅρκου). Having established tabernacles for himself and his property according to kin (ἑαυτῷ τε ἰδίᾳ καὶ τοῖς οἰκεταῖς αὐτοῦ κατὰ συγγενείας πηξάμενος σκηνάς), at that time Abraham first established the feast of tabernacles for seven days (TM, JP: ἡμέρας; LG: ἡμέραις), which Israel even now celebrates in the feast of tabernacles.

The Logothetes preserve an abstract of material based on *Jubilees* 15–16. The account of Abraham's settlement at the "well of the oath" and his establishment of the feast of tabernacles is extremely close to the preserved Ethiopic text.[184] Parts of the above text appear to be a literal rendering from a Semitic original. The expression διαφθείρει δὲ καὶ αὐτό ἄπαν τῆς γῆς ἀνάστημα (TM 22.9–10) is difficult to understand unless one supposes that a translator has rendered τὸ ἀνάστημα from the Hebrew "hayequm."[185] The passage dealing with the fire rained down by God on the Pentapolis reveals the hand of an editor, who has substituted the Pentapolis for "Sodom and Gomorrah and Zeboim and the region of Jordan" (cf. *Jub.* 16.5). Whether or not the notice that prefaces this passage—explaining the origins of the Saracens—is a modernization from Africanus himself or is a later gloss by an epitomator is difficult to ascertain.[186]

2) While furnishing virtually the same *Jubilees*-based passage, Cedrenus has removed their notice about the origins of the Saracens, substituting in its place a more extensive etymology of the term drawn from Syncellus (Ced. 50.22–51.1; cf. Sync. 113.12–16): "From Ishmael the Saracens are called Ishmaelites. They changed their name to Saracens, deeming it unworthy to be called by the slavish name Hagarenes. But some say that

---

[184] Cf. *Jub.* 16:11; 16:20–21;. cf. Charles note ad loc. (*Jub.* 16:20–31).

[185] So see a variant reading of the Septuagint at Gen. 7:4(A): καὶ ἐξαλείψω πᾶν τὸ ἀνάστημα (= Heb. *kol-hayequm*) ἣν ἐποίησα, ἀπὸ προσώπου τῆς γῆς.

[186] It is not beyond the range of possibilities that the association of Hagarenes, Ishmaelites, and Saracens was taken from Africanus' chronicle. It is certainly well attested in 4th-century chronicles. Eusebius has it in his *Canons* (24a): "Abraham fathered Ishmael from his servant-woman Hagar, from whom came the race of Ishmaelites, who were later called Hagarenes and finally Saracens." Epiphanius uses the same nomenclature in the chronological introduction to his *Panarion* 4.1.7 (ed. Holl, 180.10–12). On Christian use of the terms Saracens, Ishmaelites, and Hagarenes as designations for the Arabs, see Irfan Shahîd, *Byzantium and the Arabs in the Fourth Century* (Washington, D.C., 1984), 126–27, 279–80; idem, *Rome and the Arabs* (Washington, D.C., 1984), 105 (note 63), 124.

Sarah sent Hagar away bereft (κενήν) of an inheritance." Although Cedrenus has either taken this directly from Syncellus or from the same source, the second etmology of Saracen, linking it to Sarah, is already attested in John of Damascus (675–ca. 745).[187]

The War between Esau and Jacob

As has been noted above (pp. 205–6), Syncellus and the Logothetes have related accounts of this event. Cedrenus and George the Monk have similar versions, as does Michael Glycas:

1) Syncellus 123.22–124.14:

> From Genesis: Isaac said to Esau in his blessings, "There shall come a time when you shall loosen his yoke from your neck, and you will pay the penalty with death (πλημμελήσῃς εἰς θάνατον).'
>
> From Josephus: In the 153rd year of Isaac Jacob returned to him from Mesopotamia. When Isaac looked up and saw the sons of Jacob, he blessed Levi as high priest and Judah as king and ruler (ηὐλόγησε τὸν Λευὶ ὡς ἀρχιερέα καὶ τὸν Ἰούδαν ὡς βασιλέα καὶ ἄρχοντα). And Rebecca petitioned Isaac in old age to exhort Esau and Jacob to love one another ('Η Ῥεβέκκα ἤτησε τὸν Ἰσαὰκ ἐν τῷ γήρᾳ παραινέσαι τῷ Ἡσαῦ καὶ τῷ Ἰακὼβ ἀγαπᾶν ἀλλήλους). And he counseled them and foretold that if Esau would rise up against Jacob, he would fall by his hands (ἐὰν ἐπαναστῇ τῷ Ἰακὼβ ὁ Ἡσαῦ, εἰς χεῖρας αὐτοῦ πεσεῖται). So after Isaac died, Esau, incited by his sons, mustered his people and marched out for combat against Jacob and his sons. But closing the gates of the tower (τὰς πύλας τῆς βάρεως), Jacob appealed to Esau to recall the familial injunctions. But since he was not restrained, but rather was running riot and making reproaches (τοῦ δὲ μὴ ἀνεχομένου, ἀλλ' ὑβρίζοντος καὶ ὀνειδίζοντος), Jacob, pressured by Judah, drew out his bow and shot Esau, striking him on his right breast (βιασθεὶς Ἰακὼβ ὑπὸ τοῦ Ἰούδα ἐνέτεινε τόξον καὶ πλήξας κατὰ τοῦ δεξιοῦ μαζοῦ τὸν Ἡσαῦ κατέβαλε). When he died, the sons of Jacob opened the gates and killed

---

[187]*De Haeresibus* 101 (PG, 94. 764A): Σαρακενοὺς δὲ αὐτοὺς καλοῦσιν, ὡς ἐκ τῆς Σάῤῥας κενοὺς, διὰ τὸ εἰρῆσθαι ὑπὸ τῆς Ἀγὰρ τῷ ἀγγέλῳ· Σάῤῥα κενήν με ἀπέλυσεν; see Gelzer, *SJA*, 2. 188–89; 292. Jerome (*Commentary on Ezechiel* 8.25.1–7, CC Series Latina 75, 335) also associates the name of Saracen with Sarah, although in a slightly different way. He says that the "Ishmaelites and the Hagarenes" are "now called Saracens, falsely taking for themselves the name of Sarah, whence, that is, they might appear to have been descended from a freeborn mistress."

most of them (τοῦ δὲ θανόντος ἀνοίξαντος τὰς πύλας οἱ υἱοὶ Ἰακὼβ ἀνεῖλον τοὺς πλείστους). *This is reported in the Little Genesis* (ταῦτα ἐν λεπτῇ Γενέσει φέρεται).

2) LG 23.3–23.19 (cf. Cramer 2. 255.29–256.11); TM 23.20–24.2:

When he was eighty-seven years of age, Jacob fathered Levi. Rebecca petitioned Isaac to summon Esau and Jacob and reconcile them (ἠξίωσε τὸν Ἰσαὰκ ἀγαγεῖν Ἡσαῦ καὶ Ἰακὼβ καὶ διαλλάξαι αὐτούς) and at the same time admonish them both to swear an oath of peace with one another and confirm a covenant of fraternal friendship. Now having done this, he foretold to Esau that "if you would rise up against Jacob, you would fall by his hand (προεῖπε τῷ Ἡσαῦ ὅτι ἐὰν ἐπαναστῇς τῷ Ἰακὼβ ἐμπεσῇ εἰς χεῖρας αὐτοῦ)." And first Rebecca, and not much later Isaac died, leaving the perquisites of primogeniture to Jacob. And the sons of Esau provoked their father against Jacob and his sons. And having been outfitted for combat, they went out with their armies for combat. And having closed the gates (θύρας; TM: πύλας) of the city, he (Jacob) advised Esau to remember the familial injunctions and warnings. But when he (Esau) was not restrained, but was rather running riot, Jacob, since Judah was encouraging him, drew his bow and shot Esau, striking his right breast (τοῦ δὲ μὴ ἀνεχομένου, ἀλλὰ μᾶλλον ὑβρίζοντος, τοῦ Ἰούδα παρακαλέσαντος ἐνέτεινε (TM: + τὸν) τόξον Ἰακώβ, καὶ πλήξας κατὰ τοῦ δεξιοῦ μαζοῦ τὸν Ἡσαῦ κατέβαλε). And when he died, the sons of Jacob opened the gates and went out and killed almost everyone (πάντας σχεδὸν ἀνεῖλον).

3) Cedrenus 60.21–61.15:

Rebecca, as *Josephus says in his Antiquities,* petitioned Isaac to summon Esau and Jacob and reconcile them (ἠξίωσε τὸν Ἰσαὰκ ἀγάγειν Ἡσαῦ καὶ Ἰακὼβ καὶ διαλλάξαι αὐτούς). Now having done this, and having admonished them at the same time, he had them swear an oath of peace with one another and confirm a covenant of spiritual friendship. He foretold to Esau that "if you would rise up against Jacob, you would fall by his hand (προεῖπε τῷ Ἡσαῦ ὅτι ἐὰν ἐπαναστῇς τῷ Ἰακὼβ, ἐμπεσῇ εἰς τὰς χείρας αὐτοῦ)." After the death of Isaac, the sons of Esau provoked their father against Jacob and his sons. And having been outfitted for combat, he went out with his armies for combat. And after he closed the gates (θύρας) of the city, he (Jacob) was advising Esau to remember the familial injunctions and warnings. So when he (Esau) was not restrained, but was rather running riot, Jacob, with Judah encouraging him, drew his bow and shot Esau, striking his right breast (τοῦ δὲ μὴ ἀνεχομένου ἀλλὰ καὶ μᾶλλον ὑβρίζοντος, τοῦ Ἰούδα παρακαλέσαντος ἐνέτεινε τὸ τόξον Ἰακώβ, καὶ πλήξας κατὰ τοῦ δεξιοῦ μαζοῦ τὸν Ἠσαῦ κατέβαλε). And when he died, the sons of Jacob opened the gates and went out and killed almost everyone (πάντας σχεδὸν ἀνεῖλον). And first Rebecca, and not much later Isaac died, leaving the perquisites of primogeniture to Jacob.

4) George the Monk 113.20–114.16:

Isaac and Rebecca, after the return of Jacob, summoned both Jacob and Esau. And after counseling them and making them swear to make peace with one another and at the same time to confirm a covenant of filial friendship, they died, first Rebecca, and not much later Isaac as well, having bequeathed the rights of primogeniture to Jacob. After this, Esau, provoked against Jacob by Amalek his son through a concubine, assembled his tribes and rushed out in battle against him and his sons, as *Josephus says* (ὥς φησιν Ἰώσηπος). And when he had closed the gates of the city, to which he had fled, Jacob urged Esau from the wall to recall the familial commandments. But when he (Esau) was not restrained, but was rather running riot and making reproaches and threatening to destroy him (τοῦ δὲ μὴ ἀνεχομένου, ἀλλὰ καὶ μᾶλλον ὑβρίζοντος καὶ ὀνειδίζοντος καὶ ὀλοθρεύσειν αὐτὸν ἀπειλοῦντος), Jacob drew his bow and shot Esau, striking his right breast. And when he died, the sons of Jacob immediately slipped out and slew nearly everyone. And then the prediction of Isaac was fulfilled, which said to Esau, 'if you remove the yoke of your brother from your neck you will pay the penalty of death.'

5) Michael Glycas 263.13–264.6 (ed. I. Bekker):

And according to the account of Moses, Esau and Jacob made a truce with each another. But Josephus in his narrative about these things adds the following as well. As he was dying, Isaac conversed with Jacob and Esau concerning harmony between them. But when he died, Esau pursued Jacob. So he (Jacob) went into a certain city, and peering out from above, reminded him of the familial injunctions. But he was not persuaded. And drawing his bow he shot Esau in the chest. Then was fulfilled the prophecy of Isaac, "whenever you remove the yoke of your brother from your neck, then you will com-

mit an offense worthy of death (πλημμέλειαν πλημμελήσεις θανά-
του)." And these are the words of Josephus. But it is not necessary to
receive them as if they were true. For the words "you will commit an
offense worthy of death" are an addition of Josephus. For in the
prophecy (of Isaac) there is found nothing written like this.

Before the formal citation, Syncellus, under the heading "From Genesis," recounts Isaac's prophesy to Esau. The last part of the citation, describing the penalty of death which will be incurred as a result, is a gloss
from *Jub.* 26:34. In Syncellus' excerpt the description of the conflict appears under the rubric "From Josephus." In fact, what the *Antiquities* does
have to contribute about Jacob's return to Isaac contradicts the chronology presented here; according to *Ant.* 1.345, Rebecca was already dead
when Jacob returned to Isaac. The concluding words of the passage, however, assign its origins to *Jubilees*. As is characteristic of them, the Logothetes leave the passage unascribed. All five accounts describe essentially the
same sequence of events, often using very similar language.[188]

For most of this passage Cedrenus represents a secondary form of an
earlier tradition found in the Logothetes. The variants from the parallel
passage in the Logothete chronographers are the result of inadvertent error, or condensation.[189] The most obvious deviation from their account is
the attribution of the whole report to Josephus, which may show the influence of Syncellus. However, Cedrenus, unlike Syncellus, nowhere associates this report with *Jubilees;* and this particular passage does not reveal
the fairly overt evidence of conflation with Syncellus that we find in other
places.

George the Monk's account reveals some striking and unexpected affinities with Syncellus'. He too attributes the passage to Josephus. The
expression τοῦ δὲ μὴ ἀνεχομένου, ἀλλὰ καὶ μᾶλλον ὑβρίζοντος καὶ
ὀνειδίζοντος is closer to Syncellus than the other witnesses here. At the
end of this passage George appends the notice about the fulfilment of

---

[188] See esp. Ced. 61.7–11; Sync. 124.9–13; George Mon. 114.6–12; LG 23.13–17 (cf. Cramer, 2. 256.6–10); TM 23.29–32.

[189] The omission of the report of Isaac's and Rebecca's death required Cedrenus to append this notice to the end of the story. Cedrenus also omits the words τὰς πύλας ἀνοίξαντες from the last sentence in the Logothetes' report (cf. LG 23.18). Among the other minor variants from the Logothetes, see 1) Ced. 61.1; LG 23.7 = TM 23.23 (the placement of ὃ δὴ καὶ ποιήσας); 2) Ced. 61.2–3: τῆς πνευματικῆς οἰκειότητος; LG 23.6 = TM 23.22–23; τῆς ἀδελφικῆς οἰκειότητος; 3) Ced. 61.6–7: καθοπλισθεὶς . . .ἦλθε πρὸς πόλεμον; LG 23.12–13 = TM 23.28: καθοπλισθέντες . . .ἦλθον πρὸς πόλεμον; 4) Ced. 61.7–8; TM 23.29: τῆς πόλεως τὰς πύλας; LG 23.13: τὰς θύρας τῆς πόλεως (cf. Sync. 124.10: τὰς πύλας τῆς βάρεως); 5) Ced. 61.8: τῶν προγονικῶν ἐντολῶν; LG 23.14 = TM 23.30: τῶν γονικῶν ἐντολῶν; 6) Ced. 61.12: ἐξῆλθον; LG 23.18: ἐπεξῆλθον.

Isaac's prophecy. Like Syncellus, it includes the *Jubilees*-based prediction that when Esau loosed the yoke of servitude he would pay the penalty of death. Michael Glycas seems to have derived his story from George the Monk. Like him, he attributes the whole story to Josephus, including Isaac's prediction that when Esau removed the yoke of his brother, he would pay the penalty of death. Michael even goes so far as to castigate Josephus for including this prediction, which, as he knows, is not found in Genesis.

Taken in conjunction with excerpts from the same or similar works in the Syriac chronicles, the several citations from *1 Enoch* and *Jubilees* and related pseudepigrapha witness the great interest of Christian chronographers in the Jewish non-canonical literature. A complete analysis of this largely neglected corpus of material would prove useful not only for the study of the Christian use and interpretation of Jewish sources of the Second Temple period, but for the textual history of the Jewish pseudepigrapha as well. In general, Gelzer's instincts were probably correct in recognizing that the citations from the Jewish pseudepigrapha in the non-Syncellus tradition (best represented in the "Logothete" chronographers) often attest a stage in the history of their Greek transmission that is earlier than that reflected in Syncellus, and that partially originates, at least indirectly, in Africanus' chronicle. We can, however, add more precision to the discussion of the transmission of these sources once we abandon the notion that any of these chronicles are direct transcriptions of pseudepigrapha either from Africanus or the Alexandrian chronographers, or even had access to complete copies of these earlier chronicles.

All of the sources examined here are variously characterized as a collection (ἐκλογή), epitome (σύνοψις), or anthology (συναγωγή) of earlier works, not as transcripts or even digests of one or two earlier sources. As an aid in assembling a cross section of views on primordial history, Byzantine chronographers consulted anthologies and epitomes of earlier works. These epitomes had the purpose of simply collecting and compiling a sampling of opinions on a particular issue in chronography; the works represented could range over a wide spectrum of sources, both Jewish and Christian. For antediluvian history some of these authorities might include Chrysostom, Ephrem, Africanus, Eusebius, Panodorus, Annianus, Epiphanius, Gregory, Josephus, and *Jubilees*. In other cases, the epitomator might choose to leave the sponsor of a particular view unidentified; instead opinions are associated only rather vaguely with "some of the elders," or "some Christian historians."

Secondly, these epitomators operated largely as neutral compilers of various opinions. This is most evident in the manner in which they have culled material from Africanus. As we have seen, Africanus himself, after setting out competing opinions about the interpretation of Genesis 6 or the meaning of the word "Hebrew," favored one view over another; a later epitomator would then simply extract from Africanus the differing views, without preserving Africanus' own stated preference. As a result, the Byzantine chronographers who know Africanus only through one of these compilations sometimes preserve vestiges of very old views that Africanus himself had in the third century already discarded. At the same time, it must also be said that the Byzantine chronographers' dependence on such compilations has frequently produced the kind of sterile, disjointed, and incoherent presentation that is notoriously characteristic of them.

The final observation has to do with the influence of intermediaries on the textual character of several of the primary sources preserved in the chronographers. None of the chronographers' citations from the diverse literature of the Hellenistic period reflects firsthand knowledge of them. This includes the several Jewish works of the Second Temple period. Nor can they be said to have been extracted directly from a single earlier chronicle (Gelzer notwithstanding). It is certainly clear that Africanus and Panodorus served as an important reservoir of source material for the Byzantine chroniclers, but this has occurred only through intermediaries. Even those chronicles (namely, Syncellus and the Logothetes) whose excerpts from the Jewish pseudepigrapha exhibit relatively uniform textual traits cannot in all cases be classified as directly derivative of one source. For Cedrenus and George the Monk the character of their citations is even less uniform. Heterogeneity is most visible in the case of *Jubilees*. Chronographers freely combine paraphrases from that work with citations from numerous other sources, among them Eusebius, Josephus, Epiphanius, Eupolemus, and Malalas. When they are identified at all, traditions from that work are attributed variously to "Little Genesis," the "Little Genesis of Moses," "Moses," "divine Scripture," "the Apocalypse of Moses," and "Josephus." In the case of a later chronographer like Michael Glycas, the constant recycling of *Jubilees* traditions has produced an ironic result. Glycas will sometimes vilify Josephus for views that the latter never espoused; they originated in *Jubilees* and only through repeated use were gradually foisted upon the *Antiquities*.

Understanding the energy that Byzantine chronographers devoted to epitomizing and collecting excerpts from a variety of works has a practical application for the comparative study of their pseudepigraphic citations with parallel material in other chronicles, most notably the Syriac chronographers. As has already been suggested, Michael Syrus clearly knows at least some of his pseudepigraphic excerpts (*1 Enoch*) through the mediation of Annianus.[190] Other Syriac chroniclers who quote from the pseudepigrapha also cite Annianus and Africanus as authorities. This includes the Syriac anonymous chronicle *ad annum Christi 1234*, a chronicle that includes extensive excerpts from *Jubilees*. This would create strong *prima facie* evidence that the Byzantine and Syriac chronographers knew a text of these sources with related textual ancestries.

Yet if we compare the Byzantine chronographers' excerpts with the parallel passages from these writings in the Syriac chroniclers, it is difficult to suppose that the Syriac and the Greek citations share a common ancestry. The *Jubilees* citations in the anonymous Syriac chronicle are consistently more literal and more extensive than their Greek counterparts.[191] On the other hand, Syncellus and all the other Byzantine chronographers who refer to *Jubilees* furnish only paraphrases and summaries from that work.

Now digesting and abbreviating texts was a practice that Byzantine chronographers regularly engaged in. As is clear from the form in which the *Aegyptiaca* of Manetho circulated (not to mention the Syriac epitomes of Eusebius' own chronicle), distilling the main ideas from much longer sources must have been a fairly commonplace practice for chronographers. As we have seen, the excerpts from the Jewish pseudepigrapha in the Byzantine chronicles exhibit the same characteristics. For this reason, we need not conclude, as Tisserant did, that the more literal Syriac text in the anonymous chronicle proves that the author had at his disposal a text of *Jubilees* translated directly from the Hebrew original.[192] What may just as well have happened is that the Syriac chronographers simply translated their extracts from a Greek form of *Jubilees* that had not been subjected to the editorial hand of a Byzantine epitomator.[193]

---

[190] See above, pp. 177–78, 187–88.

[191] Syriac text of this chronicle is edited by I.-B. Chabot, in CSCO 81, Scriptores Syri 36; Latin translation by Chabot in CSCO 109, Scriptores Syri 56.

[192] Cf. Tisserant, "Fragments syriaques," 55–86; 206–32.

[193] In the introduction to his chronicle the anonymous chronicler names as his authorities Annianus the monk and Africanus (27). Note also that many of the *Jubilees* citations in this chronicle are a more literal rendering of similar citations found in the Byzantine chronographers, e.g., the language spoken by the serpent before his condemnation (31), the stelae discovered by Cainan (46), Abraham in the temple of idols (51–52), and the war between Jacob and Esau (56–57).

Conclusion

However often they might seek to qualify or diminish the reliability of the surviving witnesses to it, historians of antiquity, perhaps not much unlike historians today, were fascinated by the remote past. Christian chronographers had their own reasons for wanting to know as much as they could about earliest times. But they were not immune to the problems of reconstructing an absolute chronology from creation. It is in Eusebius' chronicle that we find the most focused discussion of the problems. While inclined to exempt Genesis from thoroughgoing historical scepticism, Eusebius left the door open for further inquiry by his studied disapproval of any attempts to establish a continuous chronology that would include either the creation of the world, the creation of Adam, or even the period before Abraham.

This stance was entirely consistent with Eusebius' moderate temperament and his own stated opposition to chiliastic chronography. Alexandrian chronographers after him would not share the same scepticism, however. Since Clement, Christian chronographers in Alexandria had experimented with the era from creation. But the task had in the fifth century acquired a special urgency for them, and we should not be surprised to find that it was in Alexandria that Eusebius' chronicle was destined to encounter some of its most vocal critics. In the pagan/Christian controversy in Alexandria of late Antiquity, the question of the age and duration of the universe was the one most vigorously contested, and Christian chronographers quite properly felt that they had something important to contribute to the dialogue.

The discussion naturally spilled over into the question of the proper use of extra-biblical sources. More than any other branch of Christian learning, chronography felt a keen attraction to non-biblical sources, especially those dealing with primordial history. The scope of the undertaking demanded it, and there was always the expectation that these sources would validate Genesis, at the same time reminding the Greeks of the poverty of their own sources. Then, too, lurking just beneath the surface was a frustration, rarely acknowledged openly, with the sketchiness of the information that could be teased out of the first several chapters of Genesis. When Syncellus warns his readers not to let curiosity about things concerning which Genesis is silent divert their interest to other sources, we know that this was directed to those who were doing exactly that. Other sources could offer far more rewarding answers to the kinds of questions that the ancients naturally wanted to ask about the remote past—how were records kept then, how did the ancients reckon time, how did civilization begin, which peoples were the oldest?

Berossus and Manetho were the principal staples here. More or less by default, they had become the literary property of Jewish and Christian apologists and chronographers, who, it must be said, often used them in an extremely undisciplined way, seizing on parallels and overlooking or minimizing the numerous places where they diverged from Genesis. But Christian and Jewish apologists were not able to maintain their monopoly on the ethnic histories of the Orient. If Josephus and an earlier generation of Christian apologists might point to the antiquity of Chaldean and Egyptian historical documents as evidence for the inferiority of Greek culture, pagan controversialists would soon appeal to the same records as documentable proof for the unreliability of Genesis' account of creation. The reversal must have injected a note of sobriety into Christian apologetic, for we find some of the apologists drawing away from these sources, if not, as Africanus did, rejecting them outright.

Characteristically, Eusebius stood somewhere in the middle of the discussion, recognizing the value of histories like those of Berossus and Manetho as instruments of apologetic, but cognizant of the difficulties of reconciling them with Genesis. We have no sense from him that Eusebius was unhappy with his rather tentative handling of Chaldean and Egyptian chronology in the first book of his chronicle. For Eusebius, the difficulties that they raised were an object lesson for those who had unreasonable expectations for scientific exactitude in chronography. The lesson, meant as a caveat for future generations of chronographers, was lost on Eusebius' Alexandrian successors. Among the many deficiencies that they were able to identify in his work, his vacillating treatment of Berossus and Manetho stood out as one of his greatest failings.

Later, Syncellus, on this one issue, would find himself uncomfortably allied with Eusebius, a chronicler of whom he was normally critical. What for Panodorus in fifth-century Alexandria had been a problem of overriding interest—how to recover the ethnic histories of the Chaldeans and Egyptians—had become for Syncellus a quest of very little merit, far too accommodating to discredited sources, and one that could only confuse the unsophisticated. One has only to follow the transmission of these same sources from Syncellus through Scaliger to see that Syncellus had not laid the question to rest. After the publication of Scaliger's *Thesaurus Temporum,* European chronographers of the sixteenth and seventeenth centuries would revive the same controversy. Marsham, Jackson, and many of the other European chronographers after Scaliger invoke the names of Syncellus, Panodorus, Annianus, Eusebius, and Africanus almost as if they were contemporaries. The long transmission of these sources and the continuity in interpretation of them are an eloquent reminder of how tradition-bound the discipline of chronography could often be.

Abbreviations

AAAScHung	*Acta Antiqua Academiae Scientiarum Hungaricae*
AbhAkBerlin	*Akademie der Wissenschaften, Abhandlungen,* Berlin
ANF	*The Ante-Nicene Fathers,* ed. A. Roberts and J. Donaldson
AO	*Acta Orientalia*
APOT	*Apocrypha and Pseudepigrapha of the Old Testament,* 2 vols., ed. R. H. Charles
AThANT	*Abhandlungen zur Theologie des Alten und Neuen Testaments*
BCH	*Bulletin de correspondance hellénique*
BiblGr	*Bibliotheca Graeca,* ed. J. Fabricius
BSOAS	*Bulletin of the School of Oriental and African Studies*
BZ	*Byzantinische Zeitschrift*
Canons	*Die Chronik des Hieronymus,* ed. R. Helm
CBQ	*Catholic Biblical Quarterly*
CC	Corpus Christianorum
CCAG	Catalogus codicum astrologorum graecorum
Chronica	*Die Chronik des Eusebius aus dem Armenischen übersetzt,* trans. J. Karst (Book 1)
ConBibOT	Coniectanea biblica, Old Testament
CP	*Classical Philology*
CSCO	Corpus scriptorum christianorum orientalium
CSEL	Corpus scriptorum ecclesiasticorum latinorum
CSHB	Corpus scriptorum historiae byzantinae
DenkAkWien	*Denkschriften der (kaiserlichen, österreichischen) Akademie der Wissenschaften,* Vienna
ERE	*Encyclopedia of Religion and Ethics,* ed. James Hastings

ET	English Translation
FGrH	*Die Fragmente der griechischen Historiker,* ed. F. Jacoby
FHG	*Fragmenta Historicorum Graecorum,* ed. C. and T. Müller
GCS	Die griechischen christlichen Schriftsteller der ersten drei Jahrhunderte
HSM	Harvard Semitic Monographs
HTR	*Harvard Theological Review*
HUCA	*Hebrew Union College Annual*
JAOS	*Journal of the American Oriental Society*
JJS	*Journal of Jewish Studies*
JNES	*Journal of Near Eastern Studies*
JP	(Ps-)Julius Pollux (ed. I. Hardt)
JQR	*Jewish Quarterly Review*
JSJ	*Journal for the Study of Judaism in the Persian, Hellenistic and Roman Period*
JTS	*Journal of Theological Studies*
LCL	Loeb Classical Library
LG	Leo the Grammarian (ed. I. Bekker)
MVAG	*Mitteilungen der vorderasiatisch-ägyptischen Gesellschaft*
OLZ	*Orientalistische Literaturzeitung*
OS	*Oudtestamentische Studiën*
PAAJR	*Proceedings of the American Academy of Jewish Research*
PE	Eusebius, *Praeparatio Evangelica*
PG	Patrologia Graeca, ed. J. P. Migne
PL	Patrologia Latina, ed. J. P. Migne
PO	Patrologia Orientalis
PVTG	Pseudepigrapha Veteris Testamenti Graece
RAC	*Reallexicon für Antike und Christentum*
RB	*Revue biblique*
RE	*Realencyclopädie der klassischen Altertumswissenschaft,* ed. Pauly-Wissowa-Kroll
REG	*Revue des études grecques*
RGG	*Religion in Geschichte und Gegenwart*
RhM	*Rheinisches Museum für Philologie*
RHR	*Revue de l'histoire des religions*
RSR	*Recherches de science religieuse*

SBLDS	Society of Biblical Literature Dissertation Series
SBLMS	Society of Biblical Literature Monograph Series
SBLSCS	Society of Biblical Literature Septuagint and Cognate Studies
SBLSP	*Society of Biblical Literature Seminar Papers*
SC	Sources chrétiennes
SitzungsberAkBerlin	*Sitzungsberichte der Akademie der Wissenschaften*, Berlin
SitzungsberAkMünchen	*Sitzungsberichte der Akademie der Wissenschaften*, Munich
SitzungsberAkWien	*Sitzungsberichte der Akademie der Wissenschaften*, Vienna
SJA	H. Gelzer, *Sextus Julius Africanus und die byzantinische Chronographie*
SVTP	Studia in Veteris Testamenti Pseudepigrapha
TM	Theodosius Melitenus (ed. L. Tafel)
TU	Texte und Untersuchungen zur Geschichte der altchristliche Literatur, ed. Oscar von Gebhart and Adolf Harnack
ZDMG	*Zeitschrift der Deutschen Morgenländischen Gesellschaft*
ZNW	*Zeitschrift für die Neutestamentliche Wissenschaft*

Bibliography

I. Texts and Translations

A. Individual Authors

Agapius. *Historia universalis*. Ed. L. Cheikho. CSCO 65, Scriptores Arabici 10. Louvain: 1954.

———. *Kitab al-'Unvan*. Ed. and trans. A. Vasiliev. PO 5.4, pp. 565–691. Paris: 1910.

Anastasius Sinaita. *Anagogicarum contemplationum in Hexaemeron Libri Duodecim*. PG 89, cols. 851–1078. Paris: 1865.

———. *Viae Dux*. Ed. K.-H. Uthemann. CC Series Graeca 8. Turnholt: 1981.

Augustine. *On the City of God*, Books 12–15. Trans. Philip Levine. LCL, vol. 4. Cambridge: 1966.

———. *Questions on the Heptateuch*. CC Series Latina 33. Turnholt: 1958.

Bakhayla Mīkā'ēl (Zōsīmās). *The Book of the Mysteries of the Heavens and the Earth and other works of Bakhayla Mīkā'ēl (Zōsīmās)*. Trans. E. A. W. Budge. London: 1935.

Bar Hebraeus. *The Chronography of Gregory Abu'l Faraj, commonly known as Bar Hebraeus*. Ed. and trans. E. A. W. Budge. 2 vols. London: 1932.

———. *Scholia on the Old Testament: Genesis–II Samuel*. Ed. and trans. M. Sprengling and W. C. Graham. Oriental Institute Publications 13. Chicago: 1931.

Berossus. *The Babyloniaca*. Trans. S. M. Burstein. Sources from the Ancient Near East 1.5. Malibu: 1978.

Al–Bīrūnī. *The Chronology of Ancient Nations*. Trans. C. E. Sachau. London: 1879.

Cedrenus: Georgius Cedrenus. *Compendium Historiarum*. Ed. I. Bekker. 2 vols. CSHB. Bonn: 1838–39.

Censorinus. *De die natali*. Ed. F. Hultsch. Leipzig: 1867.

Chaeremon. "Fragments inédits des historiens grecs no. 1: Chaeremonis *Aegyptiaca*." Ed. E. N. Sathas. *BCH* 1 (1877), 127–33.

———. *Chaeremon: Egyptian Priest and Stoic Philosopher*. Ed. and trans. P. W. van der Horst, Études préliminaires aux religions orientales dans l'Empire Romain 101. Leiden: 1984.

Cicero. *De natura deorum*. Trans. H. Rackham. LCL. Cambridge: 1979.

Clement of Alexandria. *Stromata* 1–6. Ed. O. Stählin. Vol. 2. 3rd ed. GCS 52 (15). Berlin: 1960.

Cosmas Indicopleustes. *Topographie chrétienne*. Ed. and trans. W. Wolska-Conus. 3 vols. SC 141, 159, 197. Paris: 1962–70.

Diodorus of Sicily. *Library of History*. Trans. C. H. Oldfather. LCL, Vol. 1. Cambridge: 1968.

Elias of Nisibis. *Opus chronologicum*. Ed. and trans. E. W. Brooks and I.-B. Chabot. CSCO 62–63, Scriptores Syri 21–24. Louvain: 1954.

Ephrem. *Sancti Ephraem Syri in Genesim et in Exodum commentarii*. Ed. and trans. R.-M. Tonneau. CSCO 152–53, Scriptores Syri 71–72. Louvain: 1955.

———. "Ephrem le Syrien, Hymne sur le Paradis." Trans. J. Daniélou. *Dieu Vivant* 22 (1952), 77–86.

Epiphanius. *Panarion*. Ed. K. Holl. 3 vols. GCS 25, 31, 37. Leipzig: 1915–33.

Eusebius of Caesarea. *Eusebi Chronicorum Libri Duo*. Ed. A. Schoene. 2 vols. Berlin: 1866–75.

———. *Die Chronik des Eusebius aus dem Armenischen übersetzt*. Trans. J. Karst. GCS 20, *Eusebius Werke* 5. Leipzig: 1911.

———. *Die Chronik des Hieronymus*. Ed. R. Helm. 2nd ed. GCS 47, *Eusebius Werke* 7.1,2. Berlin: 1956.

———. *Demonstratio Evangelica*. Ed. I. A. Heikel. GCS 23, *Eusebius Werke* 6. Leipzig: 1913.

———. *Praeparatio Evangelica*. Ed. and trans. E. H. Gifford. 4 vols. in 5 parts. Oxford: 1903.

———. *Praeparatio Evangelica*. Ed. K. Mras. GCS 43.1,2. Berlin: 1954–56.

Eusebius of Emesa. *L'héritage littéraire d'Eusèbe d'Émèse. Étude critique et historique. Textes*. Ed. É. M. Buytaert. Bibliothèque du Muséon. Louvain: 1949.

George the Monk. *Chronicon*. Ed. C. de Boor. 2 vols. Leipzig: 1904.

Gregory of Nazianzus. *Die fünf theologischen Reden*. Ed. J. Barbel. Düsseldorf: 1963.

Hippolytus of Rome. *Die Chronik des Hippolytos*. Ed. A. Bauer. TU 29.1 N.F. 14 (1905–6), 1–287.

Iamblichus. *De Mysteriis*. Ed. É. des Places. Paris: 1966.

Isho'dad of Merv. *Commentaire d'Išo'dad de Merv sur l'Ancien Testament I. Genèse*. Ed. and. trans. C. Van den Eynde. CSCO 126, 156, Scriptores Syri 67, 75. Louvain: 1955.

Jerome. *Hebraicae Quaestiones in Libro Geneseos*. CC Series Latina 72.1.1. Turnholt: 1959.

Joel. *Chronographia Compendia*. Ed. I. Bekker. CSHB. Bonn: 1836.

John Chrysostom. *Joannis Chrysostomi Homiliae in Matthaeum*. Ed. F. Field. 2 vols. Cambridge: 1839.

Josephus. *Against Apion*. Trans. H. St. J. Thackeray. LCL. Vol. 1. London: 1976.

———. *Antiquities*. Books 1–4. Trans. H. St. J. Thackeray. LCL. Vol. 4. Cambridge: 1967.

Julius Africanus. *Lettre d'Africanus à Origène*. Ed. and trans. N. de Lange. Paris: 1983.

(Ps-)Julius Pollux. *Historia Physica seu chronicon ab origine mundi usque ad Valentis tempora*. Ed. I. Hardt. Munich: 1792.

Lactantius. *Divine Institutes*. Trans. W. Fletcher. *ANF*, 7. 9–223.

Leo the Grammarian. *Chronographia.* Ed. I. Bekker. CSHB. Bonn: 1842.

Malalas: John Malalas. *Chronographia.* Ed. L. Dindorf. CSHB. Bonn: 1831.

Manetho. Trans. W. G. Waddell. LCL. Cambridge: 1940.

———. *Manethonis Apotelesmaticorum qui feruntur libri vi.* Ed. H. A. T. Köchly. Leipzig: 1858.

Michael Glycas. *Annales.* Ed. I. Bekker. 2 vols. CSHB. Bonn: 1836.

Michael the Great. *Chronique de Michel le Grand patriarche des Syriens jacobites traduite pour la première fois sur la version arménienne du prêtre Ischôk.* Ed. Ch. V. Langlois. Venice: 1868.

———. *Chronique de Michel le Syrien, Patriarche jacobite d'Antioche, 1126–1199.* Ed. and trans. I.-B. Chabot. 3 vols. Paris: 1899–1910. Rpr. in 4 vols., Brussels: 1963.

Moses bar Cepha. *Commentaria de Paradiso ad Ignatium fratrem.* PG 111, cols. 481–608. Paris: 1863.

Moses of Chorene. *History of the Armenians.* Trans. R. W. Thomson. Harvard Armenian Texts and Studies 4. Cambridge: 1978.

Origen. *Contra Celsum.* Trans. H. Chadwick. Cambridge: 1953.

Orosius: Paul Orosius. *Pauli Orosii historiarum adversum paganos libri VII.* Ed. C. Zangemeister. CSEL 5. Vienna: 1882. Rpr. Hildesheim: 1967.

———. *Seven Books of History against the Pagans.* Trans. I. W. Raymond. New York: 1936.

Philaster. *Sancti Filastrii episcopi Brixiensis diversarum hereseon liber.* Ed. F. Heylen. CC Series Latina 9. Turnholt: 1957.

Philo. *The Posterity and Exile of Cain.* Trans. F. H. Colson and G. H. Whitaker. LCL. Cambridge: 1968.

———. *On the Creation of the Universe.* Trans. F. H. Colson and G. H. Whitaker. LCL. London: 1971.

———. *Questions and Answers on Genesis.* Trans. R. M. Marcus. LCL, Supplement 1. Cambridge: 1971.

———. *Allegorical Interpretation of Genesis.* Trans. F. H. Colson and G. H. Whitaker. LCL. London: 1971.

Plato. *Timaeus.* Trans. R. G. Bury. LCL. Cambridge: 1975.

———. *Laws.* Trans. R. G. Bury. LCL. Cambridge: 1967.

Pliny. *Natural History.* Trans. H. Rackham. LCL, 10 vols. Cambridge: 1938–71.

Proclus Diadochus. *Procli Diadochi in Platonis Timaeum Commentaria.* Ed. E. Diehl. 3 vols. Leipzig: 1903.

Seneca. *Quaestiones Naturales.* Trans. T. H. Corcoran. LCL. 2 vols. Cambridge: 1971–72.

Simplicius. *Commentaria in Aristotelem graeca: De caelo.* Ed. I. L. Heiberg. Berlin: 1893.

Suidas. *Lexicon.* Ed. A. Adler. Lexicographi Graece 1 (in 5 parts). Leipzig: 1928–38.

Syncellus: Georgius Syncellus. *Ecloga Chronographica.* Ed. A. A. Mosshammer. Leipzig: 1984.

———. *Georgius Syncellus et Nicephorus CP.* Ed. W. Dindorf. 2 vols. CSHB. Bonn: 1829.

Tatian. *Address to the Greeks.* Trans. J. E. Ryland. *ANF,* 2. 65–83.

Theodosius Melitenus. *Chronographia.* Ed L. Tafel. Monumenta Saecularia, Kön-

242 Bibliography

iglich Bayerischen Akademie der Wissenschaften zur Feier ihres hundertjährigen Bestehens, 3.1. Munich: 1859.

Theophanes. *Chronographia*. Ed. C. de Boor. 2 vols. Leipzig: 1883. Rpr. Hildesheim: 1963.

———. *The Chronicle of Theophanes*. Trans. H. Turtledove. Philadelphia: 1982.

Zonaras: John Zonaras. *Annales*. Ed. M. Pinder. CSHB. Bonn: 1841.

B. Collections

Assemani, G. S. *Bibliotheca Orientalis*. 3 vols. in 4. Rome: 1719–28.

Berthelot, M. P. E. and Duval, R. *Histoire des sciences. La chimie au moyen âge*. 3 vols. Paris: 1893. Rpr. Osnabrück: 1967.

Boll, F. et al. *Catalogus codicum astrologorum graecorum*, Vols. 1–6. Brussels: 1904–6.

Charles, R. H., ed. *The Apocrypha and Pseudepigrapha of the Old Testament in English*. 2 vols. Oxford: 1913.

Charlesworth, J. H., ed. *The Old Testament Pseudepigrapha*. Garden City: 1983.

Cramer, J. A. *Anecdota Graeca*, Vol. 2. Oxford: 1839. Rpr. Hildesheim: 1967.

Denis, A.-M. *Fragmenta pseudepigraphorum quae supersunt graeca, una cum historicorum et auctorum Judaeorum Hellenistarum fragmentis*. PVTG 3. Leiden: 1970.

Holladay, C. R. *Fragments from Hellenistic Jewish Authors* 1. Chico: 1983.

Jacoby, F. *Die Fragmente der griechischen Historiker*. 3 vols. Berlin and Leiden: 1923–58.

Mai, A. *Scriptorum veterum nova collectio*. 10 vols. Rome: 1825–31.

Müller, C. and Müller, T. *Fragmenta Historicum Graecorum*. 5 vols. Paris: 1841–70.

Nock, A. D. and Festugière, A.-J. *Corpus hermeticum*. 4 vols. Paris: 1946–54.

Robinson, J., ed. *The Nag Hammadi Library in English*. New York: 1977.

Routh, M. J. *Reliquiae Sacrae*. 5 vols. Oxford: 1846–48.

Scott, W. *Hermetica*. 3 vols. Oxford: 1924–26.

Stern, M. *Greek and Latin Authors on Jews and Judaism*. Vol. 1: *From Herodotus to Plutarch*. Jerusalem: 1974.

C. Anonymous Works

Anonymi auctoris Chronicon ad annum Christi 1234 pertinens. Ed. and trans. I.-B. Chabot. CSCO 81, 82, 109, Scriptores Syri 36, 37, 56. Louvain: 1952, 1953.

The Book of the Cave of Treasures. Trans. E. A. W. Budge. London: 1927.

Chronicon paschale. Ed. L. Dindorf. CSHB. Bonn: 1832.

(Ps-)Clementine. *Homilien*. Ed. B. Rehm. GCS 42. Berlin: 1953.

———. *Recognitionen in Rufins Übersetzung*. Ed. B. Rehm. GCS 51. Berlin: 1965.

Eine alexandrinische Weltchronik. Ed. A. Bauer and J. Strzygowski. *DenkAkWien* 51. Vienna: 1905.

Enoch, Book of. M. Black. *Apocalypsis Henochi Graece*. PVTG 3. Leiden: 1970.

———. R. H. Charles. *The Ethiopic Version of the Book of Enoch*. Anecdota Oxoniensa Semitic Series 11. Oxford: 1906.

———. M. Knibb. *The Ethiopic Book of Enoch: A New Edition in the Light of the Aramaic Dead Sea Fragments*. 2 vols. Oxford: 1978.

————. J. T. Milik. *The Books of Enoch: Aramaic Fragments of Qumrān Cave 4.* Oxford: 1976.

Incerti auctoris Chronicon anonymum Pseudo-Dionysianum vulgo dictum. Ed. and trans. I.-B. Chabot. CSCO 91, 104, 121, Scriptores Syri 43, 53, 66. Louvain: 1952–59.

Jubilees. R. H. Charles. *The Book of Jubilees or the Little Genesis.* London: 1902.

————. H. Rönsch. *Das Buch der Jubiläen oder die Kleine Genesis.* Leipzig: 1874.

————. E. Tisserant. "Fragments syriaques du Livre des Jubilés." *RB* 30 (1921), 55–86, 206–32. Rpr. in *Recueil Card. Eugène Tisserant.* 2 vols. Louvain: 1955, 1. 25–87.

The Royal Chronicle of Abyssinia 1769–1840, with Translation and Notes. Trans. H. Weld Blundell. Cambridge: 1922.

Septuaginta. Vol. 1, Genesis. Ed. J. W. Wevers. Göttingen: 1974.

Sibylline Oracles. Ed. J. Geffcken. GCS 8. Leipzig: 1902.

The Testament of Adam. Ed. S. E. Robinson. SBLDS 52. Chico: 1982.

II. SECONDARY LITERATURE

Adler, W. "Berossus, Manetho, and 1 Enoch in the World Chronicle of Panodorus." *HTR* 76 (1983), 419–44.

————. "Abraham and the Burning of the Temple of Idols: Jubilees' Traditions in Christian Chronography." *JQR* 97 (1986–87), 95–117.

Alexander, P. S. "The Targumim and Early Exegesis of 'Sons of God' in Gen. 6." *JJS* 23 (1972), 60–71.

————. "Notes on the 'Imago Mundi' of the Book of Jubilees." *JJS* 33 (1982), 197–213.

Alfaric, P. *Les écritures manichéenes.* 2 vols. in 1. Paris: 1918–19.

Allacci, Leo. "De Georgiis et eorum scriptis diatriba." In J. Fabricius, *Bibliotheca Graeca,* 10. 631–51. Hamburg: 1709–28.

Alonso-Núñez, J. M. "An Augustan World History: The *Historiae Philippicae* of Pompeius Trogus." *Greece and Rome* 34 (1987), 56–72.

Bang, T. *Caelum Orientis et prisci mundi triade exercitationum literariarum representatum.* Hauniae: 1657.

Bartelmus, R. *Heroentum in Israel und seiner Umwelt. AthANT* 65. Zurich: 1979.

Bauer, A. *Beiträge zu Eusebios und den byzantinischen Chronographen. SitzungsberAkWien,* phil.-hist. Klasse 162.3 (1909).

Beausobre, Isaac de. *Histoire critique de Manichée et du Manichéisme.* 2 vols. Amsterdam: 1734–39.

Beck, H. G., "Zur byzantinischen 'Mönchschronik'," *Speculum Historiale.* Freiburg, Munich: 1965, pp. 188–97.

Bernays, J. *Joseph Justus Scaliger.* Berlin: 1855. Rpr. Osnabrück: 1965.

Bickerman, E. *Chronology of the Ancient World.* 2nd Edition, Ithaca: 1980.

————. "The Septuagint as a Translation," *PAAJR* 28 (1959). Rpr. in *Studies in Jewish and Christian History* 1. Leiden: 1976, pp. 167–200.

Bidez, J. "Bérose et la Grande Année." In *Mélanges Paul Fredericq: Hommages de la Société pour le Progrès des Études Philologique et Historique.* Paris: 1904, pp. 9–19.

244 Bibliography

————. "Les Écoles Chaldéenes sous Alexandre." *Annuaire de l'Institut de Philologie et d'Histoire Orientales* 3 (1935), 41–89.

Böckh, A. *Manetho und die Hundsternperiode.* Berlin: 1845.

Boker, R. "Zeitrechnung." *RE* 9.2 (1907), 2386–94.

Boll, F., Bezold, C., and Gundel, W. *Sternglaube und Sterndeutung.* 4th ed. Leipzig, Berlin: 1931.

Bousset, W. "Die Beziehungen der ältesten jüdische Sibylle zur chaldäische Sibylle." *ZNW* 3 (1902), 23–49.

Bredow, C. G. "Dissertatio de Georgii Syncelli Chronographia." Originally delivered to the literary society of Paris. Published in vol. 2 of Dindorf's edition of Syncellus, pp. 3–49.

Breebaart, A. B. "Weltgeschichte als Thema der antiken Geschichtsschreibung." *Acta Historica Neerlandica* 1 (1966), 1–21.

Brock, S. "A Fragment of Enoch in Syriac." *JTS* 19 (1968), 626–31.

————. "Abraham and the Ravens: A Syriac Counterpart to Jubilees 11–12 and Its Implications." *JSJ* 9.2 (1978), 135–52.

Broek, R. van den. *The Myth of the Phoenix.* Études préliminaires aux religions orientales dans l'Empire Romain 24. Leiden: 1972.

Brown, T. S. *The Greek Historians.* Lexington: 1973.

————. *Timaeus of Tauromenium.* University of California Publications in History 55. Berkeley: 1958.

————. "Euhemerus and the Historians." *HTR* 39 (1946), 259–74.

Burn, A. R. *Persia and the Greeks.* New York: 1962.

Chaîne, M. *La chronologie des temps chrétiens de l'Égypte et de l'Éthiopie.* Paris: 1925.

Charlesworth, J. H. *The Pseudepigrapha and Modern Research.* SBLSCS 7. Rev. ed. Chico: 1981.

Chesnut, G. F. *The First Christian Histories.* 2nd ed. Macon: 1986.

Christensen, A. *Les Kayanides.* Det Kgl. Danske Videnskabernes Selskab. Historisk-filologiske Meddelelser 19.2. Copenhagen: 1931.

Chwolson, D. *Die Ssabier und Ssabismus.* 2 vols. St. Petersburg: 1856.

Collins, J. J. *The Sibylline Oracles of Egyptian Judaism.* SBLDS 13. Missoula: 1974.

Colonna, M. E. *Gli storici bizantini dal IV al XV secolo. I. Storici Profani.* Naples: 1956.

Conybeare, F. C. "On the Date of Composition of the Paschal Chronicle." *JTS* 2 (1901), 288–98.

————. "The Relation of the Paschal Chronicle to Malalas." *BZ* 11 (1902), 395–405.

Cornelius, F. "Berossos und die altorientalische Chronologie." *Klio* 35 (1942), 1–16.

Croiset, A. and Croiset, M. *Histoire de la littérature grecque.* 5 vols. Paris: 1887–1899.

Croke, B., and Emmett, A. M., eds. *History and Historians in Late Antiquity.* Sydney: 1983.

Cumont, F. "La fin du monde selon les mages occidentaux," *RHR* 103 (1931), 29–96.

Denis, A. M. *Introduction aux pseudépigraphes grecs d'Ancien Testament.* SVTP 1. Leiden: 1970.

Des Vignoles, A. *Chronologie de l'histoire sainte.* 2 vols. Berlin: 1738.

Dilke, O. A. W. *Greek and Roman Maps.* Ithaca: 1985.

Drews, R. *The Greek Accounts of Eastern History.* Cambridge: 1973.

———. "Assyria in Classical Universal Histories." *Historia* 14 (1965), 129–42.

———. "The Babylonian Chronicles and Berossus." *Iraq* 37 (1975), 39–55.

Eisler, R. ΙΗΣΟΥΣ ΒΑΣΙΛΕΥΣ ΟΥ ΒΑΣΙΛΕΥΣΑΣ. Heidelberg: 1929–30.

Emereau, C. *St. Ephrem le Syrien: son oeuvre littéraire grecque.* Études critiques de littérature et de philologie byzantines. Paris: 1918.

Fabricius, J. A. *Codex pseudepigraphus Veteris Testamenti,* 1. 2nd ed. Hamburg, Leipzig: 1722.

Feldman, L. H. "Hellenizations in Josephus' Portrayal of Man's Decline." In *Religions in Antiquity.* Edited by J. Neusner. Studies in the History of Religions 14. Leiden: 1968, pp. 336–53.

Festugière, A.-J. *La Révélation d'Hermès Trismégiste.* 4 vols. Paris: 1949–54.

Finegan, J. *Handbook of Biblical Chronology.* Princeton: 1964.

Fowden, G. *The Egyptian Hermes: A Historical Approach to the Late Pagan Mind.* Cambridge: 1986.

Fraade, S. D. *Enosh and His Generation.* SBLMS 30. Chico: 1984.

Fraidl, F. *Die Exegese der siebzig Wochen Daniels in der alten und mittleren Zeit.* Graz: 1883.

Freudenthal, J. *Alexander Polyhistor und die von ihm erhaltenen Reste jüdischer und samaritanischer Geschichtswerke.* Breslau: 1874–75.

Frick, C. "Kritische Untersuchungen über das alte Chronikon, die ägyptische Königsliste des Eratosthenes und Apollodoros, das Sothisbuch und die ägyptische Königsliste des Synkellos." *RhM* N.F. 29 (1874), 252–81.

Fruin, R. J. *Manethonis Sebennytae Reliquiae.* Dissertatio philologica inauguralis. Leiden: 1847.

Gager, J. *Moses in Greco-Roman Paganism.* SBLMS 16. Nashville: 1972.

Ganszyniec, R. "Kyraniden." *RE* 12.1 (1924), 127–34. Supplemented by W. Kroll.

———. "Studien zu den Kyraniden." *Byzantinische-Neugriechische Jahrbucher* 1 (1920), 353–67.

Gassendi, P. *Viri illustris Nicolai Claudii Fabricii de Peiresc, senatoris Aquisextensis, Vita.* 3rd ed. Quedlinburg: 1706–8.

Gelzer, H. *Sextus Julius Africanus und die byzantinische Chronographie.* 2 vols. Leipzig: 1885–88. Rpr. in one volume. New York: 1967.

———. "Die vorflutigen Chaldäerfürsten des Annianos." *BZ* 3 (1894), 391–93.

Gerland, E. "Die Grundlagen der byzantinischen Geschichtschreibung." *Byzantion* 8 (1933), 93–105.

Ginzel, F. K. *Handbuch der mathematischen und technischen Chronologie.* 3 vols. Leipzig: 1906–14.

Ginzberg, L. *The Legends of the Jews.* 7 vols. Philadelphia: 1909–38.

———. *Die Haggada bei den Kirchenvätern und in der apokryphischen Litteratur.* Berlin: 1900.

Gluck, T. *The Arabic Legend of Seth, the Father of Mankind.* Unpublished Yale Dissertation, 1968.

Goetz, Hans-Werner. *Die Geschichtstheologie des Orosius*. Darmstadt: 1980.

Grabbe, L. "Chronography in Hellenistic Jewish Historiography." *SBLSP* 1979, 43–68. Edited by P. J. Achtemeier. Missoula: 1979.

Grabe, J. E. *Spicilegium ss. patrum*. 2 vols. Oxford: 1698–99.

Grafton, A. T. "Joseph Scaliger and Historical Chronology: The Rise and Fall of a Discipline." *History and Theory* 14 (1975), 156–85.

Grelot, P. "La géographie mythique d'Hénoch et ses sources orientales." *RB* 65 (1958), 33–69.

———. "La légende d'Hénoch dans les Apocryphes et dans la Bible: origine et signification." *RSR* 46 (1958), 5–26, 181–210.

Grumel, V. *La chronologie*. Traité d'études byzantines. Bibliothèque byzantine. 2 vols. Paris: 1958.

Gutschmid, A. von. "Die Sothis, die alte Chronik und die Pandorischen (*sic*) 3555 Jahre von Hephaestos bis Nektanebos II." *Kleine Schriften* 1. Edited by Franz Rühl. Leipzig: 1889, pp. 226–43.

———. "Untersuchungen über die syrische Epitome der Eusebischen Canones." *Kleine Schriften* 1. Edited by F. Rühl. Leipzig: 1889, pp. 417–47.

———. "Ist Manethos Zeitrechnung cyclisch oder streng historisch?" *Kleine Schriften* 1. Edited by F. Rühl. Leipzig: 1889, pp. 253–277.

———. "Zu den Fragmenten des Berosos und Ktesias." *Kleine Schriften* 2. Edited by F. Rühl. Leipzig: 1889, pp. 97–114.

———. "Zur Kritik des Διαμερισμὸς τῆς γῆς." *Kleine Schriften* 5. Edited by F. Rühl. Leipzig: 1894, pp. 263–73.

Haase, F. "Die armenische Rezension der syrischen Chronik Michaels des Grossen." *Oriens Christianus* 5 (1915), 60–82.

Hartman, S. S. *Gayōmart*. Uppsala: 1953.

Havet, E. *Mémoire sur les écrits qui portent les noms de Bérose et de Manéthon*. Paris: 1873.

Heidegger, J. *De historia sacra patriarcharum exercitationes selectae*. Amsterdam: 1688–89.

Heidel, A. *The Babylonian Genesis*. 2nd ed. Chicago: 1951.

Helck, H. W. *Untersuchungen zu Manetho und den ägyptischen Königslisten*. Untersuchungen zur Geschichte und Altertumskunde Aegyptens 18. Berlin: 1956.

Helm, R. *Eusebius' Chronik und ihre Tabellenform*. *AbhAkBerlin*, phil.-hist. Klasse 4 (1923). Berlin: 1924.

———. "Hieronymus' Zusätze in Eusebius' Chronik und ihr Wert für die Literaturgeschichte." *Philologus*. Suppl. 21.2. Berlin: 1929.

———. "Die neuesten Hypothesen zu Eusebius' (Hieronymus') Chronik." *SitzungsberAkBerlin*, phil.-hist. Klasse 21 (1929), 371–408.

Hengel, M. *Judaism and Hellenism*. 2 vols. ET by John Bowden. Philadelphia: 1974.

Henning, W. B. "The Book of the Giants." *BSOAS* 11 (1943–46), 52–74.

———. "Ein Manichäisches Henochbuch." *SitzungsberAkBerlin*, phil.-hist. Klasse 5 (1934), 27–35.

Hirsch, F. *Byzantinische Studien*. Leipzig: 1876. Rpr. Amsterdam: 1965.

Honigmann, E. *Die sieben Klimata und die* ΠΟΛΕΙΣ ΕΠΙΣΗΜΟΙ. Heidelberg: 1929.

Hunger, H. *Die hochsprachliche profane Literatur der Byzantiner.* Handbuch der Altertumswissenschaft 12.5.1. Munich: 1978.

Huxley, G. L. "On the Erudition of George the Synkellos." *Proceedings of the Royal Irish Academy* 81.C.6 (1981), 207–17.

Ideler, L. *Lehrbuch der chronologie.* 2 vols. Berlin: 1831.

———. *Handbuch der mathematischen und technischen Chronologie.* Berlin: 1825–26.

Jackson, J. *Chronological Antiquities.* London: 1752.

Jacoby, F. *Apollodors Chronik.* Philologische Untersuchungen 16. Berlin: 1902.

———. *Atthis.* Oxford: 1949.

———. "Hekataios" (4). *RE* 7.2 (1912), 2750–69.

———. "Ktesias" (1). *RE* 11.2 (1922), 2032–73.

Jansen, H. L. *Die Henochgestalt.* Oslo: 1939.

Jansma, T. "Investigations into the Early Syrian Fathers on Genesis." *Studies on the Book of Genesis. OS* 12 (1958), 69–181.

Jaubert, A. "Le calendrier des Jubilés et les jours liturgiques de la semaine." *VT* 7 (1975), 35–61.

Jeffreys, E. M. "The Attitudes of Byzantine Chroniclers towards Ancient History." *Byzantion* 49 (1979), 199–238.

Jellicoe, S. *Studies in the Septuagint: Origins, Recensions and Interpretations.* New York: 1974.

———. *The Septuagint and Modern Study.* Oxford: 1968.

Johnson, J. W. "Chronological Writing: Its Concepts and Development." *History and Theory* 2 (1962–63), 124–45.

Johnson, Marshall D. *The Purpose of the Biblical Genealogies.* SNTS Monograph Series 8. Cambridge: 1969.

Keseling, P. "Die Chronik des Eusebius in der syrischen Überlieferung." *Oriens Christianus* Series 3, 1 (1927), 23–48, 223–41; 2 (1927), 33–56.

Kircher, Athanasius. *De Arca Noe.* Amsterdam: 1675.

Klein, R. W. "Archaic Chronologies and the Textual History of the Old Testament." *HTR* 67 (1974), 255–63.

Kleingünther, A. "Πρῶτος Εὑρετής." *Philologus,* Suppl. 26.1. Leipzig: 1933.

Klijn, A. F. J. *Seth in Jewish, Christian and Gnostic Literature.* Supplements to Novum Testamentum 46. Leiden: 1977.

König-Ockenfels, D. "Christliche Deutung der Weltgeschichte bei Euseb von Cäsarea." *Saeculum* 27.4 (1976), 348–65.

Komoróczy, G. "Berosos and the Mesopotamian Literature." *AAAScHung* 21 (1973), 125–52.

Krall, J. *Die Composition und die Schicksale des Manethonischen Geschichtswerkes. SitzungsberAkWien,* phil.-hist. Classe 95 (1879 [1880]), 123–226.

Kröger, K. H. *Die Universalchroniken.* Akademisches Rat an der Universität. Münster: 1976.

Kroll, W. "Manethon" (2). *RE* 14.1 (1925), 1102–6.

Kronholm, T. *Motifs from Genesis 1–11 in the Genuine Hymns of Ephrem the Syrian.* ConBibOT Series 11. Lund: 1978.

Krüger, M. J. "Die Chronologie im Buche der Jubiläen." *ZDMG* 12 (1958), 279–99.

Krumbacher, K. *Geschichte der byzantinischen Litteratur.* Handbuch der klassischen Altertumswissenschaft 9.1. 2nd Edition. Munich: 1897.

Kubitschek, W. *Grundriss der antiken Zeitrechnung.* Handbuch der Altertumswissenschaft 1.7. Munich: 1928.

———. "Kastor" (8), *RE* 10.2 (1919), 2347–57.

Lambert, W. G. "Berossus and Babylonian Eschatology." *Iraq* 38 (1976), 171–173.

Lange, Wilhelm. *De annis Christi libri duo.* Leiden: 1649.

Laqueur, R. "Manethon" (1). *RE* 14.1 (1928), 1060–1101.

———. "Synkellos" (1) RE zweite Reihe 4.2 (1932), 1388–1410.

Lauth, F. J. *Manetho und der Turiner Königspapyrus.* Munich: 1865.

Lehmann-Haupt, C. F. "Neue Studien zu Berossus." *Klio* 22 (1929), 125–60.

Lenormant, M. Fr. *Essai de commentaire des fragments cosmogoniques de Bérose.* Paris: 1871.

Lepsius, R. *Die Chronologie der Aegypter.* Berlin: 1849.

———. "Über die Manethonischen Bestimmung des Umfangs der aegyptischen Geschichte." *AbhAkBerlin,* phil.-hist. Klasse 7 (1857), 183–208.

Lewis, G. C. *An Historical Survey of the Astronomy of the Ancients.* London: 1862.

Lewy, H. *Chaldaean Oracles and Theurgy.* Publications de l'Institut Français d'Archéologie Orientale. Recherches d'archéologie, de philologie et d'histoire 13. Cairo: 1968. New edition by M. Tardieu. Paris: 1978.

Lovejoy, A. O. and Boas, G. *Primitivism and Related Ideas in Antiquity.* Baltimore: 1935.

Luck, G. *Arcana Mundi.* Baltimore: 1985.

Ludolph, H. *Historia Aethiopica.* Frankfurt: 1681.

Meyer, Ed. "Das chronologische System des Berossus." *Klio* 3 (1903), 131–34.

———. *Aegyptische Chronologie.* Berlin: 1904.

———. *Geschichte des Altertums.* 5 vols. Stuttgart: 1884–1902.

Milik, J. T. "Problèmes de la littérature Hénochique à la lumière des fragments araméens de Qumrân." *HTR* 64 (1971), 333–78.

———. "Recherches sur la version grecque du Livre des Jubilés." *RB* 78 (1971), 545–57.

———. "Turfan et Qumran. Livre des Géants juif et manichéen." *Tradition und Glaube. Festschrift für K. G. Kuhn zum 65. Geburtstag.* Edited by G. Jeremias, H.-W. Kuhn and H. Stegemann. Göttingen: 1971, pp. 117–27.

Momigliano, A. "Pagan and Christian Historiography in the Fourth Century A.D." *The Conflict between Paganism and Christianity in the Fourth Century.* Edited by Arnaldo Momigliano. Oxford: 1963, pp. 79–99.

———. "Time in Ancient Historiography." *History and Theory.* Beiheft 6. Middletown: 1966, pp. 1–23.

———. "Historiography on Written Tradition and Historiography on Oral Tradition." *Studies in Historiography.* London: 1966, pp. 211–20.

———. "The Origins of Universal History." *Settimo Contributo alla Storia degli Studi Classici e del Mondo Antico,* Storia e Letteratura Raccolta di Studi e Testi 161. Rome: 1984, pp. 77–103.

Morhof, D. G. *Polyhistor Literarius, philosophicus et practicus.* Lübeck: 1714.

Mosshammer, A. A. *The Chronicle of Eusebius and Greek Chronographic Tradition.* Lewisburg: 1979.

Neugebauer, O. "The 'Astronomical' Chapters of the Ethiopic Book of Enoch (72–82)." *Royal Danish Academy of Sciences and Letters* 40.10. Copenhagen: 1981.

———. "Die Bedeutungslosigkeit der 'Sothisperiode' für die älteste ägyptische Chronologie." *AO* 17 (1938), 169–95.

———. *Ethiopic Astronomy and Computus. Sitzungsberichte der Oesterreichischen Akademie der Wissenschaften,* phil.-hist. Klasse 347. Vienna: 1979.

———. *The Exact Sciences in Antiquity.* 2nd ed. Providence: 1957.

———. "Notes on Ethiopic Astronomy." *Orientalia* 33 (1964), 49–71.

———. "The Origin of the Egyptian Calendar." *JNES* 1 (1942), 396–403.

Nickelsburg, G. W. E. *Jewish Literature between the Bible and the Mishnah.* Philadelphia: 1981.

Nolan, F. "On the Use of Cycles in Settling the Differences of Chronologists." *Transactions of the Royal Society of Literature* 3 (1839), 1–70, 287–362.

Opelt, I. "Epitome." *RAC* 5 (1962), 944–73.

Ortiz de Urbina, I. *Patrologia Syriaca.* 2nd ed. Rome: 1965.

Parker, R. A. *The Calendars of Ancient Egypt.* Studies in Ancient Oriental Civilization 26. Chicago: 1950.

Peet, T. E. *Egypt and the Old Testament.* Liverpool: 1923.

Pessl, H. von. *Das chronologische System Manethos.* Leipzig: 1878.

Pfeiffer, A. *Henoch, descriptus exercitatione philologica ad Gen. 5.22.23.24.* Wittenberg: 1670.

Plessner, M. "Hermes Trismegistus and Arab Science." *Studia Islamica* 2 (1954), 45–59.

Poole, R. L. *Chronicles and Annals.* Oxford: 1926.

Praechter, K. "Quellenkritische Studien zu Kedrenos." *SitzungsberAkMünchen,* phil.-hist. Klasse 2.1 (1897), 1–107.

Quasten, J. *Patrology.* 3 vols. Utrecht: 1950. Rpr. Westminster, Maryland: 1983.

Rajak, T. "Josephus and the 'Archaeology' of the Jews." *JJS* 33 (1982), 464–77.

Reinink, G. J. "Das Land 'Seiris' (Šir) und das Volk der Serer in jüdischen und christlichen Traditionen." *JSJ* 6 (1975), 72–85.

———. "Das Problem des Ursprungs des Testamentes Adams." *Orientalia Christiana Analecta* 197 (1972), 387–99.

Reitzenstein, R. *Poimandres. Studien zur griechisch-ägyptischen und frühchristlichen Literatur.* Leipzig: 1904.

Renan, E. "Fragments du livre gnostique." *Journal Asiatique* 5.2 (1853), 427–71.

Rubinkiewicz, R. *Die Eschatologie von Hen 9–11 und das Neue Testament.* Oesterreichische Biblische Studien 6. Klosterneuburg: 1984.

Russell, D. S. *The Method and Message of Jewish Apocalyptic.* Philadelphia: 1964.

Samuel, A. E. *Greek and Roman Chronology: Calendars and Years in Classical Antiquity.* Handbuch der Altertumswissenschaft 1.7. Munich: 1972.

Scaliger, J. J. *Thesaurus Temporum.* 2 vols. Leiden: 1606. Rpr. Otto Zeller: 1968.

Schmidt, N. "Traces of Early Acquaintance in Europe with the Book of Enoch." *JAOS* 42 (1922), 44–52.

Schnabel, P. "Apokalyptische Berechnung der Endzeiten bei Berossos." *OLZ* 9 (1910), 401–2.

———. "Die babylonische Chronologie in Berossos' *Babyloniaka*." *MVAG* 5 (1908), 1–10.

———. *Berossos und die babylonisch-hellenistiche Literatur*. Leipzig: 1923. Rpr. Hildesheim: 1968.

Schreckenberg, H. *Die Flavius-Josephus-Tradition in Antike und Mittelalter*. Leiden: 1972.

Schwartz, Ed. "Apollodoros" (61). *RE* 1.2 (1894), 2855–66.

———. "Berossos" (4). *RE* 3.1 (1897), 309–16.

———. "Chronicon paschale." *RE* 3.2 (1899), 2460–77.

———. "Eusebios" (24). *RE* 6.1 (1907), 1370–1439.

———. *Christliche und jüdische Ostertafeln. Abhandlungen der königlichen Gesellschaft der Wissenschaften zu Göttingen*. N.F. 8.6 (1905).

———. "Die Königslisten des Eratosthenes und Kastor mit Excursen über die Interpolationen bei Afrikanus und Eusebios." *Abhandlungen der königlichen Gesellschaft der Wissenschaften zu Göttingen*, phil.-hist. Klasse 40.2 (1894–5), 1–96.

Seel, O. "Panodoros." *RE* 18.3 (1949), 632–35.

Serruys, D. "De quelques ères usitées chez les chroniqueurs byzantins." *Revue de philologie*, n.s. 31 (1907), 151–89.

———"Les canons d'Eusèbe, d'Annianos, et d'Andronicos d'après Élie de Nisibe." *BZ* 22 (1913), 1–36.

———. "Les transformations de l'aera alexandrina minor." *Revue de philologie* n.s. 31 (1907), 251–64.

Shahîd, I. *Rome and the Arabs*. Washington, D.C.: 1984.

———. *Byzantium and the Arabs in the Fourth Century*. Washington, D.C.: 1984.

Sirinelli, Jean. *Les vues historiques d'Eusèbe de Césarée durant la période prénicéene*. Publications de la section de langues et littératures 10. Paris: 1961.

Smith, K. F. "Ages of the World, Greek and Roman." *ERE* 1, 192–200. Edinburgh: 1908.

Soden, W. von. "Berossos." *RGG* (3) 1 (1957), 1069.

Sorabji, R. *Time, Creation and the Continuum*. Ithaca: 1983.

Speyer, W. *Die literarische Fälschung im heidnischen und christlichen Altertum*. Handbuch der Altertumswissenschaft 1.2. Munich: 1971.

Spoerri, W. "Berossus." *Der kleine Pauly* 1 (1964), 1548.

———. *Späthellenistische Berichte über Welt, Kultur und Götter*. Schweizerische Beiträge zur Altertumswissenschaft. Basel: 1959.

Sticker, B. "Weltzeitalter und astronomischen Perioden." *Saeculum* 4 (1953), 241–49.

Stone, M. E. "The Books of Enoch and Judaism in the Third Century B.C.E." *CBQ* 40 (1978), 479–92.

Susemihl, F. *Geschichte der griechischen Litteratur in der Alexandrinerzeit*. 2 vols. Leipzig: 1891–92.

Swain, J. W. "The Theory of the Four Monarchies: Opposition History under the Roman Empire." *CP* 35 (1940), 1–20.

Tannery, M. "Psellus sur la Grande Année." *REG* 5 (1892), 206–11.

Tarn, W. W. "Ptolemy II." *Journal of Egyptian Archaeology* 14 (1928), 246–60.

Tcherikover, V. *Hellenistic Civilization and the Jews.* ET by S. Applebaum. Philadelphia: 1959.

Unger, G. F. *Chronologie des Manetho.* Berlin: 1867.

VanderKam, J. C. *Textual and Historical Studies in the Book of Jubilees.* HSM 14. Missoula: 1977.

Vollot, H. *Du système chronologique de Manethon.* Beaune: 1867.

Wacholder, Ben Zion. "Biblical Chronology in the Hellenistic World Chronicles." *HTR* 61 (1968), 451–81.

———. *Essays on Jewish Chronology and Chronography.* New York: 1976.

———. *Eupolemus, a Study of Judaeo-Greek Literature.* Monographs of the Hebrew Union College 3. Cincinnati and New York: 1974.

———. "Pseudo-Eupolemus' Two Greek Fragments on the Life of Abraham." *HUCA* 34 (1963), 83–113.

Waerden, B. L. van der. "Das grosse Jahr und die ewige Wiederkehr." *Hermes* 80 (1952), 129–55.

Walter, N. "Zu Pseudo-Eupolemus." *Klio* 43–46 (1965), 282–90.

Wardman, A. E. "Myth in Greek Historiography." *Historia* 9 (1960), 403–13.

Wartmann, D. "Kosmogonie und Nilflut." *Bonner Jahrbücher des Rheinischen Landesmuseum* 166 (1966), 62–112.

Weill, R. *La fin du moyen empire égyptien.* Paris: 1918.

West, M. L. *Early Greek Philosophy and the Orient.* Oxford: 1971.

Wickham, L. R. "The Sons of God and the Daughters of Men: Genesis VI 2 in Early Christian Exegesis." *OS* 19 (1974), 135–47.

Wolska, W. *La topographie chrétienne de Cosmas Indicopleustès.* Bibliothèque byzantine, Études 3. Paris: 1962.

Worstbrock, F. J. "Translatio Artium. Über die Herkunft und Entwicklung einer kulturhistorischen Theorie." *Archiv für Kulturgeschichte* 47 (1965), 1–22.

Index

DATE DUE

HIGHSMITH   # 45220